TERRORISTS' TARGET SELECTION

Terrorists' Target Selection

C. J. M. Drake

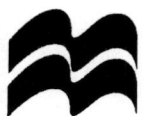

First published in Great Britain 1998 by
MACMILLAN PRESS LTD
Houndmills, Basingstoke, Hampshire RG21 6XS and London
Companies and representatives throughout the world

A catalogue record for this book is available from the British Library.
ISBN 0-333-72006-7

First published in the United States of America 1998 by
ST. MARTIN'S PRESS, INC.,
Scholarly and Reference Division,
175 Fifth Avenue, New York, N.Y. 10010

ISBN 0-312-21197-X

Library of Congress Cataloging-in-Publication Data
Drake, C. J. M., 1962–
Terrorists' target selection / C.J.M. Drake.
p. cm.
Includes bibliographical references and index.
ISBN 0-312-21197-X (cloth)
1. Terrorism—Philosophy. 2. Terrorism—Psychological aspects.
3. Victims of terrorism. I. Title.
HV6431.D73 1997
303.6'25—dc21   97-38269
                                                                  CIP

© C. J. M. Drake 1998

All rights reserved. No reproduction, copy or transmission of this publication may be made without written permission.

No paragraph of this publication may be reproduced, copied or transmitted save with written permission or in accordance with the provisions of the Copyright, Designs and Patents Act 1988, or under the terms of any licence permitting limited copying issued by the Copyright Licensing Agency, 90 Tottenham Court Road, London W1P 9HE.

Any person who does any unauthorised act in relation to this publication may be liable to criminal prosecution and civil claims for damages.

The author has asserted his right to be identified as the author of this work in accordance with the Copyright, Designs and Patents Act 1988.

This book is printed on paper suitable for recycling and made from fully managed and sustained forest sources.

10 9 8 7 6 5 4 3 2 1
07 06 05 04 03 02 01 00 99 98

Printed and bound in Great Britain by
Antony Rowe Ltd, Chippenham, Wiltshire

In memory of my father

Contents

List of Figures   viii
List of Tables   ix
Acknowledgements   x
List of Abbreviations   xi

1   Introduction   1

2   Terrorist Typologies   5

3   Ideology   16

4   Strategy   35

5   Tactics   54

6   Capabilities   73

7   Target Protection   98

8   The Security Environment   120

9   External Factors   144

10   Decision-making   163

11   Target Selection   175

Notes   183
Bibliography   243
Index   267

List of Figures

2.1	A simple model of terrorism	8
4.1	Provisional IRA: logical strategy	37
4.2	Provisional IRA terrorist strategy	37
4.3	PIRA rationale for attacking British soldiers	44
10.1	Provisional IRA command structure	166
11.1	Constraints on terrorist target selection	176
11.2	Process of terrorist target selection	180

List of Tables

3.1	Killings in Northern Ireland perpetrated by Loyalist and Republican groups, 1969–1993	32
3.2	Categories of people killed, wounded or kidnapped by communist terrorist groups in Italy and West Germany	33
4.1	Lethal mass casualty bomb attacks in Italy against civilian targets, 1969–1993	48
4.2	Civilians killed by terrorist groups in Algeria in 1994	50
6.1	Relative size and rate of fire of machine-guns, 1884–1970	94
7.1	Security force deaths in Northern Ireland, 1970–1993	113
7.2	British Army fatalities and fatal incidents caused by Irish republican groups, 1970–1993	114
7.3	British Army fatalities and fatal incidents caused by Irish republican groups, 1970–93	115
8.1	Levels of terrorist and security force activities in Northern Ireland, 1980–1989	130
8.2	Police officers killed by terrorists as a percentage of terrorist killings	137
9.1	Categories of opinion relating to the Provisional IRA and the Red Army Faction	146
10.1	Location of fatalities across the parliamentary constituencies in Northern Ireland, July 13, 1969 to July 12, 1989	173

Acknowledgements

In the course of my research I have incurred numerous debts. First and foremost my family has provided the moral and material support without which I could not have coped. For this and for much else I am profoundly grateful.

The University of St Andrews, the David Russell Trust, and the School of History and International Relations at the University of St Andrews, all provided financial assistance without which any question of my carrying out research would have been purely academic.

I would like to thank my Ph.D. supervisor, Professor Paul Wilkinson, for his forbearance and guidance, and several other members of the Department of International Relations at St Andrews for their encouragement. I am also indebted to the library staffs at the universities of St Andrews, Aberdeen, Bradford, the School of Oriental and African Studies in London, and the Linenhall Library in Belfast.

It is invidious to single out people for friendship, but amongst several others I would particularly thank Robin and Ailsa (and Katie), Mike, and Magnus for tolerating me as a Departmental colleague, and Antonio, Joao, Shaun, and Luis for their friendship and forbearance as flatmates. I am particularly grateful to Bruce and Fiona for their friendship and hospitality, and for Bruce's indefatigable proofreading and commentary on my work. To Jim and Maggie I would like to add particular thanks.

In keeping with tradition, any mistakes in this work are my responsibility.

List of Abbreviations

Abbreviations for groups, organisations, posts and publications. The countries listed here refer to where these originated, where they are based, or where they mainly operate.

Please note that it has become conventional in the literature to drop foreign accents. For the most part I have followed this convention throughout.

17N	Epanastaiki Organosi 17 Noemvri (Revolutionary Organisation 17th November). Greece.
ACDEGAM	Asociacion de Campesionos y Ganderos del Magdelena Medio (Peasants and Ranchers of the Magdelena Medio). Colombia.
AD	Action Directe (Direct Action). France.
AIS	Armee islamique du salut (Islamic Salvation Army). Algeria.
ALF	Animal Liberation Front. United Kingdom.
ALN	Acao Libertadora Nacional (Action for National Liberation). Brazil.
ANUC	Asociacion Nacional de Usuarios Campesinos (National Association of Peasant Users). Colombia.
AP/RN	*An Phoblacht/Republican News*. Ireland/United Kingdom.
B2J	Bewegung 2 Juni (June 2nd Movement). Germany.
BR	Brigate Rosse (Red Brigades). Italy.
BR/PCC	Partito Comunista Combattente (Fighting Communist Party). Italy.
CCC	Cellules Communistes Combattantes (Fighting Communist Cells). Belgium.
CIA	Central Intelligence Agency. United States of America.
DC	Democrazia Cristiana (Christian Democrats). Italy.
Dev Sol	Devrimci Sol (Revolutionary Left). Turkey.
EOKA	Ethniki Organosis Kypriakou Agoniston (National Organisation of Cypriot Fighters). Cyprus.
ETA	Euzkadi ta Askatasuna (Basque Homeland and Liberty). Spain/France.

FARC	Fuerzas Armadas Revolucionarias de Colombia (Revolutionary Armed Forces of Colombia).
FBI	Federal Bureau of Investigation. United States of America.
FIS	Front Islamique du Salut (Islamic Salvation Front). Algeria.
FLN	Front de Liberation Nationale (National Liberation Front). Algeria.
GAL	Gruppos Antiterroristas de Liberacion (Anti-terrorist Liberation Group). Spain/France
GIA	Groupes Islamique Armee (Armed Islamic Group). Algeria.
GSG9	Grenzchutzgruppe 9 (Border Protection Unit 9). Germany.
HRU	Hostage Rescue Unit.
INLA	Irish National Liberation Army. United Kingdom/Ireland.
JRA	Japanese Red Army. Japan.
LTTE	Liberation Tigers of Tamil Eelam. Sri Lanka.
MI5	Security Service (formally Military Intelligence section 5). United Kingdom.
MI6	Secret Intelligence Service (formally Military Intelligence section 6). United Kingdom.
MAS	Muerte a Secuestradores (Death to Kidnappers). Colombia.
MK	Umkhonto we Sizwe (Spear of the Nation). South Africa.
OAS	Organisation Armee Secrete (Secret Army Organisation). Algeria and France.
OIRA	Official Irish Republican Army. United Kingdom/Ireland.
OP	Observation post.
PCC	Partitio Comunista Combattente (Fighting Communist Party). Italy.
PCI	Partito Comunista Italiano (Italian Communist Party).
PIRA	Provisional Irish Republican Army. United Kingdom/Ireland.
PFLP	Popular Front for the Liberation of Palestine. Israel/Jordan.
PFLP–GC	Popular Front for the Liberation of Palestine General Command. Israel/Jordan.

PKK	Partiye Karkaran-e Kurdistan (Kurdistan Workers Party). Turkey, Iraq, Iran, Armenia, Azerbaijan, Syria.
PL	Prima Linea (Front Line). Italy.
PLO	Palestinian Liberation Organisation. Israel/Jordan.
RAF	Rote Armee Fraktion (Red Army Faction). Germany.
RIR	Royal Irish Regiment. United Kingdom.
RUC	Royal Ulster Constabulary. United Kingdom.
RZ	Rote Zellen (Revolutionary Cells). Germany.
SAS	Special Air Service. United Kingdom.
SL	Sendero Luminoso (Shining Path). Peru.
SLA	Symbionese Liberation Army. United States of America.
UDA	Ulster Defence Association. United Kingdom.
UDR	Ulster Defence Regiment. United Kingdom.
UP	Union Patriotica (Patriotic Union). Colombia.
UVF	Ulster Volunteer Force. United Kingdom.
VCP	Vehicle check-points.
WGH	Wehrsport Gruppe Hoffmann (Hoffman Military Sports Group). Germany.

1 Introduction

Trying to find out why terrorists do what they do is a bit like trying to solve a good fictional murder in that one is dealing with the elements of motive, method, and opportunity. However, the plot is reversed. With the classic murder one starts with a victim, and has to determine the motive, methods, and opportunity involved in order to discover the perpetrator. With terrorist target selection on the other hand, the motives are known, the means can usually be estimated, and the opportunities are fairly plentiful. What one has to determine is who or what is likely to be the victim.

This study is not an attempt to forecast how particular terrorist groups will act, nor an attempt to predict future trends in terrorism. That would require a longer book, would become rapidly dated, and can be done perfectly adequately elsewhere. The purpose of this study is simply to determine those factors which influence the selection of physical targets by terrorist groups, and attempt to describe how those factors interact.

When examining terrorism, an important point to bear in mind is that as well as the physical target upon which an attack is carried out, terrorists intend to affect one or more psychological targets – that is, those individuals or groups of people whose behaviour the terrorists wish to influence.[1] This relationship between the physical target which is attacked and the psychological target which is affected is central to understanding why terrorists attack the targets which they do. For the sake of simplicity the term *target* is, unless otherwise qualified, confined to those people or things which are physically attacked.

A DEFINITION OF TERRORISM

Initially, it is necessary to define what is meant by the terms *terrorism* and *terrorist*. By doing this one can differentiate terrorism from other types of political violence which a group may use.[2] The elements which differentiate terrorist acts from other forms of political violence are: that the specific acts of violence come as a surprise to the people whose person or property is attacked; that the violence is intended to make the psychological target or targets of the violence behave in a particular way by the use of recurrent intimidatory violence; and that there is always an underlying, if not explicit, threat that future violence may be serious and even lethal. The violence is not necessarily aimed physically at the psychological target, but at making it behave in a particular way.

Although the term terrorism has been adopted for this type of political violence, what is important is not generally the induction of terror as an end in itself, but that the succession of attacks is meant to create a psychological reaction in a person or group of people – the psychological target or targets – to make them act in a way which the attacker desires.[3] The use of violence may also be a way for the attackers to vent their anger at a given person or group of people, rather than being part of a carefully calculated campaign. However, to be considered acts of political terrorism, the violence must be associated with a political conviction, however incoherently understood or expressed.

Accordingly, *terrorism* is defined here as the recurrent use or threatened use of politically-motivated and clandestinely organised violence, by a group whose aim is to influence a psychological target in order to make it behave in a way which the group desires.

There is still the problem of defining what one means by terming a person or a group as terrorist. Both Gearty and Clark label specific acts as terrorist acts, rather than label groups as terrorist in themselves. Thus Clark describes ETA as a political group which from time to time may use terrorism, rather than as a terrorist group.[4]

This is a credible argument, but it assumes a group is only a one-dimensional body. However, in the same way that it is possible for somebody to be a socialist, a stamp collector, and a teacher – the one activity not excluding the others – so it is possible for a political group to also be a terrorist group if it carries out terrorist acts. This does not mean the group is solely, or even mainly, dedicated to terrorism, but it does mean that it carries out terrorist acts. Thus, for the purposes of this thesis, a terrorist is somebody who in some form actively assists or participates in an act of terrorism, and a terrorist group is one which carries out terrorist acts.

THE PARAMETERS OF RESEARCH

This study is concerned with the activities of non-state terrorist groups and not with all forms of terrorism. It does not examine the actions of states or state bodies, except when they have an impact on terrorist groups. In some cases, terrorist acts are clearly carried out directly by the military, police, intelligence, or other branches of the state apparatus. This type of terrorism includes both the operations of intelligence agents against recalcitrant émigrés, as allegedly practiced by the Libyan intelligence agencies in the 1980s, and the liquidation of internal critics, as practiced by the Argentine military government of the late 1970s and early 1980s.[5] Such activities do not fall within the scope of this thesis as this is terrorism by the state.

Some critics argue that in carrying out research on non-state terrorism one is ignoring the far larger phenomenon of state terrorism, thus demonstrating some form of right-wing, pro-western outlook.[6] This argument assumes that research is meant to fulfil a political agenda, rather than to satisfy curiosity. It is rather like condemning medical researchers who concentrate on examining the common cold as being in favour of cancer.

There are other types of government involvement in terrorism which, though not direct, nevertheless indicate the strong involvement of a government or its agencies. For example, with the Spanish group GAL (Gruppos Antiterroristas de Liberacion – Anti-terrorist Liberation Group), which assassinated suspected Basque activists in southern France, and death squads in the Philippines and Latin America which have killed suspected dissidents, the line between state terrorism and non-state terrorism has been blurred. In these cases reports indicate that the state – or at least elements within the state apparatus – appear to have supported the formation of these groups, and possibly provided them with resources.[7] In other cases, state support has taken the form of providing existing groups with training and material backing, for example the support given in the early 1980s by the governing Congress Party in India to the Sikh militant Sant Jarnail Singh Bhindranwali, and to the Tamil separatists of the Liberation Tigers of Tamil Eelam (LTTE) in Sri Lanka.[8] Another example is weapons, training, and safe haven given to the Red Army Faction – originally a terrorist group in West Germany – by the East German intelligence services.[9] Finally, there are cases in which members of state agencies become involved in terrorism of their own volition, without the apparent support of the government, for example the alleged connivance of sections of the Italian intelligence agencies with fascist terrorists in the 1960s and 1970s.[10]

Although a very high proportion of terrorist attacks could be described as arson, this study concentrates mainly on groups which constitute serious threats to life, or cause extensive damage to property.[11] Likewise, much of the evidence is based upon the actions of longer-lived and better known groups.

A small number of terrorist groups gain more attention due to their longevity, lethality, or the prominence of their victims. As Moss and Pisano have shown with communist and fascist terrorist groups in Italy, and Pearce has demonstrated with conservative death squads in Colombia, tens or even hundreds of small groups may be responsible for many more terrorist acts than the larger terrorist groups within their respective countries.[12] However, publicity and therefore research interest, inevitably concentrates upon those which carry out the more spectacular or lethal acts.

2 Terrorist Typologies

INTRODUCTION

Although each terrorist group's campaign is unique, for reasons of comparison it is useful to construct categories which can be applied across all groups. The classification of methods and targets brings some sort of order to the disparate methods used and types of people and things attacked by terrorist groups. Classifications of strategies and ideologies are examined later.

TYPES OF TERRORIST OPERATION

There are several types of terrorist operation.[1] The typology employed in this section is based upon the nature of the operation. The categories are:

- Assassination
- Discriminate attack
- Mass casualty attack
- Abduction
- Siege
- Hijacking
- Sabotage
- Mass destruction attack

More than one category of attack may be used in a single operation. For example, a large bomb could be intended to cause both mass casualties and mass destruction, although in practice most large bombings are primarily intended to cause one or the other.

Assassination: An assassination is an attack which is intended to kill a specific person or specific people. The target need not be well known or powerful, but the attack must have been aimed at killing that person or those people in particular. For instance, a lethal attack on a police officer, which is aimed at killing any police officer, is not an assassination because the object of the attack is not a specific person. However, if a specific police officer is selected as a target and killed, then it is an assassination. Other people may be killed or injured in the course of an assassination attempt, but these casualties are incidental, or are at most secondary targets – such as bodyguards – who have to be eliminated so the terrorists can attack their primary target. This was the case with the Tamil suicide bomber who killed the Congress Party leader and former Indian Prime Minister, Rajiv Gandhi, together with herself and about 20 bystanders at an election rally in Madras in April 1991.[2]

Discriminate attack: A discriminate attack is one where the aim is not necessarily to harm specific individuals, but to kill or injure people who fall within a specific category – be it racial, religious, or occupational. An example of this would be attacks on uniformed police officers, but it could apply to a broader group, such as any member of a particular religious or ethnic group. Other people may be harmed in the attack, but this is incidental to the objective.

Mass-casualty attack: A mass-casualty attack is one in which the aim is to kill or injure as many people as possible with little regard as to who is harmed. To call such attacks indiscriminate would not accurate, as most attacks contain a degree of discrimination with regard to the people or objects damaged, or the location of the attack. At the very least, terrorists tend to ensure that their own supporters are not injured. An example occurred in April 1986 when Nizar Hindawi – a Jordanian reportedly working for Syrian intelligence – duped his unsuspecting pregnant girlfriend into carrying a bomb on board an aeroplane. By specifically choosing an Israel-bound flight belonging to the Israeli airline El Al he showed a degree of discrimination in that a high proportion of victims were likely to be Jewish or Israeli.[3]

Abduction: An abduction is an operation where a person is seized and taken to a secret place where they are held pending their release or death. Such incidents frequently take the form of kidnappings where the terrorists attempt to gain some form of benefit – usually a ransom or the release of prisoners – in return for the release of the person abducted. In other cases there may be no intention to free the victim. In September 1990 a PIRA unit stopped a minibus just after it had crossed from the Republic of Ireland into Northern Ireland, and abducted an RUC officer. He was interrogated, then shot dead.[4]

Siege: Sometimes termed a barricade and hostage incident, a siege occurs when terrorists seize hostages and then barricade themselves behind cover with the intention of holding them until their demands are met. Usually such operations are pre-planned, as occurred when Arab-Iranians seized the Iranian Embassy in London in April 1980, and held the people there hostage. The terrorists' chief aim was to publicise their demand for autonomy for their area of Iran, but they also demanded safe conduct out of Britain and the release of 91 prisoners held in Iran.[5] Terrorists who are trying to evade capture may seize hostages and try to bargain their way out of captivity, as happened in London in December 1975 when four PIRA members fleeing the police, broke into a flat and seized the couple who lived there. The terrorists demanded a getaway aeroplane, but one of them later admitted they were playing for time, in the hope that other PIRA members would recover equipment from their safe house.[6]

Hijacking: A hijacking is an operation where the terrorists seize control of a vehicle, such as an aircraft, ship, or car, often seizing the occupants as bargaining counters with a government or some other actor. The Dawson's Field incident of 1970, where PFLP members hijacked three aircraft of different nationalities, is an early example of hijacking aircraft in order to exert pressure on several governments and publicise their cause.[7]

Sabotage: An act of sabotage is an attack intended to cause damage to a specific material target. Examples include the numerous incendiary attacks which the Provisional IRA carried out on commercial premises in Northern Ireland and England throughout the late 1980s and early 1990s.[8] There is always the possibility that someone will get hurt, as happened in February 1978 12 people were killed and 23 injured by a PIRA blast-incendiary bomb at the La Mon House Hotel near Comber, county Down, Northern Ireland.[9]

Mass-destruction attack: A mass-destruction attack is intended to cause a large amount of material damage. Prime examples would be the two massive bombs which the PIRA detonated in the City of London in April 1992 and April 1993, where *Lloyd's List* quotes insured losses at £350 million in the former case and £650 million in the latter.[10] The potential for injuries or fatalities in such attacks is enormous. Three civilians were killed and over 75 injured in the 1992 explosion, and one was killed and over 50 injured in that of 1993.[11]

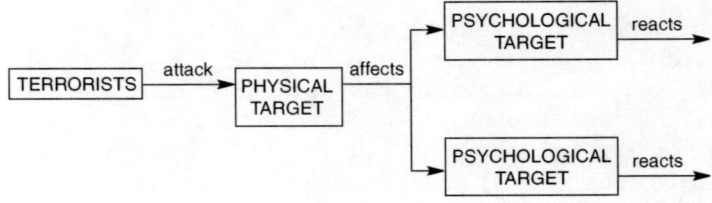

Figure 2.1 A simple model of terrorism

CLASSIFICATION OF TARGETS

When examining terrorists' target selection, one must be aware that there is usually more than one intended target for an operation. As well as the physical target which is attacked there is also the psychological target or targets whose behaviour the terrorists wish to affect. In practice, a single attack may be intended to influence the behaviour of more than one psychological target. If one wanted to construct a simple model of how terrorism works, it would be something like Figure 2.1.

There are a few terms which are used in this study in relation to types of target which it would be useful to know. A soft target is one which has little or no protection and a hard target is one which has a substantial degree of protection. Apart from this, targets are classified, first according to the degree of preparation which goes into the terrorist operation, and second according to the purpose of the attack.

Not all targets are painstakingly selected beforehand. On the one hand there are pre-planned attacks, where terrorists have deliberately selected the target before carrying out the attack. Examples of this would be highly complex operations like the kidnapping of former Italian Prime Minister Aldo Moro in April 1978, or the assassination of the Spanish Prime Minister Admiral Luis Carrero Blanco in December 1973.[12] Pre-planned attacks need not be aimed at specific individuals. For instance, the bombing of Bologna railway station in Italy in August 1980, which killed 85 people, required advance planning to select the target and assemble the bomb.[13]

On the other hand there are opportunist attacks on what can be deemed targets of opportunity. These occur when a person or thing, falling within the class of what the terrorists concerned regard as targets, suddenly becomes vulnerable to attack and the terrorists take advantage of the opportunity. This is more likely to happen where the terrorist group has selected categories of people as legitimate targets – for example police officers or members of an ethnic group – rather than specific individuals. Catholics in Northern Ireland have been abducted and killed after they wandered into areas where members of loyalist terrorist groups have been present.[14] Similar attacks by European fascists often result following heavy drinking on the part of the attackers when an identifiable target happens along.[15] Such attacks are also more likely to occur when the terrorist group is large, because the more group members there are, and the more geographically dispersed they are, the more chance there is of them encountering a target. Targets which have similar characteristics – for example soldiers – can be deemed as either pre-planned targets or targets of opportunity depending on the nature of the attack.

CATEGORISING TARGET BY PURPOSE OF ATTACK

Another way to classify targets is according to the potential effect of attacking them.[16] However, categorising targets by the purpose of the attack requires the need to know – or at least have a well-informed theory about – the attackers' motives. A complication is that not every terrorist attack is accompanied by a communiqué.[17] When they are, as with any political group there is the question as to whether what they say represents an attempt to put an acceptable gloss on their actions.[18]

In order to classify targets by the terrorists' purpose the following terms are used.

- Symbolic
- Functional
- Logistical
- Expressive

These relate to the reason why the terrorists are believed to have selected these people or things as targets. Of course, a target may be attacked for more than one reason.

SYMBOLIC TARGETS

Symbolic targets are those where the primary motive for the attack is to prompt a reaction in the psychological target. This can be for a number of purposes. Terrorists may attack a target so as to draw attention to the group and their cause. For instance, following the PIRA assassination of Lord Mountbatten in August 1979, when a New Zealand journalist rang the Sinn Fein office in Belfast to ask why a harmless old man like Mountbatten had been killed, the Sinn Fein official reportedly asked the journalist why he was ringing from New Zealand.[19] According to a member of the PIRA Army Council:

> Killing this man had the aim of making the world understand – and first and foremost the British – that there is a state of war in this country. Given his personal importance there was inevitably going to be enormous publicity attached to this operation.... we had no hatred for him as a person. It is the society, the military and the political machine he symbolized that we were aiming at.[20]

Similar comments were made by the IRA man Dan Breen, concerning the unsuccessful attempt in Dublin in December 1919 to assassinate Lord French, Lord Lieutenant of Ireland and a commander of the British Army in France during the First World War. Breen states that the IRA held no spite against French, but concludes that if the attempt on French had been successful, people around the world would have thought 'Ireland must have a grievance. What is it?'[21]

Targets do not have to be prominent in order to have a symbolic value. Peter Gurney, former head of the Explosives Section of London's Metropolitan Police Anti-Terrorist Squad, has divided PIRA attacks in England into what he terms 'spectaculars' and 'pot-boilers'.[22] Pot-boilers, which in the rest of this study are termed *irritants*, are low-level attacks where the aim is to cause inconvenience and aggravation as a niggling reminder to the psychological target or targets that the terrorists are a problem which will not go away until they have got what they want. The aim of irritants is to keep up a constant minimum level of aggravation and inconvenience. Even certain killings, such as the killing of individual soldiers and police officers in Northern Ireland, can come into the category of irritants when they have become relatively commonplace.

Spectaculars are attacks intended to cause serious damage and distress. As Gurney points out, this may be in order to put the terrorists' campaign, and hence their cause, at the top of the political agenda. There are precedents where the terrorists have carried out but not claimed spectaculars because they hope the resultant chaos will further their cause. As will be seen later, this has been the case with the fascist and Mafia bombings in Italy between the 1960s and 1990s.

An unknown person can take on a symbolic value because of the office they hold or the job they perform. For example, in the Basque Country members of the Spanish Civil Guard (Guardia Civil) are frequently killed by ETA, while in Northern Ireland uniformed members of the British Army or the RUC are killed by the PIRA, not because they pose an immediate threat to the terrorists, but because they provide a readily recognisable symbol of what the group is fighting against.[23]

FUNCTIONAL TARGETS

Functional targets are people or objects whose destruction removes a threat to the terrorist group. The most obvious example would be the case of a terrorist being confronted by an armed opponent where he had to either kill the opponent or risk being killed or apprehended. Such cases may occur when the police have trapped a terrorist who then tries to shoot his way out in order to avoid death or arrest. For example, in October 1974 the Red Brigadist Roberto Ognibene shot dead a Carabinieri marshal when attempting to escape from a patrol which had lain in wait for him at a BR safe-house.[24]

However, the threat need not be so immediate. Police or intelligence officers who are involved with the investigation of terrorist groups are a prime target. These people are primarily functional targets because, as a 1978 British Army report on PIRA noted, they pose a direct threat to the terrorist group.[25] One of the great successes of the IRA in the rebellion of 1919–21 was to paralyse the British intelligence system through the systematic elimination of police and intelligence operatives. As an IRA agent noted, even if a dead detective was replaced, the new man would not have his knowledge of the situation.[26] The successful elimination of such people can also be exploited for its propaganda potential. Hence, in 1977 the Sinn Fein newspaper, *Republican News*, carried PIRA statements applauding the killings of an RUC detective in Derry, and of a British Army intelligence officer.[27] However, this publicity is a secondary benefit of such attacks.

In addition to focusing on individuals, facilities used by investigators have also been targeted. In September 1992 a 2,000 lb. PIRA bomb destroyed the forensic science laboratories in Belfast. The destruction of the laboratories – which in 1991 handled nearly 32,000 items involved in over 5,000 cases – hampered the attempts of the authorities to build up cases against terrorist suspects.[28]

LOGISTICAL TARGETS

Logistical targets are those which are attacked in order to provide or safeguard the group's resources. Any terrorist organisation which deploys a number of more or less full-time operatives, has to obtain money in order to secure safe houses, rent cars and hotel rooms, buy weapons, and carry out other essential activities. In countries where it is necessary to carry identity documents, premises have been raided to obtain the necessary paperwork. Thus on November 16th 1971 the Red Army Faction raided the town hall at Neustadt am Ruebenberge and stole blank passports, identity cards, and official seals. Five days later they raided the town hall in Langgonns, Hessen, and took identity cards and more official stamps.[29]

The methods used to obtain money, materials, or personnel vary considerably. Straightforward methods such as bank robbery can net fairly large sums in little time. From 1879 until the early 1900s, bank robbery was a common method used by Russian revolutionary groups to secure sufficient funds.[30] More recently, Carlos Marighela, who led the Action for National Liberation (Acao Libertadora Nacional – ALN) in Brazil in the late 1960s, saw bank robbery as a useful source of funds and also useful training for other activities.[31] Robberies have been committed by groups as diverse as the Red Army Faction, the PIRA, the PLO, and the remnants of the French Secret Army Organisation (Organisation Armee Secrete – OAS).[32] In March 1992 it was reported that during the troubles in Northern Ireland £18 million had been taken in 17,000 robberies within the Province.[33]

Another method is to kidnap people. This can take the form of seizing a person and then hiding them until a ransom is paid. Alternatively the victim can be held until comrades of the kidnappers are released from prison. The kidnappers can present a list of several demands. Behind the demands lie the threat that the hostage will be killed if the kidnappers' terms are not met.

On September 19, 1974 the Montoneros, an Argentine Peronist group, kidnapped two sons of the founder of the grain and flour company Bunge y Born. Both were senior executives in the company. One was released early for health reasons, the other was released on June 20, 1975 after a number of conditions had been met, the most important being the payment of $60 million.[34] Other kidnappings achieve more modest sums. In March 1983 ETA kidnapped the president of a bank which had recently collapsed. Initially the group demanded 1,200 million pesetas (£6 million), but eventually released him on payment of 150 million pesetas (£750,000).[35] However, ETA has also instituted a form of extortion termed a 'revolutionary tax'. The group contacts wealthy individuals and threatens to kill them unless they pay a certain amount to ETA annually.[36] If the victims pay, they are not harmed. If they do not they may be kidnapped, killed, or deliberately wounded.[37]

Kidnappings aimed at obtaining the release of comrades from imprisonment have also occurred fairly frequently. The Uruguayan National Liberation Movement (Movimiento de Liberacion Nacional – MLN), also known as the Tupamaros, carried out a number of kidnappings in the early 1970s including the Chief Public Safety Advisor at the US Embassy – who was killed, and a number of ambassadors.[38] Likewise, in 1989 and 1990, members of the Medellin cocaine cartel took journalists, businessmen, and the manager of a football team hostage. The cartel seized these hostages to prevent the Colombian Government from apprehending members of the cartel members' families, and to prevent the extradition of cartel members to the USA.[39]

Attempts to obtain money through a form of kidnapping can be far more overt, as happens in the case of hijackings, or in sieges where terrorists hold hostages within a building. In these cases, no attempt is made to conceal the general whereabouts of the hostages, although their precise location within the aircraft or building might not be known. The aim is to trade the safe return of the hostages for the release of the terrorists' colleagues.

For example, in June 1985, Trans-World Airways Flight 847 from Athens to Rome was hijacked by members of the Lebanese Shia Islamic group Hizbollah, demanding the release of 766 Lebanese prisoners held in Israel, and the withdrawal of Israeli troops and the Israeli-created South Lebanese Army (SLA) from southern Lebanon.[40] On June 15 one of the hostages, a US Navy diver, was shot dead at Beirut. The hijacking ended on June 30 after negotiations through the Syrian Government and the leader of the Lebanese Shia Moslem militia group known as the Lebanese Resistance Battalions (Afwaj al-Muqawimah al-Lubnaniyah – AMAL). The 766 Lebanese held in Israel were freed over a period of three months, although the Israelis denied that this was due to the hijacking. Most other demands were not met.[41]

The fact that a target has a logistical value does not preclude it from having a functional or symbolic value as well. When members of the Palestinian organisation Black September seized eleven Israeli athletes at the 1972 Munich Olympics, they had three aims, according to Fatah's head of security and intelligence, Abu Iyad: to affirm the existence of the Palestinian people; to gain publicity for the Palestinian cause from the saturation media coverage of the Olympics; and to force Israel to release imprisoned comrades. Although ostensibly intended to fulfil logistical objectives, and despite the death of the hostages and killing or capture of the terrorists, the Munich kidnappings fulfilled a symbolic objective by forcing the Palestinian question onto the international agenda.[42]

EXPRESSIVE TARGETS

Terrorism can be an emotional response to a situation, rather than a part of an overall strategy. The lone anarchists who carried out bomb and knife attacks in France in the 1890s were often motivated by personal anger at perceived injustices, rather than by political programmes.[43] Auguste Vaillant's bomb attack on the Chamber of Deputies on December 9, 1893, for which he was executed, seems to have been inspired as much by despair at his family's poverty as by any symbolic political motive.[44] Likewise, Emile Henry, who bombed the Café Terminus in Paris in February 1894, stated at his trial:

> I wanted to show the bourgeoisie that their pleasures would no longer be complete, that their insolent triumphs would be disturbed, that their golden calf would tremble violently on its pedestal, until the final shock would cast it down in mud and blood.[45]

Lupsha cites indignation as a possible motive for carrying out an act of political violence.[46] He defines indignation as an attitude and behavioural manifestations of wrathfulness because of unworthy or unjust treatment.[47] Merari refers to a similar concept in discussing 'expressive terrorism' citing the terrorist campaigns by South Moluccans in the Netherlands and the Armenian Secret Army for the Liberation of Armenia (ASALA) as examples.[48] Arguably the South Moluccan campaign was quite rational in that they perceived a need to highlight the political position of the Moluccans, and did so. On the other hand, whilst ASALA calls for an independent state in the formerly Armenian provinces of Turkey, it appears to have been largely motivated by the desire to exact revenge against the Turks for the death of 1.5 million Armenians in 1915.[49]

Revenge can also be a major motivation for specific attacks. During operations against Sikh militants and terrorists in the Punjab in June 1984, the Chief of the Indian Army Staff, General Vaidya, ordered the storming of the Golden Temple in Amritsar, the holiest Sikh shrine. The Temple was severely damaged and many Sikhs killed, including the militant leader Sant Jarnail Singh Bhindranwale. In August 1986, at Pune in southern India, Sikhs on motor cycles overtook and fired on the car of the then retired General Vaidya, killing him and wounding his wife and bodyguard.[50]

3 Ideology

INTRODUCTION

Ideology can be defined as the beliefs, values, principles, and objectives – however ill-defined or tenuous – by which a group defines its distinctive political identity and aims, and justifies its actions.[1] Some ideologies – particularly religion or separatism, but others as well – include elements of historical or even semi-mythical beliefs.[2] What is important is that ideology provides a motive – and possibly a formula – for action.

There may be a distinction between the professed ideology of a group and the actual beliefs of individual members. The organisers at the top of such groups usually believe in a fairly specific political ideology and have clear political objectives, but for many of their followers a sufficient motive for belonging to the group is provided by adherence to the group and a visceral dislike of an 'enemy', however defined. This is seen with various far-right organisations in Britain in the late 1970s and early 1980s, and in letters from imprisoned Italian fascists.[3]

Whilst ideology generally sets the limits within which terrorists select targets, different ideologies provide different targets. Furthermore, in some cases the connection between terrorist activity and political ideology may not be straightforward due to other influences. For instance, in Sri Lanka, the Punjab, and Northern Ireland, communal rivalries may account for the selection of local targets by a group which in principle bases itself upon a more abstract ideological justification.

CATEGORIES OF IDEOLOGY

The categories used to classify ideologies in this study are:

- Separatism
- Religion
- Liberalism
- Anarchism

- Communism
- Conservatism
- Fascism
- Single-issue
- Organised Crime

Separatism. The concepts of separatism and nationalism are inextricably linked. There are several theories as to what makes up a nation, and consequently several definitions of nationalism.[4] This study adopts Smith's definition of nationalism as 'an ideological movement for attaining and maintaining autonomy, unity and identity on behalf of a population deemed by some of its members to constitute an actual or potential "nation"'.[5] A separatist group is one which aims at gaining political independence from the existing form of government for a given geographical area and population, either for the purposes of gaining total independence, or to attach themselves to a state with which they feel a greater affinity. Separatist groups believe that they represent the interests and aspirations of a national group – whether or not that group realises it – by seeking to liberate them from their current 'foreign' rulers. A separatist terrorist group is one which uses terrorism for that end. Examples include ETA in the Basque region of Spain, and the Liberation Tigers of Tamil Eelam (LTTE) in Sri Lanka, who wish to set up separate states for the Basques and Tamils respectively.[6] Alternatively, separatist groups like the Greek-Cypriot group EOKA in the 1950s, or the present-day Provisional IRA in Northern Ireland, wish to secede from the existing government and join another state – in these cases Greece and the Republic of Ireland.[7]

Religion. A religion is a system of laws, customs, and possibly institutions, relating to the worship of a supernatural power. Like separatism, religion commands from its adherents a high degree of fealty to an intangible entity. As with nationality, people are generally born into their religion. Whereas they consciously choose ideologies such as communism, liberalism, or fascism, their religion and nationality is something which they generally inherit.

Members of a religious terrorist group use terrorism to promote their perception of the doctrines and political interests of their religion. This includes groups such as the Armed Islamic Group (Groupes Islamique Armee – GIA) in Algeria, Hizbollah in the Lebanon, and the Jewish Underground which flourished in parts of Israel in the early 1980s.[8] Groups promoting an extensive political role for their religion believe that their governments are morally obliged to govern according to the tenets of that religion.

This study does not examine millenarian groups which do not have definable political aims. Millenarians believe that some form of apocalyptic change is at hand, and anticipate 'collective, earthly, imminent, total, supernatural salvation'.[9] The majority of millenarian groups are not violent.[10] Where they have been – mainly in the USA – they appear to have been motivated primarily by an extreme right-wing political agenda rather than by their religious beliefs.

Liberalism. Liberalism promotes the establishment of democratic systems of government, the equality of individuals before the law, and the maintenance of the civil rights and freedom of the individual.[11] A liberal terrorist group is one which uses terrorism in order to secure a government of this nature. In Russia, for example, the People's Will in the 1870s and 1880s and the Social Revolutionaries in the early twentieth century, were primarily concerned with the overthrow of the Tsarist autocracy and the introduction of democratic reforms.[12] Likewise, the ANC's political programme – the Freedom Charter of 1955 and subsequent amendments – was not radical by democratic norms, but called for the political and legal equality of all South African citizens, a moderate redistribution of wealth, and the limited nationalisation of parts of the economy.[13] Initially, ANC violence – carried out by Spear of the Nation (Umkhonto we Sizwe – MK) – was supposed to take the shape of sabotage and self-defence, but from 1985 mass casualty bomb attacks were made on whites in general.[14]

Anarchism. Anarchism is resistant to an authoritative definition. Proudhon is quoted as saying to an admirer of his 'system'; 'My system? I have no system!'[15] Anarchists generally oppose the authority of one group of people over others, and oppose the exercise of power by the possessors of private wealth. They believe that the state is an unnecessary and oppressive institution, and wish to replace it with structures which operate on a cooperative, voluntary basis, and are directly answerable to those on whose behalf they administer.[16] An anarchist terrorist group is one which uses terrorism in order to overthrow the existing system of government, and replace it with one which accords with anarchist thought. Examples of anarchist terrorists include the French anarchists of the late nineteenth century and the Angry Brigade in Britain in the early 1970s.[17]

Communism. Communism's fundamental principles derive from the writings of Karl Marx in the third quarter of the nineteenth century and the revision and adaptation of these ideas by Lenin in the first quarter of the twentieth century. Marxist-Leninist communism professes that in any society there is a constant struggle between the ruling classes who own the instruments for the distribution of wealth and power, and the classes who work for them. In industrial societies Marx termed the capitalist ruling class as the bourgeoisie and the ruled industrial working class as the proletariat. Communists see the state as an instrument of repression which the bourgeoisie use to maintain their wealth and power. Whilst Marx saw developing class consciousness as making the victory of the working class inevitable, Lenin stated that a small, clandestine revolutionary leadership is required to provide the necessary impetus.[18] Hence the development of Marxist-Leninist communism, where a small revolutionary vanguard would lead the masses to victory and eventually true communism. Subsequent variants take into account the work of later followers of Marxism-Leninism, in particular those of the Chinese communist leader Mao Tse-tung, and Latin American communist revolutionaries such as Che Guevara and Carlos Marighela.[19]

Communist terrorist groups aim at overthrowing the existing political and economic system through the use of terrorism in the hope that the violence will politicise the masses and incite them to rise up and destroy the capitalist system. Examples of communist terrorist groups include the Red Brigades and Front Line in Italy, the Red Army Faction and the June 2nd Movement in Germany, the Shining Path in Peru, the Naxalites in India, and the Japanese Red Army.

Conservatism. There are various types of conservatism, but it does have a core of beliefs, the essence of which is defence of the existing social, economic, or political order against radical change. Where radical change has occurred, conservatives may try to achieve a reversion to the earlier state of affairs.[20] A conservative terrorist group is one which uses terrorism in order to defend the existing order or to gain a reversion to an earlier arrangement.

There have been a number of conservative terrorist groups. The OAS flourished in French Algeria in 1961 and 1962, and sought to prevent the independence of Algeria from France because its members believed that independence would harm the interests of the Europeans who had been settling there since the 1830s.[21] Similarly, the Ulster Defence Association and the Ulster Volunteer Force have both attempted to prevent the secession of Northern Ireland from the United Kingdom to the Republic of Ireland because they fear that this would harm Northern Irish Protestants.[22] In Colombia in the 1980s, several land owners, narcotics dealers, and military officers helped set up scores of paramilitary groups in order to protect themselves and their political interests against left-wing guerrillas. Several spawned death squads which intimidated or attacked their perceived opponents in trade unions, peasant movements, and reforming governments.[23]

Conservative terrorism frequently takes the form of political vigilantism, although vigilantism is not confined to conservative groups. Vigilantism has been defined as illegal acts which are intended to defend the established order from subversion.[24] Vigilantism is not necessarily a political action and can be as a method of controlling crime.[25] Rosenbaum and Sederberg note that the latter type is often portrayed as 'taking the law into one's own hands' and suggests the lynching of horse thieves by American cowboys as an example.[26] However, vigilantism can also be used as a form of political terrorism in order to consolidate existing power structures.

Fascism. Fascism is a revolutionary doctrine based upon some fairly distinct tenets. These include: a belief in the intrinsic superiority of one's self-perceived race; a desire for non-democratic authoritarian government by elites over an homogenous organic nation; and – normally – a dislike or hatred of people who are seen to be somehow different from the norm.[27] The most obvious characteristic of fascism is racialism which can range from extreme nationalism to the racial ideology of the Nazis where supposedly inferior races are deemed to be only worthy of destruction.[28]

Fascists tend to see the existing political elites as effete and corrupt, and generally yearn for strong, heroic leadership figures. Ordinary people, even the supposedly ethnically pure, are seen as a mass or herd, to be led by a strong leader.[29] Allied to this is a form of nihilism, with a propensity towards the use and glorification of violence.[30] Ultimately fascists aim to establish an organic, homogeneous society, based upon the primacy of order and loyalty to the state, or to a broader racial loyalty such as the pan-European ideal held by some European fascists.[31]

European examples of fascist terrorist groups include New Order (Ordine Nuovo – ON), a group which flourished in Italy from the 1956 until the late 1970s, the Hoffman Military Sports Group (Wehrsportgruppe Hoffman), which flourished in West Germany in the 1980s, and a smattering of small fringe groups in other European states.[32] Over the last fifteen years or so a fascist-anarchist hybrid has evolved in the USA which regards any form of government above the state level as evil, but also retains strong authoritarian and racialist views. Groups such as the 'Covenant, Sword, and Arm of the Lord', The Order, Posse Comitatus, and various other white supremacist, anti-Jewish, and anti-federal government groups, have developed a rag-bag of ideologies in the 1970s and 1980s. These proclaim that the federal government is part of a Jewish conspiracy which plans to hand America over to a dictatorial world government, and refer to the federal government as the Zionist Occupation Government (ZOG).[33] Some American anti-federalists also appear to be anarchistic in their self-proclaimed individualism and hostility to the American state, resulting in attacks on tax offices, and federal buildings and officials.[34]

Single-issue. A single-issue group is one which confines its actions to a restricted area of politics. Such groups do not intend to change the system of government or radically alter social or economic relationships – although individual members may wish to do so. Instead they try to exert influence over relatively narrow policy areas. Whilst these groups may wish to mobilise public support, they believe that if necessary their rights override the views of the majority.[35]

A single-issue terrorist group is one which uses terrorism to promote its objectives. Examples include some animal liberationists in Britain and some anti-abortionists in the USA.[36] Recently in the USA, groups opposed to various forms of development or environmental degradation have carried out acts of sabotage, but thus far have not killed or injured anybody.[37] The single-issue category does not include terrorist groups which carry out attacks linked to an issue area but who have wider ambitions. For instance, in the 1980s the Revolutionary Cells in West Germany attacked the offices of firms involved in the extension of the runway at Frankfurt Airport, whilst ETA assassinated managers and engineers involved in the construction of a nuclear power station at Lemoniz in the Basque Country.[38]

Organised Crime. A criminal group is a group which commits acts in breach of the criminal law primarily in order to obtain material benefits. The term 'organised crime' refers to groups which have a permanent or semi-permanent organisation and which tend to concentrate on those crimes which bring in a constant flow of income.[39] Depending on the laws in the state concerned this could include extortion, fraud, the production and distribution of illegal narcotic drugs, and dealing in prohibited goods such as illegal weapons. As will be seen in the chapter on capabilities, many terrorist groups use these methods to raise funds, but they are not counted as organised criminal groups as defined above because fund-raising is not their primary aim. Similarly, the use of violence and intimidation by criminal groups for purely financial gain is not terrorism. An organised criminal group is only termed as a terrorist group when it uses terrorist methods in order to achieve political objectives.

This has occurred in Italy – particularly Sicily – and Colombia, where criminal organisations have used violence to gain immunity from the law or to safeguard their interests.[40] The Mafia, for example, is not overly concerned with political affairs provided they do not threaten its power or profits, and contents itself with having placemen in the relevant official and political posts. This allows it to secure public sector contracts, pass laws which will favour its opportunities for profit, and stop laws which could harm it. It also requires the eradication of serious threats to the organisation's existence or activities. These do not just consist of those people or institutions which pose a direct challenge, but also include those people or groups which may create a political climate which is inimical to the criminals' activities. In such circumstances these groups have intervened in politics, by violent and lethal means if necessary.[41] By using violence to intimidate the authorities into placing organised crime beyond the scope of the law, these groups are pursuing an objective which is ultimately political.

Organised criminal groups do appear to prefer the ideological right. Narcotics trafficking groups in Colombia have colluded with conservative terrorist groups in attacking left-wing politicians, union organisers, and peasant leaders.[42] Likewise, the Mafia was, until the recent disintegration of the Italian political establishment, heavily involved with the Christian Democrats, with conservative economic interests and with fascist terrorist groups.[43] However, such alliances may simply reflect opportunistic opposition to the threat from reformist groups rather than a right-wing bias as such.

The categories are not mutually exclusive and it is perfectly possible for a group to hold to more than one political aspiration. Indeed, the beliefs of many groups form ideological hybrids. For instance, the categories of communist and separatist are listed separately, but the Basque group ETA – together with its political partner Herri Batasuna (HB) – has considered itself to be both separatist and Marxist.[44] In practice this caused several splits in ETA.[45] Similarly the Palestinian group Hamas can be described as both a re-

Ideology

ligious group and as a separatist group. It combines what it claims to be a true interpretation of Islamic tenets with the desire to set up an Islamic Palestinian state in the territories which now include Israel, the Israeli-occupied territories of the west bank of the Jordan, and the areas currently under the governance of the PLO.[46] Insofar as it is an Islamic group Hamas can be classified as a religious terrorist group, but it is also separatist because it advocates Palestinian autonomy from Israeli control.

THE ROLE OF IDEOLOGY IN TARGET SELECTION

A group's ideology is extremely important in determining target selection. It defines how the group's members see the world around them. Events and the actions of various people – both potential targets and other actors – are interpreted in terms of the terrorists' cause, even if the actors concerned have never given the terrorists a moment's thought. For instance, according to Patricia Hearst, Emily Harris of the Symbionese Liberation Army justified the possibility of law students being killed by a bomb under a police car on the grounds that:

> Those law students are studying to be lawyers and they'll go to work for some big, piggy, corporation, and so they are pigs too.[47]

The students' action in choosing to study law, was seen in terms of Harris' ideological mindset rather than their own perception of what they were doing. Likewise, in 1977 the Provisional IRA carried out a short-lived campaign of assassination against prominent businessmen on the grounds that the very presence of such firms was felt to underpin the British occupation of Northern Ireland.[48] Doubtless the businessmen did not see their actions in this light, but the PIRA saw them in terms of their own ideological structure, and this meant that they became targets.

When a group takes the decision to use violence, an early step is to determine who or what will be attacked. The ideology of a terrorist group identifies the 'enemies' of the group by providing a measure against which to assess the 'goodness' or 'badness', 'innocence' or 'guilt' of people and institutions. This gives rise to the idea that certain targets are somehow 'legitimate' targets. The concept of the legitimate target should not be confused with common or legal notions of guilt and innocence. For instance, members of the ALF frequently claim that although technically breaking the law, they are in fact responding to a higher law which compels them to act as they do.[49] Similarly, a member of the Provisional IRA told Tony Parker:

> I don't expect to be judged by your rules: if Brits do that, then they'll see the IRA as a lot of ruthless maniacs which by their definition I suppose we are. Ruthless, definitely yes: and maniacs if that's what people are who're never going to see sense as you define it, well yes that'd be an appropriate word. The IRA has its own logic and oh no it's not yours.[50]

An example of the difference between the terrorists' perception and that of the more generally accepted institutions, occurred in April 1991 when the Red Army Faction shot dead Detlev Rohwedder, the head of the agency responsible for overseeing the privatisation of companies formerly owned by the East German state. Following the assassination, the editorial in the London-based newspaper *The Independent* condemned the RAF as 'a tiny band of sick people representing no views beyond those concocted in their own closed minds', whilst the newspaper's obituarist called Rohwedder: 'one of the good guys on the German political scene'.[51] However, the RAF communique following the assassination accused Rohwedder – who had previously been State Secretary in the West German Economics Ministry – of having sold arms to fascist regimes in the Third World, and of having traded nuclear know-how for uranium from the apartheid regime in South Africa. They called him:

> One of those armchair murderers who daily go over dead bodies and who in the interest of power and profits plan the misery and death of millions of human beings.[52]

and went on to condemn him as a 'brutal reorganizer' when manager at Hoechst Chemicals. They also condemned the expansion of Germany, the imposition of 'free market economics' on East Germany and the Third World, and condemned the nature of capitalism and the price it exacted from those in the Third World.[53] By killing Rohwedder the RAF believed they were striking at the roots of the development of a racialist and capitalist 'Greater Germany' and were sending a message to people in the former East Germany.[54] For the RAF the killing of Rohwedder was not only an effective use of violence, it was a moral act.

Terrorists seek to identify their victims as being in some way 'guilty', and deserving of the treatment meted out to them.[55] This absolves them – at least temporarily – of feelings of guilt for their actions, because a person who is defined as an enemy deserving punishment obviously deserves to be attacked. It also legitimises the terrorists' actions in their own minds, in those of their followers, and they hope in the minds of those people who are uncommitted. Thus in July 1990 the Provisional IRA killed the Conservative MP Ian Gow with an under-car bomb because he was a close friend of the then Prime Minister, Margaret Thatcher, and was deemed to be 'central to policy decisions'.[56] He was seen as part of the 'British war machine' responsible for the British presence in Northern Ireland, and was therefore categorised as a legitimate target. His friendship with the Prime Minister, association with her policies, and steadfast support for Ulster unionism, made him an even more tempting target – according to McKittrick almost a surrogate for her.[57]

Another important effect of ideology is that it transforms people or objects into representative symbols. According to a loyalist who bombed a pub in a Catholic area of Belfast in 1974:

> We dehumanised the other side and branded them animals. We didn't think of them in terms of them being people. If we couldn't get the IRA, we would have to slaughter members of the Catholic community who after all seemed to support them.[58]

By reducing people to mere ciphers it clearly becomes easier to justify killing them. Thus, loyalist terrorists in Northern Ireland have regarded Catholics as 'taigs' – a derogatory term for Irish Catholics. In June 1994 six Catholic men drinking in a country pub were shot dead by loyalist gunmen, one of whom called them 'Fenian bastards', the Fenians being a nineteenth century republican revolutionary movement.[59] Likewise, soldiers in Northern Ireland have been seen by Irish republicans as 'Brits' to be 'stiffed' (killed) or as a 'uniform' representing the 'occupying force' in Ireland.[60]

This approach is illustrated by a Red Brigadists account of how someone is adjudged to be 'guilty' in the terrorists' terms and thus becomes a legitimate target.

> The trial begins when you single out someone on paper, that is to say, you make a person correspond to a political need ... he is not even a person any more, he has been emptied and you load him up with other crimes, other responsibilities.[61]

A repentant Brigadist, Massimiliano Bravi, has also noted:

> The ideals of justice turned into murderous violence directed against the men who represented the State (the human being totally crushed in his social role) and in our eyes they were the guardians and perpetrators of every possible injustice and social suffering. They were 'the unjust' and we were the 'avengers'.[62]

The question of guilt or innocence is thus subject to the moral imperatives of the terrorists rather than to legalities. For example, in March 1985 Ezio Tarantelli, a Professor of Economics at the University of Rome and adviser to the Italian Government, was shot dead by the PCC (Partitio Comunista Combattente – Fighting Communist Party, a faction of the Red Brigades) because they deemed him 'one of the most authoritative technical-political exponents in the service of large capital'.[63]

A similar rationalisation comes from the PIRA member interviewed by Tony Parker.

> Our definition of who the enemy is isn't one which follows the same line as yours either. We regard all people who support the armed forces of the British Government in any way as legitimate targets. ... We'll define whether someone's helping the security forces or not: it's not for you to make the definition and criticise us for not agreeing with it. I don't know if I make that clear: probably not and if that's so then I have to say it doesn't greatly matter to me.[64]

Hence, whilst a workman involved in the construction of a police station might see himself as an innocent civilian, the Provisionals see him as a 'collaborator', and therefore liable to 'execution'.[65]

Such rationalisation is not confined to terrorist groups, and is common in wartime. According to Glenn Gray:

> The basic aim of a nation at war in establishing an image of the enemy is to distinguish as sharply as possible the act of killing

from the act of murder by making of the former an act deserving all honour and praise.[66]

Thus, during the Second World War British soldiers killed their German adversaries and vice versa, despite holding little personal animosity towards them as individuals, because they were the enemy.[67] Aerial bombing raids against German cities were presented to the British people as revenge for similar raids by the German Luftwaffe, and the malignancy of the German people was cited by Churchill as one of the justifications for the raids.[68] Thus, when necessary dehumanising an enemy can be done by democratic states as well as by terrorists.

One does not have to carry out or fail to carry out some action in order to be deemed a legitimate target by terrorists. Just being who or what one is may be enough to condemn a person or institution. For example, when Japanese Red Army terrorists carried out the Lod Airport massacre in Israel in May 1972 in the cause of Palestinian nationalism, the PFLP justified the death of the Puerto Rican pilgrims who made up the bulk of the victims, on the grounds that by being in Israel they were held to have tacitly recognised the Israeli state.[69] Crenshaw makes the point that during the Algerian Rebellion of 1954 to 1962 the FLN saw bomb attacks upon European civilians as legitimate because the Europeans' very presence made them symbols of French and European authority in Algeria. Moreover, by virtue of being Europeans the death and injury of these civilians had a direct influence on the conflict because it polarised the European from the Algerian population.[70]

This approach explains how being a member of a particular religion or race can make one a target for terrorist attacks without seeming to have done anything blameworthy. For instance, a building housing the Delegation of Argentine-Israeli Associations and the Argentine-Israeli Mutual Association was bombed in July 1994.[71] As the attack was thought to be in retaliation for an Israeli attack on a Hizbollah base in the Lebanon the previous June, a Lebanese authority on the Hizbollah was asked why Jews were targeted in Argentina rather than in Israel. The reply was that:

> The Jews of Israel come from Poland, from Russia, from Europe or from Latin America ... What is the difference? It is the same.[72]

Thus, all Jews were seen as a legitimate target for attacks aimed at punishing the state of Israel, to which they were perceived to be affiliated.

Not all terrorist attacks are preceded by a detailed ideological inquiry. Where the target is readily identifiable, and any decisions as to the guilt of the target have been made, target selection is quite straightforward. Bishop and Mallie point out that the initial PIRA decision to kill British soldiers was simply resuming hostilities against a traditional enemy in a war which had never been declared over.[73] The decision that British soldiers were a legitimate target had been settled a long time ago by republican ideology. Thus, in November 1987 a PIRA spokesman noted that there was no need for a local unit to gain permission from above to carry out a bombing against soldiers.[74]

As well as determining potential targets, ideology also allows terrorists to displace the blame for their actions onto other people. The guilt of the physical target, or the actions of others – sometimes the psychological target, are held to make the terrorists' actions inevitable. For example, according to Abu Iyad the Black September kidnapping of Israeli athletes at the Munich Olympics in September 1972, was caused by the International Olympic Committee and the international community as a whole failing to accord proper recognition to the Palestinians. Likewise, he claimed that the deaths of nine of the Israelis were due to the German rescue attempt at Furstenfeldbruck Airport rather than to the terrorists decision to carry out the operation in the first place.[75] In a similar vein, the leader of a group of Palestinian hijackers who seized a Lufthansa aeroplane in October 1977 is quoted as having stated 'We don't want to shed blood... but as the imperialist fascist West German regime rejects our demands we have no choice', and at another point claimed 'What happens now is solely the fault of the fascist German government and of Helmut Schmidt'.[76] Again, the responsibility does not lie with the terrorists, but with the psychological target.

In a similar fashion Provisional IRA and republican spokesmen have claimed that all deaths in the Northern Irish conflict are ultimately the responsibility of the British for not leaving Northern Ireland.[77] Regarding specific attacks, in January 1987 PIRA claimed they were forced to bomb commercial premises in Northern Ireland by the Government's assertion that normality had returned to Belfast.[78]

Sometimes, the ideological justification for an attack is supplied after the attack has occurred rather than having been worked out beforehand. It appears that the higher levels of the Provisional IRA have justified actions by local units after the event, although they would not have sanctioned the operations they had received prior notice.[79] In Italy, Moss records that the Red Brigades in Turin in the late 1970s, often did not issue their communiqué justifying an attack until after they had seen the press reaction. They then tailored it accordingly.[80] According to Willan, during this period BR targeting was often based on slipshod research and trivial considerations. He claims that on one occasion, after they had shot and wounded the wrong person, they rewrote the original communiqué so as to give the impression that the victim had been their intended target.[81]

TARGETING PATTERNS OF DIFFERENT IDEOLOGICAL GROUPS

The influence of ideology on terrorist targeting can be seen by comparing the targets attacked by different groups. Differences between groups with different ideologies, and similarities between groups with similar ideologies, may demonstrate to a degree the extent to which ideology affects target selection.

A comparison of people killed by republican and loyalist terrorists in Northern Ireland is instructive because it illustrates differences in target selection between separatist groups and conservative groups operating within the same geographical arena, and with a background of mutual communal antipathy. In general, separatist terrorists tend to attack those people who are members of, or co-operate with, organisations which they see as representing the occupier. For instance, the Basque group ETA have frequently attacked the Civil Guard (Guardia Civil – a national paramilitary-style police force whose members are generally recruited outside the areas in which they serve), national police, and the military as their primary targets.[82] According to Clark, law enforcement officials and members of the armed forces make up 62.4 per cent of those killed by ETA and 40.5 per cent of those wounded between 1968 and 1980, whilst Llera, Mata, and Irwin estimate that policemen and military officers make up 59.1 per cent of the total fatalities caused by ETA operations between 1968 and 1988.[83] Of these, the heaviest casualties occurred amongst the Civil Guard, who were, in the 1960s and early 1970s, widely feared in the Basque provinces, and seen as symbols of Francoism and Spanish occupation.[84]

Conservative terrorists, on the other hand, use terrorism to protect the existing state of affairs and, sometimes, to protect the state from what they claim to be subversion. In the 1980s for example, the initial task of Colombian conservative terrorist groups such as Death to Kidnappers (Muerte a Secuestradores – MAS) and the Association of Peasants and Ranchers of the Magdelena Medio (Asociacion de Campesionos y Ganderos del Magdelena Medio – ACDEGAM), was supposedly to combat communist guerrillas such as the April 19th Movement (Movimiento 19 de Abril – M-19), and the Revolutionary Armed Forces of Colombia (Fuerzas Armadas Revolucionarias de Colombia – FARC).[85] However, they also targeted members of the FARC's successor political party, the Patriotic Union (Union Patriotica – UP), peasant groups, trade unionists, and other groups seeking to change the balance of political power in Colombia.[86] According to Pearce over 700 members of the UP were killed between 1985 and March 1989, and by 1994 Amnesty International estimated that the figure had risen to 1,500.[87] Hundreds of trade unionists and workers have been killed, particularly those taking strike action against their employers, together with judges and those investigating such killings.[88] Such killings have been condemned by members of the Government but the death squads have justified the killings as action against subversives.[89]

The respective patterns of ETA and the Colombian death squads are broadly similar to those of the separatist and conservative terrorists in Northern Ireland. For the republicans, and in particular the Provisional IRA which is the largest republican terrorist group, target selection is fairly simple. Anybody who is a member of the security forces, or who aids the British presence in Ireland, is automatically considered a member of the 'British war machine', and thus a legitimate target. It includes contractors who work on military or police buildings in Northern Ireland, politicians or officials involved in the formulation of policy towards Northern Ireland, unionist politicians, informers, and anybody whom the PIRA deem to be actively collaborating with the security forces.[90]

A problem faced by loyalist terrorists in Northern Ireland is that whilst republican terrorists can identify security force members relatively easily, it is difficult for loyalists to identify and target members of republican terrorist groups. As a result they have often attacked any Catholics, believing them to be sympathetic to republican terrorism, or at the very least culpable for not putting pressure on the Provisionals to stop their campaign.[91] Reports suggest that this suspicion of tacit Catholic complicity with republican terrorists is shared by many ordinary Protestants in Northern Ireland.[92] By attacking Catholics, loyalist terrorists have hoped to put pressure upon the PIRA to stop its campaign and to prevent governmental moves towards a united Ireland.[93] In October 1993 a spokesman for the Ulster Freedom Fighters said:

> We are out to terrorise the terrorists. To get to the stage when old grannies up the Falls will call on the IRA to stop, because it is ordinary Catholics that are getting hit, not the provos behind steel security doors.[94]

Sectarian attacks have also provided a means for loyalist terrorists to retaliate for republican attacks, rationalising attacking Catholics on the grounds that those killed were somehow responsible for republican actions.[95]

The pattern shown in Table 3.1 may be skewed by the gap between the terrorists' intentions and the results actually achieved. However, one can see that in their lethal attacks separatist republicans have primarily targeted the security forces. A number of people have been killed purely because they were Protestants, and a large number of attacks have involved the deaths of bystanders. Although deliberate attacks against property are not specifically represented here, the large number of 'others' killed by republicans reflects their use of bombs against both property and human targets, as bombings inevitably harm bystanders.

For the loyalists on the other hand, attacks have been mainly directed against ordinary Catholics, with a relatively small though sizeable number of republican terrorists or political activists being killed, and a fair number of other loyalists also being killed. The concentration of loyalist attacks against Catholic civilians confirms that the Catholic population as a whole is a target. The communal nature of much of the violence in Northern Ireland can be seen in the number of sectarian killings on both sides, but there is a much higher concentration of primarily sectarian killings amongst the people attacked by the loyalist groups than by the republican groups. This is what one would expect to see with a conservative terrorist group which regards a particular community as suspect or subversive.

Table 3.1 Killings in Northern Ireland perpetrated by Loyalist and Republican groups, 1969–1993

	Loyalist		Republican	
	Number	%	Number	%
British Army[a]	1	0.1	448	26.3
UDR/RIR[a]	3	0.4	236	13.9
RUC[a]	6	0.7	297	17.4
Prison officers[a]	2	0.2	25	1.5
Alleged informers	16	1.9	65	3.8
Security force workers[b]	0	0.0	35	2.1
Internal feuds[c]	46	5.4	45	2.6
Opposing terrorists[d]	28	3.3	27	1.6
Political activists[e]	32	3.8	12	0.7
Overtly sectarian[f]	670	79.3	152	8.9
Other[g]	41	4.9	363	21.3
TOTAL NUMBER KILLED	845	100.0	1705	100.1

n.b. Percentages are rounded up or down to nearest 0.1%.
[a] Includes former members.
[b] Civilian contractors and direct employees carrying out work for the security forces.
[c] Loyalists killed by loyalists and republicans killed by republicans.
[d] Republicans killed by loyalists and loyalists killed by republicans.
[e] Nationalists and republicans killed by loyalists and unionists and loyalists killed by republicans.
[f] Catholics killed by loyalists, and Protestants killed by republicans, primarily because of their religion.
[g] Excludes killings outside Northern Ireland. Excludes terrorists killed by their own bomb but includes other unintended deaths.

Source: M. Sutton, *Bear in mind these dead ... An Index of Deaths from the Conflict in Ireland, 1969–1993* (Belfast: Beyond the Pale Publications, 1994), 196–203.

There can also be notable differences in targeting between groups with apparently similar ideologies. Looking specifically at the ideology of two distinct groups – the Red Brigades in Italy and the Red Army Faction in West Germany – one finds that although the ultimate aims were similar – to overthrow the capitalist system, there were important ideological differences which translated into differences in target selection. These differences were publicised when documents captured by the Italian police in June 1988 revealed the relative failure of the RAF and the BR faction known as the Fighting Communist Party (Partito Comunista Combattente – BR/

Table 3.2 Categories of people killed, wounded or kidnapped by communist terrorist groups in Italy and West Germany

	Italy: 1970-82		W. Germany: 1967-91[a]	
	Number	%	Number	%
Police	69	23.1	9	7.7
Judicial	13	4.3	4[b]	3.4
Penal	14	4.7	0	0.0
Political	27	9.0	5[c]	4.3
Business	85	28.4	5	4.3
Media	9	3.0	17[d]	14.5
Others	82[e]	27.4	77[f]	65.8
TOTAL NUMBER	299	99.9	117	100.0

n.b. Percentages rounded up or down to nearest 0.1%.
[a] To April 2, 1991.
[b] Includes officials or politicians in judicial-related posts.
[c] Includes senior officials.
[d] Includes 16 injured in bombing of Springer Press office.
[e] Includes 17 targeted doctors.
[f] Includes 60 people killed or injured in attacks on US military facilities.

Sources: D. Moss, *The Politics of Left-Wing Violence in Italy, 1969-1985* (London: Macmillan, 1989), 38. B. A. Scharlau, 'Chronology of Major Events' (Unpublished manuscript, 1992). D. Pluchinsky, 'An Organizational and Operational Analysis of Germany's Red Army Faction Terrorist Group (1972-1991)', in Y. Alexander & D. Pluchinsky (eds), *European Terrorism Today and Tomorrow* (Washington, DC: Brassey's (US), 1992), 57-79, 84-6.

PCC) to agree a coordinated strategy – an aim of the RAF at that time.[96]

The BR and other Italian communist terrorists put a much higher premium upon the overthrow of the Italian state, whilst the RAF and other German groups generally saw their objective as the destruction of international capitalism and imperialism. Furthermore, the original anarchistic outlook of the original leaders of the Red Army Faction contrasted with the origins of the BR as a splinter from the Italian Communist Party, and translated itself into a greater concentration on symbolic targets.[97]

The targeting pattern of communist terrorist groups in Italy and West Germany can be seen in Table 3.2. Again, one must allow for discrepancies between what the terrorists intended to do and the actual result. Additionally, the small number of attacks involved in the West German example leads to single attacks distorting the overall pattern. Many of the RAF's anti-American attacks were bombs intended to cause mass casualties, with the result that the attacks on US military facilities caused a high proportion of the overall casualties inflicted, whilst a bomb attack on the Springer newspaper complex in 1972 accounted for sixteen media casualties.

Table 3.2 highlights differences between the Italian and West German cases. The RAF attacked higher-profile targets, such as US military personnel, senior business executives, and senior government officials. They tended to avoid junior officials and ordinary police officers, although police bodyguards for high-profile targets were killed. This reflected the RAF's ideological opposition to international capitalism as opposed to pursuing purely national objectives. In contrast, the Italian communist groups – with their roots in the northern Italian factories and opposition focused upon the Italian state – concentrated far more on attacking local factory managers and minor representatives of the state such as police officers and junior and middle-ranking political officials.

Ideology was not the only reason for the differences in targeting strategy. The BR had many more members than the RAF and could carry out more actions, including actions against less prominent targets. The RAF could have attacked low-profile human targets with much greater ease than the high-profile targets which were attacked, but chose not to.[98] In practice their internationalist stance meant they were not as interested as the Red Brigades in trying to agitate and provoke the population within their own country, and consequently their target selection differed.

Overall, whilst the ideology of a terrorist group is not the sole determinant of its target selection, it is important because it shapes the way in which they see the world and defines how they judge the actions of people and institutions. This in turn helps to form their views as to who or what may be seen as a legitimate target. By establishing such parameters, ideology is influential in determining their initial range of potential targets.

4 Strategy

INTRODUCTION

In this study, strategy is taken to be the plan by which a terrorist group seeks to deploy and use its resources with the aim of achieving its political objectives.[1] The role of strategic thought in determining the activities of terrorists differs greatly between groups. Since their actions are generally dictated by their own perceptions there are dangers in assuming that terrorists – or other actors in politics – always behave in a way which seems objectively rational in retrospect. In practice, the pressures connected with surviving can distort terrorists' ability to make rational decisions. However, except where their actions are wholly expressive, most terrorists do try to relate their violent acts to specific objectives.

THE PLACE OF TERRORISM IN STRATEGIC PLANNING

Terrorism is only one of a number of methods which a group may use as part of its strategy. Depending on their capabilities, their strategy may include other violent methods ranging from riots to conventional warfare, and non-violent methods such as civil disobedience and constitutional politics. The Irish republican movement's strategy, embracing political action and violence, was described by Sinn Fein's Director of Publicity, Danny Morrison, as taking power in Ireland with a ballot paper in one hand and an Armalite in the other.[2] Similarly, soon after the Provisional IRA announced their ceasefire on August 31, 1994, a Sinn Fein representative stated:

> One thing we all know is that the struggle is not over. We are into a new and important phase of the struggle.[3]

Thus, the republican campaign for a united Ireland would continue with a strategy which – for the time-being – did not include the use of anti-state violence.[4] This example, and the end of that ceasefire in February 1996, demonstrates how groups can change their strategy over time.[5]

The foundations of a terrorist group's strategy are often found in the world-view prescribed by their ideology. The ideology lays down the political objectives towards which their strategy should be directed and shapes the way in which terrorists see the world around them. It therefore shapes their choice of the most appropriate strategy to adopt. For example, the Red Brigades' leaders believed that the Italian political and economic system was reorganising due to a state of political and economic crisis, with the possibility of a *coup d'état* by the authoritarian right.[6] Their terrorist strategy, which aimed at undermining the system in order to encourage a working-class revolt, appears thoroughly logical if one accepts the basic premises of their ideology. Likewise, if one accepts that Irish republicans in the early 1970s saw the British presence in Northern Ireland as a colonial one, and bears in mind that Britain had recently divested herself of an empire – sometimes under pressure of terrorism as in Palestine, Cyprus, and Aden, it was logical for republicans to suppose that the British would withdraw if faced with sufficient violence.[7] This led to a strategy which sought to transform Northern Ireland into a liability which the British Government would be glad to get rid of.

In his study of the Provisional IRA, Smith confirms the link between ideology and strategy, stating that a group's strategy should logically proceed from its ideology, taking into account the context within which the group operates. However, he believes that in practice, the PIRA's strategy in the early 1970s derived directly from the historical ideology of militant Irish republicanism without much appreciation of other relevant factors. Instead of the logical progression shown in Figure 4.1, Provisional IRA strategy can best be described by Figure 4.2.[8] The ideological predisposition of Irish republicanism towards the use of violence determined strategy with little reference to other factors.[9]

This emphasises the point that one must not be overawed into thinking of strategy as something complex, mysterious or even well-planned. At the time, decisions may well be rushed and conducted under great pressure.[10] Despite this the long-term plans of terrorists, however crude, are still strategies. For instance in the mid-1970s a PIRA leader described their campaign as 'blattering on until the Brits leave'.[11] Whilst this might not appear to be particularly sophisticated, it outlined a credible strategy of psychological attrition with the achievement of a definite political goal – the 'Brits' leaving Northern Ireland.

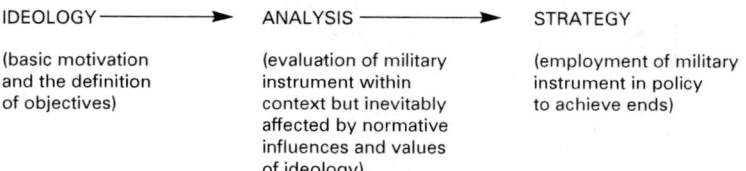

Figure 4.1 Provisional IRA: logical terrorist strategy. From M. L. R. Smith, *Fighting for Ireland?*, 140.

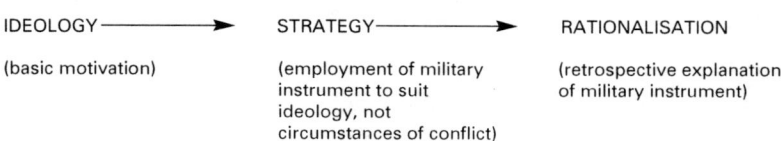

Figure 4.2 Provisional IRA strategy. From M. L. R. Smith, *Fighting for Ireland?*, 140.

Even with terrorist groups which possess a clear political objective, there sometimes appears to be little sense of planning beyond preparing for the next attack. Jenkins noted in the mid-1970s that many terrorist groups fail to progress from the tactical concerns of planning specific operations to devising a strategy to achieve their political objectives.[12] Although the terrorists know what their political objectives are, and are convinced of the need for violence to attain them, they do not know how to use violence effectively. In this situation a form of strategy through inertia can develop a momentum of its own, not being substantially altered unless it is seen to be failing.[13]

Many terrorist campaigns do not last long enough to develop beyond their initial stages.[14] The Angry Brigade in Britain only lasted as a really effective terrorist group between mid-1970 and late 1971, and became largely inactive following the arrest and conviction of the group's leaders.[15] Similarly, in Belgium the Fighting Communist Cells (CCC – Cellules Communistes Combattantes) was broken up by a number of arrests in December 1985 after carrying out 26 bombings in Belgium over a 14 month period.[16]

Other terrorist campaigns have been protracted, and in these cases it is possible or even likely that strategies will alter over time in order to adapt to changing circumstances or changes in the group's capability. It is also possible that – due to capture, death, or retirement – the people initially making strategic decisions for the terrorist group will be replaced by others with a different outlook.

Thus, Israeli assassination squads and internal feuds have killed leading members of the PLO, in Germany a number of the Red Army Faction leaders have been imprisoned over the years, and in Northern Ireland the INLA has lost leading members in internal feuds.[17]

The Provisional IRA provides an example of the changes to be seen in a groups' long-term strategy. They have changed their terrorist and political strategy – though not their political objectives – on a number of occasions. Their original strategy was to maintain a high level of violence and kill a large number of security force members in a short period of time. By the mid-1970s this strategy had been largely suppressed by an intensive security force commitment which resulted in the death or capture of several PIRA members, and demonstrated the ability of the British Government to endure a certain level of violence within the Province.[18] In response the Provisionals switched to a protracted 'long war' terrorist campaign, which consisted of a lower level of violence combined with the political mobilisation of the Catholics of Northern Ireland by Provisional Sinn Fein.[19] The objective of the long war strategy was to gradually wear down the resistance of the British Government and public by maintaining a lower but constantly irritating level of violence against a number of targets – primarily the security forces and civil and commercial targets in Northern Ireland and England, with the occasional spectacular attack executed in order to maintain a climate of apprehension.[20] In August 1994 the PIRA leadership altered its strategy again when it temporarily ceased the use of violence against the state and the economy, followed by the loyalist groups the following month.[21] However both loyalist and republican groups continued to injure or kill people whom they alleged were 'anti-social' elements such as criminals or drug traffickers, to a greater extent than they did before the ceasefire. As well as the overtly-stated aim of curbing criminality it seems likely that this also represented a strategic decision to maintain the compliant nature of the local population in case of a resumption of the conflict.[22] Thus, when the Provisionals ended the ceasefire with a bomb in the Docklands area of London in February 1996, they would not have felt the need to worry excessively about the risk of overt repudiation from the Catholic areas of Northern Ireland.[23]

This example also shows how terrorism can be integrated into a broader strategy for the purpose of achieving political goals. In general terrorists do not view their actions as uncoordinated violence and have some idea of the overall effects which they want their violence to achieve. They believe that these effects will in turn help them to achieve their political goals.

THE STRATEGIC OBJECTIVES OF TERRORIST GROUPS

The strategic objectives of terrorists are not the same as their ultimate political objectives, but are the long-term effects which they wish to impose on their psychological targets through the use of terrorism. The success of a terrorist strategy depends upon the terrorists finding the type of pressure or encouragement to exert upon a psychological target in order to produce the desired responses. For instance, terrorists wishing to gain publicity for their cause will not progress far if they confine themselves to minor acts of sabotage against unimportant buildings or institutions. Therefore they will select targets where attacks will gain attention. Similarly, if the terrorists wish to intimidate a specific group of people into behaving in a certain manner, it would probably be a waste of effort – and possibly counter-productive – to cause a widespread panic by killing several people with mass-casualty bomb attacks. Such actions might not affect the intended psychological target and could be counter-productive.

Crenshaw identifies a number of psychological reactions – ranging from curiosity to terror – which terrorists may seek to evoke.[24] Some groups seek to maximise the impact of their actions by pursuing more than one objective. These objectives are assembled into seven categories which have been adapted from categories used by Crenshaw and Thornton.[25]

- Threat elimination
- Compliance
- Disorientation
- Attrition
- Provocation
- Advertisement
- Endorsement

Threat elimination: This is the elimination of those people, organisations, or things which pose a direct threat to the terrorists. It includes the killing of informers, effective investigators, or anybody whose actions threaten the terrorist group. The elimination of threats makes it much easier for terrorists to concentrate upon achieving other strategic objectives and ultimately their political goals. A classic example of threat elimination was the campaign of assassination which the IRA waged between 1919 and 1921 against the police, military intelligence services, and informers in Dublin and elsewhere in Ireland.[26] Likewise, the Mafia's assassination in Sicily in the summer of 1992 of the Director of Penal Affairs for Italy, Giovanni Falcone, and Palermo's Chief Prosecutor, Paolo Borsellino, led to the immediate resignation of seven other senior investigating magistrates on the island.[27]

Compliance: Compliance occurs when the psychological targets obey the will of the terrorist group for fear of attacks upon themselves or upon people or objects of value to them. The terrorists' strategic objective is to establish control in the relationship between the terrorists and the psychological target. When deployed against the civil population such a strategy may secure whatever logistic support the terrorists need and protect them against the risk of informers or internal dissidence. Ideally it should also give the terrorists sole political leadership amongst possible sympathisers, and prevent opposition from forming there.

Disorientation: A group which intends to cause disorientation aims to destroy the certainties of everyday life for the psychological target by the use, or threatened use, of violence. This strategic objective comes closest to the classical understanding of terrorism in that the aim is to create a constant feeling of anxiety in the psychological target and to destroy the psychological target's faith in the capacity of anyone to protect it. The strategic objective of disorientation can be differentiated from that of compliance in that with the latter one can obtain relief from fear by complying with the terrorists' demands, but with the former there is no certain course of action which will relieve the anxiety. The terrorists' aim is to cause anxiety in the hope that this will induce the desired reaction by the psychological target by frightening them into acting as the terrorists wish.[28] For instance, the use of indiscriminate mass casualty car-bombings by powerful drug trafficking groups in Colombia in the late 1980s and early 1990s, was aimed at producing public anxiety so as to undermine the authority of the Government and intimidate it into agreeing not to extradite drug traffickers.[29] Alternatively the campaign of selective assassination against the nobility by the People's Will in Tsarist Russia was intended in part to break the will of the ruling classes, and therefore their ability to continue ruling.[30]

Attrition: A strategic objective of attrition is one where the terrorists intend to erode the will of the psychological target by attacking physical targets on which the psychological target sets some value. Whilst not precluding large-scale attacks, the emphasis of such a strategy is upon a continual series of small-scale attacks in the hope that cumulatively these will break the psychological target's resistance. For the terrorists, it is important that the physical targets attacked are ones upon which the psychological target places a fairly high value. If it does not, then the attacks will not have the debilitating effect desired by the terrorists. A classic case of this is the Provisional IRA's campaign of attacks on the British Army and upon civil and political targets in Northern Ireland and England.[31] Such attacks – in combination with communiques threatening more of the same – have been intended to induce a British withdrawal from Northern Ireland by wearing down the endurance of the British governing classes and the British public in general.[32]

Provocation: Provocation occurs where the terrorist group carries out attacks in the hope of making the psychological target act in a way which will alienate people who were previously uncommitted, or possibly even unsympathetic towards the terrorists, as well as people who sympathise with them. For insurgent groups the aim is often to provoke repressive security measures by the authorities in order to make them unpopular and to increase the popularity of the insurgents. This idea was popular in the 1960s amongst communist Latin American insurgents such as Che Guevara and Carlos Marighela.[33]

An example of the effects of provocation was seen in Northern Ireland in May 1992, when British soldiers appear to have entered bars and assaulted civilians in Coalisland, County Tyrone. In one case this occurred after a colleague had his legs blown off by a bomb. Newspaper accounts of these and other incidents, and photographs of soldiers attacking civilians, provided a propaganda opportunity which the republican press exploited to the full.[34]

Similarly, following the six-day war of 1967 the Israeli authorities have had a policy of destroying the houses of the families or helpers of alleged Palestinian terrorists. During the intifada of the 1990s they reportedly destroyed the homes of some stone-throwing rioters.[35] According to O'Brien 1,224 houses were destroyed or sealed up by the Israeli authorities between 1967 and 1977. The Arab–British

Centre states that 135 Palestinian houses were sealed or demolished between May 1985 and July 1st 1987, whilst O'Brien states that between 1987 and 1989 this happened to a further 224 houses.[36] Such a policy seems unlikely to win hearts and minds, and the enmity created provides Palestinian terrorists with a further incentive for attacking Israelis.

However, it is not only insurgents who have provocation as an objective of their strategy. Italian fascists have carried out attacks in the hope that they will be blamed on anti-state groups, and provoke a security clampdown, an atmosphere of crisis, and ultimately calls for an authoritarian government.[37]

Terrorists seeking to provoke a response need to determine who they wish to provoke into a reaction, what type of reaction they want, and how to provoke that reaction. The Tupamaros in Uruguay in the early 1970s provoked the military into overthrowing the democratic government – which the terrorists did want, and crushing the Tupamaros with utter ruthlessness – which they did not.[38]

Advertisement: A strategic objective of advertisement is intended to make people aware of the existence of the terrorists and their cause. Operations with this objective in mind are primarily designed to publicise the group and its cause. In practice most overt terrorist activities advertise the group and their cause just by happening, but some terrorists carry out operations where the primary aim is the maximisation of publicity. A prime case of this was the spate of high-profile operations by Palestinian groups in the early 1970s, including a number of aircraft hijackings and the PLO kidnapping and subsequent killing of Israeli athletes at the Munich Olympics in 1972.[39] By carrying out such operations, Palestinian terrorist groups gained recognition of their existence, if not initially of their cause.[40]

Endorsement: Attacks aimed at gaining endorsement are calculated to mobilise support for the group concerned. The terrorists carry out attacks which they hope will receive the approval of their supporters, and possibly that of people who are merely curious or uninterested. For instance, the PFLP leader George Habash claims that the hijack of three aircraft in September 1970 – belonging to British, Swiss, and German airlines – lifted the morale of Palestinian nationalists, as well as gaining the freedom of PFLP terrorists held prisoner in these countries and irritating the Israelis.[41] The hijackings also advertised the Palestinian cause to the wider world, demonstrating how a single operation can achieve more than one strategic objective.

In other cases, terrorists may seek to gain support at the expense of groups espousing a similar ideology. Kramer refers to the 'imitative rivalry' which existed between two Lebanese Islamic groups – Hizbollah and Amal – in the mid-1980s. Although open conflict later broke out between the two, for a period of about five years the rivalry was expressed in several forms, one of which manifested itself in the form of each attempting to outdo the other in the amount of damage inflicted upon the Israelis in southern Lebanon and the Western presence in Beirut.[42] A similar rivalry seems to have existed between the Red Brigades and Front Line in Italy in the late 1970s. Moss notes that in Milan, Front Line attacks had a greater tendency to be aimed at human targets than in Florence where there was less competition from BR and therefore less reason for spectacular attacks.[43]

If they have sufficient resources terrorist groups can pursue a number of these strategic objectives simultaneously. The FLN did this during their rebellion against the French in Algeria. Amongst other actions they carried out mass-casualty bomb attacks against the European population of Algeria with the aim of disorientating and scaring them, assassinated dissident Algerians with the aim of ensuring overall compliance amongst Algerians, and killed members of the French armed forces in order to wear down the French public's support for their country's presence in Algeria.[44]

Similarly, when examining the strategy of the Provisional IRA, one can see that their aim, as detailed in their training manual, has been to achieve a number of strategic objectives.[45] (The strategic objectives are placed in brackets after the objective.)

A war of attrition against enemy personnel which is aimed at causing as many casualties and deaths as possible so as to create a demand from their people at home for their withdrawal. [Attrition and Advertisement.]

A bombing campaign aimed at making the enemy's financial investment in our country unprofitable while at the same time curbing long term financial investment in our country. [Attrition and Advertisement.]

To make the Six Counties as at present and for the past several years ungovernable except by colonial military rule. [Disorientation and Provocation.]

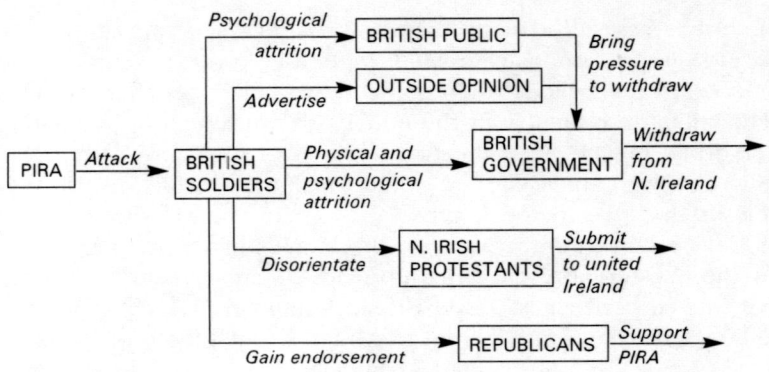

Figure 4.3 PIRA rationale for attacking British soldiers

To sustain the war and gain support for its ends by National and International propaganda and publicity campaigns. [Endorsement and Advertisement.]

By defending the war of liberation by punishing criminals, collaborators and informers. [Endorsement, Compliance, and Threat Elimination.]

Arguably the Provisionals have also attempted to achieve disorientation amongst the Protestant population of Northern Ireland and the public in England, by causing civilian casualties with bombs in public places, although they deny that this is done deliberately.[46] Thus, within the limits of their strategy, the Provisionals have pursued a number of strategic objectives simultaneously, at times putting more emphasis on one objective than on others.

One aspect of PIRA strategy – the killing of British soldiers – can be explained using the model shown earlier, in Figure 2.1. Killing soldiers fulfils a number of strategic objectives (see Figure 4.3). Ultimately, each terrorist campaign is unique and the categories discussed above are merely an attempt to bring some sort of system to their activities. Terrorist planners do not usually think in terms of neat categories, but in relation to the circumstances which they face. Furthermore, as well as the differences between the strategies of different terrorist groups, one can also find that the strategies of a single terrorist group can change over time.

THE EFFECT OF STRATEGY ON TARGET SELECTION

It can prove difficult to gauge precisely what the reaction will be to a terrorist act, or to the terrorists' overall strategy. Attacks might not produce the desired effect, and may prove counter-productive if they alienate actual or prospective supporters. Thus, to maximise the likelihood of achieving their strategic objectives terrorists should ideally select their targets carefully.

In practice the degree of strategic planning varies between groups. Some use terrorism largely as an expressive act rather than one which aims to influence other people's behaviour. The French anarchists of the 1890s have already been mentioned. More recently, some racial attacks by European fascists in the 1990s seem to have been motivated primarily by a desire to cause pain to immigrants, non-whites, and non-conformists, rather than by a discernible strategy.[47] In such cases one could say that the psychological target of the terrorist act is the terrorist himself. The strategic objectives of other terrorists appear to be planned in great detail, and are heavily derived from the ideological preconceptions of the group.

An example of this can be seen in the attempts of the Peruvian communist group Shining Path (Sendero Luminoso – SL) to apply strategic principles derived from the writings of Mao Tse-tung.[48]

The basis of Maoist military theory is guerrilla warfare: a form of warfare where semi-formed military formations seek to wear the enemy down with hit-and-run attacks, whilst avoiding full-scale battles, until the enemy is so weak that he can be defeated in open battle. Guerrilla warfare is not the same as terrorism in that the guerrillas' objective is ultimately to physically defeat the enemy in battle, either by themselves or with the assistance of other military forces.[49] Terrorism by itself cannot achieve such a military victory as it is primarily intended to have a psychological effect, but it can be used by groups involved in guerrilla warfare.

The Maoist model of rural guerrilla insurgency was based on the fact that the population of 1930s China consisted mainly of peasants. In contrast to the Marxist-Leninist concentration on urban workers, Mao saw the peasantry as a potentially revolutionary class. He believed that the role of the Chinese Communist Party was to mobilise peasants in areas where the communists had a presence. This formed secure base areas where the communists were relatively safe from attack and could assemble supplies, gain recruits, and start forming sizeable armed forces – both guerrillas and a regular 'Red' Army.[50] (Giap – who put many of Mao's ideas into practice against the French, Americans, and South Vietnamese authorities in Vietnam – points out that one way of securing such an area was to kill opponents and to gain public support by eliminating unpopular people such as landlords.[51]) Given the disparity between the initially weak communist forces and the more powerful opposition, the aim of the communists was to stay on the defensive militarily, avoiding clashes where the Red Army could be destroyed in its entirety, whilst carrying out guerrilla attacks on the advancing enemy. Once the opposition had over-extended its forces in pursuing the Red Army and the communist guerrillas, the Red Army would be able to push back the enemy offensive, thus gaining more time to consolidate.[52] At the same time the communists would go on the offensive politically, increasing their support amongst the peasantry in new areas, thus increasing their material resources and manpower.[53] Finally, after a period of military equilibrium, the now superior Red Army would take the offensive, penning the enemy into the towns and cities, and finally defeating him in open battle.[54]

Ironically, bearing in mind the school of followers which he acquired, Mao was insistent that whilst one could adopt some useful ideas from other conflicts, one could not derive universal strategic precepts from the specific circumstances of a particular conflict.[55] For Mao the relevant factors included the vast geographical size of China, the social and economic development of the country, and the relative strength of the enemy compared to the forces of the Chinese Communist Party.[56] This emphasis upon the particular circumstances of a conflict is relevant to the Peruvian example because the case of the Shining Path demonstrates how the Maoist model was adapted to local circumstances.

For over twenty years the Shining Path has conducted a rural revolutionary strategy based on the Maoist model. Indeed the original SL leader, Abimael Guzman, has seen himself as the ideological successor to Mao.[57] However, SL also grafted elements of the grievances and beliefs of the Andean Quechua indians onto their ideology, in order to construct and maintain a base of support in Ayacucho province, and has also undertaken urban operations in the Peruvian capital, Lima.[58]

From the formation of SL in 1970, until the start of the violence in 1980, Guzman spent a great deal of time building up a support base area for SL amongst the rural population in Ayacucho, working full-time on the project from 1976 onwards.[59] Since 1980 SL has fought what it has termed 'A War of Little Wars', or what Smith describes as 'a thousand little wars spread across the Andes'. Each 'little war' has involved attacking not just the government and security forces but also people whose local standing might rival that of SL, such as priests, schoolteachers, judges, police officers, businessmen, and junior officials.[60]

In the countryside, when estimating the possibilities of operating in a particular area, SL has determined the most unpopular person in the community and also the most respected. The former have been killed, whilst the latter have been persuaded or pressurised into cooperation, neutrality, or exile.[61] Where a rural village or religious community has opposed the Shining Path, or development programmes and facilities have been started which might act as an alternative focus of loyalty, SL has carried out attacks, and in some instances large-scale massacres, as a demonstration of the consequences of non-compliance.[62] Thus, in 1989 76 per cent of SL's victims were peasants or urban slum-dwellers.[63] These terrorist activities have been in addition to guerrilla attacks upon government officials, the Police, and the Army, which are intended to expel the institutions and influence of the state from areas which SL intends to take over with a final view to isolating and taking Lima itself.[64]

Due to the growth of Lima, and consequently the increased proportion of the population to be found there, SL has also carried out urban operations. It has organised urban cells, and in order to mobilise support amongst the poor migrants from country areas has tried to develop urban social programmes – whilst attacking those organised by other bodies. In addition, they detonated indiscriminate car bombs in Lima in the early 1990s, the objective being to loosen the hold of the authorities over the population by causing widespread panic.[65]

Overall the Shining Path has sought to follow Maoist strategy by building up base areas in the countryside with a view to isolating the cities. Whilst maintaining its broad allegiance to Maoist principles, SL has attempted to fit Maoist strategy to existing realities by coopting the indians' grievances and extending operations to Lima, and it has chosen its targets accordingly.

Another example of the effect of strategic considerations can be seen in the activities of Italian fascist terrorists. Table 4.1 shows some of the mass casualty bomb attacks carried out by fascist or associated groups. A 1969 document concerning the so-called 'strategy

Table 4.1 Lethal mass casualty bomb attacks in Italy against civilian targets, 1969–1993

Date	Location	Dead	Injured
December 12, 1969	Lobby of National Agricultural Bank, Milan	17	88
May 28, 1974	Anti-fascist rally, Piazza della Loggia, Brescia	8	94
August 4, 1974	Bologna–Florence Italicus train, tunnel near Bologna	12	105
August 1, 1980	Second-class waiting room, Bologna railway station	85	177
December 23, 1984	Naples–Milan Rapido 904 train, tunnel near Bologna	15	267
May 27, 1993	Car bomb outside Uffizi Gallery, Florence	5	30
July 27, 1993	Car bomb outside Royal Villa Art Gallery, Milan	5	20

Source: A. Jamieson, *The Heart Attacked*, 21. 'Uffizi gallery blast strikes at heart of Italian culture', *The Times*, May 28, 1993. 'Italians blame shadowy powers for bringing terror to Florence', *The Independent on Sunday*, May 30, 1993. 'Italian bombings leave five dead', *The Times*, July 28, 1993. 'President says bombs will not halt renewal', *The Independent*, July 29, 1993. 'Executive held over Uffizi bomb', *The European*, February 8–14, 1996. The casualty figures vary slightly from one account to another particularly with regard to the number of people injured.

of tension' from one of the Italian groups to the Aginter Press – allegedly a fascist front organisation in Lisbon – states:

> Our belief is that the first phase of political activity ought to be to create the conditions favouring the installation of chaos in all of the regime's structures. This should necessarily begin with the undermining of the state's economy as a whole so as to arrive at confusion throughout the whole legal apparatus This leads on to a situation of strong political tension, fear in the world of industry and hostility towards the government and the political parties.[66]

The document makes it clear that these actions are to be carried out in such a way as to implicate 'communist and pro-Chinese' organisations.[67] In fact the first suspects arrested for the fascist bomb attack in the Banca Nazionale dell'Agricoltura in the Piazza Fontana, Milan, on September 12, 1969, were anarchists.[68]

As well as corresponding with the strategic objectives of the Italian fascists, the strategy of tension is perfectly in line with the dictates of fascist ideology. It corresponds to the idea that the mass of people are manipulable, what Hitler called '... a herd of sheep and blockheads'.[69] The idea that a crisis is necessary before the fascists seize power accords with the precedents of Italy in 1922 and Germany in the early 1930s. In those cases the crisis was genuine, and was aggravated and exploited by the use of fascist street violence.[70] For later breeds of fascists, the necessary widespread anxiety was to be created by seemingly arbitrary explosions. Their hope was to provoke a military coup or propel the public into turning to a strong leader.[71]

A report at the time of the bomb outside the Uffizi Gallery in Florence in May 1993 linked the type of explosive used there to that used in the bombs on the Rapido 904 train in December 1984, and the May 1992 Mafia assassination of the Italian Director of Penal Affairs, Giovanni Falcone.[72] Shawcross and Young suggest that the Rapido 904 bombing was possibly carried out by a group which included fascist terrorists, the Mafia, and the Camorra, to divert attention from the Mafia's activities.[73] This, together with the apparent collusion of elements in the Italian security and criminal justice establishment, indicates cooperation between fascist groups and organised criminal groups.[74] Such an alliance is not surprising as – with the possible exception of the Rapido 904 bombing – the attacks in question have taken place at times of political turbulence when the existing political order – including the apparent immunity of organised criminal groups – was perceived to be at risk. These risks consisted of the electoral success of the Italian Communist Party in the 1970s and early 1980s, and from revelations in the early 1990s concerning organised crime and the corruption of the Italian political and business establishment.[75] In such situations there were obvious advantages for the fascist, conservative, and criminal groupings concerned, in creating a state of disorientation amongst the public, a distrust of radical change, and a desire for authoritarian government.

The conflict which began in Algeria in 1992 provides an example of terrorist strategies being carried out by religious groups where the main enemy is the indigenous government and its adherents rather than a foreign occupier or opponent. A military coup in January 1992 pre-empted the first free elections in Algeria since independence – elections which the Islamic Salvation Front (Front Islamique du Salut – FIS), was likely to win. Since then the FIS,

Table 4.2 Civilians killed by terrorist groups in Algeria in 1994

Officials	855
Lawyers and magistrates	20
Politicians and party members	13
Liberal professions	670
Teachers, academics, and students	169
Journalists	21
Religious leaders	52
Prison guards	31
Town security guards	32
Businessmen	350
Foreigners	61
Other civilians	4114

Source: Algerian Government statistics in 'PM blames civil war on the old guard', *The Independent*, 8 March 1995.

the affiliated Islamic Salvation Army (Armee Islamique du Salut – AIS), the Armed Islamic Group (Groupes Islamique Armee – GIA), and a number of other groups have carried out attacks upon a range of targets.[76]

The targets chosen by the Islamic groups vary. On the one hand they include the standard revolutionaries' targets of police officers, soldiers, and officials. According to unofficial sources, 116 police officers were killed in the last two weeks of January 1994 alone.[77] Likewise, in a two week period in mid-1994 dozens of conscripts were reportedly killed in various parts of Algeria – often having their throats cut.[78] In a single incident in January 1995 a bomb-laden van, driven by a suicide-bomber from the GIA, exploded outside the Algiers police headquarters, killing 42 people and injuring 286.[79] As shown in Table 4.2, the terrorists have also attacked several officials outside the security forces, particularly those who took over political or official posts which had been held by FIS members before the coup.[80] In November 1992, the FIS stated that all who cooperated with the Government would be 'considered as associated with the crime against the Algerian people'.[81]

The GIA has also attacked targets which represent groups or individuals which in some way represent foreign influences or secularism. The aim of such attacks is to weaken a government already heavily in debt, and reduce western cultural influence, by intimidating foreign workers – and thus foreign expertise and investment – into leaving Algeria.[82] In October and November 1993 the GIA issued threats against all foreigners living or working in Algeria, and by December 1994 over seventy foreigners had been killed, of which more than a quarter were French.[83] According to an unnamed GIA spokesman, the justification for these killings was that foreigners are the 'main coronary artery' of a plan to colonise Algeria with 'non-Muslim unbelievers', and that attacking them weakened the Algerian Government.[84] Between the outbreak of the conflict in January 1992 and December 1994, according to a report, the number of French nationals in Algeria fell from 10,000 to 1,000.[85]

An explanation of the religious aspect to this approach was demonstrated in May 1994, when the GIA claimed responsibility for the killing of a Catholic nun and priest who had run a library in the Algiers Casbah since the late 1960s.[86] The GIA stated:

> Within the framework of the policy of liquidation of Jews, Christians and miscreants from the Muslim land of Algeria, a GIA brigade organised an ambush in which it killed two crusaders who had passed long years propagating evil in Algeria.[87]

By labelling the victims as 'crusaders', the GIA hoped to draw an analogy with the Christian crusades to Palestine between the eleventh and fourteenth centuries. This pair were therefore suitable targets because they were non-Muslims, they were foreign, and they were very vulnerable. The FIS condemned these particular killings and in January 1995 was reported by *The Economist* to have 'firmly dissociated' itself from threats to foreigners, stating that the 'military dictatorship' was its enemy.[88]

The GIA has also targeted those Algerians whom it feels are supportive of the secular nature of the Algerian government. As well as disorientating the Algerian political and social elite, such attacks are intended to enforce compliance to the terrorists' political and religious norms. Those targeted have included feminists, popular entertainers, educators, writers, and other people whom they say are acting in an un-Islamic fashion.[89] Journalists have also been targeted in the onslaught on the secular professions. By February 1995 29 journalists were reported to have been killed by terrorists, 5 in the first seven weeks of 1995, and this had risen to 69 by December 1996.[90]

Education is an area of great cultural and symbolic importance to Algerian Islamist terrorists. In particular they have shown a great deal of hostility towards educational institutions or practices associated with the French. In August 1994 the GIA is reported to have said that it would bomb schools and universities in Algeria because they served the secular government.[91] It issued an instruction that girls should not be allowed to do gymnastics, female teachers should wear the veil, and all music should be banned. If these demands were not met it would destroy schools and attack staff.[92] Accordingly a number of teachers, academics, students, and their affiliated institutions have been attacked. *The Times Higher Education Supplement* reported that in 1994 over eighty teachers had been killed and 600 schools had been attacked.[93] Of the teachers killed, thirty are reported to have been teaching the French language, the GIA having condemned anyone teaching the language of the former colonial power.[94] In 1994 three universities and nine training institutes were burned or bombed.[95] According to *The Times Higher Education Supplement*, three heads of Algerian university institutions and well over fifty academics were killed between March 1993 and October 1994.[96] In February 1995 the leader of one of Algeria's student unions was shot dead on the same day that a college director was killed.[97] As a result of such attacks, by October 1994 over 1,000 academics were reported to have left Algeria.[98]

The GIA in particular, has also attempted to enforce political and religious conformity amongst ordinary Algerians. In February 1997 the GIA leader was quoted as vowing to step up the killing of 'all those who are not with us'.[99] Women who have not obeyed the terrorists' edicts on dress or education have been attacked and sometimes killed.[100] In October 1994 a car bomb exploded outside a female hall of residence at the University of Algiers.[101] In late 1996 and early 1997 Islamist terrorists carried out a series of bomb attacks and large-scale massacres in villages and in Algiers itself – using methods such as beheadings and throat-cutting to emphasise their demand for obedience.[102] These killed over 300 people in January and early February 1997, many of whom, according to Fisk, were relatives of government-formed militias. The onset of Ramadan was cited as a possible reason for this upsurge in violence.[103] However, the FIS has claimed that Algerian intelligence agencies have infiltrated the GIA, and perpetrated massacres in order to discredit all Islamic groups.[104]

The targets attacked by the Algerian Muslim terrorist groups represent an attempt to attain a number of strategic objectives. Attacks on the universities, secular intellectuals, and others deemed to be anti-Islamic are a clear attempt to disorientate the ruling elite in Algeria. Together with the more widespread attacks on ordinary civilians, they also represent an attempt to enforce compliance with the terrorists' political and religious demands. As well as the desire to strengthen adherence to the terrorists' religious precepts, such terrorism strengthens the terrorists' hold over the civil population, and their consequent ability to extract support and resources from them. The deaths of targets with a functional and symbolic value such as soldiers, police officers, and officials, have an attritional aspect in that they have damaged the Government's material ability to combat the terrorists, and they have also demonstrated the weakness of the state. Meanwhile the killing of foreigners has advertised the terrorists' cause and damaged the Algerian economy.

SUMMARY

Whilst the ideology of a terrorist group sets out the moral parameters within which they operate, the selection of targets is also affected by the effect or effects which they wish their violence to achieve. In practice, whilst terrorists may have fairly simple political aims, they may pursue a number of strategic objectives in order to achieve that aim. The strategic objectives which they set themselves affects the targets which they choose because they hope that by attacking such targets, they will maximise the pressure upon the psychological target to behave in a certain fashion.

5 Tactics

INTRODUCTION

Although terrorist operations vary in their methods and objectives, they usually involve certain stages, even though the terrorists themselves may not be conscious of them. These are:

- Setting up a logistical network
- Selecting potential targets
- Gathering information on potential targets
- Reconnaissance of potential targets
- Planning of operation
- Insertion of weapons into the area of operations
- Insertion of operators into the area of operations
- Execution of the operation
- Withdrawal of operational team
- Issue of communiqués

Some operations, may require a great degree of planning, or the acquisition of detailed information, for instance a kidnapping or hijacking requires the captivity of the hostage, receipt of ransom or released colleagues, and any other actions. Others, like racial attacks, can be carried out on the spur of the moment when a victim happens along.

SETTING UP A LOGISTICS NETWORK

A terrorist group's logistics consist of the support structure necessary to sustain it. A logistics network includes the means to transport weapons and personnel, to house members of the group without arousing suspicion, and generally to allow the group to function. It includes the provision of safe houses, weapons dumps, vehicles, and whatever identity documents might be appropriate. For a prolonged terrorist campaign to be sustained at a fairly high level of intensity, some form of logistics network is necessary, so that members of the group have places to stay, places to hide their weapons, and are able to sustain themselves without being discovered.

In cases where members of the terrorist group have not yet been detected and forced into clandestinity by the authorities, some of the features of the logistical structure may be superfluous. This has largely been the case with 'part-time' terrorists – such as members of the Revolutionary Cells in Germany and the 'irregular' members of the Red Brigades in Italy – who only devote some of their time to terrorist activities.[1] These terrorists can lead a relatively ordinary life while operating as terrorists, openly using their own identity, vehicles, and residences, until they are detected. Once they have been identified as terrorists they can become so dependent upon the logistical infrastructure that it becomes difficult to carry out basic functions of normal life – such as renting or buying accommodation and buying food – without running the risk of detection.[2] For this reason some terrorist groups set up a logistics network before they start using violence. In Cyprus, Grivas spent the best part of three years setting up EOKA, and its infrastructure before the terrorist campaign began.[3] McKittrick reports that the Provisional IRA is thought to have set up a network of safe houses and weapons dumps in Great Britain in the mid-1980s, soon after they received large shipments of weapons and explosives from Libya. However their campaign of sustained terrorist violence in England did not begin until 1988, after the logistical structure for the campaign had been set up.[4]

Setting up a logistics network for one operation is only necessary when the operation itself is complex. The kidnappings of Schleyer in Germany in 1977, and of Moro in Italy in 1978, necessitated the renting or purchase of flats in which to hold the abductees whilst negotiations were carried out for the terms of their release.[5] Similarly, in the aftermath of the assassination of Rajiv Gandhi by the LTTE in April 1991, the Indian police unearthed a large network which was set up in order to support the operation.[6] On the other hand, for one-off attacks upon targets of opportunity, or for isolated low-intensity attacks, a specifically dedicated logistics structure is not necessary and would probably be an encumbrance.

For vigilante groups which are tolerated by the authorities or some of their agencies, the requirements for a clandestine support network are not great. In Colombia, conservative death squads seem to have operated with a high degree of impunity, and consequently members of these groups have not had to live a particularly clandestine life.[7] Likewise, unlike the Provisional IRA and the Ulster

Volunteer Force (UVF), the Ulster Defence Association (UDA) was not banned in Northern Ireland until July 1992. As a result, whereas people whom the authorities could prove to be PIRA members have had to live clandestine lives because PIRA membership is an offence – albeit one difficult to prove, members of the UDA were not so constrained until July 1992.[8]

In contrast, the problems of trying to sustain a clandestine existence provided communist terrorist groups in Italy with some of their greatest problems. Under Italian law, people are required to carry identification documents and there are laws which require people renting out accommodation to register the tenants of the residence. This makes it much more difficult to maintain clandestinity and makes it imperative for the group concerned to assemble a network which allows activists to remain underground in safety.[9]

THE SELECTION OF POTENTIAL TARGETS

The selection of potential targets is the process by which terrorists decide which targets they might attack, before they have taken into account other factors which determine which targets they will attack. The decision to attack certain people or things need not necessarily be well thought out before an operation takes place. Whilst with a pre-selected target this is normally the case, where a target of opportunity presents itself, there is little if any planning. Provided the general category of targets has been agreed – in however rudimentary a fashion – it is quite possible the terrorists will carry out an attack immediately.[10] For instance Jimmy Brown, leader of the republican splinter group known as the Irish People's Liberation Organisation (IPLO), was killed in Belfast in August 1992, when he stopped his car by a man he knew. The pedestrian unexpectedly produced a gun and shot Brown dead.[11]

When operations are pre-planned, a number of people or things may be selected on the basis of their ideological legitimacy as targets, with the intention of choosing one of them as the final target after other factors have been considered. This occurred when Aldo Moro was kidnapped by the Red Brigades in March 1978. The Brigadists' aims were to capture a leading politician in order to: draw attention to the cause of the Red Brigades, highlight the impotence of the Italian state, prevent the then likely political alliance between the Christian Democrats and the Communist Party, and capture and question a leading Christian Democrat about the corruption at the heart of the Italian state.[12] They also demanded the release of Red Brigadists being held prisoner.[13] However, the BR had also considered kidnapping the Prime Minister – Giulio Andreotti, or a former Prime Minister and President of the Senate – Amintore Fanfani.[14] It was only after the BR decided Fanfani's personal routine was too unpredictable and Andreotti's protective security too tight, that they decided to kidnap the relatively routine and poorly protected Moro.[15] Whilst the selection of Moro, Fanfani, and Andreotti as potential targets was based on the BR's ideology and strategy, other factors determined that Moro was selected.

GATHERING INFORMATION ON POTENTIAL TARGETS

Once the range of potential legitimate targets has been decided upon, the group can carry out the research necessary to discover where the targets are likely to be located. The ideal is where members or sympathisers of the terrorist group have personal knowledge of the activities of potential targets. The Russian anti-Tsarist terrorist Savinkov, who was active in the early twentieth century, describes the usefulness of Tatiana Alexandrovna Leontyeva, the daughter of the Vice-Governor of Yakutsk province and an aristocrat by birth. She was well connected with 'rich and official St Petersburg', had the opportunity of being presented at the Imperial Court, and with time could become a lady-in-waiting to the Empress. Although she wished to be an active terrorist, Savinkov preferred her to gather information whilst unknown to the police as a terrorist sympathiser.[16]

More recently, in July 1977 the Chief Executive of the Dresdner Bank, Jurgen Ponto, let Susanne Albrecht – the daughter of a family friend – into his house with two of her friends. He was shot dead during the ensuing Red Army Faction kidnap attempt.[17] In the aftermath the Federal Interior Minister commented that few senior German businessmen or officials did not have a terrorist within their immediate or more distant social circle, a point was which was echoed by *The Times*' correspondent in 1993.[18]

Sometimes sympathisers just happen to be in the right place at the right time. According to Coogan, during the Irish Rebellion of 1919–1921 the Post Office in Dublin put the cousin of Michael Collins – effectively the operational leader of the IRA – in charge of handling secret coded messages. The cousin of another IRA man was a typist in Dublin Castle – at that time the headquarters of the British administration in Ireland – where she had access to information which included the names and addresses of intelligence operatives.[19] Additional sources of information were: some detectives in the political 'G' section of the Dublin Metropolitan Police (DMP), policemen with access to the RIC cipher codes, a secretary in the headquarters of the 6th Army Division in Cork, and a senior civil servant in Dublin Castle.[20]

More recently, both republican and loyalist terrorists in Ireland have received information from well-placed sympathisers. The Provisional IRA has obtained highly sensitive information from the RUC, the prison service, the Northern Irish Civil Service, and the Gardai in the Republic of Ireland, either by intimidating people within these organisations, or through sympathisers who work in them.[21] Similarly, members of the security forces in Northern Ireland have passed information on suspected republicans to loyalist terrorists, thus locating targets for assassination.[22]

Alternatively, terrorists can gain access to secret information by electronic means. In the mid-1970s the Provisional IRA was found to have been intercepting security force communications with phone taps, and by the mid-1980s at the latest was able to intercept radio messages by the use of scanners capable of intercepting radio communications. This allowed PIRA units to locate and either avoid or attack security force units.[23] Likewise, in 1995 Fisk reported that units of the Armed Islamic Group in Algeria were said to have radio scanners which they used to intercept messages to police patrols.[24]

Electronic eavesdropping has also aided the assassination of specific people. Pearce states that narcotics traffickers in Colombia tapped the telephone of the Attorney General, Rodrigo Lara Bonilla, before his assassination in April 1984.[25] Similarly, the Sicilian Mafia reportedly learned of the movements of Palermo's Chief Prosecutor, Paolo Borsellino, by tapping his mother's telephone. Borsellino and five police bodyguards were killed in July 1992 by a bomb placed outside his mother's flat.[26]

Information can often be gleaned from publicly available sources. A brief examination of the 1988 copy of *Who's Who* provides a very useful list of private addresses for anyone wishing to cut a swathe through the British political elite.[27] For their campaign of assassination in England the Provisional IRA are believed to have identified the home addresses of prominent individuals from several open sources such as *Who's Who*, the *Civil Service Year List*, the *Army List*, and television broadcasts.[28] Somebody's presence in such sources thus makes it more likely that they will be selected as a target than somebody who is not in them. This can have drawbacks for the group carrying out the research because they may be using outdated information. When the PIRA set off a bomb at the former home of a former Conservative Party Treasurer Lord McAlpine in June 1990, *The Independent* reported that it was still listed as his home in the then current edition of *Who's Who*.[29] In the same way, when the PIRA tried to assassinate the former Cabinet Secretary, Lord Armstrong, in August 1990, they placed a bomb under a car parked in the drive of a house which he had moved from, but which was listed as his home in the 1976 *Who's Who*.[30]

The information revealed after police raids on safe houses can be quite revealing about the ways in which terrorists gather information. When the police searched a flat in November 1990, which had allegedly been used by two PIRA men, they found a 1979 copy of *Who's Who* together with a list of potential targets.[31] On the list were Sir Charles Tidbury – chairman of the William & Mary tercentenary trust and a former worker for the Conservative Party – with details showing his London and country addresses, and car registrations of two neighbours. Also found were details concerning two previous Northern Ireland Secretaries, Roy Mason and James Prior, senior politicians including Sir Geoffrey Howe, Douglas Hurd, Sir Geoffrey Johnson-Smith – a Conservative MP, Major-General Sir Julian Thompson, General Sir Michael Trant, Sir John Fieldhouse – former Chief of the Defence Staff, and Major-General Sir John Acland. Newspaper photographs of some of these people were also attached. On another occasion the police found a list with the names of various senior and middle-ranking politicians and businessmen, at a safe house in Luton. The terrorists had also noted the private addresses and family details of senior military personnel, and had made notes describing the most convenient routes to their homes.[32]

Other terrorists also use such methods. On July 6, 1977 Willy Peter Stoll – a member of the Red Army Faction – visited the Hamburg Institute of International Economics and requested information on Jurgen Ponto – the Chief Executive of the Dresdner Bank, and Hans-Martin Schleyer – the President of the West German Employers Federation. He claimed this was for a thesis on leading economists.[33] Ponto was shot dead on July 30, 1977 during the attempt to kidnap him. On September 5, 1977 Schleyer was kidnapped and six weeks later was killed. Likewise, according to Schiller, members of the Berlin-based June 2nd Movement used a book entitled *The Rich and Super-Rich in Austria* when selecting a target for abduction. They chose an Austrian textile manufacturer, Michael Palmers who was described in the book as often moving large sums of money, and who preferred payment in cash.[34] June 2nd Movement (Bewegung 2 Juni – B2J) kidnapped him in November 1977, receiving a payment of DM 4.3 million in return for his release.[35]

An article in a newspaper might give a terrorist many details which would prove useful in planning an attack. In April 1994, an article in *The Spectator* outlined several details concerning the then British Permanent Representative to the European Community, Sir John Kerr.[36] It identified the type of car in which Kerr travelled and what his chauffeur looked like, allowing the assassin or kidnapper to positively identify the target. It also gave useful details about Sir John's travel arrangements. This would make him a more tempting target than somebody about whom the potential assassins or kidnappers knew nothing.[37]

It may seem too much emphasis has been placed upon the possible effect of the release of a relatively small amount of information, but people have been picked out as possible targets on the basis of seemingly insignificant snippets of knowledge. In 1972 the Basque group ETA selected the Spanish Prime Minister, Admiral Carrero Blanco, as a likely target for kidnapping or assassination when they discovered that he attended Mass at the same church at nine o'clock every morning. He was killed by a car-bomb in December 1973 as he returned home from Mass.[38]

Furthermore, terrorists often attack targets in cars. Cars are easily stopped and surrounded or blown up. Once stopped they offer little in the way of escape.[39] According to Russell and Miller 95 per cent of abductions occur when the victim is in transit between home and work and 80 per cent whilst the victim is in a vehicle whilst Scotti states that 85 per cent of all kidnappings and assassinations occur whilst the victim is in transit, though the term 'transit' is undefined.[40] In a comparative sample of political and non-political murders in Northern Ireland, Lyons and Harbinson found that whereas 85 per cent of the non-political murders were committed in the home of the victim with only 12 per cent occurring when travelling, with political murders only 6 per cent occurred in the home whilst 74 per cent occurred when travelling.[41] A number of British diplomats have been abducted or assassinated over the past three decades, so a high-profile diplomat such as Kerr would have been a prime target.[42]

RECONNAISSANCE OF POTENTIAL TARGETS

For a pre-planned attack to succeed, the terrorists must establish where the target will be at a specific time. Obviously this is not a problem in the case of a fixed unprotected target, such as a building. Similarly, if the intention is to leave a bomb in a public place where it can cause the maximum damage, then the terrorists do not need to carry out much in the way of reconnaissance. However, if the target is a specific person or mobile object it is usually necessary to establish where the target will be at a given time.

Even if a target is immobile, terrorists need to know whether it is protected in order to gauge the degree of force needed to overcome any protective security, and to plan their escape after the operation has been carried out. The withdrawal of the operational team is examined later, but – with the exception of attackers who do not expect to survive the attack themselves – most operations are planned on the assumption that they will only proceed if there is a reasonable chance of the attackers escaping.[43] Apart from the natural desire to survive on the part of the individual, most terrorist groups are not large enough to be able to risk heavy losses on a regular basis.

The priority for terrorists seeking to attack a human target is to establish whether the target has a routine. Most people do, unless they deliberately vary it in order to avoid becoming a target. The requirements of work or other patterns in life, mean that most lives are governed by the clock. In January 1982 Italian police found written details concerning the observation of a Rome magistrate's routine by potential assassins.

> In the morning he opens the curtains around 7.30. Between 8.15 and 8.25 the men of his escort arrive outside the house. There are usually 3 of them: one stays at the wheel, the second gets out and looks around, the third goes up to the house and comes back with him. Between 8.30 and 8.40 . . .[44]

Reports concerning the observation of security force patrols by ETA and the Provisional IRA show that reconnaissance is used to establish the routine of members of enemy organisations, as well as that of specific individuals. For example, in relation to a planned Provisional IRA ambush of a British Army patrol in Belfast in May 1980, Dillon notes how the terrorists observed that vehicles were slowed down or stopped by the traffic lights at a busy junction. The ambushers commandeered a house overlooking the junction and, with an M60 medium machine-gun and rifles, waited for a military vehicle to appear. In this case it was in vain as the ambushers were themselves under surveillance, and the house was stormed at the cost of one soldier killed.[45]

Reconnaissance is sometimes carried out by a separate terrorist unit to the one which actually carries out the attack. In line with the reorganisation of the Provisionals into a tightly-run cell system in the late 1970s, Dillon notes that the reconnaissance of a potential target will often be carried out by an intelligence cell, with the attack itself being carried out by an Active Service Unit (ASU).[46] In the same fashion, Clark lists the reported activities of an intelligence cell of ETA which was arrested in May 1980. For four or five Sundays in a row they monitored the movements of a former Mayor of Bilbao in order to pass the information to an ETA assassination team. The resulting attack was unsuccessful. The same group gathered information on the Civil Guard patrols which protected the airports at Bilbao and Vitoria, and obtained photographs, blueprints, and other information concerning electric power plants in Vizcaya Province, together with a list of people occupying key positions in the plants. They also gathered information concerning two members of the national police force who lived in Algorta.[47]

Even for a target which is immobile, terrorists may carry out reconnaissance to ensure that the operation can be carried out according to plan. Katayama states that three members of the Japanese Red Army flew to Tel Aviv in September 1971 to reconnoitre Lod Airport.[48] Likewise, two suspected PIRA members are reported to have been seen reconnoitring a Royal Marine training base in Devon in June 1990 whilst under police surveillance, and police believed that PIRA members observed the Royal Marine barracks at Deal in Kent for two weeks before they bombed it in September 1989.[49] Another raid on a PIRA safe house outside London found, amongst other things, Ordnance Survey maps of the areas around Salisbury Plain and Aldershot, areas which contain military bases.[50]

PLANNING THE OPERATION

Terrorist groups do not plan their operations in a uniform fashion. With small autonomous groups, such as the first generation of the Red Army Faction in Germany or small units of loyalist terrorists in Northern Ireland, planning took the form of a general discussion by those directly involved, although the process was often dominated by forceful members of the group.[51] On the other hand the Red Brigades, at least in their most successful period in the mid-1970s, had what Caselli and della Porta term a 'centralised and oligarchic bureaucracy'.[52] Theoretically, plans were approved by the Executive Committee and delegated to local groups for execution. However, Moss states that there were considerable differences between the theory of a highly centralised BR organisation and the practice of a fairly decentralised one where local groups picked their own targets and disregarded orders from above.[53] In the Provisional IRA, because the control of weapons is usually at the brigade or battalion level – one level above the active units – plans generally have to be cleared at the level above the unit which would carry out the attack, but again there have been exceptions.[54]

Having selected potential targets, and carried out a detailed reconnaissance to detect vulnerabilities, the terrorists next determine how to attack the target. This aspect of the operation may be quite sketchy. When a target of opportunity – such as a sectarian target in Belfast – suddenly presents itself to a terrorist group, little in the way of planning is necessary.[55]

On other occasions a great deal of time may be spent on planning attacks. This can be seen from the above-mentioned attempt to ambush a British Army in Belfast in May 1980. By the mid-1980s PIRA spokesmen admitted that it has become increasingly difficult to kill British soldiers.[56] The way in which individual Army patrols were coordinated in mutually supporting patterns, and operating in tandem with strategically placed observation posts, made it difficult for terrorists to be sure that they could get away safely after an attack.[57] This meant that more planning became necessary for such attacks to be successful.

THE INSERTION OF WEAPONS INTO THE AREA OF OPERATIONS

The weapons used by terrorists can vary from the crudest of weapons up to extremely sophisticated explosive devices. According to Feldman a UDA gunman has stated:

> You can go in and terrorize your next-door neighbour if you have a hammer in your hand.[58]

On the other hand the Red Army Faction bomb which killed the President of the Deutsche Bank, Alfred Herrhausen, in 1989, was detonated by a photoelectronic cell which projected an infra-red beam across a road onto a reflector which returned it. When Herrhausen's car broke the beam the bomb exploded.[59]

Knives or heavy, blunt objects can be used against people or objects which have little in the way of protection.[60] The Naxalites, an Indian Maoist movement which flourished in West Bengal in the late 1960s and early 1970s, used knives partly because of the psychological effect which such ferocious methods would have upon the landowning class, whom the Naxalites wished to scare out of rural areas.[61] Such weapons also have the advantage that if one is stopped by the police with a knife or a hammer, it is possible to make up some form of explanation. As a result such weapons, whilst limited in the amount of damage which they can do, are relatively easily transported to the place of an operation. Trying to explain away a pistol or a quantity of explosives could be somewhat difficult.[62]

Other weapons are more difficult to get into the area where the operation is to take place. From the terrorists' point of view, the ideal would be for the attackers to carry the weapons to the area of operations, use the weapons, and then withdraw. Sometimes this happens. In 1977 Patricia Clough described how the typical maiming attack was carried out by communist terrorist groups in Italy.

> The scene is almost always the same: the victim leaves his home for work at the usual hour and on the way to his car, bus stop or office, notices two or three young people in jeans standing idly in the street. As he approaches they pull out pistols, aim carefully at his legs and fire repeatedly. He falls, shouting for help, while his assailants run to a waiting car and are driven off at speed.[63]

In cases like this the pistols appear to be carried to and from the attack by the terrorists. The risk is that they may be apprehended either before or after the operation, and arrested for possession of an illegal weapon if not killed in a gun-fight. If forensic evidence such as ballistics tests can link the weapon to terrorist operations, the person found in possession of the weapon could be charged with participation in whatever killings, woundings, or other offences, have been carried out with that weapon.

For this reason some groups use couriers to move weapons to the place of attack, or to a safe house which is close to the point where the attack is to take place, and then remove them after they have been used. Thus a gunman can only be caught in possession of a gun for the short period when he is using it or waiting for the target to appear.[64] The courier on the other hand should be somebody who is not suspected by the authorities, who is not likely to arouse suspicion, and who is dispensable.

Getting bombs into the area of operations is in some ways similar to the problems involved in moving guns, except that some bombs are far bulkier. Small bombs can be carried on the person. The incendiary devices used by the PIRA as part of their campaign against businesses are no larger than a cassette tape holder, and can easily be carried into a shop and then placed so as to cause damage.[65] Bulkier bombs can also be moved into position if adequately disguised. One PIRA member has noted:

> if someone is to carry a bomb in a pram, it is better that a woman is pushing the pram, because a man doing that might attract attention.[66]

Women seem to be frequently used to carry guns or bombs – for example in Cyprus and Algeria – on the supposition that the security forces and other security staff will be less likely to search a woman or suspect her of terrorist involvements.[67]

Large bombs have been carried in vehicles. Putting a bomb into a car or another form of vehicle is a common way of getting it into the proximity of the target.[68] In March 1985 an attempt was made – allegedly with the connivance of the CIA and the Lebanese intelligence agencies – to kill the spiritual leader of the Hizbollah, Sheikh Fadlallah, with a massive car bomb in Beirut. The attempt failed, but eighty people were killed in the explosion.[69] The bombing of the Israeli Embassy in London in July 1994 was carried out with a bomb placed in the boot of a car which was then parked close to the Embassy.[70] Extremely large bombs have been placed in larger vehicles. The bombs which devastated the Baltic Exchange in the City of London and damaged the A5 flyover at Staples Corner in April 1992 were placed in vans, and the bomb which wrecked buildings around Bishopsgate, again in the City, in April 1993 was placed in a truck.[71]

In some terrorist campaigns, bombs are brought to the area of the operation by what are termed suicide bombers. These are people who carry the bomb to the target and detonate it whilst so close to the explosion that they are likely to be killed themselves. This method is neither new nor necessarily confined to religious groups. In 1881, an assassin from the People's Will was killed by the powerful bomb which he threw at the carriage of Tsar Alexander II, whilst Savinkov describes how Social Revolutionaries carried bombs to the vicinity of their intended targets and detonated them in the expectation, not necessarily realised, that they too would be killed in the explosion.[72]

Suicide bomb attacks have often been used by the Sri Lankan LTTE. This method was used in the assassinations of Rajiv Gandhi at Madras in April 1991 and Sri Lanka's President Premadasa in May 1993, whilst suicide bombers have also killed several ordinary members of the Indian and Sri Lankan military by running into troop emplacements and convoys with explosives strapped to their bodies.[73] Islamic groups have also used suicide bombers, usually driving vehicle bombs into protected targets, such as the highly lethal Hizbollah attacks in Beirut on the US Embassy in April 1983 and September 1984, on the US Marine Barracks in October 1983, and on the US Embassy in Kuwait in December 1983.[74] However, unprotected targets have also been attacked by suicide bombers. In April 1994 a suicide car bomb attack was made on a school bus at Afula in Israel by a member of the Palestinian Islamist group Hamas, killing 8 people including the bomber, apparently in revenge for the massacre of 29 Muslims in the Hebron mosque by Baruch Goldstein, a Jewish settler.[75]

There have also been cases where people have been tricked or intimidated into planting bombs by terrorists. As an example of trickery, the case of Nizar Hindawi and the bomb he planted on his Israel-bound girlfriend has already been mentioned. However, the use of such dupes seems to be quite rare.

More common is the application of intimidation. The use of 'proxy' bombs by the Provisional IRA has been fairly common in Northern Ireland, and more recently in England. In some cases a person is held by members of the group and told that friends or members of his family, who are also being held by the terrorists, will be harmed if he does not drive a vehicle containing a bomb to the location of the target. In other cases, as happened to a pair of London cab-drivers in June 1992 and April 1993, they are told that a bomb has been placed in their vehicle, and that they are to drive to a particular spot. They are warned that if they disobey, the bomb will be remotely detonated from a car following them. Usually the person has enough time to get away from the vehicle before it explodes.[76] However, in a refinement of that tactic, on October 24, 1990, PIRA groups held the families of three men hostage and tied the men into vehicles which they were told to drive into British Army checkpoints. Two of the bombs detonated, killing 6 soldiers and one of the drivers and injuring another 35 people.[77] In all three cases the Provisionals claimed that the men concerned were 'collaborators', people carrying out work which the PIRA deemed to be helping the security forces – for instance, the dead driver was a kitchen assistant for the Ministry of Defence.[78] However, the Provisionals stopped using this method, apparently due to the revulsion which it caused amongst their own supporters.[79]

THE INSERTION OF THE OPERATOR OR OPERATIONAL TEAM

The successful execution of a terrorist operation demands that the relevant operational member or members of the terrorist group are able to get into a position where they can attack the target. In some cases this means getting physically close to the target and staying close to the target when the attack takes place. At other times this is not necessary.

Where there is little protection for a human target whom the terrorists have decided to kill, a close quarter assassination is a simple option. This merely requires that the assassin gets close to the target, kills him or her, and gets away. In an interview in 1983, the then INLA leader Dominic McGlinchey pointed out the importance of getting close to the target for attacks with a gun.

> I usually like to get in close, to minimise the risk for myself. It's usually just a matter of who gets in first and by getting in close

you put your man down first.... I wouldn't be as good as they are at shooting it out over distances because I don't get the opportunity for weapons and target training like they do. So I believe in getting in close.[80]

Of course access is much easier if one of the terrorists is a relation or supposed friend of the target.

Gun attacks can also take place from a longer range, obviating the need to overcome close protection around the target as long as the gun and ammunition are powerful enough. As mentioned, in April 1991 the Red Army Faction assassinated Detlev Rohwedder, the head of the agency responsible for privatising or liquidating companies in the former East Germany. As he worked in the study of his Dusseldorf villa, he was shot dead from across the street by a sniper using a precision made rifle.[81] In August 1993 a police raid in Belfast found, amongst other weapons, a Tejas 0.50 calibre rifle, reported to be capable of firing armour-piercing rounds up to a range of between one and three miles. During that period a similar rifle was being used to kill soldiers and police officers in the Northern Irish border areas.[82]

Bombing can be easier than shooting as terrorists can often plant bombs quite openly. An indiscriminate bombing can be carried out by leaving down a seemingly innocuous bag or package in a public place such as a litter bin in a railway station. In February 1991, a PIRA bomb in a litter-bin at Victoria Station in London killed one man and injured 43 people.[83] With such a bombing it is not necessary to overcome any security arrangements or inspections. However, in some cases bombers have been detected on closed circuit television (CCTV) recordings examined after the event. Thus, in March 1993 two English-born members of the Provisional IRA were recognised and arrested after the police released still pictures from a security camera which showed them planting a bomb outside Harrods department store in London.[84]

Other attacks have overcome security checks, for example the PIRA's bombing of the Grand Hotel at Brighton during the 1984 Conservative Party Conference. One terrorist had booked a room in the hotel on September 15, 1984. When a colleague arrived, they assembled and planted the bomb, together with a detonator adapted from the timer device from a video recorder, behind the side panels of a bath. The explosives were wrapped in cellophane to mask their smell. The terrorists left the hotel around September 18,

1984. The bomb was not detected, and on October 12, 1984 it killed 5 people, injured 34, and nearly killed members of the British Cabinet.[85]

At other times getting the assailants close to the target can involve rather more effort. The problems which the terrorists can face include avoiding recognition before the attack is carried out, and overcoming the physical security protecting the target. An example of how both were achieved in one operation is provided by the abduction of Aldo Moro, the President of the Italian Christian Democratic Party and a former Prime Minister who was kidnapped in Rome on March 16, 1978, and held for 55 days before being killed.

When the Red Brigades were planning to kidnap Aldo Moro one of the problems they had to overcome was the physical security provided by five armed bodyguards, two in the car containing Moro, and three in an escort car which followed. They decided to overcome this by killing all of the bodyguards with overwhelming firepower. This involved a number of terrorists armed with automatic weapons. The problem was how to place a number of people with sub-machine guns in the proximity of the ambush site in Via Fani in such a way as not to arouse suspicion. The kidnappers had noticed that the area around the Via Fani was popular with staff from the Italian airline Alitalia. Consequently they bought caps and stole material similar to that used by Alitalia, and made uniforms from it. Each terrorist in the firing team carried a leather bag similar to those used by Alitalia staff to carry clothes, toiletries and so forth necessary when flying abroad; except in this case they carried sub-machine guns. The firing team was able to shelter by a bar which had gone out of business. On the morning of March 16, 1978, a white Fiat 128 estate car with diplomatic licence plates overtook Moro's convoy in the Via Fani, and deliberately reversed into Moro's car. The escort car was unable to stop and hit Moro's car from behind. The driver and passenger in the Fiat 128 got out and shot the bodyguards in Moro's car whilst the men in Alitalia uniforms took their guns from the bags, stepped out from the cover afforded by the bar, and raked the escort vehicle with gunfire. The wounded bodyguards were finished off with shots to the head whilst Moro, who had not been wounded, was dragged from his car and bundled into a waiting Fiat 132 which drove off. Thus the abductors succeeded in getting close and neutralising Moro's security by using cars to stop his car, by disguising some of the abductors in airline uniforms so that they would not be spotted as terrorists

THE EXECUTION OF A TERRORIST OPERATION

The Moro kidnap demonstrates that the main characteristic of a terrorist operation is speed. The aim is to carry out the operation in such a way that the active part has been concluded before the target or any possible reinforcements have had the time to react effectively. According to Scotti the Moro abduction took only 45 seconds from the moment when Moro's car was stopped to the bundling of Moro into the van.[87] In the 1950s George Grivas recommended that ambushes of military patrols or convoys should not be allowed to last for more than five minutes.[88]

Bombings or attacks with guns should only take as long to execute as is needed to fire a shot or detonate a bomb. Indeed, as with the Brighton explosion, a person placing a bomb need not be in the vicinity when it explodes if it has a timer, anti-handling device, or any mechanism which is capable of triggering an explosion without needing the bomber to positively detonate the device. Close quarter bomb attacks are dangerous for the perpetrator, although obviously this is not a problem for suicide bombers. However, as in Northern Ireland, small explosive devices such as hand grenades or small bombs can be thrown at either human targets, or at material targets such as vehicles or buildings, sometimes with lethal effect.[89]

The main requirement of a terrorist attack is that the job is done properly. Apart from the publicity, and possibly the shock to the psychological target, of an unsuccessful attack, there is little point in attempting to kill somebody or destroy something and then failing to do it. It represents a waste of resources, leaves clues, and provides the enemy with the opportunity to protect that target against future attacks. For this reason an effective terrorist operation should be conducted in such a way as to minimise the chance of failure. Thus, Rajiv Gandhi's assassin, an LTTE suicide bomber, walked right up to him before setting off her explosives.[90] Likewise, as mentioned above, the INLA leader Dominic McGlinchy liked to 'get in close'.[91] Indeed, various accounts of terrorist gun attacks at close-quarters have shown that assailants frequently shoot the victim a number of times – once or twice to get them on the ground and then a few shots into the head to make sure they are dead.[92]

THE WITHDRAWAL OF THE OPERATIONAL TEAM

Once the operation has been executed the most important factor for the terrorist is the ability to escape. Except in the case of suicide bombers, proxy bombers, hijackings, and sieges, terrorists plan their operations on the assumption that the attackers must get away immediately after the operation has been carried out. Even when the terrorists do remain in the public eye for a while, they usually have escape plans. For example, when in December 1975 a terrorist group, led by Carlos, stormed the Vienna conference of OPEC (Oil and Petroleum Exporting Countries), and took the various government ministers there hostage, one of their demands, which was achieved, was that they were flown to a safe haven.[93]

Where an attack involves leaving a bomb to explode some time afterwards, the withdrawal of the terrorists is not really a problem. However, in other cases someone has to remain in the vicinity of the target until the operation is concluded. Examples of this include a shooting, or a bomb which requires that the terrorist can see the target when detonating the device – for example a remote-controlled land-mine.[94] In these cases the terrorist group must plan some form of getaway before carrying out the operation.

The most obvious example of the need for a getaway plan is when an abduction takes place. For the Moro kidnapping mentioned above, the escape route was well planned. After the bodyguards had been eliminated, Moro was bundled out of his car into a waiting Fiat 132 and driven off. One of the abductors left on a motor-cycle whilst the others left in a Fiat 128. The Fiat 132 was only driven for a relatively short distance, before Moro was transferred to a Fiat van. This was driven to an underground car park, where Moro was put into a packing case which was loaded into another Fiat van. From there Moro was taken to a safe flat which had been prepared in the Via Montalcani in Rome.[95]

Even less sophisticated operations require an escape route. When carrying out sniper attacks, the Provisional IRA and the INLA place a premium on having a 'runback', that is a secure, short, escape route from the vicinity of the attack to a safe house or a car which will get them away from the area.[96] When the escape route is not planned or reconnoitred sufficiently the results can be fatal for the terrorists concerned. In February 1992 a Provisional IRA unit, consisting of at least four men, attacked an RUC station with a truck-mounted heavy machine-gun and automatic rifle fire. They planned to dump the truck in a church car-park a mile away and transfer into cars that they had left there. They had made no attempt to secure the change-over site before the truck returned. A British Army unit – probably Special Air Service operating on the basis of inside information – was lying in wait and killed four Provisionals.[97]

THE ISSUE OF COMMUNIQUÉS

Terrorist groups sometimes issue communiqués after an operation in order to justify the attack, and to propagate their political beliefs. The previously-mentioned PIRA assassination of Lord Mountbatten is a case in point, but as Alexander and Pluchinsky's collection of European terrorist communiqués demonstrate, some terrorist groups have a desire to explain and justify their actions to a wider audience.[98]

On the other hand several groups do not claim responsibility for operations. Moss has noted that 80 per cent of terrorist attacks in Italy between 1968 and 1980 went unclaimed.[99] In some cases groups may positively deny their actions. For instance, the LTTE strenuously denied responsibility for the assassination of Rajiv Gandhi in May 1991, despite the fact that the Indian police unearthed an extensive LTTE network which was almost certainly involved in the plot.[100] After the assassination of the Sri Lankan Minister of State for Defence, General Wijeratne, in March 1991, the new Defence Secretary brushed aside denials of responsibility by the Tamil Tigers on the basis that they never claim responsibility for their terrorist operations.[101]

SUMMARY

Terrorist attacks often involve a number of steps which make a successful result more likely. These include: choosing potential targets; gathering information; planning the attack; executing the attack; ensuring that the terrorists get away afterwards – with the exception of suicide attacks; and issuing communiqués. The extent to which they carry out those stages effectively can determine the success of an operation, or indeed whether the terrorists survive.

6 Capabilities

INTRODUCTION

The capability of a terrorist group can be defined as its ability to carry out terrorist operations. Thus, some groups may be capable of carrying out operations against hard targets whilst others may only be capable of attacking relatively soft targets. Three factors determine the capabilities of a terrorist group: the quality of the group's leadership, the membership of the group, and the material resources available.

THE QUALITY OF LEADERSHIP

Terrorist groups are usually created by a leader or nucleus of leaders. These formulate and explain an ideology which has the capacity to attract adherents and spur them on to action. The leaders then have to devise ways of translating the ideology and the desire for action into concrete terrorist operations. Having done this they must be able to justify these actions in terms of their ideology.

With the Red Brigades for example, this nucleus was formed in 1969–1970 by Renato Curcio and Mara Cagol of the Metropolitan Political Collective in Milan, and ex-members of the Federation of Young Italian Communists (FGCI – Federazione Giovanile Comunista Italiana) such as Alberto Franceschini.[1] Similarly, Yasser Arafat, Salah Khalef (later known as Abu Iyad), and other Palestinian students studying in Cairo in the early 1950s, mobilised support within the Palestinian Student's Union and formed al-Fatah, which became the core of the Palestine Liberation Organisation when it was founded in 1964.[2] In other cases the formation of the group can be more diffuse. The Berlin-based June 2nd Movement consisted of a number of groups, what Scharlau terms *cliques*, which clustered around a common leadership. In fact B2J was a relatively small organisation whose estimated membership varied between thirteen people in 1971 and forty in 1976.[3] Likewise, the Ulster Defence Association originated in the formation of several separate Protestant and loyalist vigilante groups in urban areas of

Northern Ireland in 1970, and these only adopted the loose confederal structure of the UDA in the early summer of 1971.[4]

Where a group has a pre-history of sorts, such as the PIRA, or has an institutional base, such as MAS in Colombia, there may be a tradition or a skeletal framework to fall back upon. With the Provisional IRA in 1970, a skeleton structure and historical tradition were already in place, and a core of people existed to keep an almost defunct organisation from going out of existence. Thus the leaders did not have to start from scratch. Likewise, with MAS in 1981, a nucleus of leaders existed in the drug-trafficking groups, the military, and other governmental and business institutions.

A nucleus may fail to attract adherents or supporters to the cause and the group will fail to maintain sufficient momentum to stay in existence. This appears to have been the case with many of the small Italian communist and fascist groups, but it might equally be applied to a group such as the Angry Brigade in Britain, which was very active for a short period but did not long survive the arrest of the leading members of the group.[5] Alternatively, when several members of the PIRA leadership were imprisoned or interned in the early 1970s, the group merely continued to operate in an uncoordinated and more violent fashion under the decentralised control of less experienced and less politically conscious young activists.[6] Some smaller groups – for example the Revolutionary Organisation November 17th (Epanastaiki Organosi 17 Noemvri – 17N), a highly nationalistic Greek communist terrorist group, have only ever consisted of a small core and have concentrated upon carrying out meticulously planned high-profile operations.[7] Thus there has been no need for them to expand much beyond the original small nucleus.

The ability of the terrorist leadership is important. A degree of intelligence is obviously an advantage in a terrorist leader, but this should not be confused with formal academic ability. The fact that terrorists tend to start their activities at an early age may mitigate against them being in a position to enter further or higher education. Furthermore, the material success which further education can bring may divert such people from the risks inherent in terrorism. However, the leaders must be capable of translating their political ideology into a set of beliefs which are attractive and comprehensible to the other members at the very least, and ideally to supporters and potential sympathisers as well. A former PIRA member notes that one reason why a particular Derry Provisional rose in the organisation in the 1970s was that:

He was articulate and could explain publicly where we were at. That was unusual in the IRA and it secured his place very early on and kept him there because he is still able to think.[8]

Similarly, one of the reasons why Gudrun Ensslin was able to lead the first generation of the RAF, in combination with the forceful Baader, was her ability to translate the group's actions and beliefs into the pseudo-Marxist jargon which appealed to other members of the group.[9]

Another notable factor amongst terrorist leaders is a high degree of dedication and single-mindedness with regard to the political cause involved. Bowyer Bell, who has met various terrorist and insurgent leaders over the years, refers to their 'very deep and very narrow political beliefs' and their inability to see a realistic alternative to the use of violence in achieving their aims.[10] When reading the biographies or autobiographies of terrorist leaders such as Savinkov, Collins, Begin, Grivas, or MacStiofain, one is struck by their driven nature.[11] The belief that their cause is honourable, and their willingness to subordinate all other concerns to the demands of the organisation, means that whilst terrorist leaders might have a strong sense of values, they are also capable of rationalising acts of great ruthlessness. For instance, following the British execution of two members of the Jewish terrorist group Irgun Zvai Leumi (National Military Organisation – Irgun) in Palestine in 1946, Menachim Begin – the head of the Irgun – ordered that two British soldiers should be abducted and hanged in order to dissuade the British from carrying out any more executions. In addition the soldiers' bodies were booby-trapped with explosives.[12]

One of the most important qualities of terrorist leaders is the ability to learn from their own experience and from that of others. In February 1991 a PIRA spokesman describing operational aspects of PIRA's strategy stated that new tactics were discussed before an operation and their effectiveness was analysed afterwards.[13] Sean MacStiofain, the PIRA's former chief of staff, has noted that by 1972 the Provisionals had built up a fund of experience which the British authorities would be unable to remove.[14] A practical example of the use of such experience can be seen in the development of the 'one-shot sniper'. Essentially, rather than getting caught up in a gun-battle with the better-armed, better-trained, and more numerous British troops, from late 1972 the PIRA used snipers who would fire one shot and then retreat to a safe place before they could be located and caught or killed.[15] An earlier example of the ability of an Irish republican leader to learn from experience is shown by Coogan's account of Michael Collin's actions in 1920 following the IRA ambush of a Dublin police detective. Although hit several times and mortally wounded, the detective was able to run to his house. Collins ensured that in future members of his assassination squad would carry .45 calibre pistols instead of the lighter .38s.[16]

Terrorist leaders can also learn from the experience of other groups. During the 1950s, those members of the IRA who were destined to form the core of the Provisional IRA in the 1970s, were imprisoned in England with members of the Greek-Cypriot terrorist group EOKA. By their own account they learned from them.[17] According to various sources PIRA members have also consulted books on guerrilla warfare and insurgency by the likes of Barry, Begin, Guevara, Mao, and Taber.[18] Similarly, in 1970 Marighela's 'Handbook of Urban Guerrilla Warfare' or 'minimanual' was published by Giangiacomo Feltrinelli – a publisher who in 1969 set up the Partisan's Action Group (Gruup di Azione Partigiani – GAP) a forerunner to the Red Brigades. This book provided the BR leadership with a blueprint for organising a revolutionary communist group and for its subsequent strategy.[19]

Some groups have drawn direct lessons from the experiences of others. As mentioned, some West German communist terrorists received training from Palestinian groups in the 1970s.[20] Similarly, after a suicide bombing by Hamas in Tel Aviv on October 19, 1994 which killed 22 people and injured 45, a spokesman for the group claimed that Hamas leaders had learned how to carry out such operations from the Lebanese Islamist group Hizbollah when Hamas leaders were exiled to southern Lebanon by the Israelis.[21]

However, it would be over-stating the case to say that terrorists always necessarily learn from their own, or other people's, experience. For instance the Red Brigades knew that whilst the public reacted ambivalently to attacks on politicians and business managers, attacks which killed ordinary people or police officers were widely unpopular and damaged support for the group.[22] Nevertheless, in January 1979 they caused mass protests – and vast damage to their cause – when they shot dead a popular worker who had denounced a work colleague for distributing BR literature.[23] In general, if the communist terrorists in Europe in the 1980s had any great capacity to learn, they would have realised that whilst tactically successful, in strategic terms their campaigns were largely futile.

Leadership within terrorist groups can operate at a number of levels. Where the operational group is part of a larger organisation – such as the Shining Path, the LTTE, or Hizbollah – a fairly rigid hierarchy may be formed with fixed lines of command delegating some powers of decision to the lower levels.[24] With smaller terrorist groups which still cover a wide geographical area, for example the Provisional IRA and the Red Brigades, organisational structures generally have some form of hierarchy, with an overall leadership cadre and a chain of command over the various sub-groups below. Within these sub-groups there are also likely to be leadership structures – whether formal or informal – with certain people making operational decisions. Where the members of these sub-groups also try to develop ideological policies independent of the overall leadership, there is a possibility of splits developing within the organisation, examples being the split between the Official IRA and the INLA, and between the Red Brigades and the Milan-based Walter Alasia Column of BR.[25]

In a very small group whose members live in the same area, it is unlikely that a formal bureaucratic pattern of organisation will evolve. Group structures are normally informal, and leadership roles tend to devolve upon those with the most forceful or persuasive character. As mentioned, Andreas Baader was able to exercise leadership of the original Baader-Meinhof group by his rude and forceful behaviour. Similarly Lenny Murphy, who led a UVF group in the Shankill Road area of Belfast, appears to have commanded his group through a combination of charisma, audacity, and fear.[26] According to Hearst, Donald DeFreeze, who called himself Cinque Mtume, appears to have controlled the other eight members of the Symbionese Liberation Army (SLA) in California through a combination of bombast, constant criticism, and occasional violence.[27] In such cases the group's effectiveness – or at least its levels of activity – may be enhanced by a determined and forceful leader.

Obviously, one of the main determinants of the effectiveness of a terrorist leader is his ability to plan operations and to link them to the political objectives of the group. Whilst terrorist leaders like Baader and Murphy ruled through force of character, other terrorist leaders attain their position through respect for their operational or political abilities. George Grivas, who led the Greek-Cypriot EOKA against the British in the 1950s, had been a staff officer in the Greek Army before the Second World War, and he meticulously laid down both the organisation of EOKA and gave personal consent to many of the operations carried out by EOKA members.[28] Likewise, the leading Derry member of the Provisional IRA mentioned above reportedly receives a great deal of respect because of his operational abilities and his perceived willingness to assume the same risks as his subordinates.[29] According to one republican source he, '... has the respect and confidence of the volunteers. He's seen as their man. They trust him'.[30]

Although a degree of political astuteness – the ability to match violent methods to political objectives and explain the connection between the two – appears to be a prerequisite for the overall leadership, this is not necessarily the case for operational leaders.[31] Whilst PIRA leaders such as Francis Hughes and Jim Lynagh were very effective operationally, their reported lack of political sophistication means they would not necessarily have made effective leaders of the overall republican movement.[32]

On the subject of operational ability, Bruce notes that amongst the Scottish supporters of the loyalists in Northern Ireland, it was accepted that a man could be a good organiser, but 'just not cut out for the rough stuff'.[33] However, most groups appear to want at least a degree of demonstrated operational competence. Thus, the rise of the criminologist Giovanni Senzani, to the leadership of the Naples column of the Red Brigades in the early 1980s is only partially explicable by his ability to link the operations of the BR to wider theoretical precepts. Like his rival BR leader Mario Moretti – who was presented as being more straightforwardly 'militarist' – Senzani also planned operations.[34]

A final characteristic which can determine the effectiveness of a terrorist group's leadership is experience. The psychologist David Canter has noted that non-political criminals become more competent with experience, and there is little reason to suspect that the same does not apply to terrorists.[35] Although the stresses of a prolonged clandestine or semi-clandestine life may lead to exhaustion or disillusion, the more experienced the group leaders are, the more likely it is that their competence will improve. The existence of a high degree of continuity amongst the PIRA leadership has been noted by Bowyer Bell and is one reason for their high degree of competence.[36] In November 1991 a security forces source described the PIRA as 'very, very good' and noted that they made very few mistakes due to having twenty-two years experience.[37] At the same time another security force source said that the PIRA leaders were 'better than ever before' and described some of their operations as 'brilliant, in terrorist terms'.[38] For groups which lose their leadership cadre early in the campaign, acquiring such a degree of competence would be much more difficult.

Ultimately a terrorist group is dependent upon its leadership – whether formally or informally designated – to provide it with the impetus for action, and to maintain the momentum once it has started. The leaders of a terrorist group at the overall command level have to be able to articulate the ideology of the group in such a way as to attract and retain enough support to keep the group in existence, and to translate the ideology into a strategy. Leaders at the operational level have to be able to translate this strategy into operations. Ideally these leaders must be capable of thinking beyond the next operation. The greater the ability of the terrorist leaders, the more likely it is that the group will select targets which serve their political and ideological purposes.

THE MEMBERSHIP OF THE GROUP

For the purposes of this study a member of a terrorist group is somebody who plays an active role in terrorist operations or in actively carrying out support and logistical functions such as the collection and analysis of information, weapons procurement, the maintenance of arms dumps and safe houses, and the movement of weapons. It does not include sympathisers, or even supporters if their role does not go beyond providing passive support or taking part in legal activities such as overt fund-raising or political campaigning.

An aspect of a terrorist group which contributes to its ability to carry out operations is the number of members which it has. It is a fairly obvious point that the more members which a group has the more operations it can carry out. In addition, a larger terrorist group can obtain more information in relation to possible targets because it has a greater number of people who can acquire or simply overhear potentially useful information. Of course it may be the case that a smaller group has better targeting information on specific targets because it has members who are in the right place or move in suitable circles. The People's Will in 1880s Russia was fortunate to possess members who had access to members of the Tsarist court. One member, a skilled workman in the Winter Palace in St Petersburg, planted a bomb below the Tsar's dining room in February 1880, killing ten people and narrowly failing to kill the Tsar himself.[39] In general, however, a larger terrorist group – such as the PIRA – will have more members in less crucial but potentially useful areas, such as the civil service, as well as simply having more members who are likely to pick up casual gossip.[40]

The size of the terrorist group will also determine, to a degree, the complexity of the operations which they can carry out. Relatively simple operations such as assassinations, mass-casualty bombings, and similar attacks do not require the participation of many terrorists. However, an operation such as the abduction of a high-profile person is more complex and requires an assault team, somebody to sort out the logistics such as transport, safe houses, and possibly any subsequent communications with the authorities or any other interested parties. The Moro kidnapping of 1978 involved an assault team of at least six or seven people, with another two to four acting as drivers or blocking off the Via Fani as Moro was dragged from his car and the bodyguards were killed. Ten BR members were found guilty of involvement with the abduction and murder of Moro, and arrest warrants were issued for two more.[41] An alternative route was taken by ETA in 1973, when they decided to kill rather than kidnap the Spanish Prime Minister Carrero Blanco because killing him was easier and required fewer resources.[42] Thus, the size of the group can determine the types of operation which it can carry out.

A terrorist group's capability is also affected by the quality of its members. The individual calibre of terrorists can be defined as their ability to carry out terrorist operations effectively. Generally, terrorists have to carry out operations which are deemed illegal in the country where they are conducted, all the time trying to avoid the attentions of the security forces or other enemies. The better they are at planning and carrying out operations, and at evading death or capture in the process, the more effective they are as terrorists. Thus, their calibre is a mixture of intelligence, ability to carry out technical tasks such as bomb-making and the use of firearms, and nerve.

The technical ability of terrorists varies considerably. It is not necessary for somebody to be well-trained in military techniques for them to be able to carry out certain types of terrorist operation. Uncomplicated attacks against relatively undefended targets do not require much in the way of training. In the late 1960s and early 1970s many of the attacks carried out by the Naxalites in

India were stabbings against soft targets such as traffic policemen, wealthier peasants, and lower-ranking members of the Communist Party of India (Marxist).[43] Such attacks were suitable for the poorly armed Naxalites, suited the Santal tribals who were initially heavily involved with the rural aspects of the Naxalite campaign, and had a greater psychological impact than attacks with guns or explosives would have done.

However, for terrorists wishing to carry out more complex operations, training in the use and construction of weapons is extremely useful. Groups may train their own members. However, in other cases training may be provided by other terrorist groups due to some feeling of solidarity or for mutual advantage. For example, from the late 1960s the PLO helped to train members of the June 2nd Movement and the Red Army Faction, whilst reports suggest that in the 1980s members of Italian and German fascist groups received training from Christian Falangists in the Lebanon and from Palestinian groups.[44] In these cases the trainers felt they had a common enemy to those whom they trained − western imperialism or zionism in the case of the Palestinians and communism in the case of the Falangists.

Some governments have also provided terrorists with training, due to support for the terrorist's cause, or to discomfit an enemy. One example of this occurred in the mid-1980s when members of the LTTE received training from the Indian armed forces at training camps in the province of Tamil Nadu.[45] This was before the ill-fated intervention of the Indian Peace-Keeping Force in Sri Lanka between 1987 and 1990. Similarly, the East German Stasi provided training and a safe haven for members of the RAF and B2J, apparently because aiding the activities of these groups was seen as a way of destabilising the western alliance system.[46]

It is also possible for security force members to join terrorist groups on their own account. Members of the armed services or other security force members who become involved with terrorist groups can be divided between those who are still in the security forces when their terrorist involvement occurs, and those who have already left. The former case includes the involvement of 59 military officers in the MAS conservative death squads in Colombia. Although the definite involvement of the authorities is not proven, there is a strong suspicion that the officers were acting with at least tacit support from some governing elements.[47] In the early 1990s members of Colombian police units are also alleged to have carried out the killings of suspected left-wing terrorists, political activists and human rights campaigners, as well as killing vagrants, petty thieves and other people deemed 'undesirable' by traders and other commercial elements.[48] In Northern Ireland, serving members of the UDR/RIR have been involved in loyalist terrorists' activities, including attacks on Catholic targets. According to Ryder, between the regiment's formation in 1970 and March 1979, over thirty UDR members were convicted of serious terrorist offences. This included five convicted of murder, five of manslaughter, ten of arms and explosives offences, and four of serious assaults.[49]

Former members of the military or other security forces can also provide a degree of expertise for terrorist groups. Maxime Frerot, the bomb-maker for the communist Direct Action (AD – Action Directe) group based around Lyons in France, was originally trained in the use of explosives when carrying out his national service as a paratrooper in the French Army.[50] Similarly, Bruce mentions that the expertise of ex-servicemen made a contribution to the activities of loyalist terrorist groups in Northern Ireland. Reportedly, some UDA and UVF members joined the UDR in order to receive training and to gain access to weapons and intelligence. However, Bruce notes that the existence of locally recruited security forces provides a legal way of defending the existing political order for those who might otherwise join the loyalist terrorists, and speculates that this drain of talented recruits has left the loyalists with a poorer talent pool to recruit from.[51]

A good bomb-maker does not necessarily require military training as expertise can come from elsewhere. Joseph O'Connell, who constructed the detonator devices for the bombs used by a PIRA unit active in London and south-eastern England in the mid-1970s, had previously worked as a radio operator and electronics trainee for the Marconi electronics company in Cork.[52] In practice a terrorist bombing campaign does not need many bomb-makers. As long as the method of priming the bomb is simple enough to be carried out by untrained people, and there are sufficient people prepared to carry the bombs to their targets, the bombs themselves can be constructed by a small number of bomb-makers.[53] However, failure in this respect can be costly. Between 1969 and 1993 over one hundred PIRA members were killed by the premature explosion of their own bombs, just over one-third of the total number of PIRA members killed.[54]

As well as technical ability, the personal characteristics of terrorists can be important. Terrorist groups often consist of people who knew other members of the group socially before they became group members. This can reinforce loyalties and frustrate penetration. In some cases the connections may be based around family networks. Provisional IRA members, and to a lesser degree INLA members, frequently have other members of their family – fathers, mothers, brothers, uncles and so forth – in the organisation as well as close friends.[55] Likewise, Islamic paramilitary groups in the near east, for example Hizbollah and Hamas, appear to be frequently organised around family ties.[56] In the Lebanon one result of this has been that some terrorist operations – including the taking of western hostages in the Lebanon – have been partially aimed at gaining the freedom of imprisoned family members.[57]

In other cases the links within the group are between friends and acquaintances. According to Marnham, nine members of the Lyons-based cell of Direct Action seem to have been recruited by their former schoolteacher.[58] Communist terrorists in Italy and West Germany also seem to have recruited people who were already in the circle of friends or were the acquaintances of group members.[59] In ETA, cells have often consisted of people who were members of the same *cuadrilla* – the term for the groups of young people who socialise together in the towns and villages of the Basque country – or were recruited by older fellow members of one of the semi-political hill-climbing clubs common to the area.[60]

When considering the rationality of terrorist behaviour, it is important to note that terrorist group members are, in general, psychologically normal. The fact that terrorists are frequently killers or the accomplices of killers may make them seem abnormal to an observer for whom lethal violence is largely an abstract concept. However, the ability to kill or injure people against whom one has no personal animosity is not confined to terrorists. Members of the armed forces are trained to kill and may often have to kill other combatants in wartime but, as Ellis shows, Allied soldiers were also capable of killing unarmed German soldiers, whilst in March 1968 ordinary American troops massacred between 200 and 700 Vietnamese villagers in the village of My Lai.[61] Similarly, in the aptly titled *Ordinary Men*, concerning a German field police unit during the Second World War, Browning shows how working- and middle-class, middle-aged conscripts from Hamburg followed orders to shoot dead Jewish men, women, and children in cold-blood. Over time they became hardened, and hence more willing to kill.[62]

Research concerning non-terrorists confirms the ability of ordinary people to inflict pain in appropriate circumstances. In the 1960s the psychologist Stanley Milgram carried out a series of experiments which demonstrated that subjects were willing to inflict powerful electric shocks upon other people if ordered to do so by a person in authority.[63] Likewise, an examination of torturers employed by military governments in Greece and Argentina found that at the point of recruitment – apart from signs of authoritarianism, obedience, and ideological sympathy for the government – there was little evidence that they were particularly different from their peers.[64] Although the experience of killing may lead to the individual becoming calloused, there is little reason to assume that people who kill or torture as part of their profession are psychologically different to ordinary people.

Research about terrorists generally confirms this view. Studies by Lyon and Harbinson, and Heskin in Northern Ireland, and by Ferracuti and Bruno in Italy, suggest that insurgent terrorists are at least as intelligent and emotionally stable as normal people.[65] On the other hand fascist terrorists in Italy do seem to exhibit signs of emotional instability and aggression whilst those in Germany were less well qualified and had jobs of lower status than their left-wing counterparts.[66]

An exception to the view of the terrorist as a psychologically normal person comes from Jerrold Post who, largely but not wholly on the basis of studies carried out by the German government, has speculated that terrorists are 'marginal, isolated, and inadequate individuals from troubled family backgrounds'.[67] Post, and the German psychiatrist Lorenz Bollinger, believe that terrorists frequently display the characteristics of a process termed splitting, whereby one's strengths are attributed to oneself, but weaknesses and failings are projected outwards and blamed upon others. This process is reinforced by the ideology of the group.[68] However, Post also notes that there is no evidence to suggest that terrorists are psychopaths, and that on the contrary, evidence suggests that they are in most respects normal.[69] The problem with Post's approach is not that it is necessarily wrong with regard to terrorism in Germany, but that it is not necessarily applicable elsewhere.

One notable difference which Post notes is that people who join terrorist groups which have a degree of support from their host community are more likely to have well-adjusted characters then people who join groups which appear to be divorced from the community. Members of the Basque group ETA or the communist Red Brigades in Italy have received support in the past because of their identification with causes which were felt to have some historical justification – the Basque struggle in the first instance, and the anti-fascist partisan war between 1943 and 1945 in the second. However the Red Army Faction had relatively little popular support and consequently the group members became more isolated from the world outside the group.[70] This view of terrorists having a more stable outlook because they can relate to an ordinary community life is borne out by Clark's study of ETA, and also by White and White's study of the Provisional IRA.[71] Consequently, the inward-looking nature of the group may be reinforced in groups with few supporters or sympathisers amongst whom they can relax and obtain moral support.

Another characteristic is that terrorists tend to be recruited when they are young. From a study of 18 terrorist groups, Russell and Miller suggest that the average urban terrorist is between 22 and 25.[72] Studies of individual groups tend to bear this out. From an analysis of 67 PIRA members killed in Belfast between 1969 and 1988, White and White found that the average age at recruitment was 19 years and 4 months.[73] Clark found that ETA recruits tended to be in their mid-twenties when recruited or first arrested, and Weinberg and Eubank found that in Italy the majority of members of left-wing groups (72.8 per cent) and right-wing groups (80.1 per cent) were under 29 years old when first identified as terrorists.[74] There is some difference in age between ordinary terrorists who tend to be in their late teens and twenties, and the leaders of the groups who tend to be a few years older.[75] Other studies of specific terrorist groups show this pattern of young ordinary members, with leaders who are a few years older, to be quite common.[76] There are exceptions. The average age of the German left-wing terrorists surveyed was higher on average than for most other groups, but this disguises the fact that members of the Red Army Faction in Germany were much older on average than members of the contemporaneous June 2nd Movement.[77] Italian right-wing leaders tend to be quite a bit older than the average, and their ordinary members are somewhat younger.[78]

A possible consequence of the driven nature of terrorist leaders and the youth of their followers is that terrorists tend to be impatient by nature. In an article on the importance of organisational factors in analysing terrorism, Crenshaw has noted that 'Terrorists are often individuals who are impatient for action', and that they give action priority over talk.[79] The comments of some terrorists seem to bear this out. In a letter in 1971, Michael Baumann, who was later to join the June 2nd Movement in Germany, wrote:

> WORDS CANNOT SAVE US! WORDS DON'T BREAK CHAINS! THE DEED ALONE MAKES US FREE! DESTROY WHAT DESTROYS YOU![80]

Similarly, Hall notes a loyalist group in Northern Ireland terming itself the 'Ulster Militants' stating:

> We do not believe in defence but attack... but we got sick and tired of training with only a general idea of what we were supposed to be training for. We wanted action and were not allowed to have any.[81]

Other statements by loyalist terrorists reinforce this view of the primacy of action.[82]

Similarly, the impatience of Irish republicans has historically been reflected in a low opinion of 'politicians' rather than 'soldiers'.[83] Burton has observed that out of all the young men he saw in west Belfast in the early 1970s, the PIRA members were the ones who appeared to have an aura of 'urgent activity' about them and one of O'Brien's interviewees notes that in the early 1970s active PIRA membership was 'exciting' for youngsters.[84] As one former PIRA activist said of his youthful actions, 'You can't let politics ruin a fuckin' war'.[85] This is not to say that all terrorists are necessarily impulsive. Guzman spent ten years laying down the foundations for the violent campaign of the Shining Path in Peru, whilst the amount of time which some groups will spend in planning a single operation is testament to their patience.[86]

An important characteristic of some terrorists is their persistence in the face of adversity and the ultimate possibility of death. O'Malley describes the Irish republicans he has met as:

> highly intelligent, extraordinarily motivated, relentlessly committed to their course of action, imbued with a puritanical obsession – you might even say a tyrannical obsession – with wanting to do right and to be seen to do right, which makes their actions all the more frightening.[87]

To take three PIRA members for example, Jim Lynagh was imprisoned for four years in Northern Ireland and for four years in the Republic, Dessie Grew was imprisoned four times, whilst Mairead Farrell spent nearly ten years in prison. All three remained active members and were subsequently killed on operations.[88]

Likewise, with the German communist terrorist Inge Viett, who was a member of first the June 2nd Movement and then the Red Army Faction. She escaped from prison twice, in 1973 and 1976, and shot a policeman who tried to arrest her in Paris in 1981, before 'retiring' to East Germany in 1983. She appears to have simultaneously been an agent for the East German Ministry for State Security (Ministerium fur Staatssicherheit or Staatssicherheitsdienst known as the MfS or Stasi) and was arrested in 1990 after German reunification.[89]

A characteristic of terrorists which is not often remarked upon is the degree of courage which is sometimes necessary in the commission of their actions. Several terrorists have been willing to die in pursuit of their aims. Between 1969 and 1993, 256 members of the Provisional IRA were killed by the security forces, by rival terrorist groups, or by the premature detonation of their own bombs.[90] Their determination is well illustrated by the willingness of prisoners to fast to death in pursuit of political status or other changes in prison conditions. Between 1974 and 1981 twelve Irish republicans died on hunger strike – two in England in 1974 and 1976, and ten during the H-Block hunger strikes of 1981.[91] Similarly, in West Germany two RAF members starved themselves to death in order to change their prison conditions – Holger Meins in November 1974 and Sigurd Debus in April 1981.[92] In addition, there is the previously mentioned example of the members of groups such as Hamas, Hizbollah, and the LTTE who carry out suicide attacks. Whilst terrorists generally use methods which minimise the risks to themselves, and often carry out attacks which are perceived as callous, it is wrong to assume that they lack courage.[93]

The capability of ordinary terrorists can be seen as an amalgam of the skills and abilities which they possess. These in turn can determine the types of operations which they are capable of carrying out. For example, there would be little purpose in entrusting somebody who had little training or technical sense with firing a complex portable anti-aircraft system. Thus, to an extent, a terrorist's ability may be measured according to his technical ability with weapons. In addition, personal abilities such as intelligence and courage are also useful, because it is more likely that someone possessing these attributes will carry out an operation successfully. Lastly, as a rule, the more terrorists which a group possesses the greater the number and complexity of the operations which they can carry out. However, in order for their capabilities to be put to the best use, they need suitable weapons.

THE WEAPONS AVAILABLE

Even if a terrorist group has very talented leaders and highly trained and committed members, its capability is limited without suitable weapons. This does not mean that a group needs masses of the latest and most sophisticated weaponry, but the availability of such weapons can extend its capability, provided its members are able to use them.

The means by which a terrorist group can obtain weapons are many and varied. During the Second World War a communist resistance group adopted the slogan:

> Any household has a knife; if you have a knife, you can get a pistol; if you have a pistol, you can get a rifle; if you have a rifle, you can get a machine-gun. Get on with it comrades: get armed![94]

As Foot notes, this may seem somewhat ambitious, but some groups have gained their initial armaments by raiding the resources of the police and military. Throughout 1970 Japanese communist terrorists raided a number of the small two to three man urban police huts – known as a koban – in order to obtain weapons.[95] Similarly, in May 1979 *Corriere della Serra* reported that five members of a group calling themselves the Proletarian Combat Squad (Squadre Proleterie di Combattimento) had raided a police section house in Turin, taking the uniforms, weapons, and identity (ID) cards from two policemen.[96]

Some terrorist groups – mainly espousing conservative or fascist ideologies – have been supplied with weapons by sympathisers within the security forces. Groups which have members serving in the security forces will generally have little difficulty in obtaining some weapons. In Colombia and other parts of Latin America, it seems likely that terrorist groups which are linked to the police, military or military-approved paramilitary groups have either used their ordinary service weapons when carrying out attacks, or have obtained unregistered weapons and ammunition.[97] During the recent troubles in Northern Ireland, loyalist terrorists have raided UDR depots using inside information to obtain weapons, and on occasion have also been directly supplied with weapons by sympathisers or members within the regiment.[98]

Terrorists can also obtain weapons on the legal and illegal arms markets. The relatively unrestricted gun laws in the USA have made it possible to openly purchase small arms up to the level of automatic and semi-automatic rifles in gun shops.[99] In the early 1970s many of the Armalites obtained by the PIRA were bought in the USA in small consignments and then smuggled over to Ireland.[100] The Red Brigades also appear to have bought some weapons from Italian gun shops, using false identity papers to make their purchases.[101]

With the break-up of the Soviet Union and the eastern bloc, weapons formerly held by the Soviet Army and newly developed weapons appear to have come onto the market in the west, whilst, a television programme about Bulgarian arms dealers indicates that they would not enquire too closely as to the final destination of weapons which they supply.[102] The low costs of arms manufacturers in the former Soviet bloc and far east allow them to develop cheap small arms which would be suitable for a terrorist group. A report in September 1994 stated that whereas a standard European-made hand-grenade cost about £8 one made in China cost £3, and whilst a sophisticated European rifle cost about £400 a Russian-made AK47 cost about £60.[103] In addition, some recent Russian weapons are extremely well-suited for use by both security forces and terrorists alike. These include a small silenced pistol, a silenced assault rifle based upon the AK47 which is reportedly capable of penetrating body armour, and a silenced sniper rifle. In addition a new 350mm long handgun has been developed which is capable of firing automatic bursts, has an extending stock so that it can be fired from the shoulder, and is said to be capable of penetrating all types of military body armour.[104] Such weapons would be extremely useful to a terrorist group.

As well as buying weapons on the open market, terrorists can obtain them from foreign supporters or sponsors who are not directly involved with the group concerned, but who wish to either help the group or harm the enemies of the group. Governments can be extremely useful suppliers of weapons and other resources as they have access to money and the arms market, and can obtain weapons without too many questions being asked. If necessary, governments can move weapons around the world using the diplomatic bag and store them in embassies.[105] Reported examples of governments supplying weapons and other forms of aid to terrorist groups include Iranian aid to the Lebanese Shia Islamic group Hizbollah, and US aid to the conservative Nicaraguan Counter-revolutionaries (contrarevolucionarios – Contras) who fought the Sandanista Government of Nicaragua in the 1980s.[106]

The greatest material boost which the Provisional IRA received in recent years was the shipments of arms from the Libyan Government of Colonel Gaddafi. Gaddafi had supplied weapons to the Provisionals in the early 1970s as part of his general opposition to 'imperialism', but in the mid-1980s he appears to have supplied large quantities to the PIRA because of the police siege of the Libyan Embassy in London in April 1984 following the fatal shooting of a policewoman and the subsequent expulsion of Libyan diplomats.[107] According to *The Economist* the RUC estimated that by November 1987 the Libyans had given the PIRA six tons of Semtex plastic explosive, twenty SAM-7 anti-aircraft missiles, about 1,500 Kalashnikov AK47 automatic rifles, 1.5 million rounds of ammunition, fifty RPG7 rocket launchers, ten flame throwers, and a number of medium and heavy machine-guns.[108] According to McKittrick, the shipments provided the Provisionals with enough weaponry to continue their campaign for at least another decade.[109]

An interesting case of terrorists receiving indirect help from a government may be found in the case of Afghan mujahedeen fighting Soviet occupiers in the 1980s, who obtained Stinger anti-aircraft missiles and training in their use from the US Government.[110] In 1993, a report in *The Independent* suggested that Algerians who fought alongside the mujahedeen in Afghanistan had turned up in the civil war in Algeria, whilst the possible use of anti-aircraft missiles in terrorist attacks against aircraft has become a major concern of the US Department of State.[111] The concern is particularly acute as reports suggest that some of the Stingers were diverted to Iran, a state which the US Government has long regarded as being a sponsor of anti-American terrorist groups and activities.[112]

The influence of foreign sponsors on the selection of terrorist targets has varied. As well as providing safe haven and training, the East German Stasi appears to have recruited West German communist terrorists as agents. However, the extent to which this affected target selection is not clear.[113] On the other hand, although

James Adams claims that the PIRA plan to bomb a military parade in Gibraltar in 1988 was an intended payoff to Gadaffi for the arms by humiliating Britain on the international stage, there is little evidence suggesting that PIRA allows outsiders to influence their attacks.[114]

In other cases this type of relationship has greatly influenced the types of target selected by a terrorist group. The Palestinian group Fatah Revolutionary Command (FRC) run by Sabri al-Banna – otherwise known as Abu Nidal, has had a number of sponsors throughout the years. The FRC has been provided with shelter and training facilities as well as weapons and logistical support by, respectively, the Iraqi, Syrian, and Libyan Governments over a number of years since the mid-1970s. As a result, the relationship between the FRC and the sponsoring governments has resembled that of a mercenary group and its paymasters, with the terrorists carrying out attacks to suit the political interests of their sponsors as well as attacking their own favoured targets.[115]

As well as receiving weapons, some terrorists have made weapons themselves. The manufacture of home-made guns is not particularly common because of the relative availability of guns on the open market or from sponsors. However, primitive home-made pistols were used by the Mau Mau in Kenya in the 1950s, and in the late 1960s and early 1970s the Naxalites of West Bengal used pipe-guns triggered by pulling a string.[116] Even in developed countries there have been cases of home-made guns being manufactured. In October 1990 a former member of the British Army was jailed in Northern Ireland for making sub-machine guns for the UDA. The components were clandestinely manufactured by workers at the Shorts aircraft factory in Belfast and supplied to the man, who assembled the guns at a workshop in county Down.[117] Similarly, in February 1992 French police arrested a man thought to be ETA's quartermaster, in a villa near Bayonne. Police found home-made pistols and sub-machine guns based upon the Israeli Uzi.[118] However, most terrorists use mass-manufactured guns.

A home-made weapon which the Provisional IRA has used since 1972 with moderate success has been the home-made mortar using cut-down oxyacetylene canisters as the tube, and with home-made projectiles. Although there is some dispute over the accuracy of these mortars, with several civilians having been injured by stray projectiles, the mortars have been used with some effect since 1979.[119] The development of mortars has allowed the PIRA to carry out several attacks against security force targets in Northern Ireland which had been protected against attack from bombs, guns and rockets by the use of reinforced barriers. In February 1985 a mortar attack on an RUC station in Newry, county Down, killed nine police officers when the canteen was hit.[120] However, a subsequent mortar attack in Newry in November 1986 injured 35 civilians.[121] Mortars have also been used in England: to attack the British Cabinet at 10 Downing Street in February 1991, and to carry out two attacks on London's Heathrow Airport in March 1994.[122]

Bombs are commonly assembled by terrorists themselves. Guidebooks such as *The Anarchist Cookbook* give directions for the construction of relatively simple devices, and recently bomb-making information has become available on the Internet.[123] Powerful and sophisticated weapons can be constructed using components readily available in electronics and other shops. After the arrest of a Japanese Red Army member near New York in April 1988, police officers found that many of the components of his bombs had been bought from ordinary electronics and department stores.[124] Likewise, in June 1990 a bomb-expert in the RUC told an American court that the PIRA had detonated bombs from a distance by using rewired radar detectors readily available in the electronics chain store Radio Shack.[125] More recent reports suggest that the Provisionals have also used a photoflash slave unit as a detonator, attaching it to a bomb and setting it off from up to 800 metres with a flashgun.[126] Other examples of the use of everyday merchandise in bombs includes the use of the timers from video-recorders to detonate bombs weeks or even months after they have been primed, and the use of small electronic timers in incendiary devices.[127] The availability of electronic goods is unavoidable in a mass consumer society, but it does make it easier for terrorists to obtain the components necessary to construct sophisticated explosive devices, and thus extends their range of possible targets.

Some home-made bombs are relatively low-powered anti-personnel devices, such as the low-powered grenades used by the Naxalites in Calcutta in 1970–1, and PIRA's nail-bombs consisting of cans packed with explosive and nails or other shrapnel.[128] Similar hand-thrown grenades, such as the 'drogue' bombs used by the Provisionals from the late 1980s onwards, have proved capable of penetrating lightly armoured vehicles because although the outer shell of the bomb was made from household items such as baked bean tins, they contained the relatively powerful plastic explosive Semtex.[129]

Booby-trapped home-made bombs have also been used by the Provisionals including a bomb inside a football which was placed inside the perimeter of an RUC station in county Antrim – doubtless in the hope that a police officer would move the ball or even kick it, and a bomb inside a tin of chocolates which was given to a soldier manning a checkpoint in county Tyrone as a 'Christmas present'.[130]

The explosive components of a bomb can also be home-made. The IRA used home-made explosives in the bombing campaign in England in 1939–1940, and since the early 1970s the Provisionals have used various mixtures of ammonium nitrate and fuel oil (ANFO), of sodium chlorate and nitro-benzene (COOP), and later of ammonium nitrate and nitro-benzene (ANNI).[131] These bombs could sometimes be quite destructive. Recent large PIRA bombs based on similar components and weighing well over 1,000 pounds caused massive destruction in the centre of Northern Irish towns and in the City of London in the early 1990s, and were also used to attack military and police facilities.[132] In April 1995 a similar bomb, thought to consist of about 5,000 pounds of ammonium nitrate-based fertiliser and fuel oil, destroyed a federal government building in Oklahoma City, killing 168 people and injuring about 500.[133] These bombings demonstrate that the lack of a powerful pre-manufactured explosive need not prevent terrorists from carrying out mass-casualty or mass-destruction attacks.

A recent development in the use of home-made weapons was the manufacture of the nerve gas sarin by a Japanese religious group, the Supreme Truth sect (Aum Shinri Kyo). The release of sarin on the Tokyo underground in March 1995 killed twelve people and injured up to 5,500, and Japanese police reportedly believe the group was also responsible for the death of seven people from similar nerve gas poisoning in Matsumoto, Nagano Prefecture in June 1993. At the time of the Tokyo attack in March 1995 the cult was coming under increased surveillance and pressure from the police due to suspected abductions by the cult.[134] Later reports have noted that the Tokyo attacks were concentrated on parts of the underground network close to police headquarters.[135]

The weapons available to terrorists are very important in determining the targets which they can hope to attack successfully. The clandestine nature of terrorist operations means that smaller firearms are generally more suitable because they can be easily concealed when being moved and when approaching the target. Similarly,

Table 6.1 Relative size and rate of fire of machine-guns, 1884–1970

Model and Year	Length (Inches)	Weight (Pounds)	Rate of fire (Rounds/minute)
Maxim (1884)	46.50	40.00	600
Thompson (1928)	33.75	10.75	800
Ingrams MAC 10 (1970)	10.50	6.25	1145

Source: I. V. Hogg & J. Weeks, *Military Small Arms of the 20th century* (London: Arms & Armour Press, 1977), 98, 101–2, 220.

the possession of silencers for firearms means an attack can be carried out without guards or bystanders being aroused. According to Ryder a PIRA assassin used a silenced pistol to kill a police officer in a pub in Newry, county Down, in June 1981.[136] The tendency towards the miniaturisation of guns demonstrated in Table 6.1 has aided terrorists.[137] Unlike the other guns the Ingrams can be fitted with a silencer. Both ETA and the UVF are reported to have received Ingrams'.[138]

The trend towards miniaturisation can be most clearly seen in the reduction of size of different versions of the highly successful Israeli Uzi sub-machine gun of the 1950s. Whereas the original Uzi weighed 8.9 lbs and was 18.9 inches long, the newer mini-Uzi weighs 6.3 lbs and is 14.7 inches long.[139] More recently a semi-automatic pistol version has been developed weighing 4.7 lbs with a length of 9.5 inches.[140] Longer-range firearms are also relatively small. The American Armalite, which the PIRA used from the early 1970s onwards, was easily folded-up for the purposes of storage and concealment.[141] This trend towards smaller weapons, whilst useful to law enforcement officers who also need concealed weapons, has undoubtedly aided terrorists.

Explosives have also become more powerful and more stable over the years. When a group of French royalists unsuccessfully tried to assassinate Napoleon Bonaparte in December 1800, they placed a barrel of gunpowder on a cart along a route which he was known to take. The primitive time fuse failed to function properly and the bomb detonated after Napoleon had passed.[142] However, in the nineteenth century developments in the manufacture of explosives transformed their role as a weapon of political protest.[143] The invention of dynamite provided revolutionaries with a much more powerful explosive than had been hitherto available, whilst the invention of nitroglycerine, and its stabilisation with gelatine, provided a stable, powerful, and portable explosive – gelignite – used by Fenian bombers in 1880s London.[144]

More recently the development of stable, durable, and powerful plastic explosives has given terrorists greater flexibility in their use of bombs. For instance, the Libyan shipments of the plastic explosive Semtex made a great difference to the PIRA's capabilities. It is stable, malleable, and powerful – about 1.3 times as powerful as TNT according to Gurney – and a powerful explosion can be obtained from, for example, a two pound under-car bomb.[145]

THE FINANCIAL BASE

Terrorist groups need money to buy weapons and their components, to rent or buy transport and accommodation, acquire or forge documents, and provide for the living expenses of their members. Conceivably, a group such as the Animal Liberation Front in Britain or the Revolutionary Cells in Germany, can get by without large funds because most of their members are part-time terrorists who have jobs or other means of sustenance, and who do not use particularly sophisticated weaponry for their operations. However, a group with a substantial number of full-time members has to maintain a structure of safe houses, courier links, and weapons dumps. These generally require money, although some can be provided free by sympathisers.

Several terrorist groups gain funding by carrying out bank robberies, kidnappings, and by extorting money from businesses, private citizens, and even governments, with the threat that refusal to pay will result in violent retribution. Groups have also obtained money through legal and semi-legal methods. In addition to methods which rely on violence or the threat of violence, the Provisional IRA is reported to have obtained money through illegal methods such as tax fraud, smuggling, and the operation of unlicensed gaming machines, as well as from legitimate methods such as public collections, pubs, drinking clubs, taxi firms, shops and other legitimate businesses which both raise money, and allow the Provisionals to launder illegally obtained money.[146]

Another lucrative source of funds for some terrorist groups has been the drugs trade. In Peru the Shining Path has raised much of its income through 'taxes' on traffickers, whilst also taking steps to prevent the major traffickers from forcing down the prices charged by peasant coca growers. According to Rummrill the Shining Path raised $25–30 million when coca prices were at their height in August 1989.[147] In Colombia, communist, conservative, and criminal terrorist groups have also raised money from drugs trafficking. When, in the early 1980s, the communist Colombian Armed Revolutionary Force (Fuerzas Armadas Revolucionarias Colombias – FARC) raised money by extorting protection money from narcotics traffickers, death squads were set up and financially supported by narcotics traffickers and other wealthy groups in order to kill and intimidate suspected communists and other threats to the traffickers and the Colombian economic elites.[148] In Northern Ireland members of the loyalist Ulster Volunteer Force, and of the republican Irish People's Liberation Organisation, have been active in importing and distributing drugs in the province.[149]

Some terrorist groups have been financially supported by governments. According to Ranstorp, Hizbollah received an estimated $30 million from the Iranian government in 1985, rising to $64 million in 1988 and possibly over $100 million by the 1990s – although much of this went to support Hizbollah's social and political activities. Shultz reports that Iran also gave the Palestinian group Hamas $30 million in 1992 and $20 million in 1993.[150] Likewise, in 1983 the US Congress approved an allocation of $24 million for the CIA to spend on the Nicaraguan Contras – before the Boland Amendments technically restricted the uses to which US aid to the Contras could be put – and approved a further $100 million in October 1986. This was in addition to moneys diverted to the Contras from the covert sale of American weapons to Iran in the mid-1980s.[151]

In other cases governments have provided money as the price of preventing terrorist attacks. Seale claims that Abu Nidal's Fatah Revolutionary Command raised $50 million from Saudi Arabia and other Gulf states. If they failed to pay the money demanded, his organisation attacked targets such as diplomats and civil aircraft belonging to that state, as well as bombing civilian targets within the state.[152]

THE IMPORTANCE OF DOCUMENTATION

Terrorists frequently need documents so as to obtain access to target areas, to pass security checks at ports, airports and other international crossing points, and to maintain a clandestine existence.

Some groups, such as the Fatah Revolutionary Command, have the ability to forge documents.[153] Likewise, a police raid on a PIRA safe house in Luton in 1990 found, amongst other things, a number of forged Home Office passes.[154]

In other cases documents have been obtained by force. When the Proletarian Combat Squad raided the Turin police section house in April 1979, as well as taking the weapons of two police officers they also took their ID cards.[155] Some of the earliest actions of the Red Army Faction in Germany involved raids on town halls in order to obtain official stamps, blank passports, and blank ID cards.[156] In August 1985 an RAF group shot dead a US soldier – Edward Pimental – outside a Wiesbaden nightclub and stole his ID card. The following day they used it to enter the US Air Force base at Rhein-Main. The bomb which they planted there killed two Americans.[157]

Lastly, terrorist groups can be supplied with documents by sympathetic or sponsoring governments. According to Seale Abu Nidal's Fatah Revolutionary Command has in the past been supplied with documents – particularly passports – by both Iraq and Libya. Real passports are of much more value than forged ones, giving terrorists a false but verifiable identity and the scope to travel across borders and within countries with little hindrance.[158]

SUMMARY

When selecting their targets, terrorists' options are circumscribed by their capabilities. The weapons possessed by a group do much to determine which targets can be attacked. However, the terrorists' capability is also affected by the ability of a group's leaders to motivate ordinary members and plan operations whilst the quality of their ordinary members determines whether their weapons and other resources are used effectively. Furthermore, although groups with few full-time members and relatively primitive weapons can function without a large financial base, more sophisticated groups need the money to pay for weapons and other resources such as ID and travel documents.

7 Target Protection

INTRODUCTION

A practical problem which confronts terrorists wishing to carry out an attack is the extent to which the target is protected. Some targets, such as an unarmed civilians and unguarded buildings, are largely unprotected. Others, such as senior politicians and officials, or government ministries and embassies, may have elaborate and expensive forms of protection in order to preempt attacks or to protect the targets if an attack takes place.

A general rule of thumb is that terrorists will always have opportunities to carry out attacks because not all potential targets can be protected all of the time due to limits on resources. Providing a high-level of protection is expensive. During the most serious period of the terrorist threat in Italy, between the mid-1970s and early 1990s, the security services are reported to have provided 3,681 bodyguards to protect 671 assorted politicians, judges, and businessmen. The average cost of an armoured car in Italy was estimated at $70,000.[1] Likewise, in 1990 personal protection costs were reported to take up over 5 per cent of the budget of London's Metropolitan Police.[2] Such protection cannot be given to all potential targets, and this fact creates vulnerabilities.

Another rule which can be applied to the protection of targets is that the less public knowledge there is about the target the better. Terrorists cannot attack a target if they do not know where it is. As mentioned, the necessary information can often be gleaned from publicly available sources.[3] The aim of potential targets must therefore be to assume as low a profile as is commensurate with their responsibilities and a tolerable lifestyle. In its guidelines to American families living abroad the US State Department advises:

> A single concept, more than any other, should permeate all planning activities, namely 'LOW PROFILE'. In other words, DO NOT draw attention to yourself as an American by driving a big American car, subscribing to U.S. magazines, etc; blend in to local environs.[4]

Wurth notes that business executives who are felt to be potential targets should remove their names and addresses from telephone books and company directories.[5] The practice of minimising knowledge about the movement of potential targets can reach to the very top. Geraghty quotes a 1987 article in *The Mail on Sunday* which noted that although the then Prime Minister, Margaret Thatcher, was to begin a high-profile campaign concerning the future of Britain's inner cities, the details of the places she was to visit and the times when she was to visit them were withheld for security reasons.[6]

However, with some targets a low-profile policy is impossible because they could not carry out their normal business if this was done. For example, the precautions necessary to provide absolute protection for an embassy and its staff would divert so much manpower from its primary mission and would make it so inaccessible to those with whom it is meant to do business, that it could not function effectively.[7] Likewise one cannot readily imagine politicians in a democracy adopting a low profile during an election – or indeed at any other time – because this would necessarily conflict with the public side of their profession.

A distinction can be made between static targets – which remain in roughly the same place for a relatively long period, and mobile targets which are generally moving. An obvious example of a static target would be a building, but human targets – such as a person in their home or giving a speech at a podium – would also fall into this category. The most obvious mobile target would be a moving car, or more pertinently the occupant or occupants of the car. However, it could also include a walking person, or a material target such as a moving train. For the purposes of this study, a temporarily immobile target – such as an aeroplane at an airport, a train in a station, or a parked car – counts as a static target because it is deliberately immobile for a period at the time when it is attacked. It follows from this that the same person can be a mobile target when he is in a moving car and a static target when he is in a small area for a length of time. A third type of target is an urban area, such as a town or city, which, whilst containing several specific targets, may also be under a general threat of terrorist attack.

THE PROTECTION OF STATIC TARGETS

The protection of static targets differs from that of mobile targets. With static targets, reliance is placed on controlling access to the area where a potential target is located. Detectors and barriers may be set up to deter, detect, and deflect an attack, and to provide the means of reacting if an attack takes place. The amount of protection afforded to a static target will vary according to its perceived importance, the resources available, and the risk of an attack taking place. Whilst a normal person or building will not usually have much in the way of protection, with more heavily guarded static targets the protective measures are more sophisticated and also exert control over an area. In these cases protection is not dependent upon one particular measure, but upon several layers or rings of defensive measures and barriers which make up an integrated system of physical protection. Their function is to detect threats, assess the nature of intrusions, and delay intruders long enough for sufficient response forces to either neutralise the threat or, if necessary, evacuate the target.[8]

With a high-profile human target out of doors the terrorists will almost certainly encounter armed bodyguards. A heavily guarded person will be protected by establishing an outer ring of bodyguards to control access, keep an eye on incomers, and detect any possible dangers. These bodyguards will ideally be able to observe anybody coming close to the target. Those bodyguards closer to the target deal with any immediate threat, if necessary by placing themselves between the target and the attacker.[9] Although bodyguards may not be able to stop a determined attacker, part of their deterrent effect is that an attacker would not escape, and would quite probably die, after an attack.[10]

For example at a parade held in Donegall Place, Belfast in September 1993 to commemorate the seventy-fifth anniversary of the founding of the Royal Air Force, it was possible to get within about five to ten yards of the Northern Ireland Secretary, the military Commander of Land Forces in Northern Ireland, and the Lord Mayor of Belfast. The first two at least would have been prime targets for the Provisional IRA. Around these people were a number of what appeared to be plain-clothes bodyguards. In the vicinity were several armed police officers and soldiers in uniform patrolling, stopping vehicles from entering the area, and checking the bags of pedestrians though not searching the pedestrians themselves.

A surveillance helicopter hovered constantly overhead. Given the security precautions an attacker with a grenade or concealed weapon could have launched a brief attack, but it is highly unlikely that they would have escaped or indeed survived.[11]

If the static target concerned is a high-profile person, there is a fair chance that the bodyguards, and possibly the target, will be protected by some form of body-armour.[12] As Prime Minister, Margaret Thatcher was frequently accompanied by uniformed armed police officers wearing bullet-proof vests whilst a reporter who accompanied the Sinn Fein President Gerry Adams for a few days in late 1993 reported that Adams wore a light bullet-proof jacket.[13]

Protecting buildings or people within the buildings is different in that permanent physical barriers and other protective devices can be installed. At the most basic level the physical protection of buildings consists of little more than reinforcing the usual access points – such as doors or windows – through which an assailant may gain access. For example, in Northern Ireland in July 1994 a group of armed UFF members attempted to gain entry to a mainly Catholic pub in Annaclone, county Down, on a day when the pub contained about forty people watching the football World Cup Final on television. The terrorists' intention was to spray the people in the pub with gunfire, killing as many of them as possible. A similar attack on a west Belfast betting shop in February 1992 had killed five people, whilst attacks on rural pubs in October 1993 and June 1994 had killed eight and six people respectively.[14] However, the Annaclone attack was foiled because the landlord, fearing a similar attack on his pub, had locked the heavy outer doors to the pub when the football match started. Unable to get through the doors the UFF members fired through the windows, but only succeeded in injuring people with the flying glass.[15] In a similar fashion, after Sinn Fein members were increasingly targeted by loyalist groups in the late 1980s and early 1990s, some protected their homes with front doors toughened with Macrolan perspex on the back, and with steel internal doors beyond these to prevent anybody from gaining access to the rest of the house.[16] The upgrading of protective measures by Sinn Fein members was specifically recognised by the UFF. In a statement in October 1993 they specifically referred to 'the provos behind steel security doors' when justifying their attacks on ordinary Catholics instead.[17]

Terrorists attempting to gain access to a more heavily protected building would encounter a greater number of obstacles. Where buildings, such as the police stations in Northern Ireland, are at risk of attack from gunfire, bombs, and mortars or rockets, they may be protected by concrete blast-walls, high wire-fencing, metal-sheeting, and other forms of barrier, as well as having watch-towers, lighting, and closed circuit television (CCTV) aimed at detecting attacks as soon as possible.[18] Entry to restricted areas is generally limited to specific people entering through a few access points – normally doors or gates with security barriers. Terrorists seeking to gain access through these points would have to get past guards checking ID cards, or alternatively open locked doors which only open on the insertion of an electronic card or 'key' which is read by a sensor. The security system automatically unlocks the door if the correct card is presented, but the terrorist would need such a card – or would need to be able to get hold of one. Sensor systems are often supplemented by entry-phones or the need to type in a Personal Identification Number (PIN) on a key pad at the door – rather like the codes used by cash dispensers outside banks.[19] Thus, to gain entry through conventional access points without causing a disturbance the terrorists would probably need a convincing ID card, possibly an electronic card which matched the records on a computer, and would have to know the appropriate PIN.

For more easily accessible targets such as sports events and airports, barriers such as walls, fences, and ditches – possibly reinforced with barbed wire, razor wire, or other edged materials – restrict entry to access points where controls can be applied.[20] In the best-protected complexes terrorists would encounter barriers designed to make it physically difficult to enter the protected area except through guarded access points. At night these barriers may be illuminated by powerful lights, ensuring that the dark offered no cover.[21] Even if the terrorists surmounted the first set of barriers they might encounter guard dogs and patrolling security guards.[22]

In addition they would quite probably be detected by intruder detection systems such as acoustic cables which detect sound or vibration, and passive infra-red detectors which detect body-heat and movement.[23] If CCTV is installed the intruders might be seen by security staff in a central control room, thus allowing the guards or their supervisors to determine the scale of the intrusion. Whilst few physical barriers are totally impregnable, if proper alarms are in place they can give a warning of intrusion to the defenders of the target and impose a delay upon an intruder which gives the defenders time to assess the nature of the threat and to react to it. Even if the terrorists are not caught immediately, video recordings attached to the CCTV system can allow them to be identified after the event, and provide evidence of their presence.[24]

Unless the terrorists' aim is simply to plant a bomb inconspicuously they will have to neutralise whatever resistance they encounter before attacking the primary target. There is a good chance that an important target will be protected by armed guards of one form or another. Most airports have armed guards on the premises, and the same applies for many of the premises which terrorists may wish to attack.

Having accomplished their task, the terrorists still have to get away. First they must evade or neutralise any guards who are still present. They then need to get clear of the target area before reinforcements arrive. Due to the risk of such intervention, the greater the delay or likely delay which the terrorists encounter in penetrating the defences of the protected area, the less likely it is that terrorists wishing to survive will try an attack, or persist with it once resistance has started to slow them down.[25] Although an individual or a small group faced by terrorist intruders may have to rely on the resources available on site, larger organisations or government installations can hope for a quicker response. A PIRA member in Belfast reckoned that the British Army could seal off an area within two to three minutes of an incident taking place.[26] It is also estimated that armed police officers could be sent to any of the foreign embassies in London within a similar period, whilst the helicopters operated by the Metropolitan Police can reach any spot in London within fifteen minutes.[27] Incidents at targets with a lower priority may not receive such a rapid or appropriate response. In 1990 a senior civil servant at the Ministry of Defence estimated that an unarmed police presence could reach a Royal Ordnance factory in the Thames Valley area within three minutes of the alarm being given, but conceded that an armed presence would take rather longer.[28]

Explosives may be also be smuggled into a building, as happened when a vehicle-bomb exploded in an underground car park beneath the World Trade Centre in New York in February 1993, killing six and injuring 1,000.[29] As mentioned, the bomb which killed five people and nearly killed British Cabinet members at the Grand Hotel in Brighton during the 1984 Conservative Party Conference, had been smuggled into a room and hidden behind the side-panels of a bath.[30] Since the Brighton bombing, events such as political party conferences have required extremely costly and overt security measures with room-sweeps, baggage checks, and the presence of armed policemen.[31]

Smuggling guns or bombs onto an aeroplane is more difficult as precautions are generally taken to prevent hijacks or bomb attacks. At airports dogs may be used to sniff for concealed weapons or explosives, but various forms of manufactured detectors are more commonly used.[32] In addition, whereas previously a terrorist was able to check in baggage containing a bomb and then not board the aeroplane, many airlines now have baggage reconciliation systems which should ensure that baggage which is not attributable to a boarded passenger will be removed and will not fly.[33]

If terrorists wish to plant a time-delayed bomb in areas open to the public – such as shops or railway stations – the risk of detection is not such a problem because there is generally little in the way of protective measures. It is possible that somebody might notice a suspicious package and notify the authorities. In the case of an attack on a specific person or object, a search may find the bomb before it is due to explode.[34] However, the main risk to a terrorist is of being seen on CCTV and either captured at the time or having his movements recorded and being identified.

THE PROTECTION OF MOBILE TARGETS

As noted, attacking human targets in transit is a popular method amongst terrorists.[35] The target is particularly vulnerable whilst in a car because cars are comparatively easy to ambush, easily surrounded, and hard to get help to, whilst the target is trapped in a confined space and can do little to evade the terrorist attack.[36] A member of the INLA commenting on the PIRA assassination of RUC officers claimed that nine times out of ten the Provisionals shot a police officer when getting in or out of his car, or would put a bomb in the car.[37] A terrorist who knows where a target's journey will start and end, has located at least two definite points where an attack can take place. If the target's route is also known then the terrorist's options grow even wider.

For the terrorist wishing to attack a specific mobile target, the first objective is to determine a definite time when the target will be in a particular location, and will be vulnerable.[38] Thus, the aim of the target and the people responsible for defending it will be to prevent the assailant from gaining such information, if possible by adopting a low profile, if not by restricting the knowledge which becomes available. Consequently an intended target may make it difficult to predict where he will be at a given time by, for example, varying the routes which he takes to and from work and the times at which he takes them.[39] During the recent troubles in Northern Ireland, judges have frequently changed routes and cars between offices and court in an attempt to avoid falling into a recognisable routine.[40] This can cause problems for the terrorist, but as Tony Slinn, editor of *International Security Review*, notes:

> You may change your route to work each day, but when you drive out of your front gate, you've got to turn either right or left, and the terrorist knows this too.[41]

Clutterbuck states that for this reason most abductions take place close to the target's home.[42]

The assassination of Reinhard Heydrich, Nazi Governor of Bohemia-Moravia, by Czech partisans in Prague in May 1942, shows what can happen if attackers gain knowledge about a target's movements. Local members of the Czech resistance obtained information about Heydrich from the domestic staff who worked for him and the German garrison in a castle outside Prague. A watchmaker in the castle established a date and time when Heydrich was to be driven to the airport via his office in the city. The partisans ambushed Heydrich, mortally wounding him with a bomb thrown at the car.[43]

Having identified the movements of the target the terrorists have to overcome whatever protective measures have been taken. The terrorists' approach to these measures will depend upon the nature of the operation. If the aim is to destroy the target any method will suffice as long as it causes the necessary damage without compromising other aims the terrorists may have, for example by killing uninvolved bystanders. If however the aim is abduction, a more subtle use of violence is necessary in order to ensure that the intended hostage is not killed prematurely.

The forms of protection for a mobile human target can vary greatly. In the case of an unguarded pedestrian there is none, in which case a knife or a heavy blunt instrument would suffice for an assassination. This occurred in May 1882 when the Chief Secretary for Ireland and his Under-Secretary were stabbed to death in Phoenix Park, Dublin, by members of a small republican secret society.[44] Several ordinary victims of terrorist attacks have been killed when unarmed and away from cover, although guns rather than knives or blunt objects tend to be the more common instruments of dispatch in the West. The terrorists' task could be complicated if the targets is wearing some form of body-armour. From 1971 onwards, uniformed members of the security forces on patrol in Northern Ireland have often worn flak jackets or other forms of body armour as a matter of course.[45] A PIRA spokesman acknowledged that as the body-armour of the security forces was improved, the terrorists found it more difficult to kill them whilst they were on duty.[46]

Terrorists seeking to attack a heavily protected mobile target will encounter rather more in the way of obstacles, and need some idea as to how well the target is protected. There is little point in shooting at a car if it is too heavily armoured for the bullets to penetrate. A car which has been protected as much as possible will have reinforced body-panels, bullet-proof glass, protection for features such as the engine, radiator, and petrol tank, 'runflat' tyres capable of absorbing hits from high-velocity bullets, and a means of communicating with possible reinforcements.[47] Such a car may be proof against several types of gunfire and relatively small explosions. For instance, in January 1981 at Tynan Abbey in county Armagh, Northern Ireland, PIRA members encircled an armour-reinforced RUC car, and poured several bursts of gunfire into it without harming the occupants.[48]

However, few armoured cars can protect the occupants against a very large explosion. When ETA set off a culvert bomb under the car of Spanish Prime Minister, Admiral Carrero Blanco in December 1973, the resulting explosion threw his car over a five-storey building killing him and his driver.[49] Likewise, the Chairman of the Deutsche Bank, Alfred Herrhausen, was killed by an explosion in November 1989 despite being protected by a 2.8 ton armoured Mercedes. Members of the Red Army Faction placed a shaped shrapnel bomb on the back of a pedal-cycle which was placed on the side of the road where Herrhausen was likely to be sitting and at the height where they reckoned that Herrhausen would be sitting in the car. The bomb, containing 22 to 40 pounds of TNT as a propellant, blasted an armoured door into Herrhausen and threw the car over 80 feet across the street. Whilst Herrhausen bled to death his chauffeur only received relatively minor injuries.[50] Against such devices there is little defence short of travelling in an armoured personnel carrier or taking to the air in a helicopter. Even then the former can be vulnerable to mines or anti-tank rockets, and the latter to heavy machine-guns or portable surface-to-air missiles.[51]

If the terrorist operation is to be an abduction, a major problem will be the presence of bodyguards. Not all targets have government-supplied bodyguards, but targets perceived as important are often heavily protected.[52] With a mobile target the role of a bodyguard is to prevent attacks by taking evasive measures if an attack seems imminent, and failing that to protect the target once an attack occurs.[53] Ideally the target's car will be accompanied by one or more cars containing armed bodyguards. If the terrorists manage to stop a car containing a government-protected target they must reckon upon the bodyguards having guns and being proficient in their use.[54] In such cases, time constraints mean that the bodyguards have to be neutralised swiftly, probably by killing them as in the Moro case.

THE PROTECTION OF AN URBAN AREA

In January 1991, the head of the London Emergency Planning Information Centre conceded:

> Frankly, if a terrorist group really wanted to make a mess of London, they could.... We would not be able to cope. By that I mean we would be limited to chasing after the effects of a disaster.[55]

The very size of a major city makes it difficult to protect all possible targets, particularly if the range of targets is broad. During the PIRA bombing campaign in England – and particularly London – in the early 1990s, Terry Kirby pointed out that a guard could not be mounted over every railway line and shop doorway.[56] As long as a terrorist group is operating effectively, it is simply impossible to provide absolute physical protection to the entire transport and commercial structure of a major city. Attempts to do so over the long-term would be prohibitively costly and would deplete the resources available to protect specific potential targets. The French Government discovered the vulnerability of a major city during a series of bomb attacks carried out in Paris between December 1985 and September 1986 by a pro-Iranian group. The explosions, which were in busy areas, killed thirteen and injured 250. Although suspects were finally convicted for the attacks, it was investigative action taken after the attacks which achieved this. During the attacks the Government was almost helpless.[57]

A degree of protection can be afforded to an area by the deployment of large numbers of soldiers. Such measures can make it difficult for terrorists to operate in the areas where these measures are implemented because of the danger of interception on the way to or from an attack. A similar reasoning appears to have been behind the decision of the security organiser for the 1984 Olympic Games in Los Angeles to deploy 12,000 uniformed – though unarmed – security guards in addition to the normal law-enforcement agencies.[58] (This is assuming that the terrorists do not have the backing of sympathetic elements of the security forces, or indeed have members within the security forces. If they do then the terrorists may find their path is smoothed quite considerably.)

Intense surveillance of an area can also make it difficult for terrorists to carry out their operations undetected. As noted above, the installation of CCTV can afford blanket coverage of a defined area to the police in a control room, and if necessary the recordings can provide evidence in any subsequent trial.[59] This can be supplemented by observation posts. For a long time an observation post on the top of Divis Flats allowed the British Army to observe much of west Belfast, whilst covert observation posts in the roofs of houses or in abandoned buildings supplied information over the radio concerning suspicious activities.[60] This was supplemented by up to three helicopters equipped with surveillance equipment constantly hovering over the district.[61] Helicopter surveillance is also used in London by the Metropolitan Police during public events, such as the Trooping of the Colour.[62]

The setting up of checkpoints can also disrupt terrorist operations by making it difficult for them to move or carry out operations undetected. Following a number of PIRA bombings in London and Manchester, a series of checkpoints were set up in both cities.[63] A police superintendent in London commented at the time:

> Terrorists have to move about and transfer their weapons from location to location. The presence of this type of road-block should have a deterrent effect as they run a risk of being detected.[64]

Such methods have been common in the Catholic urban areas in Northern Ireland throughout the recent troubles, with west Belfast being ringed by checkpoints.[65]

The deployment of checkpoints can be reinforced by restricting the number of access points open to traffic in a defined part of an urban area. Following the damage caused by two massive vehicle bombs in the City of London in 1992 and 1993, vehicle access to the City was closed-off at 18 points and restricted to 7 entry points which had police check-points.[66] Again, such measures were common in Belfast from the 1970s up to the mid-1990s.[67] In his study of a Catholic enclave of Belfast in the early 1970s, Burton reports that of the 16 roads into 'Anro', only three were open, and these were frequently manned by soldiers at checkpoints. The others were barricaded with dragon's teeth, sheet metal, or concrete lumps.[68] More recently, reports about west Belfast and PIRA activities in the Markets area of Belfast confirm that access points from Catholic areas have been limited in order to restrict terrorist activities.[69]

Ultimately the very design of an urban area may be affected by the desire to hamper terrorists' operations. Such considerations are not new to town-planning. The broad, straight Parisian boulevards planned by Hausmann in the 1860s were designed to allow charges by the police, infantry, and cavalry to be more effective, and to make it difficult for rebels to erect barricades successfully.[70] More recently, town planning in Northern Ireland appears to have taken security considerations into account. According to Ryan the Belfast motorway system built in the 1980s took account of the need to ensure rapid access to potentially troublesome estates. Also, whereas in Great Britain pedestrian-only zones and restricted parking areas are patrolled by parking wardens, in Northern Ireland the security forces are in control.[71] Ryan's view is at least partly borne-out by a 1983 newspaper report which stated that the security forces were involved in aspects of town-planning in Belfast through a coordinating committee in the section of the Northern Ireland Office which dealt with urban-planning.[72] The main aim appears to have been to cut down on the number of 'sectarian interfaces' where members of one community came up against the other. The segregation was effected by walls and wide roads with access points controlled by the security forces. Despite the long-term social consequences, the move towards greater segregation seems to have been grounded in peoples' desire for safety within their own religious community, and may seem desirable in terms of immediate security concerns.[73]

Thus a terrorist in a heavily protected urban area who seeks to transport weapons or carry out an operation, will encounter a number of problems. Gaining access to a protected area in a vehicle may only be possible through certain access points. If the terrorist is already wanted for an offence and is recognised, or merely lacks sufficient proof of identification, he could be detained at a checkpoint. Similarly, such a search could find weapons or other incriminating materials. Even if he avoids this, once he carries out an operation there is a strong possibility that he will be located within minutes and, if under observation from the air or on CCTV, he will find it difficult to evade detection and interception by the security forces.

When examining the use of protective measures against terrorist or other attacks, it should be borne in mind that the systems put in place may not function properly. Skimping on costs by paying low wages to security guards can lead to poor quality guards or guards becoming tired due to working overtime or taking second jobs to make up their income.[74] Whilst dogs can also be used to detect intruders and to detect explosives concealed within vehicles or within other objects, like humans they can also become tired and lose concentration if used for overly-long periods.[75] In practice some CCTV systems are badly maintained and do not operate, or even if they do the video-recording facilities do not work.[76] According to a recent report the police have found that in many shops the camera surveillance systems produce such poor quality pictures that it is nearly impossible to identify suspects on them, although this can sometimes be overcome by equipment which enhances video images.[77] As to restricting access to an area, after a protective perimeter was set up around the City of London in late 1993 journalists found that it was still possible to drive vehicles in without being examined.[78] Thus, there can be, and often are, shortcomings in security systems. On the other hand, without careful and lengthy observation, or a source on the inside, it would be a rash terrorist who took such shortcomings for granted when planning an attack.

TARGET PROTECTION AND TERRORIST TARGET SELECTION

Terrorists confronted by a target which has been protected against their desired method of attack have three choices: they can give up altogether, they can seek to attack the same target by different means, or they can attack a different target. It is difficult to determine the extent to which protective measures deter potential terrorists from carrying out attacks because one cannot measure events which have not happened. Studies concerning ordinary criminal activities seem to show that overt protective measures deter criminals from carrying out attacks at the site where the measures are in place. American studies indicate that the overt presence of guards is a major factor which bank robbers take into account when deciding whether to rob a particular bank.[79] Similarly, since the installation of closed circuit television cameras backed up by mobile police units, street crime in Newcastle-upon-Tyne's town centre reportedly dropped by 20 per cent whilst in Airdrie it dropped by three-quarters.[80]

Although this may hold true for ordinary criminals, it may not always be the case for terrorists, whose motivation is political rather than financial. The existence of protective measures may prompt the terrorists to vary the methods used to attack a given target. Although this may involve greater risks, higher costs, or just the need to spend more time working out ways of overcoming the protective measures in place, the terrorists may deem this worthwhile. By attacking a well-protected target they will have demonstrated their ability to attack whatever targets they wish, intimidating other potential targets and possibly securing more attention for their cause.

There are a number of examples of this. In their first telephone communiqué after the abduction of the former Italian Prime Minister Aldo Moro in April 1978, the Red Brigades stated:

> This morning our organization brought the attack to the heart of the state. You'll hear from us again as soon as possible. Moro is only the beginning.[81]

Mario Moretti, who is said to have planned the operation, subsequently stated:

> In Rome at that moment there were tens of thousands of police and carabinieri dispersed throughout the metropolitan area, but in Via Caetani, for those few minutes, we were superior.[82]

Similarly, after the RAF's assassination of Alfred Herrhausen, their communiqué stated that:

the perpetrators of this [imperialist] system must know... that they will not have any place in the world where they can be safe from the attacks of the revolutionary guerrilla units.[83]

By attacking hard targets some terrorists hope to give an impression of omnipresence – that they can attack whatever targets they wish.

The Provisional IRA has long held this attitude. In the early 1970s a PIRA member said of bomb attacks in the heavily-guarded centre of Derry city:

> Once the security forces decided to put security barriers around the town our strategy was then to break through them. It was – how many bombs can you get inside their net? Every bomb we got inside was looked upon as a victory for us.[84]

Similarly, in April 1993, after the destruction caused by their second large bomb in the City of London, the Provisionals boasted of their ability to pierce the increased security measures which had been put in place after the first big bomb in April 1992.

> These latest attacks underline both the ability and the determination of our volunteers to breach whatever level of security the British authorities are capable of mounting.[85]

In addition to the physical and psychological damage caused by the bomb, the PIRA wished to demonstrate that their attacks could not be stopped by protective measures.

The practical measures which the terrorists use can either involve using a method which will overcome the protective measures in place, or a method which circumvents them. Protective measures can be overcome by using more powerful weapons, or by using a method of approach which negates their effectiveness. As an example of the former one can examine the difficulty which the Provisional IRA found in killing British soldiers in the 1980s.

Republican spokesmen repeatedly stated that they would prefer to kill British soldiers than members of the locally-recruited security forces because they were a better symbol of colonial rule, and because dead soldiers had more of an impact on British opinion.[86] Killing soldiers became more difficult over time, partly because soldiers were increasingly well-protected by newly developed body armour, and partly because the Army had adopted patrolling methods

Table 7.1 Security force deaths in Northern Ireland, 1970–1993

Year	RUC[a]	UDR/RIR[b]	Army	Total
1970–3	43	39	204	286
1974–7	63	42	71	176
1978–81	54	39	70	163
1982–5	62	31	37	130
1986–9	43	30	40	113
1990–3	27	20	22	69
TOTAL	293	201	444	938

[a] Includes RUC reserves and part-time RUC.
[b] Includes part-time UDR/RIR.
NB: This table includes nineteen security force members killed by loyalists or mistakenly killed by other security force members. The vast majority of security force deaths have been caused by republicans.
Sources: Royal Ulster Constabulary, *Chief Constable's Annual Report 1993*, 96. M. Sutton, *Bear in Mind These Dead*, 195–205.

which made it difficult to attack them and escape successfully.[87] Also, as the Troubles progressed the regular British Army made up a lower proportion of the security forces in Northern Ireland – the balance consisting of an expanded RUC and UDR – and thus provided less targets.[88] As Table 7.1 shows, the number of soldiers killed dropped greatly both in absolute terms and in proportion to deaths amongst the local security forces.

The practical problems were outlined by a PIRA spokesman.

> We would prefer to be hitting Brits than cops because of the need to focus on British rule. But because the Brits are more sophisticated and because of their body armour we have to take considerable risks. The IRA has inadequate guns to penetrate the armour so we have to get in close for head or stomach shots.[89]

As a result of the difficulties encountered in trying to shoot soldiers, throughout the 1980s the Provisionals showed a greater tendency to use explosive devices rather than guns to kill British soldiers. This can be seen in Table 7.2.

With bomb attacks on the security forces however, there was always the possibility of killing or injuring civilians, with all the problems which that implied for the image of the PIRA amongst its own supporters as well as outsiders. This occurred several times,

Table 7.2 British Army fatalities and fatal incidents caused by Irish republican groups, 1970–1993

	Deaths		Fatal Incidents	
	Shot	Explosion	Shot	Explosion
1970–1973	123	74	117	49
1974–1977	42	29	35	20
1978–1981	27	43	23	18
1982–1985	10	26	7	14
1986–1989	8	31	7	15
1990–1993	9	12	9	7

NB: A Fatal Incident is one where at least one member of the British Army, excluding the UDR/RIR, has been killed. Deaths and fatal incidents classified as caused by explosions include bombs, rockets, and mortars.
Source: Calculated from M. Sutton, *Bear in Mind These Dead*.

most notably at a Remembrance Day Parade in Enniskillen in November 1987. On that occasion 11 civilians were killed and 63 injured by a bomb which was supposed to kill members of the Ulster Defence Regiment.[90]

The problem was at least partially overcome in the early 1990s when the Provisionals obtained a more powerful gun, reported to be the Barrett L82A1 sniper rifle.[91] A similar Tejas 0.50 calibre gun was captured by the RUC during a house search in Belfast in August 1993.[92] The five-foot-long Barrett 'light-fifty' fires a heavy 0.50 calibre armour-piercing shell at a speed of 2,800 feet per second. It can penetrate steel-plate at a range of over one mile and a Barrett reportedly killed Iraqi soldiers at a range of 1,800 metres during the 1991 Gulf War.[93] It is easily capable of smashing through the flak jackets worn by the security forces in Northern Ireland and could be fired from a long distance from the patrol, thus making it easier to escape after the attack. Between September 1992 and August 1993 such a gun killed six security force members in the border areas of south Armagh and south Fermanagh.[94] The resulting increase in deaths from gunshots can be seen in Table 7.3. The problem presented by body armour was overcome by a more powerful weapon, albeit one which was awkward to transport and which was only available in small numbers.

Protective measures can also be overcome by terrorists who crash through them. The deterrent effect of protective measures is partly based on the assumption that a terrorist will not survive after carrying out an attack. Consequently, it does not apply to terrorists

Table 7.3 British Army fatalities and fatal incidents caused by Irish republican groups, 1980–1993

	Deaths		Fatal Incidents	
	Shot	Explosion	Shot	Explosion
1980	5	3	5	3
1981	4	6	4	2
1982	5	15	2	5
1983	0	5	0	5
1984	4	5	4	3
1985	1	1	1	1
1986	0	4	0	3
1987	2	1	2	1
1988	3	18	2	6
1989	3	8	3	5
1990	1	6	1	2
1991	1	4	1	3
1992	2	1	2	1
1993	5	1	5	1

NB: Excludes a Royal Navy recruiter killed by a bomb in 1988.
Source: Calculated from M. Sutton, *Bear in Mind These Dead*.

who expect to die as an integral part of the operation. This was demonstrated in the mid-1990s when the Islamic Palestinian groups Hamas and Islamic Jihad carried out a series of suicide bombings in the Gaza Strip and the Israeli-occupied west bank of the Jordan, and within Israel itself. The terrorists simply walked or drove up to the target concerned, and then detonated the bomb, killing themselves in the process.[95] In October 1994 one of the bombers recorded a message on video before carrying out an attack on a bus in Tel Aviv, killing 22 people.[96] Such people are not likely to be deterred by security measures which only threaten their lives once they have carried out an attack.

The circumvention of defences is achieved by carrying out an attack which does not rely on penetrating through the defences so much as go around them. For instance, if a target's residence is surrounded by protective barriers, bombs can be sent directly to the target as occurs when letter-bombs are sent to targeted individuals through the post.[97] However, small X-ray devices in the office or home can be installed to detect letter-bombs for people who are thought to be at risk.[98]

Where the identity of the target is general rather than specific, circumventing defences may involve attacking similar targets in a setting where they are less secure. For example, due to the increasing difficulties in killing British soldiers in Northern Ireland, PIRA attacked them in England and on the Continent. Between January 1, 1988 and December 31, 1990 they killed 14 soldiers in England and seven soldiers and air force members on the Continent, compared to 39 soldiers and one naval recruiting officer killed in Northern Ireland over the same period.[99]

Where the target is a specific person or thing, the method of attack may be changed. Again the actions of ordinary criminals show how this occurs. Due to improved bank security in Britain in recent years, bank robbers have circumvented protective measures by kidnapping the families of key holders and forcing them to open the bank without raising the alarm. Although the Home Office does not specifically link these statistics, it is notable that whilst robberies against building societies dropped from 1,086 in 1991 to 770 in 1993, with only 262 in the first seven months of 1994, the total number of kidnappings in Britain increased 70 per cent over the two-year period to the end of 1992, bringing the yearly figure to 929.[100]

Another example of a terrorist attack circumventing protective measures is provided by the PIRA attack on the British Cabinet when it met at 10 Downing Street in February 1991. Security there was increased in the 1980s by protective measures such as strengthening the structure of the building, sealing off Downing Street with high gates at one end and barriers at the other, and installing CCTV cameras and electronic sensors in the immediate area.[101] The PIRA unit circumvented the gates and other protective measures by using a home-made mortar placed in the back of a van parked in Whitehall. One shell exploded within 40 feet of the Cabinet Room.[102] Thus the PIRA largely negated the measures designed to stop attackers from gaining access to Downing Street by firing mortar shells over them.

As well as changing their methods of attack, increased protective measures around preferred targets may lead terrorists to choose different ones. This process has been examined by a group of American economists using econometric assumptions to explain patterns in international terrorism.[103] Underlying their speculations is the assumption that terrorists will act like rational people in their deployment of resources, seeking to maximise benefits and minimise costs whilst responding to restraints.[104] The economists conclude that the terrorists will almost always pick the softest possible targets commensurate with the desired gain, on the grounds that the cost of overcoming counter-measures – in terms of risk, time and resources – is significantly lower.[105]

The economists examine cases of target hardening, such as the fortification of American embassies from 1976 onwards, and the installation of metal detectors at American and other airports from 1973 onwards. These counter-measures led to a decrease in attacks on the targets thus protected, because the cost of operations against them was increased by the counter-measures. On the other hand it was found that measures which protected certain targets, without positively reducing the resources of the terrorist groups concerned, merely diverted attacks onto less well protected targets or led to different means being used to attack the same target. This is particularly the case when a similar target to the protected one could be attacked by a different, less costly method.[106]

The economists have termed this shift in targets *substitution*, meaning that the terrorists substituted a 'cheaper' target or method in place of a more 'expensive' one. Thus the fortification of American embassies led to a decrease in terrorist attempts to occupy or otherwise attack them, but led to an increase in attacks upon Americans outside the security of the embassy compounds.[107] There were also signs of substitution from aircraft hijacking into other non-aircraft hostage incidents.[108] Thus substitution can mean that rather than attack hard targets, terrorists often switch their attacks to less well-protected or softer targets.

Some of the attacks carried out by terrorist groups suggest that they commonly substitute targets. Attacks by Palestinian groups against Israeli or Jewish targets in third countries seem to be prompted, at least partly, by the fact that they are not as well protected as targets within Israel. From 1970 onwards, Palestinian groups have attacked Jewish or Israeli targets outside Israel, with incidents such as the kidnapping and killing of 11 Israeli athletes at the Munich Olympics in September 1972, and the seizure of the Italian cruise ship *Achille Lauro* in 1985 being merely some of the most prominent.[109] Hizbollah has acted in a similar fashion. In southern Lebanon in February 1992, an Israeli helicopter-gunship killed the Hizbollah Secretary-General, Sheikh Abbas al-Musawi, together with his wife and infant son. The Hizbollah did not retaliate by attacking a target in Israel. Instead the following month they attacked the Israeli Embassy in the Argentine capital Buenos Aires, killing about 30 people with a car bomb.[110] Likewise, after an Israeli helicopter-gunship assault on a Hizbollah base in the

Lebanon killed up to fifty recruits in June 1994, a bomb destroyed the Delegation of Argentine-Israeli Associations in Buenos Aires the following month, killing 96 people. Although Hizbollah did not claim responsibility for the attack, reports suggest that they were responsible.[111]

An examination of security force and related deaths in Northern Ireland during the recent Troubles also indicates a shift from harder to softer targets within the context of a declining number of deaths overall. As Table 7.1 above shows, whilst the rate of regular British Army soldiers killed declined quite steeply between 1970 and 1993, the rate of RUC and UDR deaths remained fairly constant until the mid-1980s, and declined less rapidly than that of the Army thereafter. This tendency becomes even more pronounced if one bears in mind that the figures for the Army are partly inflated by incidents where more than five soldiers have been killed in a single attack, (Warrenpoint, August 27, 1979 – 18 dead; Ballykelly, December 6, 1982 – 11 dead; Lisburn, June 15, 1988 – 6 dead; Ballygawley, August 20, 1988 – 8 dead), whereas only one single attack has inflicted similar casualties upon the local security forces (Newry, February 28, 1985 – 9 RUC dead).[112]

The reduced number of soldiers killed relative to total security force casualties can be partly explained by the reduction of regular troops as a proportion of the security forces deployed in Northern Ireland – from about 17,200 out of a total of 32,400 in 1973 to about 9,700 out of 28,900 in 1989.[113] However, as Bowyer Bell and McKeown point out, it is also due to the fact that whilst British Army members in Northern Ireland are on more or less constant alert, members of the RUC and UDR are far more vulnerable as they live within Northern Ireland and can therefore be more easily attacked off-duty.[114] In addition, from 1985 onwards the Provisionals targeted businessmen and their employees who were carrying out building work or providing services for the security forces, killing 27 between 1985 and 1993. Thus the reduction in the targeting of the regular British Army in Northern Ireland, compared to the targeting of the RUC, the UDR/RIR, and civilian contractors to the security forces, can be seen as an example of target substitution caused by the increasing difficulty of killing British soldiers in Northern Ireland.

SUMMARY

Whilst some protection might be possible against terrorist attacks, it is impossible to protect everything all of the time. The limitations on the amount of protection possible creates vulnerabilities which provide terrorists with opportunities. As a terrorist campaign progresses, one will find that whilst the people trying to protect potential targets react to attacks by protecting new targets or hardening existing ones, the terrorists can select softer targets or devise new methods or weapons to attack existing hardened targets. Occasionally terrorists may select harder targets because of the publicity value of a successful attack on such a target and the impression of strength which such an attack may give. There is, to an extent, a reciprocal relationship between the actions of the terrorists and their opponents but neither of them are necessarily limited to reactive strategies.

8 The Security Environment

INTRODUCTION

Terrorist groups are severely affected by the matrix of laws and institutions which, ideally, protect the state and the public from crime and disorder. In this study the matrix is termed the *security environment*. The basis of the security environment in a liberal democracy is the various statutes – known collectively as *the law*, as opposed to individual laws – which constitute the rules which constrain those aspects of human behaviour judged to be undesirable. The law is enforced by a group of institutions – known collectively as the *criminal justice system* – which deal with the prevention, detection and punishment of crime. The primary elements of the criminal justice system are the legal system, the police, and the penal system. These institutions carry out the procedures whereby those who break the criminal law are detected, detained, tried, and punished if found guilty.

An understanding of the components of the criminal justice system is useful in order to understand how it hampers terrorists and why members of the system are often selected as targets. The legal system includes the laws, the courts, the judiciary, and the legal profession; in short the institutions responsible for determining whether people have broken the law, and for deciding the appropriate measures to be taken against those found guilty. The police are responsible for maintaining public order, apprehending suspected law-breakers, and preparing evidence for court. They, and other security agencies, are also responsible for gathering information on potential and actual threats, and for the protection of potential targets. The penal system is responsible for the confinement of those sentenced to imprisonment for breaking the law, and in some cases it is also responsible for the rehabilitation of prisoners. The penal system includes the prisons, prison staff, and allied organisations such as the probation service. Taken together these three elements – the legal system, the police, and the penal system, make up the criminal justice system and underpin the rule of law within a state.

Where the normal policing structure can no longer maintain order, the authorities may deploy the armed forces. This will often be accompanied by comparatively repressive emergency laws and greatly strengthened powers for the security forces – that is the police, the intelligence agencies, and the military. Gwynn mentions three instances where the armed forces might be deployed to restore order: where police numbers are insufficient to maintain the existing law and the army's role is simply to reinforce the police; where civil control and the system of policing have totally collapsed and the army is needed to maintain order in the absence of the police; and where an internal war has broken out against an organised enemy.[1] The deployment of armed soldiers is a signal to demonstrators and insurgents that lethal force might be employed by the authorities, but the army should only use the minimum force necessary in support of the civil power.[2]

In a totalitarian or authoritarian state, where the state's institutions act in a repressive manner, terrorists may face the same obstacles to a much greater degree. Laws can be drafted so as to label the actions of peaceful opponents as criminal. The police may act as the partisan instruments of the government – arresting people on the grounds of mere suspicion or because of their political affiliations, whilst in some countries the police have set up official or semi-official death squads. Likewise, the prisons may serve as a means of incarcerating real or suspected political opponents, and of intimidating their friends and families. Finally, in some countries the use of military force has not been seen as a last resort to be used sparingly, but as a desirable tool of oppression. This scenario is worth bearing in mind as it is far from uncommon. As Laqueur notes and the example of Argentina between 1976 and 1983 demonstrates, it is extremely difficult for terrorists to operate in a such a security environment.[3]

THE ROLE OF THE SECURITY FORCES

For the sake of clarity in defining the respective roles of the police and the military, this study takes as its model the theoretical division of labour between the police and the military in Great Britain. In this case the police are responsible for law-enforcement and the maintenance of public order. Whilst the military can be called upon to aid the civil power, this is ideally an act of last resort and the proper role of the military is the protection of the state by deterring external threats, and by locating, identifying and physically destroying the enemy in wartime.[4]

With this model in mind, the security force response to terrorism can be divided into five broad functions:

Intelligence: The gathering and analysis of information to determine what has happened, what is happening and what is likely to happen.

Investigation: The examination of specific illegal incidents.

Protection: The defence of potential targets.

Public order maintenance: The prevention of disorder by the deployment of police or other security forces.

Armed response: The use of lethal force to eliminate a specific threat.

The effects which protective functions have upon terrorist activities were examined in the previous chapter, and together with the intelligence and investigative functions are standard police practice in states that are not experiencing an abnormal terrorist problem. The maintenance of public order and deployment of an armed response are generally only necessary in abnormal circumstances. In the case of mass violence, such as a riot, the police or other security forces may use equipment such as batons, riot shields, and tear gas to disperse those whom they deem to be disturbing public order. On the other hand if the nature of the problem is such that lives are directly threatened, then armed police or soldiers may be deployed and the person or people responsible for the danger shot dead. This occurred in Melbourne in December 1994, where armed police killed a man who had been shooting at bystanders.[5]

INTELLIGENCE

In defining what is meant by the term intelligence, the main distinction to be made is between intelligence and information. Using Northam's definitions, information is a fact or facts which come to the notice of the relevant agency. Intelligence is the product of the assessment and analysis of the information available.[6]

To carry out an effective investigation the police need to develop sufficient background intelligence. Building up a fund of information about neighbourhoods and suspects is part of ordinary police-work and is not confined to counter-terrorist work.⁷ The necessary knowledge is often obtained by collecting information from local gossip, paid agents, informants, and the interrogation of suspects or people who are suspected of possessing information.

The use of informers is a central part of the conduct of normal police operations against non-political criminals such as drug traffickers and armed robbers.⁸ Similarly, by far the most valuable background information against terrorists comes from informers within the group passing information to the security forces, thus allowing them to apprehend its members and resources. In Italy in the late 1970s the use of informers allowed General Dalla Chiesa, head of the Carabinieri anti-terrorist campaign, to capture most of the leaders of the Red Brigades and Front Line, and many ordinary terrorists, within a relatively short period.⁹

Information gained from informers can also allow the security forces to frustrate attacks. This could be done, for example, by deploying a heavy security presence in the vicinity of the target. Although ostensibly the security forces might seem to be carrying out routine operations, the terrorists would be deterred from carrying out the operation.¹⁰ In December 1991 the Chief Constable of the RUC stated that security force measures were interrupting four out of five terrorist attacks, whilst in June 1994 The Director General of the Security Service (MI5) stated that the security forces prevented around four out of five attempted terrorist operations in Northern Ireland.¹¹ A senior member of PIRA has stated that around nine out of ten operations were not carried out due to security force activities, and another PIRA spokesman has stated that thousands of operations have been cancelled.¹²

Alternatively informers can give the authorities information which in conjunction with other information and analysis produces contact intelligence. This allows the security forces to intercept the terrorists, and can lead to the capture of weapons and the apprehension or death of terrorists. In June 1993 the PIRA claimed that over a three year period an alleged informer was directly responsible for the arrest of at least six PIRA Volunteers, for the seizure of weapons, explosive devices and material, and for disclosing information about PIRA safe houses, buildings, and vehicles.¹³ He was shot dead and dumped on a rural track in county Tyrone, near the Irish border.¹⁴

The fear of intelligence operations means that terrorists have to spend a great deal of time and effort trying to evade detection. Toolis and Elliot point out that when carrying out a complex operation PIRA members often need safe houses, cars, money, and false documents, as well as the arms and ammunition necessary to carry out the attack. In order to avoid detection when making these purchases they have to use fictitious identities. They also need to arrange emergency escape routes in case they are detected.[15] Likewise, during the 1970s and 1980s members of the Red Army Faction in Germany, and Direct Action in France, obtained false documentation and constructed false identities in order to evade police intelligence systems.[16] Such precautions take up time and effort and thus disrupt terrorist operations.

Intelligence can also lead to the capture of terrorists' material resources. Following the Libyan shipments to the PIRA of the mid-1980s, the Irish Police (Garda Siochana – Civic Guard) – launched a major operation to capture weapons which had been stashed in the Republic. Between the start of 1985 and May 1993, the Gardai made 557 arms finds, discovering 825 guns, about 339,600 rounds of ammunition, 484 explosive devices, and 2,170 items of bomb-making equipment.[17] In Northern Ireland between the beginning of 1985 and the end of 1993, the RUC found 2,121 firearms and 29.6 tons of explosives, although not all of these related to PIRA or other republican groups.[18] The massive size of the Libyan shipments meant that the Provisionals still had sufficient weaponry for many years activity, but the fact remains that intelligence-related activities by the security force restricted the group's ability to function by forcing it to waste time and resources on hiding weapons and evading detection when those resources could have been used in attacking targets.[19]

Due to the threat which they pose, intelligence operatives and their informers are prime targets for any terrorist group. The classic example of the elimination of intelligence operatives occurred in Dublin on the morning of Sunday, November 21, 1920. A group of IRA assassins known as 'The Squad' located and killed between 12 and 19 British Army officers – accounts vary – the bulk of whom were intelligence officers.[20] One of the IRA's agents – himself a detective in the political 'G' Division of the Dublin Metropolitan Police – noted that the death of a detective meant the loss of his knowledge and experience to the police, a point confirmed by an Army report in 1922.[21]

This view was reinforced in June 1994 when 25 senior personnel from the RUC Special Branch, British Army Intelligence, and MI5 were killed in a helicopter crash. A columnist noted that whilst no intelligence sources or information had been lost, the experience in assessing and using the information had been. Furthermore, the personal relationships which made the system work more smoothly had been seriously disrupted.[22] For this reason British intelligence operatives and their informers are targeted by the PIRA, a point noted in a 1978 British Army report.[23] Some British undercover operatives detected by terrorists in Northern Ireland have had to call in reinforcements or shoot their way out of trouble, and some have been killed.[24] From the perspective of the terrorists the latter result would eliminate the threat posed by that person.

These considerations apply elsewhere. In his memoirs Grivas, the military head of EOKA, describes why he ordered the assassination of a member of the Cyprus Special Branch.

> For some months Superintendent E. N. Peirce, of the Special Branch, had been trying to penetrate my courier service in Limassol and we had to be rid of him.... [Following the assassination attempt] Although seriously wounded, Peirce survived; but he was in hospital for several weeks and troubled us no more. His career was at an end and I slept the better for it.[25]

Likewise, Israeli agents have been targeted by Palestinian terrorists. In January 1973 an Israeli intelligence officer, Baruch Cohen, was shot dead in a Madrid cafe by a Palestinian student whom he believed he had recruited as an agent within the circles of Palestinian exiles.[26] More recently, in February 1994, one Shin Bet officer was killed and two others wounded when they were ambushed in Beltounia, near Jerusalem, whilst on their way to a meeting. The 'Izzedine al Qassem Brigade' – the armed wing of the Palestinian Islamic group Hamas – claimed responsibility for the attack.[27] Again this was an example of terrorists diminishing the threat to themselves, and attacking the morale of their opponents, by eliminating an intelligence officer.

INVESTIGATION

The investigative role of the police during a terrorist campaign closely parallels their role in combating normal crime.[28] Their aim is to find out who has broken the law, to locate and detain the offender, and to build up a sufficient body of evidence to convict that person in a law court. To do this in the case of a terrorist incident, the police initially need enough information to give them a lead as to which organisation has broken the law. (Obviously this is not a problem if the terrorists concerned claim responsibility.) Once the police have this information, they can try to determine which person within the group committed the offence and try to locate them. However, whilst the police can use intelligence to identify and locate suspects, unless they have the power to imprison suspects without trial they must assemble sufficient evidence to convict the suspect of an offence. The evidence may come in the form of statements from witnesses or confessions from the terrorists themselves, and may be supplemented by film from covert surveillance video cameras or closed circuit television, and forensic evidence. Where membership of a specific organisation is a crime in itself, the aim may be to prove that an individual is a member of that group.

As a result of the threat which investigations can pose to terrorists, the various elements involved in the investigative process are often selected as targets. During the peak years of Red Brigade activity in Italy, in the late 1970s and early 1980s, police investigators were frequently attacked. For instance, in June 1978 Antonio Esposito, police chief for the town of Nervi and former head of the Genoa anti-terrorist squad, was shot dead by two brigadists as he travelled to work by bus. He had been involved in the investigation of a number of Red Brigade kidnappings. He also directed an operation connected with the 1976 assassination of the Genoa Public Prosecutor Francesco Coco, resulting in the arrest of suspected Red Brigadist, Giuliano Naria.[29] Other high-ranking policemen attacked by the Red Brigades include the chief of the Venice anti-terrorist squad, Alfredo Albanese, who was shot dead at a road crossing in his car in May 1980, and Nicola Simone, the deputy chief of the Rome anti-terrorist squad known as the DIGOS, whom the Red Brigades wounded during what seems to have been a kidnap attempt in January 1982.[30]

Some cases are not so straightforward. In July 1982, the head of the Naples Flying Squad, Deputy Police Commissioner Antonio Ammaturo, was shot dead with his driver and the killing was claimed by the Naples column of the BR. Ammaturo had been very active against the Camorra – the Neapolitan equivalent of the Mafia. Apparently he had also been unofficially investigating the strange circumstances surrounding the BR kidnapping of a Neopolitan Christian Democrat politician who had been released following negotiations involving the Camorra. This has led to speculation that the Naples BR was trying to obtain Neopolitan criminals' support by assassinating Ammaturo, or alternatively that the Camorra killed him as part of the price for the politician's release.[31]

As well as attacking investigators, terrorists may also kill or threaten witnesses who give evidence against their members. In January 1972 a local unit of the PIRA killed a witness who was to testify against three of their members for a comparatively minor case of arson.[32] In Northern Ireland in the early 1980s relatives of 'supergrasses' – terrorists who acted as witnesses against fellow republican and loyalist paramilitaries – were kidnapped in an attempt to make the witnesses retract their evidence.[33] Similarly, in Italy in 1981, Red Brigadists kidnapped and then killed the brother of the former Brigadist Patrizio Peci when he gave evidence in court.[34] Witnesses also form a major target for criminal groups involved in political terrorism. Since he turned state's evidence in 1984, Tommaso Buscetta has been one of the most productive state witnesses which the Italian authorities has ever used against the Mafia, with testimony linking leading Italian politicians to organised crime.[35] By March 1995 it was reported that the Mafia had killed eleven of Buscetta's relatives, partly to punish him, and doubtless partly to discourage other people from his example.[36]

Not all evidence comes from human sources. Forensic evidence has become increasingly important as a way of identifying suspects and gaining convictions in court. It includes fingerprints, DNA traces, lead residue from firearms, traces of the components of explosive devices on either skin or clothing, or any other form of substance which may be attributed to the suspect and which would prove his guilt.[37] Thus, laser technology picked up a small sweat and palm impression on a hotel register left by the PIRA member who planted the bomb at the Grand Hotel in Brighton in September 1984, leading to his identification.[38] However, the misuse or incorrect interpretation of forensic evidence can lead to wrongful convictions, like those following the 1974 Birmingham bombings.[39]

Terrorists have sought to combat the use of forensic evidence by a number of methods. Urban describes how the PIRA adopted measures to avoid leaving forensic traces, such as wearing rubber gloves when handling weapons, wearing boiler suits over normal clothes during operations, bathing soon after an operation, and also wearing balaclavas to avoid photographic identification.[40] Likewise, according to Pluchinsky, by the 1980s the Red Army Faction had become sophisticated at avoiding leaving forensic evidence behind after an operation.[41] However, terrorists can use more direct measures to combat the use of forensic evidence. In September 1992 the PIRA destroyed the Northern Irish forensic science laboratories in Belfast, with a 2,000 lb. van bomb.[42]

PUBLIC ORDER MAINTENANCE

Normally, public order maintenance consists of crowd control by the security forces – usually the police – seeking to prevent disorder or riots at events such as football matches, industrial disputes, and demonstrations. These can often be dealt with by the large-scale deployment of police officers, sometimes in riot-gear.[43] Such situations carry the risk of violence, and sometimes of death and injury, but combating a terrorist campaign requires additional measures because of the threat of deliberately targeted lethal violence.

The first job of the security forces in a terrorist campaign is to contain the terrorists by making it more difficult for them to operate. Both overt and covert methods can be used to do this. The overt methods include sending out patrols, the setting up of checkpoints, and house-searches for weapons or suspects. The purpose of carrying out overt patrols is to deny terrorists freedom of movement and to build up a detailed knowledge of the area and its inhabitants.[44] However, whilst this makes it difficult for terrorists to deploy their members for an attack, it also provides the terrorist with a slow-moving target.[45] To be effective in deterring attacks, security force patrols need to be organised around a pattern rather than haphazardly deployed in the hope of bumping into the enemy. The coordinated deployment of a number of small patrols, moving swiftly in an unpredictable pattern, denies snipers or other attackers a guaranteed escape route after they have carried out an attack.[46] This makes the execution of a terrorist attack unlikely, with the exception of attackers who expect to die in the process.[47] In his study of a Catholic area of west Belfast between September 1972 and April 1973, Burton notes that whilst the intermittent patrolling of a conventional infantry regiment was fairly ineffective, the constant patrols and ambushes carried out by the Parachute Regiment limited the freedom of action of the local PIRA, killed many of its members, and reduced it to near impotence.[48]

Other overt activities, where drivers or pedestrians have their identification documents checked and where they may be searched – for instance mobile vehicle check points (VCPs) and static road blocks – make it difficult for terrorists to move personnel, weapons, and supplies around the area affected. As noted earlier, road-blocks and vehicle check-points have been widely used during the recent troubles in Northern Ireland, and occasionally in England.[49] Duyker notes that similar intensive security operations by the Indian Army against Naxalites in Birbhum, West Bengal, between July and November 1971 severely restricted the group.[50] The scale of such operations can be very large. In the two months following the kidnapping of Aldo Moro in 1978 the various Italian security forces set up 72,000 road-blocks, and questioned 6.5 million people.[51] However, whilst such methods may disrupt the ability of terrorist groups to move people, weapons and messages in the affected area, surveys in Northern Ireland indicate that they also cause a great deal of resentment amongst people subjected to them, and this may help the terrorists by creating sympathisers and possibly recruits.[52]

As well as trying to capture terrorists and disrupt their activities with patrols and check-points, the security forces can also try to achieve the same ends by searching property. During the Moro kidnapping the Italian authorities searched 37,000 dwellings, whilst in Northern Ireland between 1970 and 1993 a total of 354,524 searches were carried out in both occupied and unoccupied houses.[53]

By searching specific houses or entire areas, the security forces can achieve a number of aims. If acting on specific information they may find terrorists or terrorist weaponry. For example, in the 1980s a Northern Irish estate agent let the security forces bug empty houses where he allowed PIRA members to hold meetings and stash weapons, and arms caches were found in house searches based upon the information provided by the bugged conversations. In February 1989 the PIRA abducted, interrogated, and shot the estate agent.[54]

In other cases the aim of house-searches is to find as much material as possible by sealing off an area and carrying out a blanket search of the buildings and people within. The need to guard against such searches means that the terrorists have to take time-consuming precautions to hide weapons. During 'Operation Shark', an attempt by four British Army brigades to carry out a cordon and search operation in Tel Aviv between July 30 and August 2, 1946, the Army checked 100,000 people, detaining 787 for further questioning,

Table 8.1 Levels of terrorist and security force activities in Northern Ireland, 1970–1989

	Security force personnel[a]	House Searches	Shootings & explosions
1970	14489	3107	366
1971	17146	17262	2778
1972	29411	36617	12010
1973	32365	74556	5996
1974	32096	74914	3891
1975	31925	30002	2202
1976	32129	34919	2774
1977	32267	20724	1447
1978	32724	15462	1210
1979	31903	6452	1150
1980	32404	4106	922
1981	30954	4104	1540
1982	30728	4045	766
1983	29147	1497	690
1984	28533	1282	527
1985	28259	812	385
1986	29103	1818	564
1987	28828	2474	910
1988	28878	4136	790
1989	28841	3027	790

[a] British Army, UDR, and RUC.

Sources: S. Bruce, *The Red Hand*, 297. Irish Information Partnership, *Agenda: Information Service on Northern Ireland and Anglo-Irish Relations*, sixth edition (London: Irish Information Partnership, 1990), 316. W. D. Flackes & S. Elliott, *Northern Ireland*, 471, 472.

and found 176 rifles, 4 machine-guns, 23 mortars, 127,000 rounds of ammunition, and a large quantity of explosives.[55]

A serious drawback for the authorities is that house searches and related activities often arouse animosity to the security forces amongst the people whose homes and lives have been disrupted. In Northern Ireland this has been exacerbated by the fact that the bulk of house searches have been concentrated in the relatively small geographical areas where republican terrorist groups have been most active, and the impact on these communities has therefore been all the greater.[56] Similarly, during the Palestinian uprising in the Israeli-occupied West Bank and Gaza Strip, Merari, Prat, and Tal claim that in early 1988 security measures such as house-searches were carried out in an 'intentionally rude' manner The intention may have been to cow the Palestinian population, but it also seems likely to increase resentment of the Israelis.[57]

As a measure of the effectiveness of a large overt security force presence in repressing terrorist activities, Table 8.1 shows the relationship between the number of security force personnel deployed, an assertive security force activity in Northern Ireland in terms of house-searches, and the number of terrorist incidents which occurred between 1970 and 1989. One must take care in drawing conclusions from statistics. As the experience of the security forces has increased over time it is possible that the number of houses which are searched has decreased as the security forces are better able to target their searches. Furthermore some blanket searches seem to occur so as to protect sources of information which would be compromised by actions which revealed too clearly the type of information possessed by the authorities.[59] Overall, there appears to be no necessary relationship between terrorist activity and the mere number of security force members deployed. However, there is a correlation between an assertive security force policy as measured by the number of house-searches carried out, and a decline in terrorist attacks. This seems to show that a rise in terrorist attacks tends to be followed by an increase in assertive security force activity and a subsequent drop in the number of terrorist attacks.

Terrorists may attack the security forces in order to prevent this from happening. In Northern Ireland in the early 1990s, the Provisional IRA sought to reduce the presence of the police in particular, and the security forces in general, in areas bordering the Republic of Ireland. By November 1992 an estimated 330 attacks on RUC stations throughout the Province had meant that any stations being built had to be heavily fortified.[60] By attacking fixed vehicle checkpoints, damaging RUC stations, and assassinating contractors or their employees who carried out repair work on them, the PIRA hoped to force the police and the other security forces back from the border.[61] Due to the withdrawal of contractors from doing work for the security forces, repair work had to be done by military engineers, thus increasing the number of military targets for the PIRA.[62] In interviews and articles the PIRA and their supporters have emphasised the isolation of Army and police barracks and the lengths to which the Crown forces have to go to keep such bases functioning.[63] Reports suggest that the PIRA's activities greatly constrained the effectiveness of the security forces in the area – particularly the police.[64]

ARMED RESPONSE

In warfare the aim is ultimately to win by concentrating superior forces against the enemy at a time and place of one's choosing.[65] As well as carrying out measures designed to hinder terrorist operations, sometimes security forces actively attempt to intercept terrorists.[66] Much of this involves covert methods such as information-gathering, surveillance, and the setting of ambushes.

This is more difficult when countering a terrorist campaign than when fighting conventional forces, or indeed a guerrilla army. In urban terrorist campaigns in particular, terrorists can conceal themselves in the anonymity of the town or city. In liberal democracies the authorities are constrained by the law which, in the absence of legislation allowing detention without trial, means that a terrorist cannot be imprisoned without sufficient evidence. The measures which were deemed tolerable for conflicts in former colonies – such as food rationing, strict controls on movement, and a rather more casual attitude towards the death of suspects – are not generally tolerated for conflicts at home.[67] By way of contrast, an uproar occurred in Germany after a known RAF terrorist was killed in questionable circumstances in July 1993, and continuing questions have been raised in Spain as to whether the Government authorised GAL death squads to kill Basque activists in France in the 1980s.[68] Thus, it is generally necessary for a counter-terrorist to amass sufficient intelligence in order to apprehend or thwart the terrorists.

In Northern Ireland attempts have been made to anticipate terrorist operations and to ambush terrorists when they are vulnerable. To make such operations legally and morally palatable they have generally taken place when the terrorists are clearly armed.[69] Such ambushes have often occurred at PIRA arms caches.[70] In order to carry out operations, PIRA members – either couriers or the gunmen themselves, have to go to these caches to pick up their weapons. If the security forces find out where these weapons are, they can deploy covert teams near the caches and apprehend or kill the terrorists at minimal risk.[71] In other cases the British Army has ambushed PIRA members about to carry out an operation, or on their way back from one.[72] The worst PIRA loss suffered in a single action occurred at Loughall, county Armagh, where eight or more terrorists were ambushed as they attempted to destroy a police station using a bomb in the shovel of a mechanical digger. The

SAS were waiting in ambush and killed eight terrorists, but also killed an uninvolved man who was driving through the area.[73]

Overall, between April 1976 and November 1987 the SAS killed 25 members of the Provisional IRA compared to 9 who were killed by uniformed troops, and 5 who were killed by the RUC.[74] In military terms, ambushing terrorists is an effective method, but as Urban points out it can create martyrs for the terrorist cause.[75] When such ambushes go wrong, an example being the shooting of an uninvolved teenager who stumbled across a PIRA arms cache in July 1978, the consequences for the authorities are damaging, let alone those for the victims.[76] However, the need to avoid such ambushes involves the terrorists in further security precautions, thus depleting their offensive capabilities.

A conspicuous example of the use of armed response units against terrorists has been the use of hostage rescue units (HRUs). Their responsibility is to release people being held by armed captors, and includes situations which are not terrorist-related. Incidents such as GSG9's (Grenzchutzgruppe 9 – German Border Police Group 9) rescue of passengers on a hijacked Lufthansa aeroplane at Mogadishu, Somalia, in 1977, and the SAS's rescue of hostages being held in the Iranian Embassy in London in 1980 have shown the utility of setting up such units.[77]

Police units such as the Washington DC Emergency Response Team (ERT) and the New York Police Department also frequently include negotiators who will attempt to persuade the hostage-takers to surrender peacefully if possible.[78] The ability to negotiate successfully is dependent upon the location of the siege. If it is on territory controlled by authorities which control the rescue unit, or which are friendly to them, this is much easier. If, however, the captives are being held in a place where the local powers are hostile to the rescuers, then the opportunities for such negotiation are limited because the authorities do not control the cordon, if there is one, around the area concerned.

When attempts to rescue hostages are unsuccessful the consequences can be grim. Even if the HRU eliminates the hostage-takers, the hostages themselves may be killed. The most notable early example of this was the death of all of the Israeli athletes taken hostage in Munich during the 1972 Olympics.[79] More recently, in November 1985 57 hostages died during an attempt by an Egyptian unit to storm a hijacked EgyptAir aeroplane at Luqa Airport in Malta.[80] The authorities may also find their prestige seriously damaged by the failure of a hostage-rescue operation. This occurred in April 1980 with the failure of an operation to rescue US diplomats being held by students in Tehran with the connivance of the Iranian authorities. Eight members of the HRU involved died when a helicopter collided with a transport aeroplane. Although the hostage-takers were not strictly non-state terrorists, the example is relevant because the mission's failure directly harmed President Carter's re-election campaign in 1980.[81]

The relevance of hostage rescue units to terrorist targeting is that the successful deployment of HRUs has made holding hostages in a siege far more dangerous for terrorists. It is difficult to ascertain whether the increased deployment of HRUs since the late 1970s has resulted in terrorists being less likely to attempt such operations. US State Department statistics concerning international terrorism – that is terrorism which involves the citizens or territory of more than one state – do not indicate any correlation between successful HRU operations and the frequency of hijackings and sieges.[82] However, the use of HRUs does seem to have altered the way in which terrorists go about executing hijackings or other forms of hostage-taking.

Terrorists often try to hold their captives in an area which is not controlled by the authorities. This is only really possible if the hostages were captured outside the jurisdiction of a state which might try to rescue them, as with the western hostages in the Lebanon in the late 1980s, or in the case of the hijacking of an aeroplane or a ship. If possible the kidnappers might also disperse the hostages around a number of geographically separate locations. This lessens the ability of potential rescuers to locate the hostages. Even if they do, they are less likely to have the confidence and resources to plan and carry out a number of simultaneous operations at different sites.[83]

The kidnappers may also move the hostages frequently so as to make it difficult for a rescue mission to be mounted. Although the western hostages in the Lebanon were often grouped in the same building they were moved around Beirut and other parts of the Lebanon.[84] Likewise, when TWA Flight 847 was hijacked in June 1985 soon after leaving Athens, the aeroplane was constantly flown between the airports at Algiers and Beirut. When in Beirut some hostages were taken from the aircraft and distributed around the city in order to make a successful rescue more difficult.[85] By making hostage rescue operations as difficult as possible, and by making it clear that the hostages will die if such an attempt is made, the terrorists can try to ensure that even if they do not achieve their original demands, those responsible for ordering a hostage rescue mission will suffer adverse political consequences.

INTERNATIONAL POLICE AND LEGAL COOPERATION

The trend towards international cooperation over matters such as intelligence sharing or the extradition of terrorist suspects creates another problem for terrorists. Such cooperation can be due to bilateral agreements between states, treaty obligations between states belonging to a common international organisation, or the conditions laid down by international law. The effect can be to make life more difficult for the terrorists. Leaving the territory of the state in which they have committed their offences may no longer mean that terrorists can relax the precautions which they take to avoid detection.

An example of an agreement affecting the ability of a terrorist group to operate is that between Spain and France. Until the mid-1980s the French authorities did little to prevent ETA from using France, and in particular the parts of the Basque region which are located in south-west France, as a haven from which to plan and launch operations. No extraditions to Spain took place. This situation changed, after a group calling themselves the Anti-terrorist Liberation Group (Gruppos Antiterroristas de Liberacion – GAL), allegedly mercenaries sponsored by elements within the Spanish state, assassinated up to 27 Basques in France between 1983 and 1987. Nine of the dead are reported to have had no provable links with ETA.[86] Following these attacks the French authorities clamped down upon ETA activities in France, extraditing 5 suspects to Spain and deporting a further 23 from France in 1984 alone.[87] Basque exiles from Spain were forbidden to live in the departments adjoining the border with the Spanish part of the Basque Country, and from 1987 onwards France extradited ETA suspects to Spain without requiring the production of an extradition warrant.[88] A series of top ETA members were arrested in France throughout the mid and late 1980s and into the 1990s, including the arrest of what were believed to be the three most senior ETA leaders in the south of the country in March 1992.[89]

This affected ETA's targeting. A state which extradites terrorist suspects may find itself coming under attack – either as a form of revenge or to discourage such action in future. ETA carried out attacks upon French business interests and material targets in the Basque Country, including Renault car dealerships, a furniture store, and French-registered vehicles. Some of these attacks coincided with extraditions, whilst an attack on a French-registered truck occurred on the evening of an ETA members' funeral.[90] According to Llera, Mata, and Irwin, ETA made over 500 attacks on French material targets over a five year period.[91] By early 1997 ETA's displeasure at the French Government's actions had not translated itself into attacks against French human targets, perhaps out of fear of even more severe actions on the part of the French authorities.

THE CRIMINAL JUSTICE SYSTEM AND SECURITY FORCES AS TARGETS

In addition to their functions, the criminal justice system and the security forces are symbols of the state. By selecting police officers as targets, terrorists – in particular those with a revolutionary ideology – may seek to encourage the masses to revolt by showing that the state is vulnerable and can be attacked.[92] If the attacks force the security forces to lower their profile or withdraw from an area this has both functional and symbolic importance. It shows that the writ of the state no longer runs in that area, allows the terrorists more freedom of action and allows them to extend their influence over the population.[93]

The targeting of law enforcement officers can also be attributed to the desire of insurgent terrorists to weaken the state itself. At the extreme, if the state can be sufficiently weakened it may collapse, or the conflict may be 'militarised' by the military taking over the government, as occurred in Uruguay in 1972 and Argentina in 1976. However, as noted above, even where the objectives of the terrorists are more modest there are sound reasons for trying to minimise the influence of the security forces in an area.

Police officers have been targets in some insurgent terrorist campaigns, though not in all. As Table 8.2 shows, in the major European terrorist campaigns of recent years the proportion of police victims has varied relative to the overall total. Not all groups have made a point of specifically targeting the police. In 1971, Ulrike Meinhof suggested that police officers who did not act against the

Table 8.2 Police officers killed by terrorists as a percentage of terrorist killings

Group responsible	Police killed	Total people killed	Police as %
Communist terrorists in Italy (1970–82)	57	131	43.5%
Provisional IRA in Northern Ireland (1970–93)	265	1653	16.0%
INLA in Northern Ireland (1970–93)	13	122	10.7%
ETA (1968–82)			
Police	62	349	17.8%
Civil Guard	103	349	29.5%
TOTAL	165	349	47.3%
Red Army Faction in Germany (1968–92)	5	25	20.0%

Sources: D. Moss, *The Politics of Left-Wing Violence in Italy*, 38. M. Sutton, *Bear in Mind These Dead*, 196. (The total number of PIRA killings excludes 102 PIRA members killed by their own bombs.), R. P. Clark, 'Patterns of Eta Violence: 1968–1980', 142n.7. D. Pluchinsky. 'An Organizational and Operational Analysis of Germany's Red Army Faction Terrorist Group (1972–1991)'. Unpublished chronology supplied by B. A. Scharlau.

Red Army Faction would not be attacked.[94] In practice, whilst they attacked senior security officials and sometimes killed the bodyguards for primary targets, the RAF did not generally attack ordinary police officers.

Other terrorist groups have attacked ordinary police officers in an attempt to lower police morale. According to a member of the Irish National Liberation Army, their group deliberately attacked police officers at home because it denied them the one place where they might hope to gain respite from the threat of assassination. Such assassinations were also intended to place pressure upon the wives of other policemen to persuade their husbands to leave the police.[95] According to *L'Espresso*, the Red Brigades also targeted ordinary police officers as well as anti-terrorist detectives so as to affect police morale.[96] BR justified these attacks on the grounds that whilst the capitalist state could replace its leading members, it could not operate without its lesser functionaries.[97] However, communiqués from BR also sought to portray some attacks as revenge for specific actions by the state. Thus, in November 1979 two carabinieri were shot dead whilst drinking coffee in a cafe in

Genoa, supposedly in revenge for the suicide of an imprisoned
Genoese BR member the previous month.[98] Later the same month,
the Red Brigades shot dead another police officer, whom they subsequently described as an 'executioner in disguise'.[99] The need for
public justifications other then mere ideology was obviously still
present.

Terrorist operations against the criminal justice system are not
merely confined to attacks on the police. In August 1983 a spokesman for the Irish National Liberation Army stated that they had
the right to destroy the criminal justice system, and that police
officers, judges, informers, and anybody else involved in the system
would be 'held accountable for their actions'.[100] Terrorist operations which are most directly concerned with the penal system are
those which are intended to free imprisoned terrorists. In October
1867 an attempt to break open the prison van containing Fenian
prisoners in Manchester resulted in the death of one of the police
escorts, whilst a bomb placed against the wall of Clerkenwell prison
in London that December killed 12 people. Neither attempt was
successful in releasing any prisoners and some of the would-be
rescuers were hanged for murder.[101] More recently, the first particularly violent act of the Red Army Faction – though it did not
use that name at the time – occurred in May 1970 when Ulrike
Meinhof and three comrades rescued Andreas Baader at gunpoint
whilst he was in a local library accompanied by a police escort.[102]

In attempting to gain the release of imprisoned comrades or affect their conditions of imprisonment, a terrorist group will not
necessarily restrict its attacks to members of the penal system. The
German left-wing terrorist groups in the 1970s, sometimes in col-
laboration with the PFLP (Popular Front for the Liberation of
Palestine), centred many operations around attempts to release
imprisoned comrades, but did not often attack prison staff.[103] These
operations included: the seizure of the West German Embassy in
Stockholm in 1975 by members of the Socialist Patients' Collective
(Sozialistisches Patienten Kollektiv – SPK) who had joined the RAF,
the Revolutionary Cells' (Revolutionaere Zellen – RZ) involvement
in the hijack which ended at Entebbe in 1976, and the 1977 RAF
kidnapping of Schleyer.[104] All centred on demands for the release
of imprisoned terrorists, several of whom were held in Germany.
In addition the PFLP hijackers of a Lufthansa jet in 1977 demanded
the release of German communist terrorists in addition to Pales-

tinians held in Germany.[105] With the exception of the Schleyer kidnapping all of these operations resulted in the death or capture of the terrorists involved and none of the operations gained the release of the terrorists.

Another reason for terrorist attacks on the penal system is the role which prisons play in legitimising or delegitimising the terrorist group. By imprisoning terrorists in the same way as ordinary criminals, the authorities may hope to morally delegitimise their activities, and by extension legitimise the moral authority of the government. Terrorists on the other hand have a vested interest in combating this view, and have used violence to reinforce their efforts to do this. This was seen in Northern Ireland after 1976 when the British government abolished the special category status for prisoners convicted of scheduled terrorist offences, and sought to bring them under the auspices of a version of the criminal justice system.[106] Between 1976 and 1981 the Provisional IRA and the INLA launched a series of protests and hunger strikes in the prisons in Northern Ireland. Additionally, between April 1976 and the end of the hunger strike in August 1981 18 prison officers at various grades were killed by the PIRA or INLA together with a retired prison officer and his wife.[107]

Terrorists have also attacked members of the penal system to highlight allegations about poor prison conditions, and force the people running the penal system to concede to prisoners' demands. For example, in Italy in the 1980s the Red Brigades and Front Line killed or injured prison officers and other people associated with the penal system in an attempt to put pressure upon the authorities to change specific aspects of the penal system, and also to continue the attack upon the state.[108] A notable example of this was the Red Brigade's kidnapping on December 12, 1980 of Judge Giovanni D'Urso, amongst whose responsibilities was the allocation of terrorists to high-security prisons. The BR demanded the closure of the high-security prison on the island of Asinara, an end to the isolation of imprisoned terrorists, and the publication and transmission of documents drawn up by BR prisoners.[109] On December 31, 1980 BR also assassinated Carabinieri General Enrico Galvaligi who was deputy director for security in the high-security prisons.[110] The Italian government closed the prison at Asinara, and some Italian newspapers and radio stations cooperated in publicising the prisoners' documents. On January 15, 1981 D'Urso was released.[111] The kidnapping achieved the objective of humiliating the Italian authorities, whilst addressing the concerns of imprisoned brigadists and allowing the BR to interrogate D'Urso in detail about the penal system and the people within it.[112]

Like the penal system, the legal system also has vulnerable potential targets. During the trial of members of the French communist terrorist group Direct Action in December 1986, one of the accused asked the judge how long police protection for the jurors would last. When the jurors were told that protection would only be provided for fifteen days, and found out that the defence had demanded and been given their names and addresses a month before the trial, a number of them declared themselves medically unfit for jury service. The trial had to be postponed. As a result, the French authorities brought in provisions for terrorist trials to replace ordinary juries with a panel of seven judges.[113] Similarly, for over one hundred years the Mafia has influenced and intimidated juries in order to prevent the imprisonment of members.[114]

Judges and lawyers can also be directly intimidated. According to Pearce, when, in 1985, the Colombian Supreme Court of Justice was about to hear an application for the annulment of the extradition treaty with the USA, each justice received the following note.

> We are writing to you to demand favourable positions for our cause. We do not accept resignations, we do not accept sabbaticals, we do not accept fictitious illnesses... Any position taken against us we shall take as an acceptance of our declaration of war. From prison, we will order your execution and with blood and lead we will eliminate the dearest members of your family.[115]

On November 6, 1985, the day when the Supreme Court was due to hear the case, the communist group M-19, probably with the backing of drug-traffickers, seized the Colombian Palace of Justice building in Bogota. In the ensuing siege 11 of the 24 Supreme Court justices died, including the four who made up the Court's constitutional arm.[116] In December 1986 the Supreme Court suspended the extradition treaty with the USA.[117]

As well as seeking to gain the freedom of their comrades, the desire to discredit the legal system by making it inoperable has also provided terrorists with a motive for attacks upon judges and lawyers. In 1976 the Red Brigades issued threats, not just against judges and prosecution lawyers, but against those who attempted to act in their defence at the collective trial of 52 alleged brigadists in Turin. In order to make it more difficult for the state to prosecute brigadists as criminals, and thus discredit the legal system, the defendants dismissed their defence lawyers. Under Italian law the state had to provide replacements, but the brigadists stated that they did not recognise the right of the court to try them, and would regard any defence lawyers nominated by the court as enemies. Accordingly, in April 1977, Red Brigadists shot dead Fulvio Croce, the President of the Turin lawyer's association, who had been given the responsibility of organising replacement lawyers for the defendants. The death of Croce made it difficult, in the short-term at least, to find lawyers willing to defend the brigadists.[118] In West Germany in the 1970s, defence lawyers were also threatened, and in some cases attacked by communist terrorist groups whose members they were defending in court, for much the same reason as the BR attacked defence lawyers.[119]

The Provisional IRA has threatened judges and lawyers involved in prosecuting suspected Provisionals.[120] As the PIRA and their supporters have made clear, they wish to place the authorities in a position where they effectively 'declare war' on the PIRA, forcing them to treat the group as morally equivalent belligerents rather than as a criminal group. As Danny Morrison – then the publicity director for Sinn Fein – stated in 1988, the important issue was the Government's assertion that it was morally superior to the PIRA, and that its use of the civil law helped to reinforce this stance.[121]

PIRA's serious attacks on the judiciary began in October 1972 when they shot and wounded a magistrate, William Staunton and on September 16, 1974 shot dead both Judge Rory Conaghan and a magistrate, Martin MacBirney.[122] They have subsequently killed another two judges and three magistrates in Northern Ireland, have made attempts on other judges and magistrates, and have frequently bombed court houses.[123] By preventing the normal legal procedures from operating, the PIRA have hoped to portray the situation between itself and the British Government as a war, and thus achieve a degree of moral parity with the Government. Consequently, after the PIRA blew up Lord Chief Justice Gibson and his wife with a car bomb in 1987, they denounced him as part of the 'war machine', and implied that he should have known the risks this involved for his family.[124]

Attacks can also be intended to intimidate defending counsel for enemy groups. Loyalist terrorists in Northern Ireland have targeted lawyers whom they think are too sympathetic – or possibly too successful – when defending republican suspects or representing the interests of the families of republicans. Patrick McGrory, a Catholic solicitor who had defended PIRA members in court, noted in the mid-1990s that although he was opposed to violence, his practice had become identified with the republican cause because of such cases, and he had been warned that he was a target for loyalist terrorists.[125] The possible consequence of such an identification was seen in February 1989 when Patrick Finucane, a solicitor who often represented republicans or their families in court, was shot dead by the Ulster Freedom Fighters – an alias of the UDA.[126]

SUMMARY

The security environment affects the targeting strategies of terrorist groups in a number of ways. In the first instance it restrains the activities of terrorists by compelling them to adopt a clandestine or semi-clandestine existence. This takes up time and makes it difficult for terrorists to move personnel and equipment, to organise attacks and to communicate between different sections of the group if it is more than a single small group. Thus an effective system of enforcing the law and public order creates a large obstacle for the terrorist, and is accordingly a target.

In addition, for insurgent terrorists an attack upon the police, the legal system, or the penal system, is also a symbolic attack upon the state. By attacking various aspects of the criminal justice system, insurgents can demonstrate their rejection of the legitimacy of the state, show the vulnerability of the state to violent revolutionary action, and demonstrate the inability of the state to counter the terrorists' cause. In addition the terrorists may hope that their attacks will provoke the authorities into repressive measures which will alienate the civil population and lead them to turn to the terrorists. Terrorists who do not have insurgent aims may attack those elements of the criminal justice system whom they wish to intimidate into obedience, or whom they suspect of subversion.

Terrorists are also liable to attack the penal system: directly by attacking prison associated staff so as to force the authorities to change prison conditions, or indirectly by taking hostages with the aim of gaining the release of their comrades.

9 External Factors

INTRODUCTION

Terrorists' actions are meant to have an effect upon their surroundings and are worthless if they do not. In turn, terrorists are affected by their surroundings. To a greater or lesser extent, a terrorist group depends upon the support of people who are not core members of their group, but who operate on its fringes or merely give it tacit support by withholding assistance from the group's opponents. As well as supporters, there is also that part of external opinion which is indifferent or even hostile to the activities of the terrorists. Apart from any other consideration, it is often those people who have no fixed opinion, or who are antagonistic to the group, whom the terrorists see as the psychological target to be influenced. Thus, the world outside the terrorist group can prove to be very important to the terrorists.

SUPPORT FOR TERRORIST GROUPS

Whilst a terrorist group may wish to affect society, society can in turn affect the terrorist group. Fitzpatrick points out that during the Irish Rebellion of 1919–21 there was no shortage of 'strong-willed and bellicose men' to lead a fight against British rule, but in some areas there was a lack of demand for such leadership.[1] The existence of a favourable environment was necessary for IRA leaders to recruit supporters and ultimately members. As this factor affects the capabilities of the group, it must be considered.

The effect of group structure is examined in the next chapter, but it is worth noting here that the structure of terrorist groups is not necessarily the same as the military or police, with their concentration on hierarchy, defined lines of command, and a fairly rigid demarcation between members of the profession and those outside. The relationship between a terrorist group and society can be likened to a series of concentric circles, with the core of terrorist leaders at the centre. In November 1987, a spokesman for the Provisional IRA used this analogy to describe the nature of their support.

Our support is in concentric rings. The centre is the republican movement; the next is the nationalist community in the north, followed by the south then solidarity groups, left groups and finally international sympathy.[2]

Similarly, Scharlau gives a diagrammatic representation of support for communist terrorist groups in West Germany which spreads outwards from the core of active terrorists in a series of concentric circles, through various levels of support, to the uninvolved areas of society.[3] Pluchinsky, on the other hand, uses the analogy of a pyramid to describe the support for the Red Army Faction, with the hard core RAF commando level at the apex and the other various levels of support broadening out into greater numbers the further away they are from the core of active terrorists.[4]

Thus, from the standpoint of a terrorist group, society can be divided into a number of categories. These are fairly distinct, though with some blurring at the edges. From the most favourable to the terrorists to the least favourable the categories used here are:

- *Members*. Those in the terrorist group who carry out violent operations or provide active support for them.
- *Supporters*. Those who support the political objectives and methods of the terrorist group, but generally do not have any role in operations.
- *Potential sympathisers*. Those who generally favour the same political objectives as the terrorist group, but do not support their methods.
- *Uncommitted*. People who have no opinions concerning the terrorist group's political objectives or methods.
- *Unsympathetic*. Those who have no opinions concerning the objectives of the terrorist group, but are opposed to their methods.
- *Opponents*. Those who are opposed to the aims and methods of the terrorist group.
- *Enemies*. Those who violently oppose the aims and methods of the terrorist group, or to whom the terrorists are violently opposed.

The size of these categories differs greatly from one terrorist group to another and the proportionate size of one category to another can also vary greatly. Thus one group may have a very small number of supporters with large sections of the population uncommitted, whilst another group may have sizeable support, but

Table 9.1 Categories of opinion relating to the Provisional IRA and the Red Army Faction

	Provisional IRA	Red Army Faction
Members	250–650 active terrorists and auxiliaries. Imprisoned terrorists.	15–25 active terrorists at commando level. 20–50 'illegal militants' at 'resistance' level. Imprisoned terrorists.
Supporters	Some of Sinn Fein. Some Northern Irish Catholics. Small number of people in Republic. Some people outside Ireland. Foreign supporters (e.g. Libyan government).	About 400 to 2000 people. Resistance level of RAF. Support groups (e.g. Red Help – Rote Hilfe). Lawyers carrying messages to and from prisons. E. German intelligence.
Potential sympathisers	Most Northern Irish Catholics. High proportion of people in Republic. Irish *émigré* groups. Some of political left outside Ireland.	'Alternative' groups (e.g. Greens). Groups on political fringe. Revolutionary groups in Third World.
Uncommitted	Bulk of foreign public opinion.	Bulk of foreign public opinion.
Unsympathetic	British Government and political elite. Much of public opinion in Great Britain.	Bulk of W. German public opinion.
Opponents	Northern Irish Protestants. Main Northern Irish unionist parties.	W. German government. Main political parties and institutions.
Enemies	Security forces. Loyalist terrorists.	Anti-terrorist security forces. 'Imperialists' & major capitalists.

be opposed by a large proportion of the population. This is illustrated by contrasting the rather different patterns of support shown in Table 9.1 for the Provisional Irish Republican Army and the Red Army Faction.[5]

Calculating support for the Provisional IRA shows how determining the size and nature of the terrorists' support is difficult because supporters may lie outside the formal structure of an organisation. Although Sinn Fein forms the political wing of the republican movement – PIRA being the military wing, it is too simplistic to see support for PIRA as being calculable from the number of votes which Sinn Fein receives. A survey in May 1989 suggested that about one-fifth of Sinn Fein voters were opposed to the use of violence for political ends, and one third believed that Sinn Fein should renounce the PIRA campaign.[6] On the other hand, a poll undertaken in the Irish Republic in 1979 showed that 42 per cent accepted the legitimacy of the PIRA's political motivation, and 21 per cent supported their activities to some degree, 8 per cent declaring moderate or strong support.[7] This is a much higher level of support than the 2 per cent to 5 per cent which Sinn Fein has been able to mobilise in elections in the south.[8] It is therefore likely that some republicans in the Irish Republic vote for the mainstream southern parties as being relevant to their everyday concerns, whilst they support the Provisionals' activities in relation to Northern Ireland.[9]

As a generalisation, and by accepting some correlation between support for Sinn Fein and support for the Provisionals, it would be accurate to say that PIRA gains most of its active support from Catholics in some rural areas and in the more deprived urban areas of Northern Ireland.[10] A smaller but useful level of support can be found in the Republic of Ireland, whilst some support can be found amongst Irish émigré groups – particularly in the USA. Supporters also include a very small amount of members of extreme left-wing groups in Great Britain and Europe, and, occasionally, foreign sponsors such as the Libyan government.[11]

TERRORISTS' INFLUENCE ON THE PUBLIC

Most terrorist acts influence the public indirectly by forming their views of the terrorists and their cause. However, terrorists may also affect the public directly by actions aimed at gaining their compliance or endorsement. Intimidation is one way of gaining compliance. It can take the form of killing, injuring, or threatening people who inform against the terrorists, who publicly defy terrorist edicts, or who merely criticise the terrorists. By such means some terrorists may hope to frighten people into compliance. Thus, as mentioned previously, Shining Path terrorists in Peru and Islamic terrorists in Algeria have attacked those individuals who have opposed them, and have carried out massacres against communities who have failed to comply with their demands.

However, the relation between terrorists and the public can be rather more complex than one of straight intimidation. In their relations with the public, terrorists may use combinations of intimidation and exhortation. Whilst some of their violent actions may be aimed at scaring people into aiding them – or at least not opposing them – others can conceivably be intended to garner their support. Some terrorists have attacked targets which they believe are unpopular with elements of the public who sympathise with the terrorists' cause. As mentioned, ETA have killed engineers at nuclear power stations in the Basque region, the Naxalites killed West Bengali landlords, and the Red Brigades kneecapped industrial managers in Italy.[12] In terms of gaining support, the success of such methods can depend on the type of society within which the terrorists operate.

The Provisional IRA is an example of a group with roots in one side of a conflict which contains strong elements of communal antagonism. PIRA is not an outside body which has imposed itself upon the working-class Catholic population of Northern Ireland, it is indigenous in much the same way that Northern Irish loyalist terrorists are indigenous to parts of the Protestant working-class.[13] As the RUC Chief Constable remarked, 'The reality is that terrorists reside and operate within each community'.[14] For many Northern Irish Catholics, PIRA members are often family members, friends of the family, former school-mates, or belong to a range of other personal relationships which might lead people to give them tacit if not active support.[15] In turn, over the years the Provisionals have become aware that such support could stop if they frequently overstep the boundaries of what is deemed by their supporters or potential sympathisers to be acceptable behaviour.[16] Thus, as well as providing support, the relationship places limits on the activities of the group.

However, the PIRA's position is reinforced by threats. They have made it clear that those who inform against the PIRA, or who help the security forces in minor ways such as working on security force bases, are liable to be killed.[17] Sutton estimates that between 1970 and the end of 1993 the PIRA killed 59 alleged informers and 27 contractors or contractor's employees who worked for the security forces.[18] This does not include people who have been injured or intimidated because of their opposition to aspects of republican political or terrorist actions. For instance the Belfast nationalists Gerry Fitt and Paddy Devlin, SDLP leader John Hume, and the 'Peace People' – a group who opposed republican violence, all had their homes attacked by republicans in the 1980s, Devlin eventually being driven out of Andersonstown by the attacks.[19]

PIRA's use of force within the community is not always unpopular, provided it is directed against those seen as outcasts. Following on from the IRA's precedent in the rebellion of 1919 to 1921, the PIRA has often acted as a vigilante force at the local level.[20] The activities of the Provisionals in the early 1970s made it extremely difficult for the RUC to police ordinary crime in some Catholic areas, giving the PIRA the opportunity to demonstrate that it could protect the Catholic community not only from outside elements such as sectarian assassins, but from 'anti-social' elements within.[21] Thus, in August 1977 the Derry City PIRA, claiming to be reacting to 'numerous complaints', warned bar and off-licence owners not to supply alcohol to under-age drinkers, with the threat of 'resulting action' if they disobeyed.[22] Fourteen years later, in 1991, the Belfast PIRA warned drug dealers that they would be held 'fully accountable' and dealt with 'militarily' for the misery which they caused others.[23] The effect of such action was seen in November 1992 when the Belfast PIRA killed one member of the IPLO (Irish People's Liberation Organisation) and wounded ten others on the grounds that they were peddling drugs in Catholic areas. The two wings of the IPLO announced that they were disbanding as a result of the Provisionals' action.[24] McKittrick remarked at the time that the action demonstrated PIRA's strength and authority in republican areas, and would allow them to claim credit for dealing with a drugs problem which the authorities had failed to deal with.[25]

Such warnings were not just issued to those supplying under-age drinkers or drug-users. In 1979 the Belfast PIRA warned of a crackdown on 'Thugs, Vandals, Sex Offenders and Muggers' and in a warning to petty criminals, in 1991 a PIRA representative stated that they would not 'permit individuals to inflict hardship on their own community unchecked'.[26] Such action can be popular. McCann reports that in December 1992 it was only after severe public pressure had been brought to bear on them to do something that the Derry PIRA knee-capped a man alleged to have sexually abused children. The man subsequently died.[27] Again in May 1994 McCann reports that similar pressure was brought to bear on the Derry Provisionals to maim members of an alleged paedophile ring, but on that occasion they declined to act.[28] Inevitably, mistakes have been made where the wrong person has been knee-capped, or a badly carried out knee-capping has resulted in the loss of a leg, but allegations have also been made that personal and political grudges have been paid off under the guise of 'punishment'.[29]

Finally, in their assumed role as defenders of the Catholic community in Northern Ireland, the Provisionals have taken action against loyalist terrorists. This role has been crucial to the Provisionals, as it was the failure to defend Catholic areas in 1969 and 1970 which led to the PIRA splitting away from the IRA in the first place. For instance, during 1993 and 1994 the Provisionals and the INLA carried out a series of attacks against alleged loyalist terrorists in an attempt to prevent increasingly successful loyalist attacks on Catholics and particularly on Sinn Fein members. In one incident, on the Shankill Road, Belfast in October 1993, a PIRA bomb intended to kill senior members of the Ulster Defence Association killed one PIRA bomber and nine Protestant civilians. Again much of the impetus for these republican attacks came from demands from republican supporters that something be done to stop the loyalist attacks. However, they resulted in a spiral of reprisal killings against Catholics.[30]

In describing the relationship between the Provisionals and the Catholic population of Northern Ireland, Moxon-Browne notes that, however comforting to the authorities, there was little reality in an image of the Provisional IRA as, 'a small band of ruthless criminals holding a cowering population to ransom'.[31] However, there are also limits to the degree of dissent which the Provisionals will tolerate without retaliation. Overall, the relationship between the Provisionals and the Catholic working-class is well summed up by Mary Holland's term of 'quiescent ambivalence'.[32]

In the case of terrorist groups operating in more homogenous societies, the amount of support may be much smaller. Whilst there was some sympathy for the Red Army Faction in 1970–1 – before they had killed anybody and had confined their attacks to low-level bombings and arson – by the late 1970s 85 per cent of West Germans polled were in favour of more severe penalties for terrorists.[33] The remoteness of their ideology from the day-to-day concerns of ordinary Germans meant that there was no reservoir of anti-state sympathy for them to tap into in the same way that the PIRA could amongst Northern Irish Catholics. In general, groups which establish a strong communal identity are in a much stronger position than those without one.

THE EFFECT OF SOCIETAL DIVISIONS ON TARGETING

Communal divisions within a society – that is divisions between communities which see themselves as distinctly different for whatever reason – can affect terrorist target selection because they affect the size and composition of the categories of support outlined above. These divisions can provide a terrorist group with supporters and sympathisers within their own community, and also define enemies in the shape of groups hostile to their community. In such a situation the terrorists may carry out attacks on the 'enemy' community in order to advertise their cause and mobilise support within their own community. On the other hand groups dependent upon fairly widespread backing have to ensure that the bulk of their attacks can be justified to their supporters in ideological terms. If they cannot, it can prove difficult to secure public cooperation by intimidation alone.

Where there are severe communal tensions based upon ethnic, religious, or economic differences, there seems to be a likelihood of terrorism aimed at asserting the dominance of one community over another, or conversely at protecting a weaker community from such dominance. In terms of fatalities, Northern Ireland is only a relatively minor example of this phenomenon. Tamil, Sinhalese, and Muslim groups in Sri Lanka have massacred large members of each others' communities in order to gain local dominance, or in revenge for previous massacres.[34] For instance, in April 1992 *The Independent* reported that members of the LTTE had killed 50 Muslim villagers, whereupon Muslims attacked nearby Tamil villages, killing twenty Tamils.[35] In no single violent incident since 1969 have twenty people been killed in Northern Ireland. (The two incidents relating to the Northern Irish conflict which involved twenty or more deaths occurred outside Northern Ireland, in Dublin in May 1974 and in Birmingham, England in November 1974.[36])

The conflict in the Indian province of Punjab in the 1980s and early 1990s provides a good example of bitter communal rivalries resulting in terrorism. The Punjab was greatly affected by the capital-intensive 'Green Revolution' in Indian agriculture in the 1960s. Whilst bringing greater prosperity if averaged out over the population, it is argued that it also produced greater differentiation between richer farmers who could afford to invest in the latest agricultural technology, and the poorer farmers who could not and thus could not survive in the new agricultural economy.[37] Oberoi claims that this process of differentiation forced the higher-caste *jat* Sikhs, who often made up the farming class, to work amongst lower-caste *harijans*, thereby causing much resentment amongst the jats and exacerbating the religious differences between the Sikh and Hindu groups in the province.[38] Since the early 1980s Sikh terrorists have deliberately killed unarmed Hindu civilians living in the Punjab – including some large-scale massacres – in order to force them out of the province with the aim of creating the homogeneous Sikh state of Khalistan.[39] By their words and actions some religious and separatist Sikh terrorist groups clearly wish to sharpen differences between members of their own religion and other communities, and these have been exacerbated by the economic tensions between the communities.[40]

Some societies seem more prone to support the activities of terrorist groups or other law-breakers, particularly where respect for the systems of government and justice have been eroded. Hobsbawm and Angiolillo both explore the existence in peasant societies of what Hobsbawm terms *social bandits*, that is bandits who receive popular support because they are seen to stand for the alleviation of injustice and symbolise resistance to unpopular authority.[41] This idea has similarities with the position of PIRA in Northern Ireland, ETA in the Basque country, and various Islamic separatist groups in the Kashmir province of India, where a substantial number of people have seen insurgent groups as reactions to existing injustices or to the behaviour of the security forces.[42] In such circumstances support for terrorism is likely to be higher than in a society where the law is respected.

Such attitudes are not restricted to separatist conflicts. A poll conducted in Italy in the early 1960s demonstrated a high degree of public alienation from the governmental and economic systems at a time of relative economic prosperity in Italy.[43] Only 3 per cent of Italians polled expressed pride in their governmental and political institutions – compared to 30 per cent in Mexico, and 3 per cent expressed pride in the Italian economic system – compared to 24 per cent in less economically developed Mexico.[44] This disillusion extended across people with varying degrees of political participation.[45] One must be careful in drawing conclusions from such data, but it is noticeable that during the industrial unrest of the 1970s, Italian industrial workers were relatively ambivalent in their attitude towards Red Brigade attacks on politicians and industrial managers.[46] On the other hand the BR killing of ordinary workers, or of police bodyguards and uniformed police officers, prompted huge demonstrations and widespread public opposition to the Red Brigades, forcing the brigadists to make defensive and defamatory comments about the police officers killed.[47]

Groups which do not have a wide base of support, generally those whose ideology is more abstract, are not so bound by the need to satisfy a broad section of public opinion. On the other hand, without such support they are very much dependent upon their own resources and cannot hope to expand, a position which is probably sustainable only by groups such as large drugs traffickers, which already possess sufficient resources. However, the way in which terrorist actions are perceived can also depend upon the medium through which they are received.

TERRORISTS AND THE MEDIA

The media has undoubtedly had an effect on the activities of terrorists wishing to publicise their cause or other concerns through the media, because they have to ensure that they carry out actions which are sufficiently newsworthy. Gerry Adams has described violent acts by the Provisional IRA as 'armed propaganda' because they put the issue of the British presence in Ireland onto the political agenda.[48] Schmid and de Graaf quote a PIRA spokesman in the early 1970s as noting that, for publicity purposes, one bomb in London's Oxford Street was worth ten bombs in Belfast, and over twenty years later PIRA spokesmen were still using versions of that phrase.[49] Similarly, following the PIRA mortar attack on 10 Downing Street in February 1991 the republican press noted with some satisfaction the amount of coverage which the attack generated in the British, Irish, and international press.[50]

Other groups have been similarly enamoured of the power of the media, and have chosen either their targets or the location of their attacks in order to maximise media attention. During the Algerian War of 1954 to 1962 a leader of the separatist FLN emphasised this, stating:

> Is it better for our cause to kill ten of our enemy in the countryside of Telergma, where no one will speak of it, or one in Algiers that will be mentioned the next day in the American press?[51]

Behr also recounts an FLN spokesman at the United Nations who justified bomb attacks upon European civilians in Algiers in 1956–7 by stating:

> You must realise that every time a bomb explodes in Algiers we are taken more seriously here.[52]

Several individual terrorist actions have been specifically aimed at gaining publicity. In Argentina in September 1973, members of the Trotskyist People's Revolutionary Group (Ejercito Revolucionario del Pueblo – ERP) kidnapped the executive of a newspaper and forced the paper to carry an advert urging Argentines to support Peron in the forthcoming elections.[53] Other terrorist groups have put pressure on the print and electronic media to carry statements and communiqués, usually by abducting people.[54] In June 1995 an American anarchist, known as the 'Unabomber' because of his predilection for sending parcel bombs to scientists at universities and elsewhere, stated that he would stop his activities if his 30,000-word statement on the future of industrial society was printed in major American newspapers. In the event this was done by the *New York Times* and the *Washington Post*.[55]

Some terrorists also believe that general coverage of their activities will generate publicity for their cause. Patricia Hearst – who in February 1974 was abducted in Berkeley, California, by a quasi-communist group which called itself the Symbionese Liberation Army (SLA) – claims that they were 'absolutely publicity-crazy' and were 'media-freaks' who constantly listened on the radio for mentions of themselves.[56] Similarly, according to Baumann, himself a member of the June 2nd Movement in the early 1970s, the Red Army Faction believed that media reports about guerrillas fighting in Germany would help to inspire revolution against imperialism in other parts of the world.[57]

After terrorist actions, or during them in the case of prolonged abductions, terrorists often make use of the media to issue communiqués which explain why they have carried out a specific attack, and also try to use the enhanced publicity to proselytise for their cause or to threaten further attacks if they do not get their way. During the Moro abduction between March and May 1978 the Red Brigades issued frequent communiqués – usually statements left in locations which were communicated to the newspapers – setting out BR conditions for Moro's release, and claiming to demonstrate the corruption of the Italian Christian Democrats.[58] Thus the kidnapping served to advertise the BR's claims as well as being an attempt to free their comrades.

As well as possibly encouraging those terrorists who want publicity, a further effect which media coverage may have is that of contagion, whereby media reports of terrorist violence encourage other discontented groups to use violence and possibly to adopt similar tactical methods.[59] Thus, the Red Brigades are said to have adopted the tactic of the politically motivated, high-profile kidnap from the Uruguayan Tupamaros.[60] Miller and Schmid point out that there is little empirical research to prove a link between media coverage of terrorist actions and the occurrence of similar actions elsewhere.[61] However, based on a study of 168 terrorist attacks against immigrants and asylum-seekers in Scandinavia, Bjorgo notes that such attacks tend to occur in time-related clusters, and that this is probably because one attack sets off a spate of copycat attacks elsewhere.[62] One cannot say for certain that media coverage causes some people to adopt terrorist methods or copy the methods of other terrorist groups, but it seems unlikely that it has no effect at all.

Having said this, one must not fall into the trap of over-emphasising the importance of media coverage to terrorism. To begin with, in some instances the news media may not be free to report terrorist incidents. Even in liberal democracies, governments frequently try to restrict media reporting of the actions or communications of terrorist groups or their supposed allies. In 1971 the Irish Government invoked Section 31 of the Broadcasting Act to restrict interviews with spokesmen of both the Provisional IRA and the Official IRA, and after 1972 they were banned. From 1976 until January 1994 interviews with members of Sinn Fein – the political wing of the republican movement – were also banned.[63] Between October 1988 and August 1994 the British Government banned the transmission of the voices of members of Irish republican and loyalist terrorist groups, and members of groups held to be associated with them – such as Sinn Fein.[64] In Greece it was made an offence to report the contents of terrorist statements, and in September 1991 seven newspaper editors were imprisoned for publishing the contents of communiqués by the communist terrorist group Revolutionary Organisation November 17th (17N).[65]

Governments are not the only people to suppress the media. Journalists have often been attacked by terrorists who disapprove of their politics or of what they have written.[66] Some of the attacks are not lethal. In his autobiography, Michael Baumann notes how in February 1970 members of the 'Blues' – a anarchist group in West Berlin – beat up a journalist who wrote an uncomplimentary article about them.[67] However, there are other cases where the intent has been lethal. In November 1977 Red Brigadists shot and mortally wounded Carlo Casalegno, a journalist and deputy-editor of *La Stampa* who had written articles criticising BR.[68] Likewise, in May 1984 members of the UVF shot and seriously wounded Jim Campbell, a journalist investigating the activities of a Belfast UVF group subsequently known as the 'Shankill Butchers'. The intention had been to kill him.[69] In February 1985 members of November 17th shot dead Nikos Momferatos – the publisher of Greece's largest conservative newspaper – and his driver. Momferatos was President of the Association of Athens Newspaper Publishers and a close friend of the leader of the conservative opposition New Democracy Party. 17N claimed that Momferatos' newspaper, and most other Greek newspapers, suppressed news of the American domination of Greece, of CIA activities, and of the depredations of the Greek bourgeoisie.[70] Thus, as well as eliminating an opponent the attack was intended to frighten other publishers and members of the press into compliance.

In some cases terrorist attacks on journalists have been more incessant. Since the military coup and suppression of elections in Algeria in January 1992, Islamist terrorists have attempted to silence media criticism by eliminating journalists as a class. By December 1996 the number of dead journalists was said to stand at 69.[71] Ironically newspapers have also been suppressed by the Algerian Government. According to Michael Colomes, foreign editor of the French weekly *Le Point*, the conflict in Algeria had attracted relatively little international interest because government suppression and terrorist attacks made it difficult to provide television coverage.[72]

Not all terrorist groups necessarily wish to gain widespread media attention for their actions. The effectiveness of many conservative terrorist groups in Latin America tends to depend on individual threats and the spread of rumours locally for the purposes of intimidation. For example, in Barrancabermeja, Colombia, Amnesty International reports that a group calling itself Toxicol-90 carried out 'social-cleansing' operations in the late 1980s against alleged vagrants and petty thieves, and distributed leaflets within the city warning of its intentions.[73] Likewise, news of the killings of trade unionists and workers in Colombia seem to spread by word of mouth rather than mass media coverage.[74]

Amnesty International also reports that Guatemalan trade unionists have received messages from groups – thought to be in the pay of employers or set up by them – threatening them and their families with injury, abduction, rape, or death if they do not leave their union. In some cases these threats have been carried out.[75] One note, delivered to the pregnant wife of a union activist in August 1995, threatened:

> If you love your baby, convince your husband since neither of you has taken any notice. But if he loves his baby, he will have to decide now, either leave the union or his wife and child will pay the consequences.... Ask your husband what he prefers, to have you alive or dead.[76]

The couple were subsequently told to leave the country within 72 hours.[77] In such circumstances it is likely that far from wanting media publicity the terrorists – or their backers – would seek to prevent being publicly connected with these activities, hoping that the intimidation implicit in such threats would spread to the wider psychological target – unionised workers – by word of mouth.

On some occasions terrorist groups definitely do not want any form of publicity, as when the media reports unsavoury activities or reveals terrorist plans. One of the greatest blows to the image of the Ulster Defence Association occurred in August 1987 when a television programme showed secretly-taken film of a senior UDA member trying to extort money from a television journalist posing as a businessman. As a result four UDA members were imprisoned.[78] Similarly, newspaper revelations in 1981 that some British fascists were attempting to import guns and planned to bomb the Notting Hill Carnival in London, caused great problems for the groups concerned.[79]

The publicity from operations which go wrong can also cause problems. In November 1987, eleven civilians were killed in the Northern Irish town of Enniskillen, by a bomb intended for the military guard at a Remembrance Day parade. The subsequent publicity was disastrous for the image of the PIRA amongst potential sympathisers and the uncommitted. A PIRA spokesman noted that whilst their core support was unaffected, the outer reaches were 'devastated'.[80] The views of hitherto uncommitted people may also be affected by bad publicity. Miller reports that in the aftermath of the Enniskillen bombing, polls showed a steep reduction in support in Great Britain for withdrawal from Northern Ireland, from 61 per cent in January 1987 to 40 per cent in late November 1987 – a few days after the bombing. Miller also reports a sharp reduction in support for withdrawal in the opinion polls after the Warrington bomb.[81] In practice political or strategic gains from mass casualty attacks on civilians are generally only transitory unless sustained attacks take place as with the FLN bombing campaign in Algiers.

Whatever its effect on peripheral support, supposedly bad publicity may not adversely affect the core support for terrorist groups, and the disadvantages of bad publicity may be counteracted by other benefits. For example, after a PIRA bomb killed two children in the English town of Warrington in March 1993, reports indicated that potential sympathisers in the Republic of Ireland and elsewhere were more likely to withhold support, or even actively oppose the republican movement, thus affecting its political and possibly logistical base.[82] Mitchell McLaughlin, a Sinn Fein spokesman, noted that from the republican perspective, Warrington 'didn't help'.[83] However, O'Brien and Gorman have argued that despite the opprobrium, the bombing was a PIRA success because it put the Northern Irish conflict back into the headlines in Britain.[84]

Media attention by itself is rarely vital to the continued existence of terrorist groups, rather the more active groups are newsworthy because of their continued existence. Schmid and de Graaf believe that terrorist attacks are often intended to fulfil other tactical objectives, and the resultant media attention, whilst possibly beneficial, is frequently incidental to the main purpose of an attack.[85] Thus, John Conway, the editor of news and current affairs for the BBC in Belfast, estimated in August 1988 that 78 per cent of all violent happenings there were not covered by the media.[86] Overall it seems that the mass media is more important to some terrorists than to others, and for some groups, particularly vigilante-style groups operating in a limited locality, it hardly matters at all. The media can be important to a terrorist group in that the ability to gain media attention may amplify the influence of the group and its cause, and this in turn may influence the way in which terrorist group selects its targets. Whilst there is little evidence to suggest that the prospect of getting publicity leads terrorists to attack targets which they would not normally consider legitimate, they may choose to attack those legitimate targets which have a higher news profile.

EXTERNAL POLITICAL EVENTS

Political terrorism is usually a reaction to a perceived fault in the existing order, whether it be a need to preserve the existing order in its entirety, overthrow it, or affect certain parts of it. In that sense, all terrorism is a reaction to the political environment. The reaction of terrorists to specific political events varies from group to group. Some are extremely sensitive to events, and others less so.

The way in which terrorists may react directly to a specific political event can be seen in the campaign by Hamas to destabilise the 1993 autonomy accord between Israel and the Palestine Liberation Organisation (PLO). Since the agreement – under which the PLO governs Jericho and the Gaza Strip with the possibility of this area being extended to the Israeli-occupied West Bank of the River Jordan – Hamas has sought to mobilise Palestinians and Arab governments against the agreement by provoking the Israelis into breaking the agreement and into further military repression. In order to do this bomb attacks have been carried out against civilian targets in Israel itself.[87] Between April 1994 and March 1996 thirteen suicide bomb attacks, mainly on buses or near bus queues, killed over 130 people.[88] The resultant travel restrictions on Palestinians who lived in the PLO-administered areas but worked in Israel, combined with retaliatory measures against the families of bombers, alienated Palestinian civilians. Meanwhile, Israeli pressure on the PLO administration to attack Hamas, risked making the PLO seem like Israel's puppet.[89]

Other terrorist groups have been sensitive to political events to an even greater degree. Corsun notes that November 17th in Greece appears to be particularly sensitive to political events in Greece and elsewhere.[90] Doyle notes that 17N's attacks have generally related to 'whatever is upsetting Greek public opinion at the time'.[91] Thus, in May 1988 17N bombed a number of Turkish diplomatic vehicles on the eve of a visit from the Turkish Foreign Minister, whilst a series of bombings in a wealthy suburb of Athens was intended to highlight the alleged inconsistency between the conservative Greek Government's austerity measures and the toleration of widespread tax evasion by the wealthy.[92] In early 1991 17N carried out low-level attacks against targets belonging to companies, diplomatic facilities, or other people or property whose countries had been involved on the Allied side in the war against Iraq in January 1991, and they killed a US Army sergeant in Athens in March 1991, linking the attack to the US presence in Greece and the Turkish presence in Cyprus.[93] In fact in early 1991 a number of European terrorist groups attacked targets belonging to the USA and other members of the Allied Forces.[94] These types of attack show a high degree of sensitivity to political events.

The Provisional IRA has adopted an ambivalent tone over whether they plan operations to coincide with particular dates or events. In late 1978 a PIRA spokesman denied that an upsurge in activity represented a 'winter offensive' or a 'pre-election blitz' as this would run counter to the long war strategy of attrition which the Provisionals claimed to be waging against the British.[95] Similarly, in 1983 a spokesman stated:

> Our tactics are determined by intelligence and logistics – the availability of weapons and personnel. The military struggle will not slow down to relate to Sinn Fein's political activities.[96]

Joe Austin, a senior Sinn Fein member, made a similar remark to the effect that PIRA attacks on dates symbolic to the republican movement would be self-indulgent posturing and would help the security forces by making attacks predictable.[97]

On the other hand, in March 1973 the PIRA specifically detonated a bomb in London on the day of a referendum in Northern Ireland which was likely to show that the majority of people there did not want a united Ireland.[98] In an article in March 1992, a PIRA representative was ambivalent about organising operations around political events, stating that they did not plan operations around political events such as the forthcoming British General Election.

> Operations within England and elsewhere are part of our long-term strategy and it would be playing into our enemy's hands to build any degree of predictability into our activities.[99]

However he conceded:

> it is fair to comment that operations around major political events do carry the added bonus of forcing the Irish war onto the British political agenda.[100]

Thus, whilst the spokesman denied that the Provisionals necessarily planned operations to coincide with major political events, he noted the advantages of doing so. In fact the PIRA set off two massive bombs the day after the 1992 British General Election. One badly damaged a major road flyover in west London, whilst the other in the City of London killed 3 people, injured 75 others, and caused about £350 million worth of damage.[101]

More recently, in February 1996 the Provisionals ended their ceasefire by setting off a bomb in the Docklands area of London, killing 2 people, injuring about 100, and causing damage estimated at £75 million to £150 million. They claimed they had done this because the British Government was stalling and acting in 'bad faith' over whether to allow Sinn Fein to participate in all-party talks on the future of Northern Ireland.[102] This clearly linked the attack to political developments.

Even if a political event does not have a direct influence on the terrorists' cause, occasions such as the OPEC Conference in Vienna in 1975 and the Conservative Party Conference in Brighton in 1984 provided terrorists with opportunities for kidnap and assassination respectively.[103] These attacks occurred because a lot of high-profile targets were known to be in a relatively small area on a specific date. Such opportunities may be rare, and it is hardly surprising if terrorists take them when they can.

Whilst acknowledging that terrorism is frequently a reaction to the perceived political climate in a country, one must be careful not to overstate the extent to which individual terrorist actions are linked to specific political events. Many actions, for example the PIRA killing of a police officer in Northern Ireland or the killing of an immigrant by a fascist group in Germany, are not related to a particular political event, but are part of a continuing campaign of violence with its own internal dynamic based on means and opportunities. However, on other occasions attacks by terrorist groups seem to be prompted by events – either because the terrorists are reacting to events, or because the events provide the terrorists with targets or the chance to advertise their cause by carrying out an attack at a time of heightened media attention.

SUMMARY

To a greater or lesser degree, when selecting targets terrorists have to take account of intangible factors such as public opinion and the predominant social and political atmosphere. The fact that they normally depend on supporters and sympathisers outside the group, and often wish to avoid causing the antipathy of neutrals, means that terrorists' freedom of action is constrained. Conversely the terrorists can also take steps to control the civil population. Threats, the use of vigilantism, judiciously selected assassinations and maimings, or wholesale massacres, can intimidate selected people or whole communities into cooperation with – or at least tacit acceptance of – the terrorists. Likewise, the terrorists may attack unpopular people or institutions in order to generate popular support.

When selecting their targets terrorists may try to maximise the amount and nature of the publicity they receive by choosing targets which have a high publicity value. However, this can be a double-edged sword in the case of unpopular attacks. The influence of social and economic structures can also greatly influence target selection. These structures can cause communal divisions or cleavages based on social class causing certain groups of people to be automatically deemed as enemies. Finally, political events can affect target selection. For terrorist groups wishing to influence political developments in their part of the world, the occurrence or likely occurrence of a major political event can be important in influencing target selection. Alternatively, a political event provides a useful peg – in terms of media attention already in the area – upon which to hang an operation. Lastly, political events such as conferences can provide targets in themselves because of the wealth of suitable targets which they attract.

10 Decision-making

INTRODUCTION

When examining the actions of terrorists, one must bear in mind that one is dealing with people, with all their imperfections and unpredictability, rather than some hypothetical, hyper-rational beings. Of the decision-making process itself, Arthur Schlesinger, the historian and member of Kennedy's White House staff, has noted:

> I shudder a little when I think how confidently I have analyzed decisions in the ages of Jackson and Roosevelt, traced influences, assigned motives, evaluated roles, allocated responsibilities and in short, transformed a dishevelled and murky evolution into a tidy and ordered transaction.[1]

Whilst terrorists may have fewer decisions to make than governments, they often operate with fewer resources under a great deal of psychological and possibly physical pressure. The purpose of this chapter is to examine the combined effects of the decision-making process and the vagaries of human behaviour upon terrorist target selection.

THE STRUCTURE OF TERRORIST GROUPS

Group structures vary. As already noted, terrorist groups tend to have a leader or core of leaders, with followers who might be as adept operationally as the leaders, but who are not as interested or competent in the ideology and internal politics of the group.[2] Furthermore, whilst some terrorist groups are autonomous of any other organisation, others are a sub-section of a wider organisation, as with the Hizbollah in Lebanon.[3] With some of these groups, whilst the wider movement is notionally in charge, in practice the terrorists have a great deal of autonomy if not outright independence. An example is the Combat Organisation of the Social Revolutionary Party in early twentieth century Russia.[4]

Even where the terrorist group is largely autonomous, its structure may be bureaucratic and hierarchical. The 1950s Greek-Cypriot group EOKA was highly centralised, with its commander, George Grivas, exercising strict – though not total – control over all aspects of operations.[5] However, with other hierarchically-organised groups, such as the Red Brigades, in practice operational decisions often take place near the bottom of the structure rather than descend from the top.[6] As will be seen this can have consequences for target selection and the execution of operations.

Other groups are more amorphous in structure. In small informal groups, like the early Baader-Meinhof group in West Germany or the Symbionese Liberation Army in the USA, decisions seem to have been decided by force of personality rather than by a formal decision-making process.[7] The structure of some other groups is highly diffuse, as with the Animal Liberation Front in Britain or the Revolutionary Cells in Germany. These consist of independent groups who have little if any contact with each other. They correspond through a very small number of contacts, or communicate policy lines through publications.[8] In the ALF such communications may take place through communiques and articles in journals such as the *ALF Bulletin*.[9] As Henshaw pointed out in the 1980s, there seems little point in having all operations directed from ALF headquarters as everybody knows who or what the targets are.[10] However, if a group carries out an action, and then claims it in the name of the ALF, the communique is published in an ALF supporters bulletin and is acknowledged as an ALF attack.[11] The divide between group members and non-members is therefore quite permeable. By minimising the contacts between individual groups, and between groups and the national offices, there is also less chance of the ALF being infiltrated by the police.[12] However, coordinated action between groups is difficult.

Zawodny, who served in the Polish Resistance during the Second World War, points out that there is nearly always an intrinsic tension between the need for centralised control in order to coordinate actions, and for decentralisation in order to maintain security from enemy penetration.[13] The risk of sending messages from the leadership to the active terrorists is that the messages may be intercepted by informers or enemy surveillance. The greater the number of messages, the greater the risk. This is not a great problem with small groups such as the original Baader-Meinhof group, because they only consist of one relatively small group, and do not need to take elaborate measures to transmit messages and instructions. However, if the organisation covers more than a small area in terms of geography or population then sometimes, but not always, the practice appears to be that the leaders of the group lay down the broad guidelines within which local groups operate.[14] The overall effect is that operational decisions are made by small groups either on the ground or in consultation with higher levels of the group structure. When such guidelines are not forthcoming there can be an escalation of the campaign in terms of the number and types of targets attacked. Thus, when much of the PIRA leadership was interned in 1971–2, one result was that young, aggressive, and undisciplined terrorists perpetrated a greater level of uncoordinated and indiscriminate violence than seen before.[15]

The Provisional IRA's Remembrance Day bombing in Enniskillen, provides an example of the decision-making structure failing to operate properly, and thus affecting an operation. PIRA strategy is notionally set by the bodies shown within the shaded area in Figure 10.1. However, the need to minimise internal communications for security reasons, and the differing circumstances between one area and another, have meant that units are largely allowed to operate on the basis of local initiative. Consent for specific operations comes from the brigade staff above the local unit proposing an attack. This process should mean that active terrorists choose their own targets, but within the guidelines set at the higher levels of the PIRA. In practice target selection can be affected by sectarianism, local enmities, and the shortcomings of local intelligence-collection.[16] Thus, on Remembrance Sunday in November 1987 a PIRA unit planted a bomb near the Enniskillen war memorial with the intention of killing parading members of the Ulster Defence Regiment. A PIRA spokesman later noted:

> The unit probably described it to the next most senior person as an attempt to kill three or four soldiers. Well, we try that several times a week, you don't need to have a meeting about it.[17]

Instead they killed 11 civilians, injured 63, and comprehensively damaged the PIRA's reputation.[18]

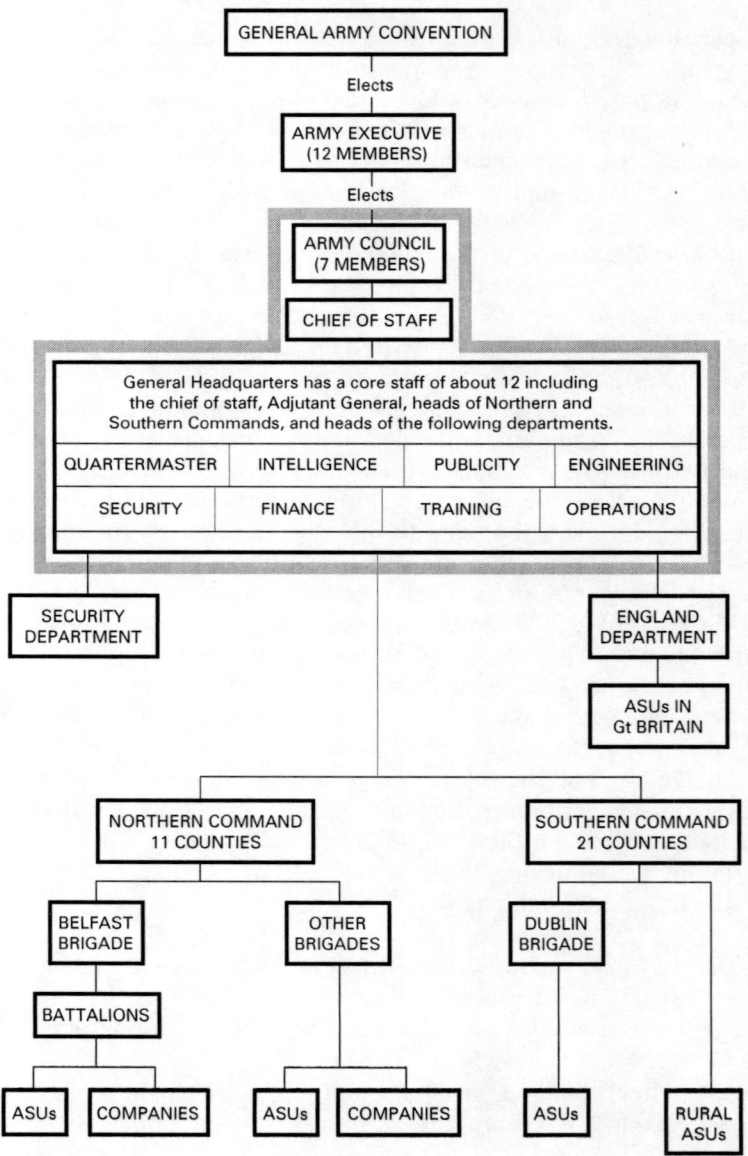

Figure 10.1 Provisional IRA command structure

Sources: M. Dillon, *The Dirty War*, 406–7. B. O'Brien, *The Long War*, 110. P. Bishop and E. Mallie, *The Provisional IRA*, 310–12. 'Behind Sinn Fein's pitch for votes...', *The Daily Telegraph*, 28 March 1997.

THE IMPACT OF CLANDESTINITY ON GROUP BEHAVIOUR

The pressures of being in a small group involved in a low-intensity conflict have been described in a study of soldiers who developed mental disorders whilst serving during the Algerian War of 1954 to 1962. Living with the constant threat of danger, in close physical proximity to each other, where individual failings could have important repercussions, caused and exacerbated tensions within the group. However, the soldiers had confidence in their leaders, and developed strong, durable friendships which led to spontaneous displays of selflessness and sacrifice. However, the morale and combativeness of the group could be broken if friends or the group leader became casualties.[19]

The degree to which the members of a terrorist group are turned in on themselves in this fashion will vary. Such introspection is not so likely in groups which can operate overtly in relatively safe havens – such as Hizbollah in the Lebanese Bekaa Valley, some of the Palestinian groups in various sponsoring countries, or conservative vigilante groups to whose activities the authorities turn a blind eye. At the other extreme, such pressures were intense for the hard-core leaders of the Red Army Faction in West Germany and members of the Red Brigades in Italy. These terrorists had to live clandestine, isolated lives in states where the degree and extent of state surveillance was high. The result appears to have been similar to that described for the soldiers in Algeria. According to the Italian Red Brigadist Adriana Faranda:

> [Clandestinity] means choosing to occupy yourself from morning till night with problems of politics, of organization, with fighting, and no longer with normal life... And when you remove yourself from society – even from the most ordinary things – when you no longer share even the most basic experiences or emotions with other people you become abstracted, removed. In the long run you actually begin to feel different – why? – because you are different.[20]

Patricia Hearst describes a similar experience when the SLA members were hiding in a house in Los Angeles.

> We were cut off from the outside world and lived in an isolated realm of our own. We had only our battery-operated radio for news.[21]

She later notes that:

> We had turned in upon ourselves in our own private worlds, and beyond ourselves we only had each other.... The atmosphere in that dirty little safehouse was overwhelmingly oppressive.[22]

In a small, cell-like organisation of this sort, the group becomes the only source of information regarding the outside world, and the sole source of security in the face of external pursuit. The group, or more likely the dominant members of the group, interprets events and ideology for the individual, determines a collective moral code, determines which targets are legitimate, and confirms the rightness of the groups' actions.

Former members of the Red Army Faction have testified to the extent to which – even before they went underground – they tended to mix only with like-minded people.[23] In such circumstances it becomes easy for judgements by the group or by individuals in the group to be affected by self-reinforcing group values rather than more generally held values. In his examination of the political socialisation of West German left-wing terrorists, Wasmund notes that individual terrorists acted as though they were absolved of responsibility for their terrorist actions by the group's ideology.[24] Even with groups such as ETA and the PIRA, whose members have links with a sympathetic community, the inevitable restrictions on the type of people they can mix with tend to reinforce the values of their group.[25]

THEORIES OF GROUP BEHAVIOUR AND TERRORIST GROUPS

There are various theories concerning the ways in which individuals interact within groups. Some of these seem to apply to the circumstances in which terrorists operate. One factor which is applicable to terrorist groups is the extent to which people are willing to conform either to authority, or to peer pressure. A number of experiments from the mid-1930s onwards have shown a fairly strong tendency for subjects to accept the judgement of their peers if they find themselves in a minority.[26] The surprising extent to which people obey those in authority – even to the extent of causing pain to others – was demonstrated by the psychologist Stanley Milgram in experiments in the early 1960s.[27]

Janis' study of decision-making in foreign policy, and the phenomenon of 'groupthink', also appears to be applicable to terrorist groups.[28] Janis defines groupthink as:

> a mode of thinking that people engage in when they are deeply involved in a cohesive in-group, when the members' striving for unanimity override their motivation to realistically appraise alternative courses of action.[29]

As a result the group overestimates its own capabilities, assumes a moral superiority relative to the enemy, closes its mind to alternatives to the agreed consensus, exerts pressure to conform upon group members, and assumes that silence on the part of group members implies consent to any decision made.[30]

This accent on conformity does seem to apply to terrorists. The Red Brigadist Adriana Faranda has noted that when one is so absorbed in a long-term commitment one accepts decisions, even if one is in a dissenting minority: 'You support the others. It's a kind of pact of obedience'.[31] Scharlau has examined the applicability of groupthink to left-wing terrorist groups in the former West Germany – in particular to the desire of the RAF leadership to escalate the level of violence following the suicide of the leaders of the RAF in Stammheim Prison in 1977. He believes that groupthink might partially explain how the leadership was able to conceive of committing acts – bomb attacks on the police – which, it turned out, the membership was not willing to endorse, and which had to be abandoned.[32]

One can also see how the Army Council of the Provisional IRA can be seen as the type of group to which groupthink could apply. The PIRA has been dominated by a small number of commanders at the level of the Army Council and Executive. Often they have known their colleagues at this level for years. Consequently decision-making is based on 'consensus, tacit agreement, like minds'.[33] Bower Bell also notes that there is an ingrained conservatism and pragmatism at the top of the organisation.[34] However, such a high degree of consensus does not appear to extend all the way through the Provisionals. It would otherwise be difficult to explain the divisions which followed the ceasefire of 1975–6.[35] Nor would it explain why the republican leadership felt it necessary to reassure the membership that the ceasefire of 1994–6 was in accordance with republican interests and was not an abandonment of the republican tradition.[36] However, the fact that the ceasefire of 1994–6 was largely observed by the Provisionals – with the permitted exception of attacks on allegedly 'anti-social' elements – demonstrates that the leadership commanded a high degree of acceptance amongst members.

The concept of 'risky shift' or 'shift to extremity' is also relevant to terrorist target selection. This is the notion that decisions made by groups tend to be more extreme than the individual preferences of group members, and are also more extreme than the average of the individual preferences of group members. A number of reasons have been attributed to this phenomenon, including the desire to conform, the desire to appear decisive, and the notion that one can afford to take riskier decisions as part of a group because one can spread responsibility if things go wrong.[37] Of interest is the fact that regular soldiers appeared more likely to take risky decisions than student reservists, who in turn took riskier decisions than other students.[38] This may be relevant because, like regular soldiers, terrorists are action-orientated. By the fact that they are willing to break the law, terrorists show that they are willing to take risks. Thus, if the concept of 'risky shift' is correct, one could expect that terrorists would take increasingly greater risks, and possibly become more reckless over time.

McKee and Franey's detailed account of a PIRA cell in London in 1974 and 1975 suggests that as time went on they were increasingly affected by a form of bravado. This ended in December 1975 when they openly carried out a gun attack from a moving car on a restaurant in the centre of London. They were chased and trapped by the police in a flat in Balcombe Street, and surrendered six days later.[39] Similarly, studies of racial attacks on immigrants in Scandinavia indicate that group members, particularly those relatively new to the group, are put under pressure by other members to carry out riskier attacks than they would do otherwise.[40]

Zawodny claims that reckless actions by the more violent or impetuous members of a group, can force the leadership to endorse such actions retrospectively for fear of losing the group's internal cohesion or even splitting the organisation.[41] Chris Hani, the head of the African National Congress' armed wing, Spear of the Nation (Umkhonto we Sizwe – MK), stated that in the 1980s he allowed bomb attacks on soft white civilian targets such as supermarkets because:

> If we don't increase our level of violence, we'll risk losing the support of young blacks in the townships.[42]

The ANC President, Oliver Tambo, also noted the difficulties of restraining the relatively untrained and embittered township youths, who increasingly made up much of MK, from attacking soft white targets.[43]

The theories of groupthink and risky shift could provide a partial explanation as to why some terrorist groups escalate their campaigns, both in the intensity of their actions and the nature of the targets which they attack. Commenting on German communist terrorist groups, Wasmund notes that a group's isolation from the rest of society, and the resultant narrowing of the channels through which reality can percolate, encourages a process by which group members encourage each other towards increasingly radical acts.[44] Those who dissent from this escalation can be isolated or threatened with expulsion. Andreas Baader, who established his leadership role in the Red Army Faction through a rather venomous and incoherent force of character, demanded conformity by threatening to expel members of the group who were not sufficiently 'tough'. Members who did not subjugate their own judgement to that of the group – for example by protesting that certain operations would endanger bystanders – were isolated by other members.[45] Having said this, an individual terrorist with a strong enough character can still defy the collective morality. When, in 1977, the RAF threatened to bomb Lufthansa passenger jets if three comrades were not released, one of their members, Hans-Joachim Klein, said that if they did this he would tell everything to the authorities. Soon afterwards Klein left the RAF.[46]

Klein's case suggests that Jenkins is correct in asserting that most terrorists operate under self-imposed moral and practical restraints, which means that they only see certain targets as legitimate.[47] He believes that left-wing terrorists tend to concentrate attacks against the personnel or institutions of the state, whilst right-wing groups carry out indiscriminate attacks in order to create a popular clamour for authoritarian government. This difference in target selection is due to ideological differences: the left-wing groups seeing themselves as acting for ordinary people, whilst right-wing terrorists see ordinary people as a disorganised mass to be manipulated through fear.[48]

Another theory which might apply to terrorist target selection, comes from the criminal psychologist, David Canter. He notes that serial murderers and rapists tend to commit their initial crimes in the vicinity of their place of residence. Later – even if they carry out their crimes away from their home area – the pattern of their attacks forms a rough circle within which their place of residence is generally located.[49] The need for a secure runback, and the desire to operate in areas with which one is more familiar, might result in similar patterns emerging with terrorist groups operating from a particular base area. It corresponds with the comment of Sean MacStiophain, PIRA Chief of Staff in the early 1970s, that PIRA members should ideally be from the locality in which they operate, so as to have a supportive environment and an intimate knowledge of the area of operations.[50] Burton also confirms that this was an important factor for PIRA members in the early 1970s.[51] On the other hand, in Northern Ireland up to the late 1970s, the security forces could often identify who was responsible for a terrorist attack by the location of the initial stages of the operation such as the hijacking of a car. Due to this the PIRA encouraged members to carry out operations away from their home area, but there is little evidence that this happened.[52]

Canter's ideas may be relevant in examining patterns of terrorism in Northern Ireland. McKeown and McKeever both note that fatalities resulting from the conflict in Northern Ireland are concentrated in particular parts of the Province.[53] McKeown demonstrates this by showing the number of deaths in areas of roughly equal population – parliamentary constituencies. This is shown in Table 10.1.

Furthermore, different types of operation seem to be more likely in some areas than in others. Those areas containing a high proportion of Catholics and a low proportion of Protestants have seen a high proportion of deaths resulting from clashes between republicans and the security forces, whilst those with a more even religious spread have a higher proportion of deaths resulting from sectarian attacks. Those areas with a high proportion of Protestants and a low proportion of Catholics have seen a relatively low level of violence overall. Thus one sees republican terrorists carrying out attacks on the security forces in relatively strongly Catholic areas such as Newry & Armagh and Belfast West, whilst sectarian attacks by both republican and loyalist terrorists are more pronounced in the Belfast North constituency.

Table 10.1 Location of fatalities across the parliamentary constituencies in Northern Ireland, July 13, 1969 to July 12, 1989.

Constituency	Armed Struggle Number	%	Sectarian Conflict Number	%	Total Number	%
N. Down	1	0.1	5	0.6	8	0.3
Strangford	18	1.2	4	0.5	23	0.8
S. Down	63	4.2	17	2.0	81	2.9
Lagan Valley	32	2.2	32	3.8	75	2.7
Upper Bann	44	3.0	50	6.0	103	3.7
Newry & Armagh	258	17.4	53	6.3	352	12.7
Fermanagh/S. Tyrone	182	12.2	35	4.2	228	8.3
Mid-Ulster	99	6.7	13	1.6	119	4.3
Foyle	235	15.8	14	1.7	275	10.0
E. Londonderry	49	3.3	8	1.0	59	2.1
N. Antrim	1	0.1	5	0.6	8	0.3
E. Antrim	18	1.2	14	1.7	24	0.9
S. Antrim	9	0.6	37	4.4	53	1.9
Belfast North	150	10.1	281	33.5	544	19.7
Belfast West	253	17.0	156	18.6	544	19.7
Belfast South	50	3.4	59	7.0	137	4.6
Belfast East	22	1.5	55	6.6	111	4.0
TOTAL	1486	100.0	838	100.1	2763	98.9

NB: Percentages rounded up or down to nearest 0.1%.
Armed Struggle category includes security force personnel and associated civilians killed by republican terrorists, republican terrorists killed by security force personnel, chance civilian fatalities, and accidental republican terrorist and security force fatalities.
Sectarian Conflict category includes Catholic civilian fatalities due to loyalist attacks, Protestant civilian fatalities due to republican attacks, and accidental or unintended Protestant victims of loyalist activities.
Source: M. McKeown, *Two Seven Six Three*, 50, 52.

The pattern also has implications for the likely location of attacks by specific terrorist units. In particular west Belfast – which has a strong concentration of Catholics in the Falls Road area and of Protestants on the Shankill Road – has a high proportion of sectarian attacks and attacks on the security forces. This suggests that terrorists on both sides tend not to operate too far from home areas to which they can quickly retreat after an operation. Thus republicans attack the security forces patrolling the Catholic areas and occasionally attack Protestant civilians in the Shankill whilst the loyalists attack Catholics in the Falls.[54] This pattern is not confined to Northern Ireland. Clark has found that the bulk of actions carried out by the Basque group ETA occur in the areas where the group receives most of its support and recruits.[55]

One should be careful here not to read too mush into apparent parallels between the actions of the serial attackers studied by Canter and the activities of all terrorists. This is particularly the case if the terrorists are prone to carry out attacks abroad – such as Palestinian groups like the PFLP and FRC – or do not have a defined territorial base – such as the Red Army Faction or Japanese Red Army. However, where the terrorist campaign is mainly concentrated in a given area, and where much of the decision-making takes place at the local level, one might see similar patterns.

SUMMARY

Terrorist groups tend to start off as informal groups, but if they survive for long they often develop a form of hierarchy. However, due to the requirements of clandestinity, decisions are often taken at the operational level by relatively small, introspective groups within the overall structure. Theories on group behaviour suggest that such groups will tend to follow an authoritative leader and will display high degrees of conformity to group decisions. This is largely borne out by experience. However, terrorists are also action-orientated and, unless strictly controlled by the leadership, may be prone to taking increasingly reckless decisions as time passes. These latter tendencies increase with the extent to which group members are isolated by clandestinity from personal opinions and judgements emanating from people outside the group. Where the terrorist campaign takes on a localised nature, as in Northern Ireland, one will find that in addition to the precepts of ideology and strategy proclaimed by the leaders of the group, decisions are likely to take into account local enmities, perceptions, and priorities.

11 Target Selection

Whilst the factors which influence terrorist target selection can be determined, it is more difficult to generalise about how they interact. This is because, despite surface similarities, each terrorist group is unique in its personnel, its ideology, and the environment within which it operates. Therefore, one must avoid creating models or theories which are so specific that, whilst they may fit some groups like a glove, are inappropriate to others.

Bearing in mind this reservation, it is still possible to construct some simple models explaining how terrorists select their targets. This process can best be seen in two stages, the process by which a target is selected, and the process by which the terrorists decide whether to proceed with an attack once they have selected a potential target. The first stage – the selection of a potential target – can best be regarded as a process by which the terrorist's freedom of action is narrowed down by the influence of various factors. Figure 11.1 shows how the dynamics behind terrorist target selection – ideology, strategy, and tactics – are constrained by these factors. The touchstone for a group's initial decisions about target selection is provided by the group's ideology. This is because the ideology lays down the initial parameters of what can be deemed acceptable behaviour by the terrorists and also enables the terrorists to judge those people who are deemed to be legitimate targets. It cannot be over-emphasised that this concept of 'legitimacy' is seen in terms of the group's beliefs and may often be far removed from what is seen as legitimate or moral behaviour by their enemies or indeed more widely. However, what it does is to set up the mental and moral framework within which the terrorists operate, and provide the terrorists with some sort of value system to which they can refer in deciding what actions they can take, or in seeking to justify them afterwards.

However, ideology does not, and indeed cannot, provide the only reference point for terrorists in selecting their targets. With the exception of some communist writers, ideologies do not generally provide political activists with a blueprint for achieving their political objectives. The decision to use terrorism is generally made in relation to the circumstances and inclination of the people involved,

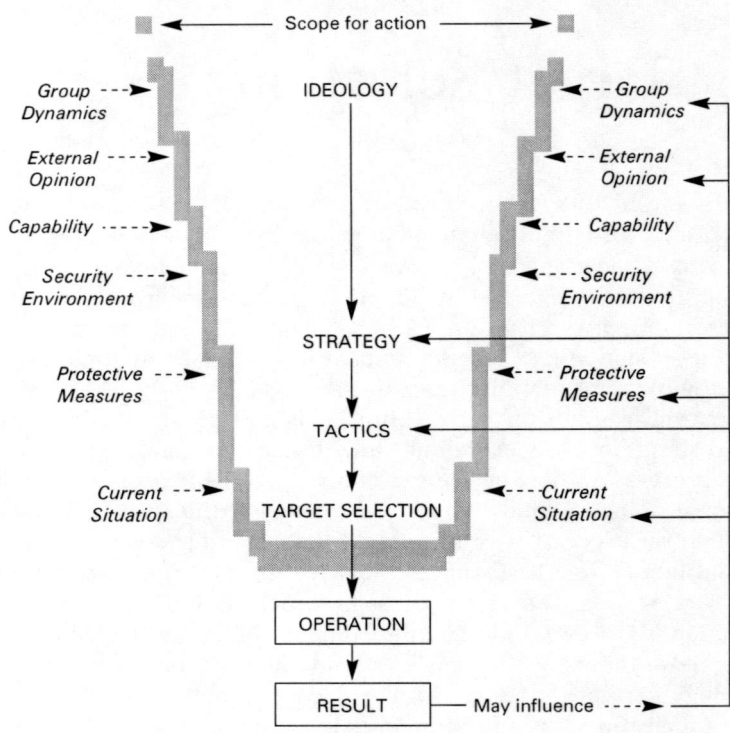

Figure 11.1 Constraints on terrorist target selection

and is rarely a necessary consequence of their ideology. Where the decision to use terrorism has been made, few groups have such a narrow range of legitimate targets or such infinite resources that they do not have to choose priorities amongst the range of legitimate targets which they could attack. The translation of political objectives into concrete actions, and hence the selection of targets is thus crucially shaped by the strategy of the group.

The strategy of the group is based on an assessment of the reactions which the terrorists wish to evoke in certain psychological targets in order to promote their political objectives. Their actions should ideally be intended to achieve strategic objectives such as advertisement, compliance, or whatever the group feels to be most appropriate, as a way of setting the ground for achieving their overall political aims. A terrorist group's strategy can be quite crude and simple. However, by determining what the terrorists wish to achieve by their use of violence, it provides a further refinement to the framework for target selection set by the group's ideology. Whilst ideology sets out the range of people and things which it is legitimate for the terrorists to attack, the strategy sets out those targets which the terrorists believe it will be beneficial for them to attack. This does not mean that the terrorists will make the right decisions in this area, and whether their strategic choices actually prove to be beneficial is a task for hindsight and historians.

However, the setting of strategy does not occur in a vacuum. Terrorists are constrained in their plans by the need for support, by their own capabilities, and by the security environment. To take the first point, terrorists generally need some support from outside the immediate confines of the group. Most terrorist groups – with the possible exception of animal rights terrorists – intend to ultimately benefit some people, whether it be an ethnic group, a social class, or some other constituency. Therefore few terrorists wish to alienate those very people whom they see themselves as helping. Furthermore, in practical terms, terrorists frequently need supporters to provide them with a potential flow of recruits, at least some of the means to get and hide weapons, and – if they have been identified and have to adopt a clandestine lifestyle – with shelter, food, and possibly documents. To retain this support, and to discourage erstwhile supporters from betraying the terrorists to their opponents or enemies, the terrorists need to ensure that their activities are not so unpopular with their supporters that they can no longer rely on their support. If the terrorists are powerful enough – for instance if they have effective control of an area – they may be able to enforce the compliance of people to their actions. However if they do not have such control, or even if they do but want active rather than enforced support, they have to tailor their actions so as to be acceptable to their supporters. If they wish to extend their support base to include potential sympathisers they must be even more selective in their attacks, but as was seen in the case of PIRA attacks on alleged criminals or against loyalist terrorists, in some cases the need to maintain the allegiance of supporters can mean carrying out attacks which may be disapproved of by neutrals. Ideally terrorists have to ensure that their actions do not needlessly repel supporters, potential sympathisers, or the uncommitted whilst still affecting the psychological target. In order to do this they must be able to justify their actions in their own ideological terms.

This particular constraint can cause problems. So far the model of target selection outlined has assumed that the strategy of a terrorist group operates within the constraints of what can be deemed as ideologically acceptable – in other words only legitimate targets are to be attacked. However, it might be the case that the terrorists concerned could gain strategic benefits by attacking a target which is not seen as being a legitimate target. For the terrorists themselves this may or may not represent a dilemma. Some terrorists may decide that attacks cannot be made against targets which do not bear some form of guilt in terms of the ideology of the terrorist group concerned, whilst others may feel that the very fact that attacking a particular target fulfils a strategic objective makes it a legitimate target. In the latter case the strategic benefits to be gained override any ideological fastidiousness. If necessary the attacks can be given some form of retrospective ideological justification. This occurred with the previously mentioned examples of the Red Brigades' killing of police bodyguards, or the RAF's killing of an American serviceman in Germany in 1985 in order to obtain his identification documents. Whilst the terrorists may attempt to justify such attacks, they can badly damage a group's support base.

The terrorists' strategic options are also circumscribed by their capabilities. Whilst the terrorists may have a long list of things which they may wish to do, they are constrained by their material resources and by the abilities of their operatives. Terrorists may make misjudgements as to their capabilities and overreach themselves, as ultimately did most of the communist terrorist groups in Europe during the 1970s and 1980s. Even at the tactical level terrorists can make serious and repeated errors of judgement – as is shown by the litany of PIRA members who have been killed by their own bombs.

Finally, the terrorists' strategy is constrained by the security environment. Initially this restricts the terrorists' freedom of action through the need to avoid police surveillance and arrest. However, if the conflict escalates it can also entail trying to survive a severe military crackdown as occurred in Uruguay and Argentina in the mid-1970s, and even to an extent in Northern Ireland at about the same time. Not only can the security environment restrict the terrorists' freedom of action, it can also result in their capability being further restricted through the loss of personnel and resources. Whilst there are opportunities for the terrorists to provoke the security forces into brutal actions which alienate the public – assuming that the security forces do not carry out such actions of their own accord – the constraints placed by their activities are far greater. For this reason the security forces are often made a terrorist target. Thus the strategic options of the terrorists are affected, and mainly restricted, by factors which in turn restrict their targeting options.

Such restrictions continue at the tactical level. The successful execution of the various types of operation outlined in the chapter on tactics is initially constrained by factors such as the capability of the group and the acceptability of certain methods. In addition to these restraints, terrorists are also constrained by the various protective measures which may be taken to defend specific targets. In the extremely unlikely event that they had only selected one specific target for their operations the effect of this may be to discourage the terrorists from carrying out any attacks. On the other hand, on the basis of strategic judgement or sheer bloody-mindedness, they may feel that despite the risks inherent in an operation, the strategic benefits – such as advertisement of their cause – to be obtained from attacking the target using the planned methods are great enough to make it worthwhile persevering.

Alternatively, as shown in Figure 11.2, if the protective measures surrounding the terrorists' initial target are too difficult to surmount using the tactics originally envisaged, the terrorists can either use a different method to attack the same target, or substitute an alternative target. The former course may be taken where the strategic benefits of attacking that particular target – such as the propaganda benefits, or the pressure put on the psychological target – are felt to be great enough to justify the increased difficulty of persisting with the attack. However, where there are a number of potential targets, attacking any of which would yield a roughly equivalent strategic benefit, there is a likelihood that the terrorists will choose to attack the softest target, as carrying out such an attack represents the least risk to the terrorists. Indeed, terrorists wary of taking too many risks may be willing to attack softer targets even if they yield lower strategic benefits than targets which are harder, on the basis that it is necessary to conserve resources for future operations. Thus a long-term strategic perspective may override the benefits which an attack may gain in the shorter term.

From the above factors it is possible to construct a general model of terrorist target selection. Firstly, the general moral framework within which terrorist activities will take place is provided by the

180 Terrorists' Target Selection

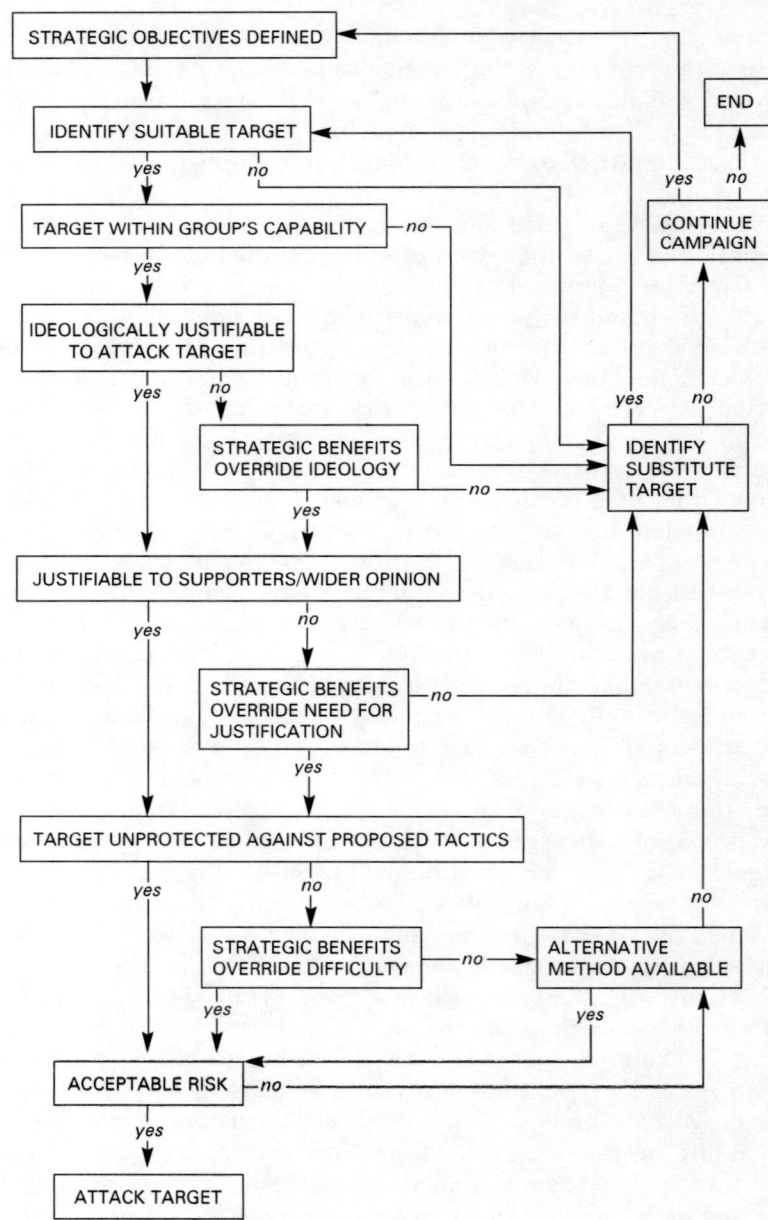

Figure 11.2 Process of terrorist target selection

ideology of the group. On the whole terrorists will tend to attack those people or institutions which they deem to be somehow guilty – or at least not innocent – of an offence in the terms of the terrorists' ideological and moral outlook.

The range of targets is refined by the strategy of the group concerned. This is important because by its nature, terrorism is a method which – with the exception of expressive attacks – is intended to yield certain benefits by causing people to react to violence or the threat of violence. Unlike conventional warfare where the destruction of the enemy may be an end in itself, a successful terrorist operation is one which, whilst it may result in the destruction of a physical target, is primarily intended to force a psychological target to react in a certain way. Thus the terrorists will generally select physical targets so as to cause the desired reaction in the psychological target. This may occasionally result in the terrorists stepping outside their proclaimed ideological framework when they perceive that the strategic benefits to be gained from such an attack are important enough to justify such action. However the terrorists also have to take into account the possibility that such attacks may damage their standing amongst supporters, with concrete consequences in terms of the loss of facilities and the possibility of betrayal.

Once the terrorists have determined the range of targets which they may legitimately attack, and have determined those which will best fulfil their strategic objectives, they are faced with a number of restrictions in terms of the group's capability, the security environment, and the protective measures taken to safeguard specific targets. The terrorists' ability to overcome or circumvent these constraints will strongly determine whether they attack their targets of choice, or whether they substitute other targets in their stead. Where the benefits from attacking any one of a range of targets are roughly equivalent, it is likely, though not certain, that they will attack the most vulnerable. Once the terrorists' ideological and strategic framework has been determined, and they have decided upon a range of legitimate targets, the options which they face are as outlined in Figure 11.2.

However, any attempt to predict terrorists' actions must be severely qualified. It must always be borne in mind that terrorists are as likely as other people to make curious decisions, misjudgements, and decisions influenced by emotional rather than logical factors. Due to the pressures caused by the danger and clandestinity under which terrorists operate, there is a possibility that, over time, they will become more blinkered and introspective, and quite possibly escalate their violence and become more reckless in their actions. The more isolated terrorists become from the world outside, the more likely it is that escalation and recklessness will occur.

Notes

1 INTRODUCTION

1. B. M. Jenkins, *International Terrorism: A New Kind of Warfare* (Santa Monica, CA: RAND Corporation, June 1974), 4–7. B. M. Jenkins, *International Terrorism: The Other World War* (Santa Monica, CA: RAND Corporation, November 1985), 9–11. M. Crenshaw Hutchinson, *Revolutionary Terrorism: The FLN in Algeria, 1954–1962* (Stanford, CA: Hoover Institution Press, 1978), 36–8, 137. J. Wright, *Terrorist Propaganda: The Red Army Faction and the Provisional IRA, 1968–1986* (London: Macmillan, 1991), 77.
2. M. Crenshaw Hutchinson, *Revolutionary Terrorism*, 20. For a list of definitions see A. P. Schmid & A. J. Jongman, *Political Terrorism: A new guide to actors, authors, concepts, data bases, theories, and literature* (Amsterdam: North-Holland Publishing, 1988), 32–8.
3. M. Crenshaw Hutchinson, *Revolutionary Terrorism*, 21.
4. C. Gearty, *Terror* (London: Faber & Faber, 1991; 1992), 151–2. R. P. Clark, *The Basque Insurgents: ETA, 1952–1980* (Madison, WI: University of Wisconsin Press, 1984), xv–xvi.
5. US Department of State, Bureau of Public Affairs, *Libya under Qadhafi: A Pattern of Aggression*, Special Report No. 138 (Washington, DC: U.S. Dept of State, January 1986), 1. R. Gillespie, *Soldiers of Peron: Argentina's Montoneros* (Oxford: Oxford University Press, 1982), 244–52. J. Burns, *The Land That Lost Its Heroes: Argentina, The Falklands and Alfonsín* (London: Bloomsbury, 1987), 20–3.
6. E. S. Herman, *The Real Terror Network: Terrorism in Fact and Propaganda* (Montreal: Black Rose Books, 1985), 21–5. E. S. Herman & G. O'Sullivan, *The Terrorism Industry: The Experts and Institutions That Shape Our View of Terror* (New York: Pantheon, 1989), xii, 45–7, 152, 157. E. S. Herman & G. O'Sullivan, "Terrorism" as Ideology and Cultural Industry', and A. George, 'The Discipline of Terrorology', in A. George (ed.), *Western State Terrorism* (Cambridge: Polity Press, 1991), 39–40, 57–62, 68–9, 77, 92–3.
7. 'Gonzalez drawn into "death squad" scandal', *The Independent*, 10 December 1988. '"Dirty war" scandal worsens', *The Independent*, 21 December 1994. 'Madrid sues over "dirty war" claims', *The Independent*, 11 January 1995. 'The noose is tightened around Felipe's neck', *The Guardian*, 23 February 1995. P. Taylor, *States of Terror: Democracy and Political Violence* (London: BBC Books, 1993), 98–104. M. S. Diokno, '"Guardians of Democracy": Vigilantes in the Philippines', and J. Caceres, 'Violence, National Security and Democratisation in Central America', in M. Kirkwood (ed.), *States of Terror: Death Squads or Development?* (London: Catholic Institute for International Relations, 1989), 48–53, 105–7.

8. M. J. Akbar, *India: The Siege Within* (Harmondsworth: Penguin, 1985), 189. M. Tully & S. Jacob, *Amritsar: Mrs Gandhi's Last Battle* (London: Jonathan Cape, 1985), 57–61, 105, 121. B. Vaughn, 'The Use and Abuse of Intelligence Services in India', *Intelligence and National Security*, 8, no. 1 (January 1993).
9. J. Schmeidel, 'My Enemy's Enemy: Twenty Years of Co-operation between West Germany's Red Army Faction and the GDR Ministry for State Security', *Intelligence and National Security*, 8, no. 4 (October 1993). B. A. Scharlau, *Left-Wing Terrorism in the Federal Republic of Germany*, Ph.D., University of St Andrews, 1991, 56–61. 'East was haven to German terrorists', *The Times*, 15 June 1990. 'More German terror suspects seized', *The Independent*, 16 June 1990. 'Arrests expose E. Germany's terrorist links', *The Independent*, 20 June 1990.
10. C. Seton-Watson, 'Terrorism in Italy', in J. Lodge (ed.), *The Threat of Terrorism* (Brighton: Wheatsheaf, 1988), 92–3, 105–6. M. Bull, 'Villains of the Peace: Terrorism and the Secret Services in Italy', *Intelligence and National Security*, 7, no. 4 (October 1992). 'Italians blame shadowy powers for bringing terror to Florence', *The Independent on Sunday*, 30 May 1993. The underlying thesis in P. Willan, *Puppet Masters: The Political Use of Terrorism in Italy* (London: Constable, 1991), is that many right-wing terrorist groups in Italy were manipulated and directed to a degree by the Italian secret services.
11. US Department of State, *Patterns of Global Terrorism: 1989* (Washington, DC: Government Printing Office, April 1990), 6. US Department of State, *Patterns of Global Terrorism: 1990* (Washington, DC: Government Printing Office, April 1991), 40.
12. D. Moss, *The Politics of Left-Wing Violence in Italy, 1969–1985* (London: Macmillan, 1989), 2. V. S. Pisano, *The Dynamics of Subversion and Violence in Contemporary Italy* (Stanford, CA: Hoover Institution Press, 1987), 38, 51. J. Pearce, *Colombia: Inside the Labyrinth* (London: Latin American Bureau, 1990), 7, 195.

2 TERRORIST TYPOLOGIES

1. B. M. Jenkins, *The Lessons of Beirut: Testimony before the Long Commission* (Santa Monica, CA: RAND Corporation, February 1984), 2.
2. 'Rajiv Gandhi assassinated in bomb blast', *The Times*, 22 May 1991. 'Rajiv Gandhi murdered by bombers at election rally', *The Independent*, 22 May 1991. 'What One-Eyed Jack knows', *The Independent*, 1 July 1991.
3. P. Wilkinson, 'Designing an Effective International Aviation Security System', *Terrorism and Political Violence*, 5, no. 2 (Summer 1993), 105. E. F. Mickolus, T. Sandler, J. M. Murdock, *International Terrorism in the 1980s: A Chronology of Events. Volume II, 1984–1987* (Ames, IA: Iowa State University, 1989), 376–8. S. Emerson & B. Duffy, *The Fall of Pan Am 103* (London: Futura, 1990), 199–200.
4. 'Murdered RUC man's body found', *The Independent*, 14 September 1990. 'IRA admits shooting of sergeant', *The Times*, 19 September

1990. B. O'Brien, *The Long War: The IRA and Sinn Fein, 1985 to Today* (Dublin: O'Brien Press, 1993), 207.

5. Sunday Times Insight Team, *Siege: Prince's Gate, London, April 30–May 5, 1980* (Feltham: Hamlyn, 1980), 31, 45, 52, 61–2. E. F. Mickolus, T. Sandler, J. M. Murdock, *International Terrorism in the 1980s: A Chronology of Events. Volume I, 1980–1983* (Ames, IA: Iowa State University, 1989), 40–2. P. Schlesinger, *Media, State and Nation: Political Violence and Collective Identities* (London: Sage, 1991), 31.
6. G. McKee & R. Franey, *Time Bomb* (London: Bloomsbury, 1988), 326–47.
7. P. Snow & D. Phillips, *Leila's Hijack War: The True Story of 25 Days in September 1970* (London: Pan, 1970). G. Rosie, *The Directory of International Terrorism* (Edinburgh: Mainstream Publishing, 1986), 94–6. G. Chaliand, *The Palestinian Resistance* (Harmondsworth: Penguin, 1972), 167.
8. 'Incendiary devices increasingly used in terror attacks', *The Independent*, 2 December 1991. 'IRA switch tactics with store firebombs, disruption of rail commuters and mortar attack on Downing Street', *The Guardian*, 11 January 1992. 'IRA claims responsibility for planting firebombs', *The Independent*, 2 September 1991. 'Mainland attacks admitted by IRA', *The Times*, 2 September 1991.
9. P. Bishop & E. Mallie, *The Provisional IRA* (London: Heinemann, 1987; Corgi, 1988), 336–7. W. D. Flackes & S. Elliott, *Northern Ireland: A Political Directory 1968–93* (Belfast: Blackstaff, 1994), 15. K. J. Kelley, *The Longest War: Northern Ireland and the IRA* (London: Zed Books, 1988), 228–9.
10. 'Insured loss may hit £150m', *Lloyd's List*, 12 February 1996.
11. 'London counts the cost of IRA bombs', *The Independent*, 13 April 1992. 'Back-to-work City defies the IRA', *The Times*, 13 April 1992. 'City bomb claims may reach £1bn', *The Independent*, 14 April 1992. 'Troubles chronology: Apr. 10', *Fortnight*, May 1992. 'IRA City bombers identified by police', *The Independent*, 15 July 1992. 'Cost will exhaust pool of insurance money', *The Independent*, 26 April 1993. 'One bomb: £1bn devastation', *The Independent on Sunday*, 24 April 1993. 'Taxpayers foot IRA bomb bill', *The Times*, 26 April 1993. 'Security to be stepped up in City after blast', 'Toll of injured rises to 51', both in *The Independent*, 26 April 1993.
12. A. Jamieson, *The Heart Attacked: Terrorism and Conflict in the Italian State* (London: Marion Boyars, 1989), 108–15. J. Agirre, *Operation Ogro: The Execution of Admiral Luis Carrero Blanco* (New York: Quadrangle, 1975).
13. The identity of the group responsible for the Bologna bombing has not been conclusively established. Four members of a fascist group were convicted of carrying out the bombing in 1988, but their convictions were overturned on appeal in 1990. C. Seton-Watson, 'Terrorism in Italy', 94. P. Willan, *Puppet Masters*, 13–14, 160–7, 170–3. S. Christie, *Stefano Delle Chiaie: Portrait of a Black Terrorist* (London: Anarchy Magazine/Refract Publications, 1984), 25, 109, 113. G. Harris, *The Dark Side of Europe: The Extreme Right Today*, new edition (Edinburgh:

Edinburgh University Press, 1994), 115, 118. C. Schaerf, G. de Lutiis, A. Silj, F. Carlucci, F. Bellucci, S. Argentini, *Venti Anni di Violenza in Italia: 1969–1988*, two volumes (Rome: ISODARCO, n.d.), 866.
14. M. Dillon & D. Lehane, *Political Murder in Northern Ireland* (Harmondsworth: Penguin, 1973), 29–35. M. Dillon, *The Shankill Butchers* (London: Hutchinson, 1989; Arrow, 1990). S. Bruce, *The Red Hand: Protestant Paramilitaries in Northern Ireland* (Oxford: Oxford University Press, 1992), 14, 173–81.
15. R. Hill & A. Bell, *The Other Face of Terror: Inside Europe's Neo-Nazi Network* (London: Grafton, 1988), 152, 153–4, 211. The question as to whether some of the more random attacks should be regarded as acts of terrorism is discussed in T. Bjorgo, 'Terrorist Violence against Immigrants and Refugees in Scandinavia: Patterns and Motives', in T. Bjorgo & R. Witte, *Racist Violence in Europe* (London: Macmillan, 1993), 34–8.
16. M. Crenshaw Hutchinson, *Revolutionary Terrorism*, xv.
17. A. P. Schmid & A. J. Jongman, *Political Terrorism*, 160.
18. M. Crenshaw Hutchinson, *Revolutionary Terrorism*, 142. J. Bowyer Bell, *IRA Tactics and Targets: An Analysis of Tactical Aspects of the Armed Struggle, 1969–1989* (Swords: Poolbeg, 1990), 27, 48, 111–12, 115.
19. K. J. Kelley, *The Longest War*, 306.
20. C. L. Irvin, 'Terrorists' Perspectives: Interviews', in D. L. Paletz & A. P. Schmid (eds), *Terrorism and the Media* (Newbury Park, CA: Sage, 1992), 78–9.
21. D. Breen, *My Fight for Irish Freedom*, revised and enlarged edition (Dublin: Anvil, 1964), 84.
22. P. Gurney, *Braver Men Walk Away* (London: HarperCollins, 1993), 213.
23. S. Segaller, *Invisible Armies: Terrorism into the 1990s*, revised edition (London: Sphere Books, 1987), 100. E. MacDonald, *Shoot the Women First* (Fourth Estate, 1991; London: Arrow, 1992), 14–15, 22, 33. J. Bowyer Bell, *IRA Tactics and Targets*, 29. G. Adams, *The Politics of Irish Freedom* (Dingle: Brandon, 1986), 121. 'IRA switch to mortar and landmine campaign', *The Guardian*, 16 March 1985. 'What's on the agenda now is an end to partition', *The Irish Times*, 10 December 1986. 'IRA rings changes to restore balance of terror', *The Guardian*, 5 May 1987.
24. A. Jamieson, *The Heart Attacked*, 86. V. S. Pisano, *The Dynamics of Subversion and Violence in Contemporary Italy*, 157. C. Schaerf et al., *Venti Anni di Violenza in Italia*, 414.
25. S. Cronin, *Irish Nationalism: A History of its Roots and Ideology* (Dublin: The Academy Press, 1980), 348. R. Fagilot, *Britain's Military Strategy in Ireland: The Kitson Experiment* (London: Zed Books, 1983), 233.
26. T. P. Coogan, *Michael Collins: A Biography* (London: Hutchinson, 1990), 78.
27. 'Derry Brigade Warning to RUC Secret Police', *Republican News*, 12 February 1977. C. Ryder, *The RUC: A Force Under Fire* (London: Methuen, 1989), 172. 'SAS Captain Executed', *Republican News*, 21 May 1977. M. Dillon, *The Dirty War* (London: Hutchinson, 1990; Arrow, 1991), 161–87. M. Urban, *Big Boys' Rules: The Secret Struggle*

against the IRA (London: Faber & Faber, 1992), 53–7. F. Holroyd & N. Burbridge, *War Without Honour* (Hull: Medium, 1989), 47, 55, 74–8.
28. 'Damage in huge blast put at £20m', *The Independent*, 25 September 1992. 'Court laboratory bombed by IRA', *The Times*, 25 September 1992. 'Brits haven't a clue', 'War News: Lab Flattened', 'IRA strikes at Diplock system's heart', *An Phoblacht/Republican News* (hereafter *AP/RN*), 1 October 1992. '"Troubles" chronology: Wed Sep 23', *Fortnight*, no. 311 (November 1992), 34.
29. S. Aust, *The Baader-Meinhof Group: The Inside Story of a Phenomenon* (Hamburg: Hoffman & Campe Verlag, 1985; London: Bodley Head, 1987), 115, 116. J. Becker, *Hitler's Children: The Story of the Baader-Meinhof Gang* (London: Granada, 1978), 234–6.
30. W. Laqueur, *The Age of Terrorism* (London: Weidenfeld & Nicolson, 1987), 112.
31. C. Marighela, 'Handbook of Urban Guerrilla Warfare', 'Guerrilla Tactics and Operations', in C. Marighela, *For the Liberation of Brazil* (Harmondsworth: Penguin, 1971), 72, 81, 111–12.
32. 'IRA suspected as raiders get away with £2m', *The Independent*, 8 January 1992. 'Brooke going soft on IRA says bishop', *The Times*, 8 January 1992. 'IRA fund-raising blamed for surge in Irish robberies', *The Independent*, 22 May 1990. P. Bishop & E. Mallie, *The Provisional IRA*, 194, 223, 391. W. Laqueur, *The Age of Terrorism*, 97. J. Adams, *The Financing of Terror* (London: New English Library, 1986; 1988), 117–20. A. Horne, *A Savage War of Peace: Algeria 1954–1962* (London: Macmillan, 1977; Harmondsworth: Penguin, 1979), 553.
33. 'Raiders target the country post offices', *The Independent*, 17 March 1992.
34. R. Gillespie, *Soldiers of Peron*, 180–2. R. Clutterbuck, *Kidnap, Hijack and Extortion* (London: Macmillan, 1987), 157–8.
35. M. Bles & R. Low, *The Kidnap Business* (1987; London: Star, 1988), 198–9.
36. R. P. Clark, *The Basque Insurgents*, 227–8. E. MacDonald, *Shoot the Women First*, 33. M. Bles & R. Low, *The Kidnap Business*, 200–14.
37. R. P. Clark, *The Basque Insurgents*, 227–8.
38. A. Labrousse, *The Tupamaros: Urban Guerrillas in Uruguay* (Paris: Editions du Seuil, 1970; Harmondsworth: Penguin, 1973), 100, 127. D. Ronfeldt, *The Mitrione Kidnapping in Uruguay* (Santa Monica, CA: RAND Corporation, 1987), 6–7, 29. For more detail of one of these kidnappings from the perspective of the victim see G. Jackson, *People's Prison*, (Faber & Faber, 1973; Newton Abbot: Reader's Union, 1974).
39. 'Drug barons threaten to kill hostages', *The Independent*, 1 November 1990.
40. J. T. Choi, *Acts of violence against civil aviation: historical survey, perspectives and responses*, Ph.D., University of St Andrews, 1992, 206–43. E. F. Mickolus, T. Sandler, J. M. Murdock, *International Terrorism in the 1980s, 1984–1987*, 219–25. G. Rosie, *The Directory of International Terrorism*, 280.
41. E. F. Mickolus, T. Sandler, J. M. Murdock, *International Terrorism in the 1980s: 1980–1983*, 468–9.

42. A. Iyad & E. Rouleau, *My Home My Land: A Narrative of the Palestinian Struggle* (Paris: Fayolle, 1978; New York: Times Books, 1981), 106, 112–13.
43. G. Woodcock, *Anarchism: A History of Libertarian Ideas and Movements* (USA: The World Publishing Company, 1962; Harmondsworth: Penguin, 1975), 286–95. J. Joll, *The Anarchists*, second edition (London: Methuen, 1979), 113–19. D. Miller, *Anarchism* (London: J. M. Dent & Sons, 1984), 111–12.
44. G. Woodcock, *Anarchism*, 292. J. Joll, *The Anarchists*, 113.
45. J. Joll, *The Anarchists*, 118.
46. P. A. Lupsha, 'Explanation of Political Violence: Some Psychological Theories Versus Indignation', *Politics and Society*, 2, no. 1 (Fall 1971).
47. P. A. Lupsha, 'Explanation of Political Violence', 102.
48. A. Merari, 'Terrorism as a Strategy of Insurgency', *Terrorism and Political Violence*, 5, no. 4 (Winter 1993), 237.
49. K. Tololyan, 'Martyrdom as Legitimacy: Terrorism, Religion and Symbolic Appropriation in the Armenian Diaspora', P. Wilkinson & A. M. Stewart (eds), *Contemporary Research on Terrorism*, (Aberdeen: Aberdeen University Press, 1987; 1989), 93. W. Laqueur, *The Age of Terrorism*, 227. J. E. Vorbach, 'Monte Melkonian: Armenian Revolutionary Leader', *Terrorism and Political Violence*, 6, no. 2 (Summer 1994), 178.
50. 'Terrorists kill India's former army chief', *Far Eastern Economic Review*, 21 August 1986. 'Vaidya killers hanged', *The Hindu: International*, 17 October 1992. M. Tully & S. Jacob, *Amritsar*, 155–91. M. J. Akbar, *India: The Siege Within*, 201–5.

3 IDEOLOGY

1. W. A. Rosenbaum, *Political Culture* (London: Nelson, 1975), 120.
2. M. Kramer, 'Sacrifice and Fratricide in Shiite Lebanon', *Terrorism and Political Violence*, 3, no. 3 (Autumn 1991), 32–3. K. Tololyan, 'Cultural Narrative and the Motivation of the Terrorist', in D. C. Rapoport (ed.), *Inside Terrorist Organizations* (London: Frank Cass, 1988), 221. A. T. Q. Stewart, *The Narrow Ground: The Roots of Conflict in Ulster*, revised edition (London: Faber, 1989), 180–1. J. Darby. 'The Historical Background', in J. Darby (ed.), *Northern Ireland: The Background to the Conflict* (Belfast: Appletree Press, 1983), 15.
3. R. Hill & A. Bell, *The Other Face of Terror*, 95, 121–2, 125, 157, 169. Searchlight, *From Ballots to Bombs: The Inside Story of the National Front's Political Soldiers* (London: Searchlight, after 1989), 16–19. C. di Giovanni, *Light from Behind the Bars: Letters from the Red Brigades and Other Former Italian Terrorists; True Stories of Terror, Agony and Hope* (Slough: St Paul Publications, 1990), 95, 99–100.
4. For a selection see J. Hutchinson & A. D. Smith (eds), *Nationalism* (Oxford: Oxford University Press, 1994). M. Williams (ed.), *International Relations in the Twentieth Century: A Reader* (Basingstoke:

Macmillan, 1989), 42–77. E. J. Hobsbawm, *Nations and Nationalism since 1780: Programme, Myth, Reality*, second edition (Cambridge: Cambridge University Press, 1992). A. D. Smith, *National Identity* (Harmondsworth: Penguin, 1991).
5. A. D. Smith, *National Identity*, 73.
6. F. Llera, J. M. Mata & C. L. Irwin, 'ETA: From Secret Army to Social Movement – The Post-Franco Schism of the Basque Nationalist Movement', *Terrorism and Political Violence*, 5, no. 3 (Autumn 1993), 106. G. Samaranayake, 'Ethnic Conflict in Sri Lanka and Prospects of Management: An Empirical Inquiry', *Terrorism and Political Violence*, 3, no. 2 (Summer 1991), 80.
7. G. Grivas – Dighenis. *Guerrilla Warfare and EOKA's Struggle* (London: Longmans, 1964), 91–2. M. Dillon, *The Dirty War*, 482.
8. 'Algerian dissident seeks UK asylum', *The Independent*, 6 August 1994. M. Crenshaw, 'Political Violence in Algeria', *Terrorism and Political Violence*, 6, no. 3 (Autumn 1994), 265, 269–72, 273. M. Kramer, 'Hizbullah: The Calculus of Jihad', in M. E. Marty & R. S. Appleby (eds), *Fundamentalisms and the State* (Chicago: University of Chicago Press, 1993). E. Sprinzak, 'From Messianic Pioneering to Vigilante Terrorism: The Case of the Gush Emunim Underground', in D. C. Rapoport (ed.), *Inside Terrorist Organizations*.
9. M. Barkun, 'Millenarian Aspects of "White Supremacist" Movements', *Terrorism and Political Violence*, 1, no. 4 (October 1989), 410.
10. M. Barkun, 'Millenarian Groups and Law Enforcement Agencies: The Lessons of Waco', *Terrorism and Political Violence*, 6, no. 1 (Spring 1994), 93.
11. D. Robertson, *The Penguin Dictionary of Politics* (Harmondsworth: Penguin, 1986), 187–8.
12. E. Crankshaw, *The Shadow of the Winter Palace: The Drift to Revolution, 1825–1917* (London: Macmillan, 1976; Harmondsworth: Penguin, 1981), 303–5. Z. Ivianski, 'Fathers and Sons: A Study of Jewish Involvement in the Revolutionary Movement and Terrorism in Tsarist Russia', *Terrorism and Political Violence*, 1, no. 2 (April 1989), 145. B. Savinkov, *Memoirs of a Terrorist* (Millwood, NY: Kraus Reprint, 1972), 175, 195. P. Wilkinson, *Political Terrorism* (London: Macmillan, 1974), 65. W. Laqueur, *The Age of Terrorism*, 38–41.
13. H. Holland, *The Struggle: A History of the African National Congress* (London: Grafton, 1989), 99, 213–14. H. W. Degenhardt (ed.), *Revolutionary and Dissident Movements: An International Guide* (Harlow: Longmans, 1988), 327–8.
14. A. P. Schmid & A. J. Jongman, *Political Terrorism*, 655–6. H. Holland, *The Struggle*, 129, 132, 138–41, 205–6.
15. G. Woodcock, 'Anarchism: A Historical Introduction', in G. Woodcock (ed.), *The Anarchist Reader* (Glasgow: Fontana/Collins, 1977), 13–14.
16. D. Robertson, *The Penguin Dictionary of Politics*, 7–8. G. Woodcock, 'Anarchism: A Historical Introduction', 21–7.
17. G. Woodcock, *Anarchism*, 286–95. J. Joll, *The Anarchists*, 130–8. D. Miller, *Anarchism*, 111–12. G. Carr, *The Angry Brigade: The Cause*

and the Case (London: Victor Gollancz, 1975). Angry Brigade, *The Angry Brigade, 1967–1984: Documents and Chronology* (Bratach Dubh Anarchist Pamphlets, 1978; London: Elephant Editions, 1985).
18. K. Marx & F. Engels, *The Communist Manifesto* (Harmondsworth: Penguin, 1967), 79–94. V. I. Lenin, *What is to be Done? Burning Questions of our Movement* (Stuttgart: Dietz, 1902; Moscow: Progress Publishers, 1947), 31, 37–43, 115–17, 125–6.
19. Mao Tse-tung, *Selected Works of Mao Tse-tung*, 3 volumes (Peking: Foreign Languages Press, 1965). Mao Tse-tung, *Basic Tactics* (New York: Praeger, 1966). C. Guevara, *Guerrilla Warfare* (New York: Praeger, 1961; Harmondsworth: Penguin, 1969). C. Marighela, *For the Liberation of Brazil*.
20. D. Robertson, *The Penguin Dictionary of Politics*, 65. R. Scruton, *The Meaning of Conservatism* (Harmondsworth: Penguin, 1980), 21. N. K. O'Sullivan, *Conservatism* (New York: St. Martin's Press, 1976), 9. R. Kirk (ed.), *The Portable Conservative Reader* (Harmondsworth: Penguin, 1982), xv–xviii.
21. A. Horne, *A Savage War of Peace*, 30–2, 441, 488. P. Henissart, *Wolves in the City: The Death of French Algeria* (London: Rupert Hart-Davis, 1971), 21, 243, 316.
22. D. L. G. Hall, *The Ulster Defence Association: A Case of Change and Continuity*, M. Social. Sc., Queen's University, Belfast, 1988. S. Bruce, *The Red Hand*. S. Nelson, *Ulster's Uncertain Defenders: Loyalists and the Northern Ireland Conflict* (Belfast: Appletree Press, 1984).
23. 'King Coke', *The Independent*, 21 July 1990. 'In Medellin, walls do not a prison make', *The Independent*, 8 August 1992. J. Pearce, *Colombia: Inside the Labyrinth*, 1, 177–8, 247. A. M. Bravo, 'Frontier culture takes to cocaine', in M. L. Smith (ed.), *Why People Grow Drugs: Narcotics and Development in the Third World* (London: Panos, 1992), 75. C. Watson, 'Guerrilla Groups in Colombia: Reconstituting the Political Process', *Terrorism and Political Violence*, 4, no. 2 (Summer 1992), 95–6.
24. H. J. Rosenbaum & P. C. Sederberg, 'Vigilantism', *Comparative Politics*, 6, no. 4 (1974), 542.
25. A. P. Schmid & A. J. Jongman, *Political Terrorism*, 46.
26. H. J. Rosenbaum & P. C. Sederberg, 'Vigilantism', 542.
27. G. Harris, *The Dark Side of Europe*, 17.
28. A. Hitler, *Mein Kampf* (London: Pimlico, 1992), 258–63, 363–9, 512. Z. Sternhell, 'Fascist Ideology', in W. Laqueur (ed.), *Fascism: A Reader's Guide; Analyses, Interpretations, Bibliography* (Wildwood House, 1976; Harmondsworth: Penguin, 1979), 328.
29. A. Hitler, *Mein Kampf*, 73–5, 165, 308, 341–2, 408–10. P. Wilkinson, *The New Fascists*, revised edition (Grant McIntyre, 1981; London: Pan, 1983), 9–10. G. Harris, *The Dark Side of Europe*, 17. D. Mack Smith, *Mussolini* (London: Weidenfeld & Nicolson, 1981; Granada, 1983), 218–19, 235. R. Drake, *The Revolutionary Mystique and Terrorism in Contemporary Italy* (Bloomington, IN: Indiana University Press, 1989), 3.
30. D. Mack Smith, *Mussolini*, 115, 216, 289. T. Sheehan, 'Myth and Violence: The Fascism of Julius Evola and Alain de Benoist', *Social Re-*

search, 48 (Spring 1981), 57–8. R. Drake, *The Revolutionary Mystique and Terrorism in Contemporary Italy*, 119, 129, 130. N. H. Jones, *Hitler's Heralds: The Story of the Freikorps, 1918–1923* (London: John Murray, 1987), 105, 111.

31. G. Harris, *The Dark Side of Europe*, 17, 28–31, 223. R. Drake, 'Julius Evola and the Ideological Origins of the Radical Right in Contemporary Italy', in P. H. Merkl (ed.), *Political Violence and Terror*, 76–7. R. Drake, *The Revolutionary Mystique and Terrorism in Contemporary Italy*, 120, 124, 128–9.

32. P. Willan, *Puppet Masters*, 43. S. Christie, *Stefano Delle Chiaie*, 18–19. H. J. Horchem, 'Terrorism in Western Europe', in R. Clutterbuck (ed.), *The Future of Political Violence: Destabilization, Disorder and Terrorism* (London: Macmillan, 1986), 152–3. G. Harris, *The Dark Side of Europe*, 107–42. B. Hoffman, *Right-Wing Terrorism in West Germany* (Santa Monica, CA: RAND Corporation, 1986), 3–4. T. Bjorgo & R. Witte (eds), *Racist Violence in Europe*, passim.

33. M. Barkun, 'Millenarian Aspects of "White Supremacist" Movements', 416–17, 430. J. Kaplan, 'The Context of American Millenarian Revolutionary Theology: The Case of the "Identity Christian" Church of Israel', *Terrorism and Political Violence*, 5, no. 1 (Spring 1993), 34, 46, 65n.28.

34. 'Militiamen go to war on American gun laws', *The Daily Telegraph*, 21 November 1994. 'Militias gird loins for the great battle', *The Guardian*, 22 April 1995. 'A holy war, home grown in America', *The Sunday Telegraph*, 23 April 1995. 'With God and gun, rugged individualism turns to hate', *The Sunday Times*, 23 April 1995. 'The Enemy Within', *The Observer*, 23 April 1995. 'FBI puzzles over "Gestapo" train wreckers', *The Independent*, 11 October 1995. 'Militia muscles in on town', *The Guardian*, 14 November 1995. 'War on the range', *The Guardian*, 22 November 1995. 'Two arrested over US tax office bomb', *The Daily Telegraph*, 29 December 1995. 'Tax grudge clue in Reno bomb plot', *The Independent*, 30 December 1995. M. Barkun, 'Millenarian Aspects of "White Supremacist" Movements', 414, 423, 428, 429. J. Kaplan, 'The Context of American Millenarian Revolutionary Theology', 38, 42, 49.

35. P. Singer, *Animal Liberation: A New Ethics For Our Treatment of Animals* (New York: Avon, 1977), 1–26. P. Singer, *The Animal Liberation Movement: It's Philosophy, Its Achievements, and Its Future* (Nottingham: Old Hammond Press, no date), 5–10. F. Ginsburg, 'Saving America's Souls: Operation Rescue's Crusade against Abortion', in M. E. Marty & R. S. Appleby (eds), *Fundamentalisms and the State*, 557, 573–4. D. Henshaw, *Animal Warfare: The Story of the Animal Liberation Front* (London: Fontana, 1989), 33–4, 92–3.

36. 'Four legs good, two legs bad: a recipe for terror', *The Independent on Sunday*, 28 August 1994. D. Henshaw, *Animal Warfare*. R. Garner, *Animal Politics and Morality* (Manchester: Manchester University Press, 1993), 215–42. 'Killing for Life', *The Independent*, magazine supplement, 10 September 1994. 'Where doctors wear bullet-proof vests', *The Daily Telegraph*, 20 October 1994. 'Vengeance', *The Economist*, 7 January

1995. B. Hoffman, *Recent Trends and Future Prospects of Terrorism in the United States* (Santa Monica, CA: RAND Corporation, 1988), 21.
37. 'The wild defence of the wild', *The Sunday Correspondent*, 3 June 1990. 'Breaking the monkeywrench', *The Independent*, magazine supplement, 2 March 1991.
38. P. Janke, 'Europe', in R. Clutterbuck (ed.), *The Future of Political Violence*, 99. R. P. Clark, *The Basque Insurgents*, 100, 105, 107.
39. P. Williams, 'Transnational Criminal Organisations and International Security', *Survival*, 36, no. 1 (Spring 1994), 106. UK House of Commons, Home Affairs Committee, *Organised Crime* (HC 18-I) (London: HMSO, 1995), x.
40. G. Falcone & M. Padovani, *Men of Honour: The Truth About the Mafia* (Paris: Edition 1, 1991; London: Fourth Estate, 1992), 160. For detailed accounts of such Mafia killings see J. Parker, *The Walking Dead: A Woman's Brave Stand Against the Mafia* (London: Simon & Schuster, 1995; Pocket Books, 1996), and A. Stille, *Excellent Cadavers: The Mafia and the Death of the First Italian Republic* (London: Jonathan Cape, 1995). R. D. Tomasek, 'Complex Interdependency Theory: Drug Barons as Transnational Groups', in W. C. Olson & J. R. Lee (eds), *The Theory and Practice of International Relations* (Englewood Cliffs, NJ: Prentice-Hall, 1994), 281–2.
41. G. Falcone & M. Padovani, *Men of Honour*, 157–9, 161–2. R. Catanzaro, *Men of Respect: A Social History of the Sicilian Mafia* (Padua: Liviana Editrice spa, 1988; New York: Free Press, 1992), 214–16. P. Williams, 'Transnational Criminal Organisations and International Security', 111. J. Pearce, *Colombia: Inside the Labyrinth*, 1, 194–5. P. D. Scott & J. Marshall, *Cocaine Politics: Drugs, Armies, and the CIA in Central America* (Berkeley: University of California Press, 1991), 76, 90. S. Strong, *Whitewash: Pablo Escobar and the Cocaine Wars* (London: Macmillan, 1995), 138–53. 'Colombian police close in on drug baron', *The Independent*, 13 April 1990. 'Colombia moves to protect lives of election candidates', *The Independent*, 5 May 1990. 'Mother's Day of mourning as car bombs kill 26', *The Independent*, 14 May 1990. 'Colombian drug dealers' bombs kill 26 shoppers', *The Times*, 14 May 1990. 'King Coke', *The Independent*, 21 July 1990. 'Going... Going... Gone', *The Guardian*, 4 December 1993. 'The king is dead... long live cocaine', *The Independent*, weekend supplement, 11 December 1993. 'Escobar dies, and the cocaine trade gets stronger', 'Obituary: Pablo Escobar', both in *The Independent*, 4 December 1993.
42. Quoted in P. D. Scott & J. Marshall, *Cocaine Politics*, 80.
43. 'A creaking system faces its final test of strength', *The Guardian*, 6 April 1993. R. Catanzaro, *Men of Respect*, 181.
44. Herri Batasuna, *The 'Herri Batasuna' the Basque Country Needs*. Herri Batasuna. *The Recognition of Democratic Rigths* [sic] *in Basque Country*, 3–4, 5. R. P. Clark. *The Basque Insurgents*, 275–6. F. Jiminez, 'Spain: The Terrorist Challenge and the Government's Response', *Terrorism and Political Violence*, 4, no. 4 (Winter 1992), 111.
45. B. Pollack & G. Hunter, 'Dictatorship, Democracy and Terrorism in Spain', in J. Lodge (ed.), *The Threat of Terrorism*, 127–30. F. Llera,

J. M. Mata & C. L. Irwin, 'ETA: From Secret Army to Social Movement', 115–16.
46. H. M. Cubert. 'The Militant Palestinian Organizations and the Arab–Israeli Peace Process', *Terrorism and Political Violence*, 4, no. 1 (Spring 1992), 32–3.
47. P. C. Hearst & A. Moscow. *Every Secret Thing* (London: Methuen, 1982; Arrow, 1983), 351.
48. 'Change of tactics by the Provos', *Financial Times*, 4 February 1977. 'Can Ulster sustain its pepperpot investment', *The Guardian*, 4 February 1977. 'Gunmen fail in bid to assassinate two leading Belfast businessmen', *The Irish Times*, 11 February 1977. 'Businessmen not expendable, unlike Brit troops', *Republican News*, 26 March 1977.
49. D. Henshaw, *Animal Warfare*, 31, 100–1.
50. T. Parker, *May the Lord in His mercy be kind to Belfast* (London: Jonathan Cape, 1993), 324.
51. 'Germany tested to its limits', *The Independent*, 3 April 1991. 'Obituary: Detlev Rohwedder', *The Independent*, 3 April 1991.
52. Red Army Faction. 'Communiqué on the Assassination of Detlev Rohwedder, President of Treuhandanstalt, in Dusseldorf on 1 April 1991', in Y. Alexander & D. Pluchinsky (eds), *Europe's Red Terrorists: The Fighting Communist Organizations* (London: Frank Cass, 1992), 79.
53. Ibid., 79–84.
54. Ibid., 82.
55. B. M. Jenkins, *International Terrorism: The Other World War*, 16.
56. 'Gow killed because of his influence on Thatcher, IRA says', *The Independent*, 1 August 1990.
57. D. McKittrick, *Endgame: The Search for Peace in Northern Ireland* (Belfast: Blackstaff, 1994), 89–90. A. Clark, *Diaries* (London: Weidenfeld & Nicolson, 1993; Phoenix, 1994), 35, 121–2, 319.
58. 'Tragedy of Ulster's relentless cycle of violence', *The Independent*, 6 February 1992.
59. 'UVF gunmen "laughed as they fled" pub massacre', *The Guardian*, 25 January 1995. S. Bruce, *The Red Hand*, 54. M. Dillon, *The Shankill Butchers*, xxiv, 24, 65, 166.
60. P. Bishop & E. Mallie, *The Provisional IRA*, 182, 195. K. Toolis, *Rebel Hearts: Journeys within the IRA's Soul* (London: Picador, 1995), 126, 357–8.
61. R. Catanzaro, 'Subjective experience and objective reality: an account of violence in the words of its protagonists', in R. Catanzaro (ed.), *The Red Brigades and Left-Wing Terrorism in Italy* (London: Pinter, 1991), 190–1.
62. C. di Giovanni, *Light from Behind the Bars*, 61.
63. Red Brigades – Fighting Communist Party, 'Communiqué on the Assassination of Ezio Tarantelli, a Rome University Economics Professor, in Rome on 27 March 1985', in Y. Alexander & D. Pluchinsky (eds), *Europe's Red Terrorists*, 203.
64. T. Parker, *May the Lord in His mercy be kind to Belfast*, 325–6.
65. '"We remain totally committed and confident in victory" – Oglaigh na hEireann', *AP/RN*, 14 February 1991. 'The IRA statement', *AP/RN*,

23 January 1992. P. Bishop & E. Mallie, *The Provisional IRA*, 421.
66. Quoted in R. Holmes, *Firing Line* (London: Jonathan Cape, 1985; Harmondsworth: Penguin, 1987), 360.
67. J. Ellis, *The Sharp End of War: The Fighting Man in World War II* (Newton Abbot: David & Charles, 1980; London: Corgi, 1982), 319–20. R. Holmes, *Firing Line*, 370, 373–5.
68. A. Calder, *The People's War: Britain 1939–1945* (London: Jonathan Cape, 1969; Granada, 1982), 566–7. M. Hastings, *Bomber Command* (London: Michael Joseph, 1979; Pan, 1981), 125–6, 135–6. M. Walzer, *Just and Unjust Wars: A Moral Argument with Historical Illustrations* (New York: Basic Books, 1977; Harmondsworth: Penguin, 1980), 256. G. Best, *Humanity in Warfare: The Modern History of the International Law of Armed Conflicts* (London: Weidenfeld & Nicolson, 1980; Methuen, 1983), 267–85.
69. W. R. Farrell, *Blood and Rage: The Story of the Japanese Red Army* (Lexington, MA: Lexington Books, 1990), 142. B. M. Jenkins, *International Terrorism: The Other World War*, 48.
70. M. Crenshaw Hutchinson, *Revolutionary Terrorism*, 19.
71. '16 killed in bomb attack on Jewish groups in Argentina', *The Independent*, 19 July 1994. 'Explosion levels building housing Jewish groups', *The Guardian*, 19 July 1994.
72. 'Hizbollah adopts an "eye for an eye" tactic', *The Independent*, 20 July 1994.
73. P. Bishop & E. Mallie, *The Provisional IRA*, 171.
74. 'Bombing "devastating" to IRA', *The Independent*, 11 November 1987.
75. A. Iyad & E. Rouleau, *My Home My Land*, 106, 111.
76. S. Aust, *The Baader-Meinhof Group*, 530. Also see P. Koch & K. Hermann, *Assault at Mogadishu* (Hamburg: Stern, 1977; London: Corgi, 1977), 139–40.
77. 'All killings and tragedies stem from British interference', *Republican News*, 25 February 1978. D. McKittrick, *Despatches from Belfast* (Belfast: Blackstaff, 1989), 86.
78. 'IRA warns of more bombs', *The Observer*, 1 February 1987.
79. M. Dillon & D. Lehane, *Political Murder in Northern Ireland*, 256. J. Bowyer Bell, *IRA Tactics and Targets*, 27, 48, 116.
80. D. Moss, *The Politics of Left-Wing Violence in Italy*, 58.
81. P. Willan, *Puppet Masters*, 201–2.
82. R. P. Clark, *The Basque Insurgents*, 40.
83. R. P. Clark, 'Patterns of Eta Violence: 1968–1980', P. H. Merkl (ed.), *Political Violence and Terror*, 136. F. Llera, J. M. Mata & C. L. Irwin, 'ETA: From Secret Army to Social Movement', 132.
84. R. P. Clark, 'Patterns of Eta Violence: 1968–1980', 136. B. Pollack & G. Hunter, 'Dictatorship, Democracy and Terrorism in Spain', 126. R. P. Clark, *The Basques: The Franco Years and Beyond* (Reno: University of Nevada Press, 1979), 170–4.
85. 'King Coke', *The Independent*, 21 July 1990. 'In Medellin, walls do not a prison make', *The Independent*, 8 August 1992. J. Pearce, *Colombia: Inside the Labyrinth*, 177–8, 247. Amnesty International, *Political Violence in Colombia: Myth and Reality* (London: Amnesty International,

1994), 52. C. Watson, 'Guerrilla Groups in Colombia', 95–6.
86. J. Pearce, *Colombia: Inside the Labyrinth*, 1, 260–1. A. M. Bravo, 'Frontier culture takes to cocaine', 75. C. Watson, 'Guerrilla Groups in Colombia', 96. P. D. Scott & J. Marshall, *Cocaine Politics*, 89.
87. J. Pearce, *Colombia: Inside the Labyrinth*, 239, 262. Amnesty International, *Political Violence in Colombia*, 1.
88. J. Pearce, *Colombia: Inside the Labyrinth*, 243, 249, 252–3, 254–5, 260–1. Amnesty International, *Getting Away with Murder: Political Killings and "Disappearances" in the 1990s* (London: Amnesty International, 1993), 74, 88–9.
89. J. Pearce, *Colombia: Inside the Labyrinth*, 196, 253, 262. Amnesty International, *Political Violence in Colombia*, 58, 61–2.
90. 'The men of war promise third violent decade', *The Independent*, 29 September 1990. '"We remain totally committed and confident in victory" – Oglaigh na hEireann', *AP/RN*, 14 February 1991. 'Freedom's soldiers laid to rest in historic Tyrone', *AP/RN*, 13 June 1991. 'UDR "comes of age": Loyalist militia renamed', *AP/RN*, 25 July 1991. 'Terrorists in and out of uniform', *AP/RN*, 4 July 1991. 'The IRA statement', *AP/RN*, 23 January 1992. 'Royal salute to Murder Regiment', *AP/RN*, 4 June 1992. J. Bowyer Bell, *IRA Tactics and Targets*, 29–32.
91. S. Bruce, *The Red Hand*, 58, 261, 277. S. Nelson, *Ulster's Uncertain Defenders*, 120. M. Dillon, *The Shankill Butchers*, 17. D. L. G. Hall, *The Ulster Defence Association*, 32–3, 81.
92. 'Gritting it out on Border farmlands', *The Irish Times*, 3 March 1983. 'Centre of hatred returns to Armagh', *The Irish Times*, 23 November 1983. J. Darby, *Intimidation and the Control of Conflict in Northern Ireland* (Dublin: Gill and Macmillan, 1986), 136–7. S. Bruce, *The Edge of the Union: The Ulster Loyalist Political Vision* (Oxford: Oxford University Press, 1994), 42–3. T. Parker, *May the Lord in His mercy be kind to Belfast*, 293–4.
93. 'Loyalist group threatens Catholic massacre', *The Independent*, 8 September 1993. 'Loyalists come out shooting to defend lost cause', *The Times*, 9 September 1993.
94. 'For Queen and Country', *The Guardian*, supplement, 19 October 1993.
95. D. L. G. Hall, *The Ulster Defence Association*, 256.
96. Red Brigades and Red Army Faction. 'Excerpts from Notes of a Meeting between the Red Brigades and Red Army Faction in January 1988', in Y. Alexander & D. Pluchinsky (eds), *Europe's Red Terrorists*, 219–27.
97. S. Aust, *The Baader-Meinhof Group*, 10–12, 63, 76–7, 146–9. J. Becker, *Hitler's Children*, 17, 62, 109, 264, 366n2.
98. For more details see: D. Moss, *The Politics of Left-Wing Violence in Italy*, 38, 79–80, 81–117, 120, 122. A. Jamieson, *The Heart Attacked*, 75–6, 93, 99, 108, 120, 188–9, 210, 212, 215–16. V. S. Pisano, *The Dynamics of Subversion and Violence in Contemporary Italy*, 163–5, 169. C. Schaerf et al., *Venti Anni di Violenza in Italia*, volume one, 736. E. MacDonald, *Shoot the Women First*, 176–7. *L'Espresso*, 24 February 1980. *L'Espresso*, 31 October 1982. S. Aust, *The Baader-Meinhof Group*, 143, 286–8. J. Becker, *Hitler's Children*, 297–8. D. Pluchinsky. 'An Organizational and Operational Analysis of Germany's Red Army

Faction Terrorist Group (1972–1991)', in Y. Alexander & D. Pluchinsky (eds), *European Terrorism Today and Tomorrow* (Washington, DC: Brassey's (US), 1992), 67, 69, 70, 71–2, 74–5. Red Army Faction. 'Communiqué on the Assassination of Alfred Herrhausen, Chairman of Deutsche Bank, in Frankfurt on 30 November 1989', Red Army Faction. 'Communiqué on the Assassination of Detlev Rohwedder', Red Brigades – Fighting Communist Party. 'Communiqué on the Assassination of Ezio Tarantelli', in Y. Alexander & D. Pluchinsky (eds), *Europe's Red Terrorists*, 68, 80, 203–4.

4 STRATEGY

1. Adapted from M. Howard, *The Causes of War* (London: Maurice Temple Smith, 1983; Unwin, 1984), 101.
2. L. Clarke, *Broadening the Battlefield: The H-Blocks and the Rise of Sinn Fein* (Dublin: Gill & Macmillan, 1987), 208. P. Bishop & E. Mallie, *The Provisional IRA*, 378.
3. 'IRA declares peace', *The Independent*, 1 September 1994.
4. B. Rowan, *Behind the Lines: The Story of the IRA and Loyalist Ceasefires* (Belfast: Blackstaff, 1995), 84. E. Mallie & D. McKittrick, *The Fight for Peace: The Secret Story behind the Irish Peace Process* (London: Heinemann, 1996), 311–12, 381–4.
5. E. Mallie & D. McKittrick, *The Fight for Peace*, 363.
6. A. Jamieson, *The Heart Attacked*, 75, 76, 81–2. D. Moss, *The Politics of Left-Wing Violence in Italy*, 59, 83, 85–6, 124. Red Brigades – Fighting Communist Party, 'Communiqué on the Assassination of Ezio Tarantelli', 205. P. Willan, *Puppet Masters*, 203.
7. M. McGuire, *To Take Arms: A Year in the Provisional IRA* (London: Macmillan, 1973; Quartet, 1973), 12, 69. P. Bishop & E. Mallie, *The Provisional IRA*, 171.
8. M. L. R. Smith, *Fighting for Ireland? The Military Strategy of the Irish Republican Movement* (London: Routledge, 1995), 140.
9. P. Bishop & E. Mallie, *The Provisional IRA*, 171.
10. J. Bowyer Bell, 'Revolutionary Dynamics: The Inherent Inefficiency of the Underground', *Terrorism and Political Violence*, 2, no. 2 (Summer 1990).
11. 'Inside the IRA', *The Sunday Times*, 3 July 1977.
12. B. M. Jenkins, *Soldiers versus Gunmen: The Challenge of Urban Guerrilla Warfare* (Santa Monica, California: RAND Corporation, March 1974), 4.
13. M. Crenshaw, 'The Concept of Revolutionary Terrorism', *Journal of Conflict Resolution*, 16, no. 3 (September 1972), 394.
14. On the longevity of various groups see Table 1 in M. Crenshaw, 'How terrorism declines', *Terrorism and Political Violence*, 3, no. 1 (Summer 1991), 76–7, and Figure 2 in Y. Alexander & D. Pluchinsky (eds), *Europe's Red Terrorists*, 47.
15. Angry Brigade, *The Angry Brigade, 1967–1984*, 40–66.
16. Y. Alexander & D. Pluchinsky (eds), *Europe's Red Terrorists*, 148–50.
17. On the changes in the leadership of the Red Army Faction see

D. Pluchinsky, 'An Organizational and Operational Analysis of Germany's Red Army Faction Terrorist Group'; and B. A. Scharlau, *Left-Wing Terrorism in the Federal Republic of Germany*. On the INLA see J. Holland & H. McDonald, *INLA: Deadly Divisions* (Dublin: Torc, 1994), 229–30, 282–99. On the policy of assassinating leading Palestinian terrorists see D. Tinnin, *Hit Team* (London: Weidenfeld & Nicolson, 1976; Futura, 1977). D. Raviv & Y. Melman, *Every Spy a Prince: The Complete History of Israel's Intelligence Community* (New York: Houghton Mifflin, 1990), 184–92, 393–8.

18. 'Ulster's rocky road to peace', *The Observer* (London), 15 December 1977. P. Bishop & E. Mallie, *The Provisional IRA*, 321. P. Taylor, *Beating the Terrorists: Interrogation in Omagh, Gough and Castlereagh* (Harmondsworth: Penguin, 1980), 80–1, 154–8, 193–4. M. Dillon, *Killer in Clowntown: Joe Doherty, the IRA and the Special Relationship* (London: Hutchinson; Arrow, 1992), 59.
19. T. P. Coogan, *The IRA* (Glasgow: Fontana/Collins, 1987), 581. L. Clarke, *Broadening the Battlefield*, 32, 35. K. J. Kelley, *The Longest War*, 233–6, 243.
20. 'The men of war promise third violent decade', *The Independent*, 29 September 1990. '"We remain totally committed and confident in victory" – Oglaigh na hEireann', *AP/RN*, 14 February 1991. 'The IRA statement', *AP/RN*, 23 January 1992. T. P. Coogan, *The IRA*, 604, 693. J. Bowyer Bell, *IRA Tactics and Targets*, 29–32. L. Clarke, *Broadening the Battlefield*, 56–7. B. O'Brien, *The Long War*, 152.
21. 'IRA declares peace', *The Independent*, 1 September 1994. 'Loyalists match IRA ceasefire', 'Combined Loyalist Military Command statement', *The Independent*, 14 October 1994.
22. L. Kennedy, 'Rough Justice', *Fortnight*, November 1995. 'How the guns kept drugs out of Belfast', *The Independent*, 21 December 1995. 'Godfathers of violence step up beatings to keep grip on power', *The Daily Telegraph*, 29 December 1995. 'Murky motives for giving drug dealers rough justice', *The Guardian*, 3 January 1996. M. O'Doherty, 'Dealing in Death', *New Statesman and Society*, 22 January 1996. B. Rowan, *Behind the Lines*. For a republican viewpoint see 'Drugs in the Six Counties: A Secret Society', *AP/RN*, 25 January 1996, and 'Drugs summit targeted North', *AP/RN*, 1 February 1996.
23. '"The ceasefire is over": IRA bombers blast London', *The Independent*, 10 February 1996. 'Bomb shatters IRA ceasefire', *The Times*, 10 February 1996.
24. M. Crenshaw Hutchinson, *Revolutionary Terrorism*, 21.
25. M. Crenshaw Hutchinson, *Revolutionary Terrorism*, 41–85. T. P. Thornton, 'Terror as a Weapon of Political Agitation', H. Eckstein (ed.), *Internal War: Problems and Approaches* (New York: The Free Press of Glencoe, 1964).
26. T. P. Coogan, *Michael Collins*, 78, 116–17, 129, 157–60. C. Townshend, *The British Campaign in Ireland, 1919–1921: The Development of Political and Military Policies* (Oxford: Oxford University Press, 1975), 41–2, 129–30. T. Barry, *Guerrilla Days in Ireland* (Dublin: The Irish Press, 1949; Tralee, Ireland: Anvil, 1962), 18–19, 99–107. E. Butler,

Barry's Flying Column: The Story of the I.R.A.'s Cork No. 3 Brigade 1919–21 (London: Leo Cooper, 1971; Tandem, 1972), 120–2.
27. 'Mafia strikes one more from its enemy hit-list', *The Times*, 20 July 1992. 'Sicilians clash with police after being banned from funeral', *The Times*, 22 July 1992. A. Stille, *Excellent Cadavers*, 373–7.
28. R. Trinquier, *Modern Warfare: A French View of Counterinsurgency* (London: Pall Mall Press, 1964), 16–17.
29. 'Mother's Day of mourning as car bombs kill 26', *The Independent*, 14 May 1990. S. Strong, *Whitewash*, 282–4.
30. G. Tarnovski, 'Terrorism and Routine', and P. Kropotkin, 'The Spirit of Revolt', both in W. Laqueur (ed.), *The Terrorism Reader*, 82, 96.
31. M. McGuire, *To Take Arms*, 69. L. Clarke, *Broadening the Battlefield*, 40–2, 56–7. T. P. Coogan, *The IRA*, 579, 604, 693. K. J. Kelley, *The Longest War*, 202–3, 210, 265. P. Bishop & E. Mallie, *The Provisional IRA*, 250, 332. B. O'Brien, *The Long War*, 23, 152. G. McKee & R. Franey, *Time Bomb*, 18–19, 308, 330.
32. 'British pay price as IRA strikes', *AP/RN*, 14 February 1991. 'The men of war promise third violent decade', *The Independent*, 29 September 1990. T. P. Coogan, *The IRA*, 604.
33. C. Guevara, 'Guerrilla Warfare – A Method', W. Laqueur (ed.), *The Guerrilla Reader: A Historical Anthology* (London: Wildwood House, 1978), 203–4. C. Marighela, 'Problems and Principles of Strategy', and 'The Handbook of Urban Guerrilla Warfare', in C. Marighela, *For the Liberation of Brazil*, 46, 95.
34. 'Paratroops accused of pub attacks', *The Independent*, 15 May 1992. 'Ulster Para officer suspended after claims of violence', *The Times*, 15 May 1992. 'Ulster brigadier "insensitive to human rights"', *The Independent*, 26 May 1992. 'Send them home', 'Coalisland exposes British army terror', both in *AP/RN*, 21 May 1992. 'Army involved in new harassment dispute in Ulster', *The Independent*, 27 May 1992. 'Picture backs claims of rifle butt assault', *The Independent*, 30 May 1992. 'British army chief removed but paras remain', 'Anglian Regiment thuggery in Derry', both in *AP/RN*, 28 May 1992. 'Six Paras face clashes charges', *The Times*, 29 September 1992.
35. S. M. Katz, *Guards Without Frontiers*, 96, 136. P. Wilkinson, *Terrorism and the Liberal State*, second edition (London: Macmillan, 1986), 158. A. Merari, T. Prat & D. Tal, 'The Palestinian *Intifada*: An Analysis of a Popular Uprising after Seven Months', *Terrorism and Political Violence*, 1, no. 2 (April 1989), 183.
36. W. V. O'Brien, *Law and Morality in Israel's War with the PLO* (New York: Doubleday, 1991), 243. No author named, *Punishing the Innocent: House Demolition and Sealing in the West Bank* (London: Council for the Advancement of Arab–British Understanding, 1987), 19.
37. S. Christie, *Stefano Delle Chiaie*, 32. P. Willan, *Puppet Masters*, 23.
38. F. Lopez-Alves, 'Political Crises, Strategic Choices and Terrorism: The Rise and Fall of the Uruguayan Tupamaros', *Terrorism and Political Violence*, 1, no. 2 (April 1989), 226, 232.
39. C. L. Irvin, 'Terrorists' Perspectives: Interviews', 78.
40. B. M. Jenkins, *International Terrorism: A New Kind of Warfare*, 6.

41. G. Chaliand, *The Palestinian Resistance*, 167.
42. M. Kramer, 'Sacrifice and Fratricide in Shiite Lebanon', 35.
43. D. Moss, *The Politics of Left-Wing Violence in Italy*, 73.
44. M. Crenshaw, *Revolutionary Terrorism*, xv, 36, 39, 44–6, 57, 41–85. A. Horne, *A Savage War of Peace*, 153–4, 231, 415–16.
45. T. P. Coogan, *The IRA*, 693. B. O'Brien, *The Long War*, 23.
46. '11 die in Cenotaph blast', *The Independent*, 9 November 1987. 'Attacks fit into a pattern of errors', *The Independent*, 13 April 1989. 'Bombings indicate new direction in mainland campaign', *The Times*, 19 February 1992. 'Damage in huge blast put at £20m', *The Independent*, 25 September 1992. '"Troubles" chronology: Wed Sep 23', *Fortnight*, no. 311 (November 1992), 34. 'IRA bombers kill child, 4', *The Independent on Sunday*, 21 March 1993. 'Tim Parry, victim of IRA bomb blast dies after ventilator is switched off', *The Independent*, 26 March 1993. D. McKittrick, *Despatches from Belfast*, 146–51. 'Brits put civilian lives at risk', *AP/RN*, 30 January 1992. 'We are doing all in our power to shorten this war', *AP/RN*, 12 March 1992.
47. T. Bjorgo, 'Terrorist Violence against Immigrants and Refugees in Scandanavia: Patterns and Motives', 38–9. Hasselbach suggests that longer-term planning has started to evolve amongst German and Austrian neo-Nazis. See I. Hasselbach & T. Reiss, *Fuhrer-Ex: Memoirs of a Former Neo-Nazi* (London: Chatto & Windus, 1996), 274–6.
48. Mao Tse-tung, 'Problems of strategy in China's Revolutionary War', *Selected Works of Mao Tse-tung*, volume 1. Mao Tse-tung, 'On Protracted War', and 'Problems of strategy in guerrilla war against Japan', both in *Selected Works of Mao Tse-tung*, volume 2. Also see V. N. Giap, *People's War People's Army: The Viet Công Insurrection Manual for Underdeveloped Countries* (New York: Praeger, 1962; Bantam, 1968) for the thoughts of one of Mao's disciples who commanded the Vietnamese communist forces to final victory over the French, Americans, and South Vietnamese between 1946 and 1975.
49. W. Laqueur, *The Age of Terrorism*, 147–8.
50. Mao Tse-tung, 'On correcting mistaken ideas in the Party', 106; 'Problems of strategy in China's Revolutionary War', 192; 'Report of an investigation of the peasant movement in Hunan'; 'Pay attention to economic work', 129–36; 'Be concerned with the well-being of the masses, pay attention to methods of work', 146, 149; all in *Selected Works*, volume 1. 'The Chinese Revolution and the Chinese Communist Party', 323: *Selected Works*, volume 2.
51. V. N. Giap, *People's War People's Army*, 17, 83.
52. Mao Tse-tung, 'Problems of strategy in China's Revolutionary War', 211–20.
53. Ibid., 202. Mao Tse-tung, 'Problems of strategy in guerrilla war against Japan', 84.
54. Mao Tse-tung, 'Problems of strategy in China's Revolutionary War', 213; 'Problems of strategy in guerrilla war against Japan', 85; 'On Protracted War', 136–40.
55. Mao Tse-tung, 'Problems of Strategy in China's Revolutionary War', 179, 181, 189; 'On Protracted War', 121.

56. Mao Tse-tung, 'On Protracted War', 197–8.
57. S. Strong, *Shining Path: The World's Deadliest Revolutionary Force* (London: HarperCollins, 1992), 71.
58. Ibid., 29, 40–3, 71, 75–6, 84–5, 91, 99–102. M. L. Smith, 'Taking the High Ground: Shining Path and the Andes', G. Gorritti, 'Shining Path's Stalin and Trotsky', both in D. S. Palmer (ed.), *Shining Path of Peru* (London: Hurst & Co., 1992), 19–20, 27, 151. T. D. Mason & J. Swartzfager, 'Land Reform and the Rise of Sendero Luminoso in Peru', 529. W. A. Hazleton & S. Woy-Hazleton, 'Sendero Luminoso: A Communist Party Crosses a River of Blood', *Terrorism and Political Violence*, 4, no. 2 (Summer 1992), 68.
59. S. Strong, *Shining Path*, 36–9. W. A. Hazleton & S. Woy-Hazleton, 'Sendero Luminoso', 66–8.
60. M. L. Smith, 'Taking the High Ground: Shining Path and the Andes', 19–20.
61. Ibid., 25. R. H. Berg, 'Peasant Responses to Shining Path in Andahuaylas', D. S. Palmer (ed.), *Shining Path of Peru*, 93. T. D. Mason & J. Swartzfager, 'Land Reform and the Rise of Sendero Luminoso in Peru', 531.
62. 'In the killing fields of Peru', *The Guardian*, supplement, 6 April 1994. S. Strong, *Shining Path*, 148–9, 181, 183. B. J. Isbell, 'Shining Path and Peasant Responses in Rural Ayacucho', D. S. Palmer (ed.), *Shining Path of Peru*, 73–4. R. H. Berg, 'Peasant Responses to Shining Path in Andahuaylas', 92. T. D. Mason & J. Swartzfager, 'Land Reform and the Rise of Sendero Luminoso in Peru', 531. S. Woy-Hazleton & W. A. Hazleton, 'Shining Path and the Marxist Left', in D. S. Palmer (ed.), *Shining Path of Peru*, 216.
63. T. D. Mason & C. Campany, 'Guerrillas, Drugs and Peasants: The Rational Peasant and the War on Drugs in Peru', *Terrorism and Political Violence*, 7, no. 4 (Winter 1995), 163–4.
64. S. Strong, *Shining Path*, 110, 121–2, 135–6. T. D. Mason & C. Campany, 'Guerrillas, Drugs and Peasants', 163.
65. 'Peru's guerrillas make slum into a "shining example"', *The Independent*, 30 November 1991. 'Car bomb kills 18 as Maoists extend terror tactics to Lima', *The Times*, 18 July 1992. 'Terror grips Peru's capital as rebels take on the state', *The Guardian*, 17 August 1992. 'The end of a long march down the Shining Path', *The Independent*, 3 October 1992. 'Maoist rebels in Peru kill 28 peasants', *The Independent*, 9 September 1993. S. Woy-Hazleton & W. A. Hazleton, 'Shining Path and the Marxist Left', 214. M. L. Smith, 'Shining Path's Urban Strategy: Ate Vitarte' in D. S. Palmer (ed.), *Shining Path of Peru*, 127–8, 136, 138. Amnesty International, *Peru: Human Rights in a Climate of Terror* (London: Amnesty International, 1991), 23–4.
66. S. Christie, *Stefano Delle Chiaie*, 32. Willan dates the document from November 1968. P. Willan, *Puppet Masters*, 23.
67. S. Christie, *Stefano Delle Chiaie*, 32.
68. A. Jamieson, *The Heart Attacked*, 22, 60. P. Willan, *Puppet Masters*, 123.
69. A. Hitler, *Mein Kampf*, 73.
70. D. Mack Smith, *Mussolini*, 56–65. A. Bullock, *Hitler: A Study in Tyranny*,

revised edition (London: Book Club Associates, 1973), 187– 250.
71. P. Willan, *Puppet Masters*, 23. V. S. Pisano, *The Dynamics of Subversion and Violence in Contemporary Italy*, 51.
72. 'Italians blame shadowy powers for bringing terror to Florence', *The Independent on Sunday*, 30 May 1993.
73. 'Mafia terrorist campaign feared', *The Independent*, 16 May 1993. T. Shawcross & M. Young, *Mafia Wars: The Confessions of Tommaso Buscetta* (Glasgow: Fontana, 1988), 299–300. P. Willan, *Puppet Masters*, 173–7.
74. 'Executive held over Uffizi bomb', *The European*, 8–14 February 1996. 'Italian police arrest the Mafia's "boss of bosses"', *The Independent*, 21 May 1996. P. Willan, *Puppet Masters*, 173–7.
75. 'Last supper at the bribery banquet', *The Independent*, 4 March 1993. 'Rotten to the core', *The Independent on Sunday*, 11 April 1993. 'Andreotti "was Mafia's man at the heart of the state"', *The Guardian*, 30 March 1993. 'Andreotti accused of ordering murder', *The Independent*, 10 June 1993. A. Stille, *Excellent Cadavers*, 390–403.
76. 'Algerian dissident seeks UK asylum', *The Independent*, 6 August 1994. M. Crenshaw, 'Political Violence in Algeria', *Terrorism and Political Violence*, 6, no. 3 (Autumn 1994), 265, 269–72, 273.
77. 'Algeria: the new horror story', *The Independent*, 9 February 1994.
78. 'Muslim rebels renew bloody campaign', *The Guardian*, 7 June 1994.
79. 'Islamist car bomb shakes Algiers', *The Guardian*, 31 January 1995. 'Suicide bomber kills 38 in Algiers attack', *The Independent*, 31 January 1995. 'Extremists tighten grip on Algeria', *The Independent on Sunday*, 5 February 1995. 'Opposition chief killed in Algeria', *The Daily Telegraph*, 6 February 1995.
80. 'Spectre of civil war stalks Algeria', *The Independent*, 28 January 1994. 'Opposition chief killed in Algeria', *The Daily Telegraph*, 6 February 1995. M. Crenshaw, 'Political Violence in Algeria', 275.
81. M. Crenshaw, 'Political Violence in Algeria', 274–5.
82. 'Algerian extremists murder 12 foreigners', *The Independent*, 16 December 1993.
83. 'French face death in Algeria', *The Independent*, 2 December 1993. 'Muslim extremists target foreigners in war on unbelievers', *The Times*, 27 December 1994. 'Stopover became martyr's graveyard', *The Guardian*, 27 December 1994. 'Fundamentally confused', *The Economist*, 7 January 1995.
84. 'Radical group is driven by violence', *The Independent*, 27 December 1994. 'Muslim extremists target foreigners in war on unbelievers', *The Times*, 27 December 1994.
85. 'Stopover became martyr's graveyard', *The Guardian*, 27 December 1994.
86. 'Islamists decry Algiers murders', *The Independent*, 10 May 1994.
87. 'Algerian Islamists admit to killings', *The Independent*, 16 May 1994.
88. 'Islamists decry Algiers murders', *The Independent*, 10 May 1994. 'A whisper from the cloisters', *The Economist*, 14 January 1995.
89. 'Feminist killed', *The Daily Telegraph*, 16 February 1995. 'Algerian theatre director killed', *The Daily Telegraph*, 14 February 1995.

'Algeria mired in war without battle fronts', *The Independent*, 1 November 1994. 'Musician killed', *The Daily Telegraph*, 17 February 1995. 'Musician shot', *The Independent*, 17 February 1995. 'Tourist threat as Algerian war crosses border', *The Independent on Sunday*, 19 February 1995. 'Algerian film producer shot in Islamic terror campaign', *The Daily Telegraph*, 8 February 1995.
90. 'Islamists kill 29th journalist', *The Independent*, 18 February 1995. 'Algeria murder', *The Daily Telegraph*, 18 February 1995. 'Cutting throats to create a Muslim state', *The Independent*, 6 December 1996.
91. 'Paris police detain 23 Algerian suspects', *The Independent*, 9 August 1994.
92. 'Algerian Islamists turn back to politics', *The Independent*, 7 September 1994.
93. 'Student leader murdered', *The Times Higher Education Supplement* (London), 24 February 1995. 'Algerian film producer shot in Islamic terror campaign', *The Daily Telegraph*, 8 February 1995.
94. 'Algiers teacher shot dead by militants', *The Daily Telegraph*, 13 February 1995.
95. 'Student leader murdered', *The Times Higher Education Supplement*, 24 February 1995.
96. 'Rector murdered by Islamic hitmen', *The Times Higher Education Supplement*, 10 June 1994. 'Murder of professor fuels fear', *The Times Higher Education Supplement*, 14 October 1994.
97. 'Student leader murdered', *The Times Higher Education Supplement*, 24 February 1995. 'Tourist threat as Algerian war crosses border', *The Independent on Sunday*, 19 February 1995.
98. 'Murder of professor fuels fear', *The Times Higher Education Supplement*, 14 October 1994.
99. 'Algerian killings stepped up', *The Guardian*, 25 February 1997. 'Algerian rebel group claims assassination', *The Independent*, 21 February 1997.
100. 'France fears upsurge of Islamic terror', *The Independent on Sunday*, 10 April 1994. 'Forget feminism, talk about survival', *The Independent*, 9 March 1995. 'Islamists kill three women', *The Independent*, 15 March 1995. 'Villagers' throats cut', *The Guardian*, 14 January 1997.
101. *The Times Higher Education Supplement*, 21 October 1994.
102. 'Algerian rebels kill 20 in bus attack', *The Independent*, 12 December 1996. 'Guillotines add a barbaric touch to Algeria's bloodbath', *The Independent*, 24 January 1997. 'Algerian militants massacre 33 villagers', *The Guardian*, 19 February 1997.
103. 'Bombers target Algiers', *The Guardian*, 22 January 1997. 'Many dead as bombs rock Algerian capital', *The Independent*, 18 March 1997.
104. 'Cutting throats to create a Muslim state', *The Independent*, 6 December 1996. 'Algerian rebel group claims assassination', *The Independent*, 21 February 1997.

5 TACTICS

1. B. A. Scharlau. *Left-Wing Terrorism in the Federal Republic of Germany*, 42, 61–2. H. J. Horchem, *Terrorism in West Germany* (London: Institute for the Study of Conflict, 1986), 6. A. Jamieson, *The Heart Attacked*, 78. G. C. Caselli & D. della Porta, 'The history of the Red Brigades', in R. Catanzaro (ed.), *The Red Brigades*, 73, 88.
2. J. Bowyer Bell, 'Revolutionary Dynamics: The Inherent Inefficiency of the Underground', 202.
3. G. Grivas-Dighenis & C. Foley (eds), *The Memoirs of General Grivas* (London: Longmans, 1964), 13–32.
4. 'Semtex stockpile the key to IRA's wider campaign', *The Independent*, 4 June 1990. 'The IRA', *The Independent on Sunday*, 22 November 1992. 'IRA mainland campaign "likely to last for years"', *The Independent*, 24 November 1992.
5. S. Aust, *The Baader-Meinhof Group*, 433–4. P. Taylor, *States of Terror*, 76. A. Jamieson, *The Heart Attacked*, 111–12. P. Willan, *Puppet Masters*, 238–9, 241–3.
6. 'What One-Eyed Jack knows', *The Independent*, 1 July 1991. 'Entering a Decisive Phase', *India Today*, 28 February 1995.
7. J. Pearce, *Colombia: Inside the Labyrinth*, 177, 196, 205.
8. J. Cusack & M. Taylor, 'The Resurgence of a Terrorist Organization – Part 1: The UDA, A Case Study', *Terrorism and Political Violence*, 5, no. 3 (Autumn 1993), 3.
9. E. MacDonald, *Shoot the Women First*, 141. G. C. Caselli & D. della Porta. 'The history of the Red Brigades', 73. D. Moss, *The Politics of Left-Wing Violence in Italy*, 55, 145. C. Seton-Watson, 'Terrorism in Italy', 103.
10. M. Dillon & D. Lehane, *Political Murder in Northern Ireland*, 29–35. M. Dillon, *The Shankill Butchers*, passim. S. Bruce, *The Red Hand*, 14, 173–81. For an account and chronology of racialist killings in Europe, including both motiveless attacks and politically directed killings, see 'Death in Europe: the toll for 1992', *Campaign Against Racism and Fascism* (London), 12 (Jan./Feb. 1993). 'Deadly Europe', *Campaign Against Racism and Fascism*, 18 (Jan./Feb. 1994). For a detailed local account of the nature of racial attacks see Director of Housing, Oldham Metropolitan Borough, *Racial Harassment Policy*, local government report (Oldham: Oldham Metropolitan Borough, 7 December 1988), 28–30.
11. J. Holland & H. McDonald, *INLA*, 334–5, 338.
12. A. Jamieson, *The Heart Attacked*, 26, 38–40, 109–10, 146, 177. D. Moss, *The Politics of Left-Wing Violence in Italy*, 155. P. Willan, *Puppet Masters*, 216–17, 271–3.
13. P. Willan, *Puppet Masters*, 219. A. Jamieson, *The Heart Attacked*, 151, 157, 160.
14. A. Jamieson, *The Heart Attacked*, 108. P. Willan, *Puppet Masters*, 222.
15. A. Jamieson, *The Heart Attacked*, 40–1, 108. P. Willan, *Puppet Masters*, 223–4.
16. B. Savinkov, *Memoirs of a Terrorist*, 79, 120. R. Hingley, *The Russian*

Secret Police: Muscovite, Imperial Russian and Soviet Political Security Operations, 1565–1970 (London: Hutchinson, 1970), 96–7.
17. D. Pluchinsky, 'An Organizational and Operational Analysis of Germany's Red Army Faction Terrorist Group', 61. S. Aust, *The Baader-Meinhof Group*, 406–8.
18. S. Aust, *The Baader-Meinhof Group*, 418. 'Culture of violence cuts deep in Bonn', *The Times*, 6 July 1993.
19. T. P. Coogan, *Michael Collins*, 82–3.
20. Ibid., 75–84, 107, 147–8. D. Neligan. *The Spy in the Castle* (London: MacGibbon & Kee, 1968).
21. 'Teenagers who enlist for terror', *The Independent on Sunday*, 5 August 1990. P. Bishop & E. Mallie, *The Provisional IRA*, 287–8. 'Informers die after policeman's betrayal', *The Daily Telegraph*, 22 March 1981. C. Ryder, *The RUC*, 242–4. 'Leaked messages from RUC' may help terrorists', *The Independent*, 18 June 1991. 'Maze officer who helped IRA to kill colleague gets life', *The Times*, 22 June 1990. 'Prison warder given life for role in IRA murder', *The Independent*, 22 June 1990. 'IRA spy jailed by Dublin court', *The Times*, 8 February 1991. 'IRA used Garda file to target man', *The Independent*, 17 April 1991. 'Dublin admits Garda leak to IRA', *The Independent*, 17 April 1991. 'Former Garda jailed for giving IRA information', *The Independent*, 1 February 1992.
22. 'Supergrass fears may have prompted poster displays', *The Independent*, 6 February 1990. 'Tories urge inquiry into smear plot allegations', *The Times*, 6 February 1990. 'RUC receives Stevens report on loyalist leaks', *The Independent*, 6 April 1990. 'Report finds RUC collusion', *The Independent*, 18 May 1990. S. Bruce, *The Red Hand*, 212–18, 261–4. D. McKittrick, *Endgame*, 154.
23. *Miami Herald*, 29 January 1979. F. Doherty, 'SIGINT used by Anti-State Forces: A Case Study of Provisional IRA Operations', in C. Bledowska (ed.), *War and Order: Researching State Structures* (London: Junction Books, 1983). M. Dillon, *The Dirty War*, 71–2. P. Bishop & E. Mallie, *The Provisional IRA*, 405.
24. 'Perfect ambush on the road to Paradise', *The Independent*, 10 March 1995.
25. J. Pearce, *Colombia: Inside the Labyrinth*, 194.
26. 'Car bombers kill another top Italian judge', *The Times*, 20 July 1992. 'Tentacles that tie down the Italian state', *The Independent*, 6 August 1992. A. Stille, *Excellent Cadavers*, 372–3.
27. A. & C. Black Ltd, *Who's Who 1988: An annual biographical dictionary* (London: A. & C. Black, 1988).
28. 'Bookworms who burrow for IRA', *The Sunday Correspondent*, 12 August 1990. S. O'Doherty, *The Volunteer: A Former IRA Man's True Story* (London: HarperCollins, 1993), 140.
29. 'McAlpine bomb indicates switch in IRA campaign', *The Independent*, 14 June 1990.
30. 'Car bomb attack on Thatcher advisor fails', *The Independent*, 7 August 1990. 'Peer target of botched car bombing', *The Guardian*, 7 August 1990.

31. '"IRA hit list and arsenal" were found in car', *The Independent*, 23 January 1992. 'Prior the top target on IRA hit list court told', *The Times*, 23 January 1992.
32. 'Arrests failed to stop attacks', *The Independent*, 7 December 1990.
33. S. Aust, *The Baader-Meinhof Group*, 423. J. Becker, *Hitler's Children*, 345.
34. D. T. Schiller, 'The European Experience', in B. M. Jenkins (ed.), *Terrorism and Personal Protection* (Stoneham, MA: Butterworth, 1985), 56–7.
35. B. A. Scharlau, *Left-Wing Terrorism in the Federal Republic of Germany*, 303.
36. 'Fine, remarkable, dirty and devious', *The Spectator*, 9 April 1994.
37. A. J. Scotti, 'Transportation Security', in B. M. Jenkins (ed.), *Terrorism and Personal Protection*, 358–9. Taylor shows how, despite route changes, it was possible for the Red Army Faction to launch an attack on the Commander of NATO forces in Europe, General Alexander Haig, in 1979, P. Taylor, *States of Terror*, 80–2.
38. J. Agirre, *Operation Ogro*, 3.
39. G. Capotorto, 'How Terrorists look at Kidnappings', in B. M. Jenkins (ed.), *Terrorism and Personal Protection*, 5.
40. C. A. Russell & B. H. Miller, 'Terrorist Targets and the Executive Target', in Y. Alexander & R. A. Kilmarx (eds), *Political Terrorism and Business: The Threat and Response* (New York: Praeger, 1979), 69. A. J. Scotti, 'Transportation Security', 354.
41. H. A. Lyons & H. J. Harbinson, 'A Comparison of Political and Non-Political Murderers in Northern Ireland, 1974–84', *Medicine, Science and the Law*, 26, no. 3 (1986), 195.
42. C. E. Baumann, 'Diplomatic Kidnappings', in B. M. Jenkins (ed.), *Terrorism and Personal Protection*. A. Selth, *Against Every Human Law: The Terrorist Threat to Diplomacy* (Rushcutter's Bay: Australian National University Press, 1988), 18–31, 182. Central Intelligence Agency, *Patterns of International Terrorism: 1980* (Washington, DC: Government Printing Office, 1981), 10. J. Gellner, *Bayonets in the Streets: Urban guerrilla at home and abroad* (Don Mills, Ont.: Collier-Macmillan Canada, 1974), 92–128. G. Jackson. *People's Prison*. J. Bowyer Bell, *IRA Tactics and Targets*, 71–2. P. Bishop & E. Mallie, *The Provisional IRA*, 308–9.
43. B. M. Jenkins, *International Terrorism: The Other World War*, 17.
44. *Corriere della Sera*, 13 January 1987.
45. M. Dillon, *Killer in Clowntown*, 83–104.
46. Ibid., 62. Details of a PIRA document captured in 1977 which outlined the reorganisation can be found in L. Clarke, *Broadening the Battlefield*, 251–3.
47. R. P. Clark, 'Patterns in the Lives of ETA members', 301.
48. Y. Katayama, *Terrorism in Japan since 1969: A study of the activities of the Japanese Red Army*, Ph.D., University of Aberdeen, 1989, 82.
49. '"IRA hit list and arsenal" were found in car', *The Independent*, 23 January 1992. 'Bandsman tells jury of escape in Deal bombing', *The Independent*, 11 December 1990.

50. 'Arrests failed to stop attacks', *The Independent*, 7 December 1990.
51. S. Aust, *The Baader-Meinhof Group*, 92–3. B. A. Scharlau, *Left-Wing Terrorism in the Federal Republic of Germany*, 176. J. M. Post, 'Hostilite, Conformité, Fraternité: The Group Dynamics of Terrorist Behaviour', *International Journal of Group Psychotherapy*, 36, no. 2 (April 1986), 216. S. Bruce, *The Red Hand*, 54–6, 114–15. M. Dillon, *The Shankill Butchers*, 47–59, 96–102.
52. G. C. Caselli & D. della Porta, 'The history of the Red Brigades', 82. A. Jamieson, *The Heart Attacked*, 84–5.
53. D. Moss, *The Politics of Left-Wing Violence in Italy*, 57.
54. 'Bombing "devastating" to IRA', *The Independent*, 11 November 1987. L. Clarke, *Broadening the Battlefield*, 252. B. O'Brien, *The Long War*, 158. P. Bishop & E. Mallie, *The Provisional IRA*, 312.
55. S. Bruce, *The Red Hand*, 54–6. M. Dillon, *The Shankill Butchers*, 65, 192–5, 198, 207.
56. 'IRA admits mounting difficulty in Ulster attacks', *The Guardian*, 7 January 1984. 'IRA rings changes to restore balance of terror', *The Guardian*, 5 May 1987.
57. M. Dewar, *The British Army in Northern Ireland* (London: Arms & Armour Press, 1985), 180–6. D. Hamill, *Pig in the Middle: The Army in Northern Ireland, 1969–1984* (London: Methuen, 1985), 119, 133, 141. M. Dillon, *The Dirty War*, 398–417. The veracity of Dewar's remarks on operational methods can be judged by the fact that they have been partially reproduced in a republican magazine. 'Operational comments of a British Army officer', *Iris*, 11 (October 1987).
58. A. Feldman, *Formations of Violence: The Narrative of the Body and Political Terror in Northern Ireland* (Chicago: University of Chicago Press, 1991), 48.
59. D. Pluchinsky, 'RAF Assassination of Alfred Herrhausen', in US Department of State, Bureau of Diplomatic Security (ed.), *Terrorist Tactics and Security Practices* (Washington DC: US Department of State, 1994), 3–9.
60. M. Dillon, *The Shankill Butchers*, 66–7.
61. B. Dasgupta, *The Naxalite Movement* (New Delhi: Allied Publishers, 1974), 40, 45–6.
62. S. Bruce, *The Red Hand*, 183–4.
63. 'Scenario for a knee-cap job in Italy', *The Times*, 23 July 1977.
64. G. Grivas-Dighenis, *Guerrilla Warfare*, 66. A. Feldman, *Formations of Violence*, 42–5. P. Bishop & E. Mallie, *The Provisional IRA*, 247–8.
65. 'New devices used in NI explosions', 12 July 1983. 'Incendiary devices increasingly used in terror attacks', *The Independent*, 2 December 1991. 'Simplicity of incendiary device makes disruption easy', *The Guardian*, 24 December 1991.
66. E. MacDonald, *Shoot the Women First*, 158.
67. E. MacDonald, *Shoot the Women First*, 73, 169. G. Grivas-Dighenis, *Guerrilla Warfare*, 66. A. Horne, *A Savage War of Peace*, 184–6.
68. B. A. Salamanca, 'Vehicle Bombs: Death on Wheels', in N. C. Livingstone & T. E. Arnold (eds), *Fighting Back: Winning the War Against Terrorism* (Lexington, MA: Lexington Books, 1986), 40–2.

69. D. C. Martin & J. Walcott, *Best Laid Plans: The Inside Story of America's War Against Terrorism* (New York: Harper & Row, 1988), 219–20. B. Woodward, *Veil: The Secret Wars of the CIA, 1981–1987* (London: Simon Schuster, 1987), 395–8.
70. 'Iran blamed for embassy car bomb', *The Times*, 27 July 1994. 'Hunt for woman car bomber', *The Daily Telegraph*, 27 July 1994.
71. 'IRA bombs were biggest ever', *The Independent on Sunday*, 12 April 1992. 'London counts the cost of IRA bombs', *The Independent*, 13 April 1992. 'Back-to-work City defies the IRA', *The Times*, 13 April 1992. 'Security to be stepped up in City after blast', *The Independent*, 26 April 1993. 'Taxpayers foot IRA bomb bill', *The Times*, 26 April 1993. B. O'Brien, *The Long War*, 272–3.
72. E. Crankshaw, *The Shadow of the Winter Palace*, 315–18. B. Savinkov, *Memoirs of a Terrorist*, 48, 58–70.
73. 'Rajiv Gandhi assassinated in bomb blast', *The Times*, 22 May 1991. 'Rajiv Gandhi murdered by bombers at election rally', *The Independent*, 22 May 1991. 'What One-Eyed Jack knows', *The Independent*, 1 July 1991. 'Suicide bomber murders president of Sri Lanka', *The Independent on Sunday*, 2 May 1993. 'Tamil Tigers blamed as bomb kills president', *The Times*, 2 May 1993. 'Dignity and death with the Freedom Birds', *The Independent on Sunday*, 26 May 1991.
74. R. Fisk, *Pity the Nation: Lebanon at War* (London: Andre Deutsch, 1990; Oxford: Oxford University Press, 1991), 478–80, 511–20. G. Rosie, *The Directory of International Terrorism*, 49–50, 51.
75. 'Hamas takes revenge for Hebron', *The Independent*, 7 April 1994. 'Nine die in suicide attack on school bus', *The Times*, 7 April 1994. 'Rabin dubbed traitor as Afula buries its dead', *The Times*, 8 April 1994.
76. 'IRA "Proxy Bombs" Blast Belfast', *The Times*, 26 July 1974. '"Human-bomb" attack fails', *The Independent*, 21 December 1990. '"Human-bomb" attack denounced', *The Independent*, 5 February 1991. 'Taxi forced to cruise West End with IRA bomb', *The Independent*, 17 June 1992. 'Mini-cab drivers "in deep shock" after hijacking', *The Independent*, 26 April 1993. 'IRA's new tactic breaches security forces' defences', *The Independent*, 25 October 1990.
77. 'IRA uses human bombs', *The Independent*, 25 October 1990. 'Seven dead in IRA "human bomb" attacks', *The Times*, 25 October 1990. 'Sitting ducks for the IRA killers', *The Sunday Correspondent*, 28 October 1990.
78. 'IRA uses human bombs', *The Independent*, 25 October 1990. 'Hume denounces IRA "cowards"', *The Independent*, 26 October 1990.
79. B. O'Brien, *The Long War*, 52, 56.
80. K. Heskin, 'The Terrorists' Terrorist: Vincent Browne's interview with Dominic McGlinchey', Y. Alexander & A. O'Day (eds), *Ireland's Terrorist Dilemma* (Dordrecht, The Netherlands: Martinus Nijhoff, 1986), 100.
81. 'German terror group admits assassination', *The Independent*, 3 April 1991. 'East German reforms hit by murder of privatisation chief', *The Times*, 3 April 1991. 'The gap left by Rohwedder', *The Economist*, 6 April 1991. B. Hoffman, 'Terrorist Targeting: Tactics, Trends, and

Potentialities', *Terrorism and Political Violence*, 5, no. 2 (Summer 1993), 16.
82. 'Long-range rifle in Ulster haul', *The Independent*, 18 August 1993. 'American sniper rifle found in arms cache', *The Times*, 18 August 1993. 'One-mile range rifle found', *The Daily Telegraph*, 18 August 1993.
83. 'Bomb warning action "too late"', *The Independent*, 19 February 1991. 'Police decided not to evacuate after "vague" phone call', *The Times*, 19 February 1991.
84. 'Video "filmed IRA bombers at Harrods"', *The Independent*, 14 April 1994. 'English-born bombers get 30 years for IRA blasts', *The Guardian*, 14 May 1994. '"Proud" IRA bombers jailed for 30 years', *The Independent*, 14 May 1994.
85. P. Bishop & E. Mallie, *The Provisional IRA*, 423–4. M. Dillon, *The Enemy Within* (London: Doubleday, 1994), 163–5.
86. A. Jamieson, *The Heart Attacked*, 113, 117. P. Willan, *Puppet Masters*, 214–15. P. W. Little. 'Abduction and Assassination Reconsidered', *TVI Report*, 8, no. 3 (1989), 17–18.
87. A. J. Scotti, 'Transportation Security', 354.
88. G. Grivas-Dighenis, *Guerrilla Warfare*, 63–4, 100.
89. 'Soldier and boy hurt in IRA "coffee jar" bomb attack', *The Independent*, 28 April 1992. 'Limpet mine raid on police car wounds 21 people', *The Independent on Sunday*, 28 June 1992. D. McKittrick, *Despatches from Belfast*, 195. B. O'Brien. *The Long War*, 154–5.
90. 'Rajiv Gandhi murdered by bombers at election rally', *The Independent*, 22 May 1991. 'What One-Eyed Jack knows', *The Independent*, 1 July 1991.
91. K. Heskin, 'The Terrorists' Terrorist', 100.
92. 'IRA kills leading Ulster politician', *The Times*, 8 December 1983. 'Attacks on perjury personnel', *AP/RN*, 8 December 1983. T. P. Coogan, *Michael Collins*, 116. T. P. Coogan, *On the Blanket: The H-Block Story* (Dublin: Ward River Press, 1980), 205, 232. P. Taylor, *States of Terror*, 106.
93. There is some dispute as to who sponsored this operation. Dobson and Payne mention Iraq, Algeria, Libya, and the PFLP as 'more obviously interested parties', with the USSR as having an interest in seeing the kidnapping succeed in weakening OPEC. Yallop on the other hand points the finger more directly at Iraq acting through the PFLP. C. Dobson & R. Payne, *The Carlos Complex: A Study in Terror*, revised edition (London: Coronet, 1978), 99, 119, 126–7. D. Yallop, *To the Ends of the Earth: The Hunt for the Jackal* (London: Jonathan Cape, 1993), 375–6, 378–9, 396–7.
94. 'IRA land-mines hard to detect', *The Guardian*, 10 April 1990.
95. A. Jamieson, *The Heart Attacked*, 110–18. P. Willan, *Puppet Masters*, 238.
96. A. Feldman, *Formations of Violence*, 42–5. P. Bishop & E. Mallie, *The Provisional IRA*, 247–8. M. Dillon, *Killer in Clowntown*, 85.
97. 'Four shot dead as army traps IRA gang', *The Times*, 17 February 1992. 'Army jubilant at killing of IRA men', 'Soldiers lay in wait for IRA gang to return', both in *The Independent*, 18 February 1992.

'Cleared IRA man shot by SAS', *The Times*, 18 February 1992. B. O'Brien, *The Long War*, 232–4.
98. Y. Alexander & D. Pluchinsky (eds), *Europe's Red Terrorists*.
99. D. Moss, *The Politics of Left-Wing Violence in Italy*, 2.
100. 'Plotting Eelam's future', *The Independent*, 15 June 1991. 'Head of Gandhi murder squad dies after siege', *The Independent*, 21 August 1991. 'Enough evidence to implicate LTTE chief', *The Hindu: International Edition*, 8 February 1992.
101. 'LTTE denies hand in killing of Wijeratne', *The Hindu: International Edition*, 16 March 1991. 'LTTE blamed for Wijeratne's killing', *The Hindu: International Edition*, 23 March 1991.

6 CAPABILITIES

1. D. Salvioni & A. Stephanson, 'Reflections on the Red Brigades', *Orbis: A Journal of World Affairs*, 29, no. 3 (Fall 1985), 491–2. A. Jamieson, *The Heart Attacked*, 70–6. G. C. Caselli & D. della Porta, 'The history of the Red Brigades', 72.
2. H. Cobban, *The Palestinian Liberation Organisation: People, Power and Politics* (Cambridge: Cambridge University Press, 1984), 21–31. A. Frangi, *The PLO and Palestine* (Frankfurt: R. G. Fischer Verlag, 1982; London: Zed Books, 1983), 95–102.
3. B. A. Scharlau, *Left-Wing Terrorism in the Federal Republic of Germany*, 179.
4. S. Bruce, *The Red Hand*, 46–50. D. L. G. Hall, *The Ulster Defence Association*, 10, 25, 42–3, 336–7.
5. See G. Carr, *The Angry Brigade*.
6. 'Defector who finds life too quiet', *The Times*, 22 February 1973. 'Internment: the big gamble for both sides', *The Independent on Sunday*, 17 November 1991. M. Dillon & D. Lehane, *Political Murder in Northern Ireland*, 247, 257–8.
7. G. Kassimeris, 'Greece: Twenty Years of Political Terrorism', *Terrorism and Political Violence*, 7, no. 2 (Summer 1995), 80. A. Corsun, 'Group Profile: The Revolutionary Organization 17 November in Greece (1975–91)', in Y. Alexander & D. Pluchinsky (eds), *European Terrorism Today and Tomorrow*, 93–4. Y. Alexander & D. Pluchinsky, *Europe's Red Terrorists*, 90.
8. K. Toolis, *Rebel Hearts*, 308.
9. S. Aust, *The Baader-Meinhof Group*, 92–3. J. Becker, *Hitler's Children*, 94, 110–11.
10. I. Salan (chair), 'Psychology of leaders of terrorist groups', *International Journal of Group Tensions*, vol. 12, 88.
11. B. Savinkov, *Memoirs of a Terrorist*. T. P. Coogan, *Michael Collins*. M. Begin, *The Revolt*, revised edition (1952; London: W. H. Allen, 1979). G. Grivas–Dighenis, *Guerrilla Warfare*. D. Barker, *Grivas: Portrait of a Terrorist* (London: Cresset, 1959). S. MacStiofain, *Revolutionary in Ireland* (Edinburgh: Gordon Cremonesi, 1975).
12. M. Begin, *The Revolt*, 288–90. R. D. Wilson, *Cordon and Search: With*

6th Airborne Division in Palestine (Aldershot: Gale & Polden, 1949), 132–4. E. Tavin & Y. Alexander (eds), *Psychological Warfare and Propaganda: Irgun Documentation* (Wilmington, DE: Scholarly Resources Inc., 1982), 229–30. L. Collins & D. Lapierre, *O Jerusalem!* (London: Weidenfeld and Nicolson, 1972; Pan, 1973), 95.

13. '"We remain totally committed and confident in victory" – Oglaigh na hEireann', *AP/RN*, 14 February 1991.
14. S. Macstiofain, *Revolutionary in Ireland*, 246.
15. Ibid., 301–2. P. Bishop & E. Mallie, *The Provisional IRA*, 247–8.
16. T. P. Coogan, *Michael Collins*, 117.
17. S. Macstiofain, *Revolutionary in Ireland*, 74–9.
18. Ibid., 43–4, 47. L. Clarke, *Broadening the Battlefield*, 30. M. Dillon, *Killer in Clowntown*, 261. R. Taber, *The War of the Flea: Guerrilla Warfare Theory and Practice* (St Albans: Paladin, 1970). M. McGuire, *To Take Arms*, 69. T. P. Coogan, *The IRA*, 693.
19. A. Jamieson, *The Heart Attacked*, 49. A. Jamieson, 'Entry, Discipline and Exit in the Italian Red Brigades', *Terrorism and Political Violence*, 2, no. 1 (Spring 1990), 1, 3–4.
20. B. Baumann, *Wie Alles Anfing. How it all Began: The Personal Account of a West German Urban Guerrilla* (Munich: Trikont Verlag, 1975; Vancouver: Pulp Press, 1977), 49–50. S. Aust, *The Baader-Meinhof Group*, 89–101.
21. 'Hamas has learnt the lessons of Lebanon', *The Independent*, 20 October 1994. B. Hoffman & D. K. Hoffman, 'The RAND–St Andrews Chronology of International Terrorism, 1994', *Terrorism and Political Violence*, 7, no. 4 (Winter 1995), 219.
22. A. Jamieson, *The Heart Attacked*, 92, 123, 126, 186.
23. 'Italian Terrorists Kill a Union Aide', *Washington Post*, 25 January 1979. 'Italian labour protest over killing', *Financial Times*, 26 January 1979. 'Hero's funeral for party victim', *Financial Times*, 29 January 1979. C. Seton-Watson, 'Terrorism in Italy', 110. A. Jamieson, *The Heart Attacked*, 100, 175–6. D. Moss, *The Politics of Left-Wing Violence in Italy*, 227, 285 n42.
24. S. Strong, *Shining Path*, 99–101. S. V. D. Samaranayake, *Political Violence in the Third World: A Case Study of Sri Lanka, 1971–1987*, Ph.D., University of St Andrews, 1990, 238–41. M. Ranstorp, 'Hizbollah's Command Leadership: Its Structure, Decision Making and Relationship with Iranian Clergy and Institutions', *Terrorism and Political Violence*, 6, no. 3 (Autumn 1994), 304–16.
25. J. Holland & H. McDonald, *INLA*, 17–118. A. Jamieson, *The Heart Attacked*, 173, 182–83.
26. M. Dillon, *The Shankill Butchers*, 8, 12, 49, 59. S. Bruce, *The Red Hand*, 173.
27. P. C. Hearst & A. Moscow, *Every Secret Thing*, 139–40, 154, 161, 198, 201.
28. G. Grivas, *Guerrilla Warfare*, 25, 47–8. D. Barker, *Grivas*, 25–9, 51–2, 79–80, 119, 139–40.
29. K. Toolis, *Rebel Hearts*, 294–6, 308, 309–10. P. Bishop & E. Mallie, *The Provisional IRA*, 197–8.

30. 'Bogside fighter turned to politics', *The Independent*, 26 August 1993.
31. K. Toolis, *Rebel Hearts*, 247. P. Bishop & E. Mallie, *The Provisional IRA*, 13, 318–20.
32. D. Beresford, *Ten Men Dead: The story of the 1981 Irish hunger strike* (London: Grafton, 1987), 152–7. L. Clarke, *Broadening the Battlefield*, 162–3. D. Hammill, *Pig in the Middle*, 268–9. P. Bishop & E. Mallie, *The Provisional IRA*, 456. M. Urban, *Big Boy's Rules*, 223–4. B. O'Brien, *The Long War*, 142.
33. S. Bruce, 'Criminality and Vigilante Politics: The Scottish Protestant Case', *Conflict Quarterly*, Spring 1986, 20.
34. *Corriere dela Sera*, 10 January 1982. 'Red Brigades key planner is betrayed', *The Daily Telegraph*, 11 January 1982. D. Salvioni & A. Stephanson, 'Reflections on the Red Brigades', 501. A. Jamieson, *The Heart Attacked*, 183–4. P. Willan, *Puppet Masters*, 326.
35. D. Canter, *Criminal Shadows: Inside the Mind of the Serial Killer* (London: HarperCollins, 1994; 1995), 214, 220, 294, 297–8.
36. J. Bowyer Bell, *IRA Tactics and Targets*, 14.
37. 'Internment: the big gamble for both sides', *The Independent*, 17 November 1991.
38. 'Internment "only way to beat IRA"', *The Independent*, 17 November 1991.
39. E. Crankshaw, *The Shadow of the Winter Palace*, 297. R. Hingley, *The Russian Secret Police*, 64.
40. 'Teenagers who enlist for terror', *The Independent on Sunday*, 5 August 1990. P. Bishop & E. Mallie, *The Provisional IRA*, 287–8.
41. A. Jamieson, *The Heart Attacked*, 113, 117, 122. P. Willan, *Puppet Masters*, 215.
42. J. Agirre, *Operation Ogro*, 2–3, 57–8, 72.
43. B. Dasgupta, *The Naxalite Movement*, 44–5, 83, 87. E. Duyker, *Tribal Guerrillas: The Santals of West Bengal and the Naxalite Movement* (Delhi: Oxford University Press, 1987), 84, 127.
44. B. Baumann, *Wie Alles Anfing*, 49–50. S. Aust, *The Baader-Meinhof Group*, 89–101. P. Willan, *Puppet Masters*, 165–6. C. di Giovanni, *Light from Behind the Bars*, 98, 104. H. J. Horchem, *Terrorism in West Germany*, 10–11, 12–14.
45. B. Vaughn, 'The Use and Abuse of Intelligence Services in India', 11–12.
46. J. Schmeidel, 'My Enemy's Enemy', 66–7. B. A. Scharlau, *Left-Wing Terrorism in the Federal Republic of Germany*, 56–61.
47. J. Pearce, *Colombia: Inside the Labyrinth*, 177. Amnesty International, *Getting Away with Murder*, 36.
48. Amnesty International, *Political violence in Colombia*, 21, 24–8.
49. C. Ryder, *The Ulster Defence Regiment: An Instrument of Peace?* (London: Methuen, 1991), 182–3.
50. P. Marnham, *Crime and the Academie Francaise: Dispatches from Paris* (Harmondsworth: Viking, 1993), 9, 11–12.
51. S. Bruce, *The Red Hand*, 216–18, 225, 271–3.
52. G. McKee & R. Franey, *Time Bomb*, 9, 61, 63, 337. M. Dillon, *The Enemy Within*, 137.

53. For accounts of such terrorist bombing operations see L. Collins & D. Lapierre, *O Jerusalem!* 116–20, 179–82. S. O'Doherty, *The Volunteer*, 69–71.
54. M. Sutton, *Bear in Mind These Dead*, 197.
55. M. Dillon & D. Lehane, *Political Murder in Northern Ireland*, 144. F. Burton, *The politics of legitimacy: Struggles in a Belfast community* (London: Routledge & Kegan Paul, 1978), 109, 22, 23. P. Bishop & E. Mallie, *The Provisional IRA*, 13, 290–1. J. Holland & H. McDonald, *INLA*, 83, 217–18, 258, 280 n.1. M. Urban, *Big Boy's Rules*, 223–4.
56. 'Spirit of hope confronts a deadlier terror', *The Daily Telegraph*, 20 October 1994. A. Ashkenasi, 'Social-Ethnic Conflict and Paramilitary Organization in the Near East', in P. H. Merkl (ed.), *Political Violence and Terror*, 317.
57. C. Coughlin, *Hostage: the complete story of the Lebanon captives* (London: Little, Brown & Co, 1992), 79, 92, 104. E. F. Mickolus, T. Sandler, J. M. Murdock, *International Terrorism in the 1980s: 1980–1983*, 468–9. E. F. Mickolus, T. Sandler, J. M. Murdock, *International Terrorism in the 1980s: 1984–1987*, 139–42. G. Rosie, *The Directory of International Terrorism*, 168–9.
58. P. Marnham, *Crime and the Academie Francaise*, 9, 16.
59. C. Novaro, 'Social networks and terrorism: the case of *Prima Linea*', in R. Catanzaro (ed.), *The Red Brigades and Left-Wing Terrorism in Italy*. A. Jamieson, *The Heart Attacked*, 103–7. B. A. Scharlau, *Left-Wing Terrorism in the Federal Republic of Germany*, 163–70.
60. R. P. Clark, 'Patterns in the Lives of ETA members', 298–9, 304–5. P. Taylor, *States of Terror*, 88–93.
61. 'Taught to kill, not to pity', *The Independent on Sunday*, 21 March 1993. R. Holmes, *Firing Line*, 366. J. Ellis, *The Sharp End of War*, 318–20. M. Maclear, *Vietnam: The Ten Thousand Day War* (London: Thames/Methuen, 1981; 1982), 373–8. M. Walzer, *Just and Unjust Wars*, 309–15.
62. C. R. Browning, *Ordinary Men: Reserve Police Battalion 101 and the Final Solution in Poland* (New York: Harper Collins, 1992; 1993), 1–2, 55–70, 77, 102, 191.
63. H. Brown, *People, Groups, and Society* (Milton Keynes, England: Open University Press, 1985), 16–19. K. Heskin, *Northern Ireland: A Psychological Analysis* (Dublin: Gill & Macmillan, 1980), 87–8.
64. L. Williams, 'Through the eyes of a torturer', *Amnesty. Campaign Journal for Amnesty International British Section* (London), May/June 1995 (issue 73).
65. H. A. Lyons & H. J. Harbinson, 'A Comparison of Political and Non-Political Murderers in Northern Ireland, 1974–84'. K. Heskin, 'The psychology of terrorism in Northern Ireland', in Y. Alexander & A. O'Day (eds), *Terrorism in Ireland* (London: Croom Helm, 1984). K. Heskin, *Northern Ireland: A Psychological Analysis*, 74–93. F. Ferracuti, 'A Sociopsychiatric Interpretation of Terrorism', *Annals of the American Academy*, 463 (September 1982), 130. F. Ferracuti & F. Bruno, 'Psychiatric Aspects of Terrorism in Italy', I. L. Barak-Glantz & C. R. Huff (eds), *The Mad, the Bad, and the Different: Essays in*

Honor of Simon Dinitz (Lexington, MA: Lexington Books, 1981), 207.
66. F. Ferracuti & F. Bruno, 'Psychiatric Aspects of Terrorism in Italy', 209. E. Kolinsky, 'Terrorism in West Germany', in J. Lodge (ed.), *The Threat of Terrorism*, 75–6.
67. J. M. Post, 'Notes on a Psychodynamic Theory of Terrorist Behaviour', *Terrorism: An International Journal*, 7, no. 3 (1984), 241.
68. J. M. Post, 'Terrorist psycho–logic: Terrorist behaviour as a product of psychological forces', in W. Reich (ed.), *Origins of Terrorism: Psychologies, Ideologies, Theologies, States of Mind* (Cambridge: Cambridge University Press, 1990), 27. L. Bollinger, 'Terrorist conduct as a result of a psychosocial process', in P. Pichot, P. Berner & K. Thau (eds), *Psychiatry: The State of the Art. Volume 6: Drug Dependence and Alcoholism, Forensic Psychiatry, Military Psychiatry* (New York: Plenum Press, 1985), 388.
69. J. M. Post, 'Terrorist psycho-logic', 26.
70. J. M. Post, 'Notes on a Psychodynamic Theory of Terrorist Behaviour', 246, 247, 250.
71. R. P. Clark, 'Patterns in the Lives of ETA members', 283–4, 293–4. R. W. White & T. F. White, 'Revolution in the City: On the Resources of Urban Guerrillas', *Terrorism and Political Violence*, 3, no. 4 (Winter 1991), 110, 115–16.
72. C. A. Russell & B. H. Miller, 'Profile of a Terrorist', in L. Z. Freedman & Y. Alexander (eds), *Perspectives on Nuclear Terrorism* (Wilmington, DE: Scholarly Resources Inc, 1983), 47.
73. R. W. White & T. F. White, 'Revolution in the City', 111.
74. R. P. Clark, 'Patterns in the Lives of ETA members', 286. L. Weinberg & W. Eubank, 'Leaders and Followers in Italian Terrorist Groups', *Terrorism and Political Violence*, 1, no. 2 (April 1989), 167, 169.
75. C. A. Russell & B. H. Miller, 'Profile of a Terrorist', 47–8. K. L. Oots, 'Organizational Perspectives on the Formation and Disintegration of Terrorist Groups', *Terrorism*, 12, no. 3 (1989), 144. L. Weinberg & W. Eubank, 'Leaders and Followers in Italian Terrorist Groups', 169.
76. I. Salan, 'Psychology of leaders of terrorist groups', 96. L. Weinberg & W. Eubank, 'Leaders and Followers in Italian Terrorist Groups', 167, 169. B. A. Scharlau, *Left-Wing Terrorism in the Federal Republic of Germany*, 129. 'Teenagers who enlist for terror', *The Independent on Sunday*, 5 August 1990. J. Bowyer Bell, 'Career Moves: Reflections on the Irish Gunman', *Studies in Conflict and Terrorism*, 15, no. 1 (January–March 1992), 74. T. P. Coogan, *The IRA*, 668–71 lists the ages of 38 IRA prisoners who escaped from the Maze Prison in Northern Ireland in March 1983. The vast majority were in their mid to late twenties, and appear to have been in their late teens to mid-twenties when first imprisoned.
77. C. A. Russell & B. H. Miller, 'Profile of a Terrorist', 47. B. A. Scharlau, *Left-Wing Terrorism in the Federal Republic of Germany*, 129.
78. L. Weinberg & W. Eubank, 'Leaders and Followers in Italian Terrorist Groups', 167.
79. M. Crenshaw, 'An Organizational Approach to the Analysis of Political Terrorism', *Orbis: A Journal of World Affairs* 29, no. 3 (Fall 1985), 474–5.

80. B. Baumann, *Wie Alles Anfing*, 72.
81. D. L. G. Hall, *The Ulster Defence Association*, 82.
82. Ibid., 75, 77.
83. C. Townshend, *Political Violence in Ireland: Government and Resistance since 1848* (Oxford: Oxford University Press), 366. P. Bishop & E. Mallie, *The Provisional IRA*, 276, 285. B. O'Brien, *The Long War*, 34. K. Toolis, *Rebel Hearts*, 294–5.
84. F. Burton, *The Politics of Legitimacy*, 111. B. O'Brien, *The Long War*, 40.
85. B. O'Brien, *The Long War*, 40.
86. S. Strong, *Shining Path*, 36–9. W. A. Hazleton & S. Woy-Hazleton, 'Sendero Luminoso', 66–8.
87. P. O'Malley, *Biting at the Grave: The Irish Hunger Strikes and the Politics of Despair* (Belfast: Blackstaff Press, 1990), 285.
88. 'Key figures allegedly behind attacks on the Continent', and 'Web of terror that spread across Europe', both in *The Independent*, 3 April 1991. B. O'Brien, *The Long War*, 142. J. Adams, R. Morgan & A. Bambridge, *Ambush: The War Between the SAS and the IRA* (London: Pan, 1988), 136–40.
89. J. Schmeidel, 'My Enemy's Enemy', 64–6. B. A. Scharlau, *Left-Wing Terrorism in the Federal Republic of Germany*, 299, 301. E. MacDonald, *Shoot the Women First*, 227–8.
90. M. Sutton, *Bear in mind these dead... An Index of Deaths from the Conflict in Ireland, 1969–1993* (Belfast: Beyond the Pale Publications, 1994), 195–205.
91. See D. Beresford, *Ten Men Dead*. L. Clarke, *Broadening the Battlefield*.
92. B. A. Scharlau, *Left-Wing Terrorism in the Federal Republic of Germany*, 93–9, 300, 304.
93. Merari argues that some of the suicide bombers in Lebanon were either coerced or duped into taking part in such operations. A. Merari, 'The readiness to kill and die: Suicidal terrorism in the Middle East', in W. Reich (ed.), *Origins of Terrorism*, 194–6.
94. M. R. D. Foot, *Resistance* (Eyre Methuen, 1976; London: Granada, 1978), 55.
95. Y. Katayama, *Terrorism in Japan since 1969*, 49. W. R. Farrell, *Blood and Rage*, 96–7.
96. 'Terroristi denudino due vigili rubando le lore divise armi a tesserini', *Corriere della Serra*, 1 May 1979.
97. Amnesty International, *Political Violence in Colombia*, 42, 52, 94–5. Amnesty International, *Getting away with murder*, 34–6.
98. S. Bruce, *The Red Hand*, 218. C. Ryder, *The Ulster Defence Regiment*, 152, 158–61, 175, 179–81. M. Dillon, *The Dirty War*, 219–20.
99. F. S. Pearson, *The Global Spread of Arms: Political Economy of International Security* (Boulder, CO: Westview Press, 1994), 61.
100. P. Bishop & E. Mallie, *The Provisional IRA*, 295–6. J. Holland, *The American Connection* (New York: Viking Penguin, 1987; Dublin: Poolbeg, 1989), 81–3. J. Bowyer Bell, *The Secret Army*, 439.
101. R. Moss, *The Politics of Left-Wing Violence in Italy*, 53.
102. '"Assassin" guns seized in raids on arms ring', *The Independent*,

25 May 1995. F. S. Pearson, *The Global Spread of Arms*, 61. R. Fleming & H. Miller, *Scotland Yard* (London: Michael Joseph, 1994), 5. *The Cook Report*, ITV, television, 13 June 1995.
103. 'The arms suppliers go to war', *The Independent on Sunday*, business supplement, 4 September 1994.
104. P. Paganacci, 'Weapons of the Russian Special Forces', *RAIDS*, UK edition (January 1995).
105. US Department of State, Bureau of Public Affairs, *Libya under Qadhafi*, 1. P. Seale, *Abu Nidal: A Gun for Hire* (New York: Random House, 1992), 105, 149, 242–3.
106. R. H. Shultz, 'Iranian Covert Aggression: Support for Radical Political Islamists Conducting Internal Subversion Against States in the Middle East/Southwest Asia Region', *Terrorism and Political Violence*, 6, no. 3 (Autumn 1994), 285, 286, 290. M. Ranstorp, 'Hizbollah's Command Leadership', 307, 310. B. Woodward, *Veil*, 177, 225–8, 275, 355–6, 388–92, 465–7, 481–3. C. Dickey, *With the Contras: A Reporter in the Wilds of Nicaragua* (New York: Simon & Schuster, 1985; London: Faber & Faber, 1986), 143, 161–2, 166–71, 180–1, 211. H. E. Vanden, 'State Policy and the Cult of Terror in Central America', P. Wilkinson & A. M. Stewart (eds), *Contemporary Research on Terrorism*, 265–7. O. North & W. Novak, *Under Fire: An American Story* (New York: HarperCollins, 1991), 249–50.
107. 'Voyage into business of terror', *The Independent*, 12 January 1991. P. Bishop & E. Mallie, *The Provisional IRA*, 246, 305–6. J. Adams, *Trading in Death: The Modern Arms Race* (London: Hutchinson, 1990; Pan, 1991), 17–30.
108. Statistics vary from one source to another. See 'Arming the IRA: The Libyan Connection', *The Economist* (London), 31 March 1990. 'Gadaffi admits training IRA elite', *The Sunday Times*, 21 June 1992. 'RUC chief proposes national police units', *The Independent*, 22 July 1992. B. O'Brien, *The Long War*, 144.
109. 'Libyan arms fuel surge in terrorism', *The Independent*, 8 May 1990. 'IRA has enough Semtex for 15 years', *The Independent on Sunday*, 19 March 1995.
110. J. Adams, *Trading in Death*, 58–64. J. Salata, 'MANPADs: The Potential for Use as a Terrorist Tactic', in US Department of State, Bureau of Diplomatic Security (ed.), *Terrorist Tactics and Security Practices*, 90–4. The acronym MANPAD stands for Man Portable Air Defence System. Another frequently used term for portable and non-portable ground-to-air missiles is SAM (Surface to Air Missile).
111. 'Algerian extremists murder 12 foreigners', *The Independent*, 16 December 1993. J. Salata, 'MANPADs', 102.
112. J. Salata. 'MANPADs', 93–4. J. Adams, *Trading in Death*, 70–1. F. S. Pearson, *The Global Spread of Arms*, 55. R. H. Schultz, 'Iranian Covert Aggression', 283.
113. J. Schmeidel, 'My Enemy's Enemy', 64–6. H. Horchem, 'The Decline of the Red Army Faction', 61, 63–5. B. A. Scharlau, *Left-Wing Terrorism in the Federal Republic of Germany*, 58–9.
114. J. Adams, *Trading in Death*, 29. M. Dillon, *The Dirty War*, 431. 'IRA

hunts for top-level mole', *The Observer*, 13 March 1988.
115. P. Seale, *Abu Nidal*, 109–51. H. Cobban, *The Palestinian Liberation Organisation*, 55, 96–7, 165.
116. H. Willmott, 'Kenya in Revolt', in R. Thompson & J. Keegan (eds), *War in Peace: An Analysis of Warfare since 1945* (London: Orbis, 1981), 111. B. Dasgupta, *the Naxalite Movement*, 83.
117. 'Ex-soldier made guns for loyalists', *The Independent*, 6 October 1990.
118. 'Spain hails arrest of ETA chief', *The Independent*, 22 February 1993.
119. 'Terrorists keep faith with a weapon that rarely kills' *The Independent*, 8 February 1991. 'The day John Major missed his lunch', *The Sunday Times*, 10 February 1991.
120. C. Ryder, *The RUC*, 310–12.
121. D. McKittrick, *Despatches from Belfast*, 206.
122. 'IRA bombers attack No 10 War Cabinet', *The Independent*, 8 February 1991. 'Mortar bombs realise worst fears of police', *The Daily Telegraph*, 8 February 1991. 'Yard "powerless" to avert new attack', *The Guardian*, 8 February 1991. 'Police comb Heathrow for more mortars', *The Independent*, 12 March 1994. 'Tanks threat turns the screw on airport bombers', *The Sunday Times*, 13 March 1994. 'Flight chaos as bomb warnings close airports', *The Independent*, 14 March 1994.
123. W. Powell, *The Anarchist Cookbook* (Lyle Stuart Inc, 1971; Secaucus, NJ: Barricade Books, 1989). 'Over-taxed and under siege', *The Independent*, 24 April 1995. 'America wakes up to its paranoid army', *The Independent*, 25 April 1995.
124. W. R. Farrell, *Blood and Rage*, xvii–xix.
125. 'IRA "using rewired US radar detectors as bomb detonators"', *The Independent*, 7 June 1990.
126. 'Photoflash bomb threat to the public', *The Scotsman*, 16 March 1994. 'IRA's "Russian roulette" detonator', *The Times*, 16 March 1994.
127. 'Security alert sent to police before bombing in Brighton', *The Times*, 15 October 1984. 'Long delay IRA fuses not new', *The Guardian*, 15 October 1984. 'RUC irked by claims of long-delay IRA bombs', *The Daily Telegraph*, 16 October 1984. P. Bishop & E. Mallie, *The Provisional IRA*, 423–6. 'Simplicity of incendiary device makes disruption easy', *The Guardian*, 24 December 1991.
128. B. Dasgupta, *The Naxalite Movement*, 79–80, 83. P. Gurney, *Braver Men Walk Away*, 116–17. D. Barzilay, *The British Army in Ulster*, vol. 2 (Belfast: Century Services Ltd, 1975), 129.
129. B. O'Brien, *The Long War*, 154–5. D. McKittrick, *Despatches from Belfast*, 195. D. McKittrick, *Endgame*, 85.
130. 'Ball bomb', *The Independent*, 31 March 1992. 'Soldier given IRA bomb in chocolates tin', *The Independent*, 24 December 1992.
131. M. Dillon, *The Enemy Within*, 27–8. J. Bowyer Bell, *The Secret Army*, 150, 153. J. Adams, *Trading in Death*, 9–10.
132. 'Biggest IRA bomb defused', *The Independent*, 6 September 1991. 'IRA City bomb was fertiliser', *The Independent*, 28 May 1992. 'Damage in huge blast put at £20m', *The Independent*, 25 September 1992. 'Shock wave of destruction was created by a deadly mixture', *The Independent*, 27 April 1993. 'Explosion could have wrecked city cen-

tre', *The Daily Telegraph*, 13 August 1993. B. O'Brien, *The Long War*, 214, 238–9.

133. 'Bomb built for damage, not slaughter', *The Independent*, 22 April 1995. 'FBI widens hunt as Republicans race to back Clinton's tough line', *The Guardian*, 25 April 1995. 'FBI piles up evidence against McVeigh', *The Independent*, 28 April 1995. 'FBI "close" to arresting bombers', *The Independent*, 22 May 1995.

134. 'Poison terror in the subway', *The Independent*, 21 March 1995. 'Religious cult suspected of gas attacks', *The Times*, 21 March 1995. 'Doom-cult linked with "sarin affair" a year ago', *The Independent*, 22 March 1995. 'Strange Aum life for cult children', *The Guardian*, 20 April 1995. 'Tokyo gas attack cult leader held', *The Guardian*, 16 May 1995. 'Aum cultists admit making nerve gas', *The Independent*, 18 May 1995. 'Aum sect guru faces trial for murder', *The Independent*, 7 June 1995.

135. 'Aum cult doctor admits making sarin nerve gas', *The Independent*, 25 October 1995.

136. C. Ryder, *The RUC*, 253–4.

137. R. Clutterbuck, 'Trends in Terrorist Weaponry', *Terrorism and Political Violence*, 5, no. 2 (Summer 1993), 130, 132.

138. R. P. Clark, *The Basques*, 155. S. Bruce, *The Red Hand*, 169.

139. E. C. Ezell, *Small Arms of the World: a basic manual of small arms*, twelfth edition (New York: Barnes & Noble, 1993), 131.

140. T. Gander, *Combat Pistols: A manual of modern handguns* (Wellingborough: Patrick Stephens Ltd, 1989), 77–80. R. Adam, *Modern Handguns* (London: Quintet, 1989), 111.

141. J. Holland, *The American Connection*, 82. P. Bishop & E. Mallie, *The Provisional IRA*, 169.

142. P. de Polnay, *Napoleon's Police* (London: W. H. Allen, 1970), 71–7. F. L. Ford, *Political Murder: From Tyrannicide to Terrorism* (Cambridge, MA: Harvard University Press, 1985), 216–17. W. Laqueur, *The Age of Terrorism*, 101.

143. J. Most, *Revolutionare Kriegswissenschaft* (New York: Drud und Berlag des Internationalen Zeitungs Beireins, 1885). Published with *The Beast of Property* (New Haven: International Workingmen's Ass'n, 1884), in one volume (New York: Kraus Reprint, 1983).

144. K. R. M. Short, *The Dynamite War: Irish-American Bombers in Victorian Britain* (Dublin: Gill & Macmillan, 1979), 1–2, 55, 64–5, 105, 128–9, 181, 205. W. Laqueur, *The Age of Terrorism*, 104.

145. 'IRA "transformed" by Libyan arms donation', *The Independent*, 7 March 1991. P. Gurney, *Braver Men Walk Away*, 151, 214.

146. 'IRA fund-raising blamed for surge in Irish robberies', *The Independent*, 22 May 1990. 'Dealing in the business of fear', *Financial Times*, 7 January 1992. 'IRA suspected as raiders get away with £2m', *The Independent*, 8 January 1992. 'Inquiry into IRA city pub links', *The Irish Times*, 9 September 1992. 'Irish pubs suspected of laundering IRA funds', *The Independent*, 28 September 1992. 'The IRA', *The Independent on Sunday*, 22 November 1992. J. Adams, *The Financing of Terror*, 197–228. D. McKittrick, *Despatches from Belfast*, 146–51.

147. S. Strong, *Shining Path*, 114, 122, 125. J. E. Gonzales, 'Guerrillas and Coca in the Upper Huallaga Valley', in D. S. Palmer (ed.), *Shining Path of Peru*, 108, 121–2. R. Rumrrill, 'The highs and lows of a cocaine economy', in M. L. Smith (ed.), *Why people grow drugs*, 86, 89.
148. C. Watson, 'Guerrilla Groups in Colombia', 88–9, 94–6. A. M. Bravo, 'Frontier culture takes to cocaine', 73, 75. J. Pearce, *Colombia: Inside the Labyrinth*, 1, 177–8, 247. Amnesty International, *Political violence in Colombia*, 52. J. Adams, *The Financing of Terror*, 269.
149. 'Terrorists "run Ulster drugs trade"', *The Independent*, 7 February 1992. 'Action against drugs puts gunmen in "policing" role', *The Independent*, 3 November 1992. 'IRA looks set for victory over terrorist faction', *The Independent*, 4 November 1992. J. Holland & H. McDonald, *INLA*, 311–13, 319–20. S. Bruce, *The Red Hand*, 194. J. Adams, *The Financing of Terror*, 289.
150. M. Ranstorp, 'Hizbollah's Command Leadership', 321. R. H. Shultz, 'Iranian Covert Aggression', 290, 297.
151. O. North & W. Novak, *Under Fire*, 21–2, 234–8. B. Woodward, *Veil*, 301, 470, 481–5, 488, 509. J. Ranelagh, *The Agency: The Rise and Decline of the CIA* (London: Weidenfeld & Nicolson, 1986; Sceptre, 1988), 718–19.
152. P. Seale, *Abu Nidal*, 28, 129–30, 204.
153. Ibid., 125, 206.
154. 'Arrests failed to stop attacks', *The Independent*, 7 December 1990. 'IRA arms cache men sentenced to 30 years in prison', 'A 42-day watch that netted top police targets', both in *The Times*, 7 December 1990.
155. 'Terroristi denudino due vigili rubando le lore divise armi a tesserini', *Corriere della Serra*, 1 May 1979.
156. S. Aust, *The Baader-Meinhof Group*, 115, 116. J. Becker, *Hitler's Children*, 234–6.
157. D. Pluchinsky, 'An Organizational and Operational Analysis of Germany's Red Army Faction Terrorist Group', 68–9. B. A. Scharlau, *Left-Wing Terrorism in the Federal Republic of Germany*, 62.
158. P. Seale, *Abu Nidal*, 23, 88, 100, 149.

7 TARGET PROTECTION

1. 'End of a bullet-proof era', *The Independent*, 21 June 1991.
2. 'Huge costs force Yard to review VIP security', *The Independent on Sunday*, 4 February 1990. 'Anti-IRA security costs must rise, police say', *The Independent on Sunday*, 23 September 1990.
3. 'Bookworms who burrow for IRA', *The Sunday Correspondent*, 12 August 1990. D. T. Schiller, 'The European Experience', 51, 57.
4. US Department of State, Overseas Security Advisory Council, *Security Guidelines for American Families Living Abroad* (Washington, DC: US Dept. of State, n.d.), 2.
5. D. E. Wurth, 'The Proper Function and use of the Private Sector Bodyguard', in B. M. Jenkins (ed.), *Terrorism and Personal Protection*, 314.

6. T. Geraghty, *The Bullet-Catchers: Bodyguards and the World of Close Protection* (London: Grafton, 1988; 1989), 18–19.
7. B. M. Jenkins, *The Lessons of Beirut*, 5.
8. G. Wardlaw, *Political Terrorism: Theory, tactics, and counter-measures*, revised edition (Cambridge: Cambridge University Press, 1989), 168–9.
9. 'SAS shield for Mrs Thatcher', *The Daily Telegraph*, 17 May 1987. *Scotland Yard: Terror*, ITV (television), 3 February 1994. D. E. Wurth, 'The Proper Function and use of the Private Sector Bodyguard', 323. R. Fleming & H. Miller, *Scotland Yard*, 146. T. Geraghty, *The Bullet-Catchers*, 204–11.
10. 'SAS shield for Mrs Thatcher', *The Daily Telegraph*, 17 May 1987.
11. Personal observation, Belfast, 12 September 1993.
12. M. Dewar, *Weapons and Equipment of Counter-Terrorism* (Poole: Arms and Armour Press, 1987), 138–75 and *passim*.
13. 'Local Hero', *Esquire* (London), December 1993/January 1994. T. Geraghty, *The Bullet-Catchers*, 206.
14. 'Loyalist gunmen kill five in new Belfast bloodbath', *The Independent*, 6 February 1992. 'Loyalist avengers slaughter five', *The Times*, 6 February 1992. '"The gunmen are savage, sinful, wicked, depraved"', *The Independent*, 1 November 1993. 'Major set to invite Hume to Ulster talks', *The Times*, 1 November 1993. 'New wave of Ulster violence feared', *The Independent*, 20 June 1994. 'Reprisal fear after Catholic pub killings', *The Times*, 20 June 1994. 'Loyalists get life terms for pub atrocity', *The Guardian*, 25 February 1995. 'UFF four get life for pub massacre', *The Independent*, 25 February 1995.
15. 'Publican's fear averted massacre', *The Independent*, 19 July 1994. 'Bar's locked doors foiled UFF gunmen', *The Guardian*, 19 July 1994.
16. 'The price of survival in a divided land', *The Independent on Sunday*, 18 October 1992. 'Local Hero', *Esquire* (London), December 1993/January 1994. 'Victimised', *Fortnight*, no. 320 (September 1993), 9. 'Sinn Fein death part of sustained assault', *The Independent*, 10 August 1993.
17. 'For Queen and Country', *The Guardian*, supplement, 19 October 1993.
18. 'State-of-the-art building for a state of siege', *The Times*, supplement, 21 November 1992.
19. PAC International, *Access Control Equipment: Data Sheet* (Stockport: PAC International Ltd, July 1993). Bel-Tech Security Products, *Bel-Pac 1000 1–2 door access control: BT1000* (Ilford, England: Bell Security Ltd). Visonic, *Company Profile & Product Catalogue*, (Biggleswade: Visonic Ltd, n.d.). R. J. Healy, 'Protecting the Office', in B. M. Jenkins (ed.), *Terrorism and Personal Protection*, 348.
20. R. Clutterbuck, *Kidnap, Hijack and Extortion*, 76. E. Best, 'An Interview with Ed Best, Director of Security at the Los Angeles Olympics', *TVI Journal*, 5, no. 2 (Fall 1984), 5.
21. 'Anti-IRA security costs must rise, police say', *The Independent on Sunday*, 23 September 1990. R. Clutterbuck, *Kidnap, Hijack and Extortion*, 73, 84.
22. 'Israel to deploy dogs on borders in attempt to curb Islamic suicide bombers', *The Guardian*, 30 January 1995. 'Israel brings in dogs',

The Independent, 30 January 1995. M. Dewar, *The British Army in Northern Ireland*, 131. D. Barzilay, *The British Army in Ulster*, vol. 2, 185–7.

23. Advanced Design Electronics and the Home Office, *The Simple Guide to Choosing an Alarm System* (Advanced Design Electronics Ltd). Modern Security Systems, *Detection Devices: Passive Infra-Red Movement Detectors* (Hemel Hempstead: Modern Security Systems Ltd, November 1992). R. Clutterbuck, *Kidnap, Hijack and Extortion*, 74.
24. 'Video filmed IRA bombers at Harrods', *The Independent*, 14 April 1994. 'English-born bombers get 30 years for IRA blasts', *The Guardian*, 14 May 1994. '"Proud" IRA bombers jailed for 30 years', *The Independent*, 14 May 1994. 'Framing the Villains', *New Statesman and Society*, 28 January 1994. 'Long lens of the law', *The Independent*, 6 July 1994. Sensormatic CamEra, *Sensormatic CamEra: The World Leader in Loss Prevention* (Warrington: Sensormatic CamEra Ltd, n.d.). Modern Security Systems, *Could YOU Use an Extra Pair of Eyes?* (Hemel Hempstead: Modern Security Systems Ltd, November 1992).
25. R. Clutterbuck, *Kidnap, Hijack and Extortion*, 73–4, 82. G. Wardlaw, *Political Terrorism*, 169–70.
26. K. Toolis, *Rebel Hearts*, 125.
27. R. Fleming & H. Miller, *Scotland Yard*, 207, 296.
28. UK House of Commons, *The Physical Security of Military Installations in the United Kingdom* (HC-171) (London: HMSO, 1990), 27–8 (paras 358–9), 58 (paras 745–7).
29. 'Death in the afternoon: bombers hit New York', *The Times*, 27 February 1993. 'New York bomb to be rebuilt', *The Times*, 29 February 1993. 'Tapes reveal role of FBI in bombing', *The Independent*, 9 November 1993.
30. 'Security alert sent to police before bombing in Brighton', *The Times*, 15 October 1984. P. Bishop & E. Mallie, *The Provisional IRA*, 423–6.
31. 'Bournemouth "under siege" in £2m security operation', *The Independent*, 9 October 1990. 'Threat to conference "extremely high"', *The Times*, 9 October 1990.
32. J. D. Baldeschwieler, 'Explosive Detection for Commercial Aircraft Security', *Terrorism and Political Violence*, 5, no. 2 (Summer 1993).
33. P. Wilkinson, 'Designing an Effective International Aviation Security System', 109, 111. J. D. Baldeschwieler, 'Explosive Detection for Commercial Aircraft Security', 100.
34. R. Fleming & H. Miller, *Scotland Yard*, 145. T. Geraghty, *The Bullet-Catchers*, 199–200.
35. C. A. Russell & B. H. Miller, 'Terrorist Targets and the Executive Target', 69. A. J. Scotti, 'Transportation Security', 354. H. A. Lyons & H. J. Harbinson, 'A Comparison of Political and Non-Political Murderers in Northern Ireland', 195.
36. G. Capotorto, 'How Terrorists look at Kidnappings', 5.
37. A. Feldman, *Formations of Violence*, 75.
38. A. J. Scotti, 'Transportation Security', 361.
39. R. Clutterbuck, *Kidnap, Hijack and Extortion*, 81. A. J. Scotti, 'Transportation Security', 356–7, 358–9.

40. 'Nightmare for the judges on 24-hour vigil', *The Guardian*, 6 January 1988.
41. Ibid.
42. R. Clutterbuck, *Kidnap, Hijack and Extortion*, 80.
43. C. MacDonald, *The Killing of SS Obergruppenführer Reinhard Heydrich: 27 May 1942* (London: Macmillan, 1989), 149–50, 166, 169–90. The account of the ambush differs slightly in M. R. D. Foot, *Resistance*, 205–6.
44. C. Townshend, *Political Violence in Ireland*, 166. J. Waldron, *Maamtrasna: The Murders and the Mystery* (Dublin: Edmund Burke, 1992), 17. R. Kee, *The Green Flag: A History of Irish Nationalism* (London: Weidenfeld & Nicolson, 1972), 383.
45. M. Dewar, *The British Army in Northern Ireland*, 196. C. Ryder, *The RUC*, 121.
46. 'IRA rings changes to restore balance of terror', *The Guardian*, 5 May 1987.
47. 'SAS shield for Mrs Thatcher', *The Daily Telegraph*, 17 May 1987. A. J. Scotti, 'Transportation Security', 361–8.
48. C. Ryder, *The RUC*, 245. M. Urban, *Big Boys' Rules*, 223.
49. 'How to murder your prime minister', *The Economist*, 29 June 1974.
50. D. Pluchinsky, 'RAF Assassination of Alfred Herrhausen', 6. D. Pluchinsky, 'An Organizational and Operational Analysis of Germany's Red Army Faction Terrorist Group', 73.
51. 'IRA claims it shot down army helicopter', *The Independent*, 12 February 1990. J. Salata, 'MANPADs'. P. Bishop & E. Mallie, *The Provisional IRA*, 246.
52. 'Huge costs force Yard to review VIP security', *The Independent on Sunday*, 4 February 1990. 'Top IRA target is stripped of his bodyguards', *The Sunday Correspondent*, 5 August 1990. 'End of a bulletproof era', *The Independent*, 21 June 1991.
53. D. E. Wurth, 'The Proper Function and use of the Private Sector Bodyguard', 320, 324–8.
54. R. Clutterbuck, *Kidnap, Hijack and Extortion*, 81–2.
55. 'Eve of destruction', *Time Out*, 16–23 January 1991.
56. 'IRA moves to strike economic targets', *The Independent*, 24 December 1991.
57. 'Terrorism's other target', *The Times*, 18 September 1986. 'Paris holds 8, says terrorist ring is broken', *International Herald Tribune*, 27 March 1987. 'How Iran's mullahs held Paris to ransom', *The Independent on Sunday*, 28 January 1990. 'Politics and the bombers of Paris', *The Independent*, 3 February 1990. '20 years for Paris bomber', *The Independent*, 10 March 1990. 'Tunisian sentenced to 20 years in prison', *Associated Press*, 10 March 1990. Y. Bodansky, *Target America: Terrorism in the US Today* (New York: SPI Books, 1993), 226–46.
58. E. Best, 'An Interview with Ed Best', 4–5.
59. 'Framing the Villains', *New Statesman and Society*, 28 January 1994. 'Long lens of the law', *The Independent*, 6 July 1994.
60. D. Hamill, *Pig in the Middle*, 238. M. Urban, *Big Boys' Rules*, 41–2. M. Dewar, *The British Army in Northern Ireland*, 185–6.

61. Personal observation: Belfast, September 1991. D. Hamill, *Pig in the Middle*, 238. M. Urban, *Big Boys' Rules*, 117–18.
62. 'Scotland Yard: Trooping the Colour', ITV (television), 10 February 1994. R. Fleming & H. Miller, *Scotland Yard*, 297.
63. 'Police set road-blocks in effort to deter IRA', *The Independent*, 7 December 1992. 'Police introduce IRA road-blocks in Manchester', *The Independent*, 8 December 1992.
64. 'Police set IRA road traps', *The Independent*, 6 December 1992.
65. 'One-dimensional policing', *Fortnight*, May 1993.
66. 'A bombshell for London's drivers', *The Independent*, 22 June 1993. 'Police to cordon off City from bombers', *The Independent*, 1 July 1993. 'Gridlock fears over City road blocks', *The Independent*, 2 July 1993. 'The Scared Mile', *The Guardian*, supplement, 3 August 1993. 'Checkpoints security in City to be scaled down', *The Guardian*, 30 January 1995.
67. 'Belfast goes to work, London goes to pieces', *The Independent on Sunday*, 24 February 1991.
68. F. Burton, *The Politics of Legitimacy*, 18.
69. 'Family defies IRA wrath over taxi firm clash', *The Guardian*, 1 June 1993. 'War News: punishment shooting', *AP/RN*, 1 April 1993. 'One-dimensional policing', *Fortnight*, May 1993.
70. D. Thomson, *Europe Since Napoleon*, revised edition (Harmondsworth: Penguin, 1966), 270.
71. M. Ryan, *War and Peace in Ireland: Britain and the IRA in the New World Order* (London: Pluto, 1994), 124.
72. 'Checkpoint Paddy, Checkpoint Billy', *The Irish Times*, 5 May 1983.
73. 'Troubles prompt moves to fortresses'', *The Independent on Sunday*, 1 November 1992. 'Apartheid deepens on streets of Ulster', *The Independent on Sunday*, 21 March 1993. 'Concern grows in Ulster as divisions continue', *The Independent*, 22 March 1993.
74. UK House of Commons, *The Physical Security of Military Installations in the United Kingdom*, xix–xx (paras 56–7), 47 (para 602), 49 (paras 625–7), 66–7 (paras 852–6). P. Wilkinson, 'Designing an Effective International Aviation Security System', 112.
75. 'Israel to deploy dogs on borders in attempt to curb Islamic suicide bombers', *The Guardian*, 30 January 1995. 'Israel brings in dogs', *The Independent*, 30 January 1995. P. Wilkinson, 'Designing an Effective International Aviation Security System', 110. M. Dewar, *The British Army in Northern Ireland*, 131.
76. 'Carlton Club camera had not been switched on', *The Independent*, 28 June 1990. 'Faults on 60% of security video-cameras', *The Independent on Sunday*, 8 July 1990. 'Video camera failed to record conference on terrorism', *The Times*, 29 September 1990.
77. 'Framing the villains', *New Statesman and Society*, 28 January 1994. 'Film aids hunt for City killer', *The Independent*, 19 December 1994.
78. 'City cordon fails to cause disruption', *Financial Times*, 6 July 1993. 'The Scared Mile', *The Guardian*, supplement, 3 August 1993.
79. A. J. Alexander, 'Getting the Most from Scarce Resources', *TVI Journal*, 5, no. 2 (Fall 1984), 28.

80. 'Framing the Villains', *New Statesman and Society*, 28 January 1994. 'Long lens of the law', *The Independent*, 6 July 1994. 'They've got an eye on you', *The Independent*, 2 November 1994.
81. A. Jamieson, *The Heart Attacked*, 120.
82. Ibid., 15.
83. Y. Alexander & D. Pluchinsky, *Europe's Red Terrorists*, 68.
84. K. Toolis, *Rebel Hearts*, 305.
85. 'The Flowers and the Tears', *Evening Standard* (London), 27 April 1993.
86. 'IRA rings changes to restore balance of terror', *The Guardian*, 5 May 1987. 'What's on the agenda now is an end to partition', *The Irish Times*, 10 December 1986. G. Adams, *The Politics of Irish Freedom*, 121.
87. 'Attack intended to mark twenty years of the Troubles', *The Independent*, 23 September 1989.
88. S. Bruce, *The Red Hand*, 297.
89. 'IRA rings changes to restore balance of terror', *The Guardian*, 5 May 1987.
90. '11 die in Cenotaph blast', *The Independent*, 9 November 1987. 'Bombing "devastating" to IRA', *The Independent*, 11 November 1987. 'IRA's toll of civilian death grows despite public stance', *The Independent*, 13 April 1989. P. Bishop & E. Mallie, *The Provisional IRA*, 459.
91. 'Provos now using deadly US rifle', *The Sunday Independent* (Dublin), 6 September 1992.
92. 'American sniper rifle found in arms cache', *The Times*, 18 August 1993.
93. 'American sniper rifle found in arms cache', *The Times*, 18 August 1993. 'Hidden Deaths', *The Independent*, magazine supplement, 20 August 1994. Y. Debay, 'The Legion tests new weapons', *RAIDS*, August 1993. R. Adam, *The World's Most Powerful Rifles and Handguns* (London: Quintet, 1991), 118.
94. 'Policeman becomes third victim of IRA sniper', *The Independent*, 26 February 1993. 'RUC men killed by sniper and bomb', *The Times*, 26 February 1993. 'Sniper kills soldier in border attack', *The Independent*, 18 July 1993. 'Victim of sniper was "dedicated soldier"', *The Times*, 19 July 1993. 'Sniper attack leads to security search', *The Independent*, 2 August 1993. 'Army searches for cover against IRA's deadly sniper', *The Times*, 2 August 1993.
95. 'Gaza in grip of suicide bombers', *The Independent*, 17 December 1993. 'Hamas has learnt the lessons of Lebanon', *The Independent*, 20 October 1994. 'Suicide bus bomber kills 22', *The Daily Telegraph*, 20 October 1994. 'Gaza suicide bomber kills 3 Israeli troops', *The Independent*, 12 November 1994. 'Bus stop bombers kill 19 in Israel', *The Independent*, 23 January 1995. 'Suicide bombers rock Middle East peace', *The Guardian*, 23 January 1995.
96. 'Israel steps up war on Hamas', *The Daily Telegraph*, 21 October 1994. 'Arab village stunned by martyrdom', *The Daily Telegraph*, 22 October 1994.
97. 'Ministers are targeted by letter bombs', *The Independent*, 26 April 1995. 'Death in the post', *The Guardian*, 15 May 1995.

98. 'Anti-IRA security costs must rise, police say', *The Independent on Sunday*, 23 September 1990.
99. M. Sutton, *Bear in Mind These Dead*, 161–76. Royal Ulster Constabulary, *Chief Constable's Annual Report 1994* (London: HMSO, 1995), 102.
100. 'Family held hostage in bank raid', *The Independent*, 9 January 1991. 'He was almost home when the nightmare began', *The Independent*, 13 May 1993. 'Gangs target families as "soft option"', *The Independent*, 14 September 1994.
101. 'Breaching the core of Whitehall's defences', *The Scotsman*, 8 February 1991.
102. 'IRA bombers attack No 10 War Cabinet', *The Independent*, 8 February 1991. 'War cabinet escapes IRA mortars', *The Times*, 8 February 1991. 'The day John Major missed his lunch', *The Sunday Times*, 10 February 1991. P. Gurney, *Braver Men Walk Away*, 1–8.
103. W. Enders & T. Sandler, 'The Effectiveness of Antiterrorism Policies: A Vector-Autoregression-Intervention Analysis', *American Political Science Review*, 87, no. 4 (December 1993). W. Enders, T. Sandler & J. Cauley, 'UN Conventions, Technology and Retaliation in the Fight Against Terrorism: An Econometric Evaluation', *Terrorism and Political Violence*, 2, no. 1 (Spring 1990). E. I. Im & J. Cauley, 'Cycles and Substitutions in Terrorist Activities: A Spectral Approach', *Kyklos*, 40, no. 2 (1987). T. Sandler, W. Enders & H. E. Lapan, 'Economic Analysis Can Help Fight International Terrorism', *Challenge* (Jan./ Feb. 1991). T. Sandler, J. T. Tschirhart & J. Cauley, 'A Theoretical Analysis of Transnational Terrorism', *American Political Science Review*, 77, no. 1 (March 1983). T. Sandler et al., 'Economic Methods and the Study of Terrorism', in P. Wilkinson and A. M. Stewart (eds), *Contemporary Research on Terrorism*.
104. W. Enders & T. Sandler, 'The Effectiveness of Antiterrorism policies', 830. T. Sandler et al., 'UN Conventions', 85.
105. T. Sandler, W. Enders & H. E. Lapan, 'Economic Analysis', 14–15. W. Enders & T. Sandler, 'The Effectiveness of Antiterrorism policies', 842. W. Enders, T. Sandler & J. Cauley, 'UN Conventions, Technology & Retaliation', 86.
106. W. Enders, T. Sandler & J. Cauley, 'UN Conventions,' 83, 96.
107. T. Sandler, W. Enders & H. E. Lapan, 'Economic Analysis' 15. W. Enders & T. Sandler, 'The Effectiveness of Antiterrorism policies', 842.
108. W. Enders & T. Sandler, 'The Effectiveness of Antiterrorism policies', 842. W. Enders, T. Sandler & J. Cauley, 'UN Conventions,' 96.
109. S. M. Katz, *Guards Without Frontiers: Israel's War Against Terrorism* (London: Arms and Armour Press, 1990), 23–31. D. C. Martin & J. Walcott, *Best Laid Plans*, 235–57.
110. 'Hezbollah chief dies in gunship attack on car', *The Times*, 17 February 1992. 'Lebanon's pain, but whose gain?', *The Independent*, 18 February 1992. 'Suicide bomber blew up embassy', *The Times*, 19 February 1992. '16 killed in bomb attack on Jewish groups in Argentina', *The Independent*, 19 July 1994. 'Bomb kills 22 at Jewish Centre', *The Times*, 19 July 1994. M. Ranstorp, 'Hizbollah's Command Leadership', 314, 339n.

111. 'Israel wreaks vengeance on Hizbollah camp', *The Independent*, 3 June 1994. 'Hizbollah bury their unseen dead', *The Independent*, 4 June 1994. 'Israel moves troops to Lebanese border', *The Guardian*, 4 June 1994. 'Explosion levels building housing Jewish groups', *The Guardian*, 19 July 1994. 'Hizbollah adopts an "eye for an eye" tactic', *The Independent*, 20 July 1994. 'Bomb alarm Britain ignored', *The Independent on Sunday*, 31 July 1994.
112. M. Sutton, *Bear in Mind These Dead*, passim.
113. S. Bruce, *The Red Hand*, 297.
114. J. Bowyer Bell, *IRA Tactics and Targets*, 29–30. M. McKeown, *Two Seven Six Three: An analysis of fatalities attributable to civil disturbances in Northern Ireland in the twenty years between July 13th 1969 and July 12th 1989* (Lucan: Murlough, 1989), 7, 21–2.

8 THE SECURITY ENVIRONMENT

1. C. Gwynn, *Imperial Policing* (London: Macmillan, 1934; 1936), 3–4, 16. Using colonial precedents, Gwynn systemised doctrine about military aid in support of the civil power. Until fairly recently, British doctrine in this area was based upon colonial experience. M. Dewar, *The British Army in Northern Ireland*, 219–20. I. F. W. Beckett, 'Guerrilla Warfare: Insurgency and Counter-insurgency since 1945', in C. McInnes & G. D. Sheffield, *Warfare in the Twentieth Century: Theory and Practice* (London: Unwin Hyman, 1988), 206–7.
2. C. Gwynn, *Imperial Policing*, 32, 14. K. Jeffrey & P. Hennessy, *States of Emergency: British Governments and Strikebreaking since 1919* (London: Routledge & Kegan Paul, 1983), 14.
3. W. Laqueur, *The Age of Terrorism*, 6, 154. Amnesty International, *Getting Away with Murder*. Amnesty International, *Argentina: The Military Juntas and Human Rights, Report of the Trial of the Former Junta Members* (London: Amnesty International, 1987). Argentina, Comision Nacional sobre la Desparicion de Personas, *Nunca Mas: A Report by Argentina's National Commission on Disappeared People* (Buenos Aires: Editorial Universitaria de Buenos Aires, 1984; London: Faber & Faber/ Index on Censorship, 1986). R. Cox, 'Total Terrorism: Argentina, 1969 to 1979', in M. Crenshaw (ed.), *Terrorism, Legitimacy, and Power: The Consequences of Political Violence* (Middletown, CT: Wesleyan University Press, 1983). J. Burns, *The Land That Lost It's Heroes*, 20–3.
4. E. Bramall, 'The Place of the British Army in Public Order', and R. Mark, 'Keeping the Peace in Great Britain: The Differing Roles of the Police and the Army', both in P. J. Rowe & C. J. Whelan (eds), *Military Intervention in Democratic Societies* (London: Croom Helm, 1985), 82–4, 85–8. J. R. Thackrah, 'Reactions to Terrorism and Riots', in J. R. Thackrah (ed.), *Contemporary Policing: An examination of society in the 1980s* (London: Sphere, 1985), 148. P. Wilkinson, *Terrorism and the Liberal State*, 46. T. F. Baldy, *Battle for Ulster: A Study of Internal Security* (Washington, DC: National Defense University Press, 1987), 115.

5. 'Melbourne gunman who killed two shot dead by police marksmen', *The Independent*, 6 December 1994.
6. G. Northam, *Shooting in the Dark: Riot Police in Britain* (London: Faber & Faber, 1989), 77.
7. British Society for Social Responsibility in Science, *TechnoCop: New Police Technologies* (London: Free Association Books, 1985), 20–4. G. Northam, *Shooting in the Dark*, 77–81. K. Oxford, 'Patterns in a Labyrinth', in A. R. Brownlie (ed.), *Crime Investigation: Art or Science* (Edinburgh: Scottish Academic Press, 1984), 10. R. Baldwin & R. Kinsey, *Police Powers and Politics* (London: Quartet, 1982), 59–82, 287–9.
8. '"I don't seek it, but . . . it could happen within 10 to 20 years"', *The Independent on Sunday*, 20 June 1993. 'Three top police informers killed', *The Independent on Sunday*, 23 May 1993. 'Rise of the gunmen', *Evening Standard* (London), 16 August 1993. K. Oxford, 'Patterns in a Labyrinth', 10. M. Maguire & C. Norris, *The Conduct and Supervision of Criminal Investigations* (London: HMSO, 1992), 15–16, 78–9, 89–95. N. Darbyshire & B. Hilliard, *The Flying Squad* (London: Headline, 1993), 79–80, 105, 214–15. M. Short, *Lundy: The Destruction of Scotland Yard's Finest Detective* (London: Grafton, 1991), 88–104. D. Hobbs, *Doing the Business: Entrepreneurship, The Working Class, and Detectives in the East End of London* (Oxford: Oxford University Press, 1989), 195–6, 203, 208, 212.
9. A. Jamieson, *The Heart Attacked*, 174, 177, 179–80, 195–8. D. Moss, *The Politics of Left-Wing Violence in Italy*, 178–80. P. Willan, *Puppet Masters*, 285.
10. M. Urban, *Big Boys' Rules*, 213.
11. 'Devastation from bomber who got through', *The Guardian*, 14 December 1991. S. Rimmington, *The Richard Dimbleby Lecture 1994: Security and Democracy – Is There a Conflict?* (London: BBC Education, 1994), 9.
12. C. Foley, *Legion of the Rearguard: The IRA and the Modern Irish State* (London: Pluto, 1992), 220. '"We remain totally committed and confident in victory" – Oglaigh na hEireann', *AP/RN*, 14 February 1991.
13. 'Informer worked for RUC for three years', *AP/RN*, 1 July 1993.
14. M. Sutton, *Bear in Mind These Dead*, 190.
15. 'Lethal mix of brutality and blunders', *The Sunday Correspondent*, 17 June 1990.
16. S. Aust, *The Baader-Meinhof Group*, 115. J. Becker, *Hitler's Children*, 234–5. S. Segaller, *Invisible Armies*, 47–8.
17. B. O'Brien, *The Long War*, 145–9.
18. Royal Ulster Constabulary, *Chief Constable's Annual Report 1993* (London: HMSO, 1994), 98–9.
19. 'Arming the IRA: The Libyan Connection', *The Economist*, 31 March 1990. 'Libyan arms fuel surge in terrorism', *The Independent*, 8 May 1990. 'RUC chief proposes national police units', *The Independent*, 22 July 1992. 'IRA has enough Semtex for 15 years', *The Independent on Sunday*, 19 March 1995.

20. T. P. Coogan, *Michael Collins*, 157–60. C. Townshend, *The British Campaign in Ireland*, 129–30.
21. T. P. Coogan, *Michael Collins*, 78. GHQ Ireland, *Record of the rebellion in Ireland in 1920–21 and the part played by the Army in dealing with it. Volume II. Intelligence* (A-2448-2), 4–5.
22. 'An incalculable loss for MI5', *New Statesman and Society*, 10 June 1994.
23. R. Fagilot, *Britain's Military Strategy in Ireland*, 233. S. Cronin, *Irish Nationalism*, 348.
24. M. Dillon, *The Dirty War*, 404–5, 478. M. Urban, *Big Boys' Rules*, 43–4, 141–2. K. J. Kelley, *The Longest War*, 275. M. Sutton, *Bear in Mind These Dead*, 108, 110.
25. G. Grivas–Dighenis & C. Foley (ed.), *The Memoirs of General Grivas*, 128.
26. Raviv and Melman place Cohen in the the Israeli domestic intelligence agency Shin Bet (Sherut ha-Bitachon ha-Kalai – General Security Service), whilst Taylor and Katz place him in the Israeli external intelligence agency Mossad (ha-Mossad le-Modiin ule-Tafkidim Meyuhadim – Institute for Intelligence and Special Tasks). D. Raviv & Y. Melman, *Every Spy a Prince*, 187–8. P. Taylor, *States of Terror*, 55–62. S. M. Katz, *Guards Without Frontiers*, 43.
27. 'Israeli agent is shot dead', *The Guardian*, 14 February 1994.
28. For an outline of normal practice concerning criminal investigations in Britain see M. Maguire & C. Norris, *The Conduct and Supervision of Criminal Investigations*. T. Colman, *Incident into Evidence: Operational Police Skills* (Maidenhead: McGraw-Hill, 1989).
29. *Corriere della Sera*, 23 June 1978. 'Red Brigades gunmen kill police chief as he rides to work on a bus', *The Times*, 22 June 1978.
30. 'Terror squad chief murdered in Venice', *The Guardian*, 13 May 1980, *Corriere della Sera*, 13 May 1980. 'Anti-Terrorist Officer Shot in Rome', *International Herald Tribune*, 7 January 1982, *The Irish Times*, 7 January 1982, *Corriere della Sera*, 7 January 1982.
31. *Corriere della Sera*, 16 July 1982, 19 July 1982, 26 July 1982, 3 August 1982, 30 August 1982. P. Willan, *Puppet Masters*, 329–35.
32. P. Bishop & E. Mallie, *The Provisional IRA*, 241. M. Dillon & D. Lehane, *Political Murder in Northern Ireland*, 53–4. 'Chronology of events: 18.1.72', in R. Bell, R. Johnstone, R. Wilson (eds), *Troubled Times: Fortnight Magazine and the Troubles in Northern Ireland 1970–1991* (Belfast: Blackstaff Press, 1991), 153.
33. 'The Armalite and the Ballot Box', *Magill*, July 1983. Also see C. Ryder, *The RUC*, 286. 'Six held as INLA hostages freed', *The Guardian*, 19 August 1983. 'Informer's wife freed as INLA rethinks tactics', *The Guardian*, 27 August 1983. 'IRA frees father of informer', *The Guardian*, 27 September 1983. 'Chronology of events: 22.12.82, 16.5.83, 25.8.83', in R. Bell, R. Johnstone, R. Wilson (eds), *Troubled Times*, 195–6, 196, 197.
34. A. Jamieson, *The Heart Attacked*, 189–90.
35. 'Supergrasses target Andreotti', *The Independent on Sunday*, 11 April 1993. 'Andreotti accused of ordering murder', *The Independent*, 10

June 1993. 'Judge deals blow to Andreotti over journalist's murder', *The Times*, 10 June 1993.
36. 'Rome turns a blind eye to Mafia's killing spree', *The Independent*, 8 March 1995.
37. 'Caught with suspicious genes', *The Independent*, 4 April 1995. 'World's first national DNA bank opens', *The Guardian*, 11 April 1995. 'We need your DNA', *The Guardian*, supplement, 21 April 1995. M. Dillon, *The Dirty War*, 32, 48. 'One day their prints will come', *The Sunday Correspondent*, 12 August 1990. B. Lane, *The Encyclopedia of Forensic Science* (London: Headline, 1992; 1993).
38. 'Police comb "bomber's lair"', *The Sunday Correspondent*, 24 September 1989. P. Bishop & E. Mallie, *The Provisional IRA*, 427. M. Dillon, *The Enemy Within*, 166.
39. C. Mullin, *Error of Judgement: The Truth about the Birmingham Bombings*, revised edition, (Swords: Poolbeg, 1990), 285–98. H. Miller, *Traces of Guilt: Forensic Science and the Fight Against Crime* (London: BBC Books, 1995), 158–9.
40. M. Urban, *Big Boys' Rules*, 115.
41. D. Pluchinsky, 'An Organizational and Operational Analysis of Germany's Red Army Faction Terrorist Group', 80.
42. 'Damage in huge blast put at £20m', *The Independent*, 25 September 1992. 'Court laboratory bombed by IRA', *The Times*, 25 September 1992. '"Troubles" chronology: Wed Sep 23', *Fortnight*, no. 311 (November 1992), 34.
43. S. Uglow, *Policing Liberal Society* (Oxford: Oxford University Press, 1988), 76–7, 80–3. G. Northam, *Shooting in the Dark*, passim.
44. M. Dewar, *The British Army in Northern Ireland*, 180.
45. D. Hamill, *Pig in the Middle*, 44.
46. Ibid., 119, 141. M. Dewar, *The British Army in Northern Ireland*, 182.
47. A. Feldman, *Formations of Violence*, 41–5.
48. F. Burton, *The Politics of Legitimacy*, 112–13.
49. 'Security alert as IRA admits bombings', *The Independent*, 5 December 1992. 'Police set IRA road traps', *The Independent*, 6 December 1992. 'Police set road-blocks in effort to deter IRA', 'Belfast security measures accepted as normal', both in *The Independent*, 7 December 1992. 'Roadblock police stop drivers at gunpoint', *The Times*, 7 December 1992. 'Police introduce IRA road-blocks in Manchester', *The Independent*, 8 December 1992. 'Home Office resists pressure for wider stop-and-search rules', *The Times*, 8 December 1992. D. McKittrick, *Despatches from Belfast*, 196–202.
50. E. Duyker, *Tribal Guerrillas*, 92–3.
51. P. Willan, *Puppet Masters*, 224.
52. A. Guelke & F. Wright, 'On a "British Withdrawal" from Northern Ireland' and A. M. Gallagher, 'Civil Liberties and the State', both in P. Stringer & G. Robinson (eds), *Social Attitudes in Northern Ireland: The Second Report, 1991–1992* (Belfast: Blackstaff Press, 1992), 49–50, 83–4. A. M. Gallagher, 'Policing Northern Ireland: Attitudinal Evidence', in A. O'Day (ed.), *Terrorism's Laboratory: The Case of Northern Ireland* (Aldershot: Dartmouth, 1995), 54–5.

53. P. Willan, *Puppet Masters*, 224. W. D. Flackes & S. Elliott, *Northern Ireland*, 472.
54. M. Dillon, *The Dirty War*, 315–25. M. Sutton, *Bear in Mind These Dead*, 168.
55. R. D. Wilson, *Cordon and Search*, 66–74. Menachim Begin, the Irgun leader and later Israeli Prime Minister, mentions having to hide in a secret compartment in his house during this operation; M. Begin, *The Revolt*, 227–9.
56. P. Devlin, *Straight Left: An Autobiography* (Belfast: Blackstaff, 1993), 147, 149. D. McKittrick, *Despatches from Belfast*, 196–202. K. Boyle, T. Hadden & P. Hillyard, *Ten Years on in Northern Ireland: The Legal Control of Political Violence* (London: Cobden Trust, 1980), 26–7. P. Bishop & E. Mallie, *The Provisional IRA*, 167, 205.
57. A. Merari, T. Prat & D. Tal, 'The Palestinian *Intifada*', 183.
58. There are some slight differences concerning the number of house searches between Flackes and Elliot, and G. Hogan & C. Walker, *Political Violence and the Law in Ireland* (Manchester: Manchester University Press, 1989), 62. For this table the figures in Flackes and Elliot have been used.
59. D. McKittrick, *Despatches from Belfast*, 198.
60. 'State-of-the-art building for a state of siege', *The Times*, Saturday Review, 21 November 1992.
61. 'Ulster checkpoints to be closed over "human bomb" raids', *The Independent*, 20 March 1991.
62. 'The Provo's easiest coup', *The Times*, 8 August 1986. 'The gunman's shadow falls across Ulster business', *Financial Times*, 11 August 1986. 'Army deploys 1,000 extra men in Ulster repair work', *The Daily Telegraph*, 7 September 1991. P. Bishop & E. Mallie, *The Provisional IRA*, 421.
63. 'War News: Guerrilla War bites deep in 1991', *AP/RN*, 2 January 1992. 'IRA destroys main British border post', *AP/RN*, 2 January 1992. 'Growing crisis for British army', *AP/RN*, 30 January 1992. 'British under pressure on check points', *AP/RN*, 11 June 1992. 'The background to the Teebane ambush', *AP/RN*, 23 January 1992.
64. 'Internment "only way to beat IRA"', *The Independent*, 17 November 1991. 'Border blues', *Fortnight*, April 1992, 25.
65. H. Strachan, *European Armies and the Conduct of War* (London: Unwin Hyman, 1983), 2, 96.
66. R. Trinquier, *Modern Warfare*, 26. F. Kitson, *Low Intensity Operations: Subversion, Insurgency and Peacekeeping* (London: Faber & Faber, 1971), 95.
67. N. Barber, *The War of the Running Dogs: The Malayan Emergency, 1948–1960* (London: 1971; New York: Bantam, 1987), 250.
68. 'Shooting mystery tarnishes German anti-terrorist squad', *The Independent*, 6 July 1993. 'Elite squad faces the axe', *The European*, 8–11 July 1993. 'Bonn "errors" in shoot-out', *The Independent*, 19 August 1993. 'Madrid sues over "dirty war" claims', *The Independent*, 11 January 1995. P. Taylor, *States of Terror*, 98–104.
69. M. Urban, *Big Boys' Rules*, 164.

70. M. Dillon, *The Dirty War*, 370–2.
71. 'IRA man killed by Army wanted for corporal's murder', *The Independent*, 10 October 1990. M. Urban, 'Who dares, need not fear inquests', *The Spectator*, 23 May 1992. M. Urban, *Big Boys' Rules*, 63, 118, 173–7. J. Adams, R. Morgan & A. Bambridge, *Ambush*, 97–100. 'IRA man killed by Army wanted for corporal's murder', *The Independent*, 10 October 1990. 'Man shot by army "had record of violence"', *The Times*, 10 October 1990. 'Web of terror that spread across Europe', *The Independent*, 3 April 1991.
72. M. Urban, *Big Boys' Rules*, 218–19.
73. Ibid., 227–37. J. Adams, R. Morgan & A. Bambridge, *Ambush*, 107–18. B. O'Brien, *The Long War*, 141–2.
74. M. Urban, *Big Boys' Rules*, 248–51, 254.
75. Ibid., 82–3. As an example of the coverage of terrorists' deaths by a sympathetic publication see, 'Freedom's soldiers laid to rest in historic Tyrone', *AP/RN*, 13 June 1991. 'Obituaries: Kevin Barry O'Donnell', *AP/RN*, 20 February 1992.
76. D. Hamill, *Pig in the Middle*, 229–31. T. Geraghty, *Who Dares Wins*, 155–60. C. Ryder, *The RUC*, 216.
77. P. Koch & K. Hermann, *Assault at Mogadishu*. Sunday Times Insight Team, *Siege*.
78. J. Teenbrook, 'ERT Negotiators', *RAIDS*, UK edition, March 1993. P. Wilkinson, *Terrorism and the Liberal State*, 145.
79. G. Rosie, *The Directory of International Terrorism*, 206–8. H. Cobban, *The Palestinian Liberation Organisation*, 54. P. Seale, *Abu Nidal*, 83–5.
80. J. Adams, *Secret Armies*, 89–95. G. Rosie, *The Directory of International Terrorism*, 106–7.
81. See C. A. Beckwith & D. Knox, *Delta Force* (London: Arms and Armour Press, 1984; Fontana, 1985). P. B. Ryan, *The Iranian Rescue Mission: Why It Failed* (Annapolis, MD: Naval Institute Press, 1985). S. E. Ambrose, *Rise to Globalism: American Foreign Policy Since 1938*, seventh edition (Harmondsworth: Penguin, 1993), 300–2. H. Smith, *The Power Game: How Washington Works* (London: Fontana, 1989), 711.
82. R. A. Friedlander (ed.), *Terrorism: Documents of International and Local Control. Volume IV: A World on Fire* (London: Oceana Publications Inc, 1984). US Department of State, *Patterns of Global Terrorism: 1983* (Washington, DC: Government Printing Office, September 1984). US Department of State, *Patterns of Global Terrorism: 1984* (Washington, DC: Government Printing Office, November 1985). US Department of State, *Patterns of Global Terrorism: 1985* (Washington, DC: Government Printing Office, October 1986).
83. P. B. Ryan, *The Iranian Rescue Mission*, 100. J. Adams, *Secret Armies*, 130.
84. C. Coughlin, *Hostage*, 110, 349, 352, 358.
85. J. Adams, *Secret Armies*, 274. J. T. Choi, *Acts of Violence against Civil Aviation*, 206–43, 210. R. Fisk, *Pity the Nation*, 607.
86. '"Dirty war" scandal worsens', *The Independent*, 21 December 1994. 'Madrid sues over "dirty war" claims', *The Independent*, 11 January

1995. 'Spain drops judge from GAL death squads inquiry', *The Guardian*, 25 January 1995. 'The noose is tightened around Felipe's neck', *The Guardian*, 23 February 1995. P. Taylor, *States of Terror*, 97–104.
87. P. Taylor, *States of Terror*, 104.
88. S. Segaller, *Invisible Armies*, 96. F. Jiminez, 'Spain: The Terrorist Challenge and the Government's Response', 118.
89. 'Visit by Chirac crowns success of co-operation on Eta raiders', *The Times*, 7 November 1986. 'Net closes in on ETA unit of "quiet men"', *The Guardian*, 16 April 1990. 'Eta reels after arrest of top leader', *The Independent*, 25 September 1990. 'Spanish alert after Eta chiefs captured', *Financial Times*, 31 March 1992. 'Spain rejoices but awaits ETA reprisal', *The Guardian*, 31 March 1992. 'Spain hails arrest of ETA chief', *The Independent*, 22 February 1993. P. Taylor, *States of Terror*, 97–104.
90. E. F. Mickolus, T. Sandler, J. M. Murdock, *International Terrorism in the 1980s: 1984–1987*, 551, 561, 629, 630, 639.
91. F. Llera, J. M. Mata & C. L. Irwin, 'ETA: From Secret Army to Social Movement', 131.
92. R. Debray, *Revolution in the Revolution? Armed Struggle and Political Struggle in Latin America* (France: 1967; Harmondsworth: Penguin, 1968), 51.
93. J. J. McCuen, *The Art of Counter-Revolutionary War: The Strategy of Counter-Insurgency* (London: Faber & Faber, 1966), 119, 154. R. Thompson, *Defeating Communist Insurgency: Experiences from Malaya and Vietnam* (London: Chatto & Windus, 1967), 114.
94. S. Aust, *The Baader-Meinhof Group*, 143.
95. A. Feldman, *Formations of Violence*, 76. See T. Parker, *May the Lord in His mercy be kind to Belfast*, 204–8.
96. *L'Espresso*, 24 February 1980.
97. *L'Espresso*, 31 October 1982.
98. Associated Press, 21 November 1979. 'Gunmen murder Italian police', *Financial Times*, 22 November 1979. C. Schaerf et al., *Venti Anni di Violenza in Italia*, 850.
99. 'Policeman shot dead as terrorists go on trial', *Financial Times*, 27 November 1979. 'Brigades victim', *The Guardian*, 28 November 1979. C. Schaerf et al., *Venti Anni di Violenza in Italia*, 851.
100. 'Informer's wife freed as INLA rethinks tactics', *The Guardian*, 27 August 1983.
101. C. Townshend, *Political Violence in Ireland*, 36–7. W. Laqueur, *The Age of Terrorism*, 104, 113. D. G. Boyce, '"A Gallous Story and a Dirty deed": Political Martyrdom in Ireland since 1867', in Y. Alexander & A. O'Day (eds), *Ireland's Terrorist Dilemma*, 14.
102. S. Aust, *The Baader-Meinhof Group*, 83–6. J. Becker, *Hitler's Children*, 124–9.
103. B. A. Scharlau, *Left-Wing Terrorism in the Federal Republic of Germany*, 91–3.
104. S. Aust, *The Baader-Meinhof Group*, 289–92. J. Becker, *Hitler's Children*, 315–22. B. A. Scharlau, *Left-Wing Terrorism in the Federal Republic of Germany*, 45. W. Stevenson, *90 Minutes at Entebbe*, 16.

105. P. Koch & K. Hermann, *Assault at Mogadishu*, 79.
106. T. P. Coogan, *On the Blanket*, 48, 161.
107. M. Sutton, *Bear in Mind These Dead*, 89–132. T. P. Coogan, *On the Blanket*, 153. L. Clarke, *Broadening the Battlefield*, 77, 92.
108. A. Jamieson, *The Heart Attacked*, 145, 150–1, 210. V. S. Pisano, *The Dynamics of Subversion and Violence in Contemporary Italy*, 157–70. D. Moss, *The Politics of Left-Wing Violence in Italy*, 38, 145. E. MacDonald, *Shoot the Women First*, 187.
109. V. S. Pisano, *The Dynamics of Subversion and Violence in Contemporary Italy*, 68. A. Jamieson, *The Heart Attacked*, 184–5.
110. V. S. Pisano, *The Dynamics of Subversion and Violence in Contemporary Italy*, 68. A. Jamieson, *The Heart Attacked*, 184.
111. A. Jamieson, *The Heart Attacked*, 184–7.
112. Ibid., 183, 184, 187. D. Moss, *The Politics of Left-Wing Violence in Italy*, 152. P. Willan, *Puppet Masters*, 326–7. V. S. Pisano, *The Dynamics of Subversion and Violence in Contemporary Italy*, 68.
113. 'Paris tested over terror trial', *The Independent*, 23 February 1987. 'Leaders of Action Directe terrorist group seized', *The Guardian*, 22 February 1987. P. Marnham, *Crime and the Académie Française*, 14.
114. R. Catanzaro, *Men of Respect*, 72–3. J. Parker, *The Walking Dead*, 65.
115. J. Pearce, *Colombia: Inside the Labyrinth*, 194. Also see S. Strong, *Whitewash*, 144.
116. S. Strong, *Whitewash*, 145–8. R. A. Hudson, 'Colombia's Palace of Justice Tragedy Revisited: A Critique of the Conspiracy Theory', *Terrorism and Political Violence*, 7, no. 2 (Summer 1995).
117. J. Pearce, *Colombia: Inside the Labyrinth*, 182, 194. S. Strong, *Whitewash*, 152–3.
118. D. Moss, *The Politics of Left-Wing Violence in Italy*, 229–33. A. Jamieson, *The Heart Attacked*, 98–9. 'Death of Turin editor shot by terrorists', *The Times*, 30 November 1977.
119. 'Uproar as terrorism trial opens in Berlin', *The Times*, 12 April 1978. 'Scuffles and insults disrupt Berlin terrorist trial', *The Times*, 13 April 1978. 'German terror trial lawyers attacked', *The Times*, 1 June 1978. 'Berlin court to rule on "terror" lawyer', *The Guardian*, 8 June 1978. 'Terror trial lawyer cleared of aiding escape', *The Guardian*, 10 June 1978. 'Kidnap trial lawyers threatened', *The Times*, 15 June 1978. 'Lawyers trapped in bitter struggle', *The Times*, 13 November 1978. S. Aust, *The Baader-Meinhof Group*, 296–7, 303–7. J. Becker, *Hitler's Children*, 323–4. B. A. Scharlau, *Left-Wing Terrorism in the Federal Republic of Germany*, 66, 303. J. Wright, *Terrorist Propaganda*, 87–8.
120. 'Nightmare for the judges on 24-hour vigil', *The Guardian*, 6 January 1988.
121. 'Declare war, says IRA', *The Guardian*, 9 March 1988.
122. R. Bell, R. Johnstone, R. Wilson (eds), 'Chronology of events: 11.10.72, 16.9.74', *Troubled Times*, 156, 166.
123. M. Sutton, *Bear in Mind These Dead*, 198. 'The background to the Teebane ambush', *AP/RN*, 23 January 1992. 'Mortar bomb blast', *The Independent*, 21 August 1993. R. Bell, R. Johnstone, R. Wilson (eds), 'Chronology of events: 2.3.82, 16.1.83, 8.4.84, 25.4.87, 9.1. 88, 23.7.88,

25.1.89, 31.7.89', *Troubled Times*, 193–4, 196, 199, 208, 210, 211, 213, 215.
124. M. O'Higgins, 'The IRA's Costly Mistakes', *Magill*, October 1987. P. Bishop & E. Mallie, *The Provisional IRA*, 453.
125. T. Parker, *May the Lord in His mercy be kind to Belfast*, 237.
126. 'IRA defence solicitor killed', 'Shooting marks broadening of targets', both in *The Guardian*, 13 February 1989. 'Hogg told by Dublin to retract remarks on Ulster solicitors', *The Independent*, 15 February 1989.

9   EXTERNAL FACTORS

1. D. Fitzpatrick, 'The Geography of Irish Nationalism: 1910–1921', *Past and Present*, 78 (February 1978), 118.
2. 'Bombing "devastating" to IRA', *The Independent*, 11 November 1987.
3. B. A. Scharlau, *Left-Wing Terrorism in the Federal Republic of Germany*, 164–5.
4. D. Pluchinsky, 'An Organizational and Operational Analysis of Germany's Red Army Faction Terrorist Group', 52.
5. 'A difficult war to win', *The Financial Times*, Northern Ireland Survey, 26 November 1991. 'Legacy of "Bloody Sunday"', *The Independent on Sunday*, 5 January 1992. M. Urban, *Big Boys' Rules*, 31–32. 'The IRA', *The Independent on Sunday*, 22 November 1992. P. Bishop & E. Mallie, *The Provisional IRA*, 391. T. P. Coogan, *The IRA*, 604. D. Pluchinsky, 'An Organizational and Operational Analysis of Germany's Red Army Faction Terrorist Group', 50, 52. H. Horchem, 'The Decline of the Red Army Faction', *Terrorism and Political Violence*, 3, no. 2 (Summer 1991), 66. B. A. Scharlau, *Left-Wing Terrorism in the Federal Republic of Germany*, 61–2, 65. J. Power, *Against Oblivion: Amnesty International's fight for human rights* (Glasgow: Fontana, 1981), 130, 133. S. Aust, *The Baader-Meinhof Group*, 231, 250–1. J. Becker, *Hitler's Children*, 305.
6. C. Irvin & E. Moxon-Browne, 'Not many floating voters here', *Fortnight*, May 1989.
7. P. O'Malley, *The Uncivil Wars: Ireland Today* (Belfast: Blackstaff, 1983), 276, 301. T. P. Coogan, *The IRA*, 594.
8. 'Labour fires first salvo on Irish privatisation', *The Times*, 30 November 1992.
9. P. O'Malley, *The Uncivil Wars*, 276, 301. K. J. Kelley, *The Longest War*, 304.
10. 'Not many floating voters here', *Fortnight*, May 1989.
11. T. Downes-Le Guin & B. Hoffman, *The Impact of Terrorism on Public Opinion, 1988 to 1989* (Santa Monica, CA: RAND Corporation, 1993), 16. J. Holland, *The American Connection*, 7–26, 114–51. 'Deutsche Terroristen helfen IRA-Kommando', *Frankfurter Allgemeine Zeitung*, 13 March 1980. 'Meinhof gang "help IRA"', *The Guardian*, 15 March 1980. 'Student anarchist who became "fixer" for IRA', *The Independent*, 9 June 1990. 'Leftwing politics led to terror campaign', *The Guardian*, 14 May 1994. J. Adams, *Trading in Death*, 17–30. 'Voyage

into business of terror', *The Independent*, 12 January 1991.
12. R. P. Clark, *The Basque Insurgents*, 100, 105, 107. B. Dasgupta, *The Naxalite Movement*, 13, 41, 44. S. Banerjee, *India's Simmering Revolution: The Naxalite Uprising* (London: Zed Books, 1984), v, 27–8. D. Moss, *The Politics of Left-Wing Violence in Italy*, 85, 89–90.
13. S. Nelson, *Ulster's Uncertain Defenders*, 15.
14. Royal Ulster Constabulary, *Chief Constable's Annual Report 1993*, 11.
15. M. Dillon & D. Lehane, *Political Murder in Northern Ireland*, 144. F. Burton, *The Politics of Legitimacy*, 109, 22, 23. P. Bishop & E. Mallie, *The Provisional IRA*, 290–1.
16. F. Burton, *The Politics of Legitimacy*, 109. See Danny Morrison's comment in Bishop & Mallie, *The Provisional IRA*, 173.
17. Gerry Adams interviewed in *Inside Story: The Informer*, BBC1 (television), 24 November 1992. 'The men of war promise third violent decade', *The Independent*, 29 September 1990. '"We remain totally committed and confident in victory" – Oglaigh na hEireann', *AP/RN*, 14 February 1991. 'The IRA statement', *AP/RN*, 23 January 1992.
18. M. Sutton, *Bear in mind these dead*, 196.
19. P. Devlin, *Straight Left*, 151–2, 285–6. L. Clarke, *Broadening the Battlefield*, 131–2, 151–2, 166. M. Rees. *Northern Ireland: A Personal Perspective* (London: Methuen, 1985), 304–5. D. McKittrick, *Despatches from Belfast*, 6. P. Bishop & E. Mallie, *The Provisional IRA*, 289.
20. M. Kotsonouris, 'Revolutionary Justice – the Dail Eireann Courts', *History Ireland*, 2, no. 3 (Autumn 1994). C. Townshend, *Political Violence in Ireland*, 335. C. Townshend, *The British Campaign in Ireland*, 68–9.
21. P. Bishop & E. Mallie, *The Provisional IRA*, 270, 246. No author named, *Volunteer Seamus Twomey*, 12. Interview with Dr Joe Hendron, 'Dispatches: Law of the Ghetto', television. J. Darby, *Intimidation and the Control of Conflict in Northern Ireland*, 159, 157–62. 'The benefits of a community police force', *Republican News* (Belfast), 27 August 1977.
22. 'Warning to Derry bar owners and off-licences', *Republican News*, 27 August 1977.
23. 'War News: IRA action against drugs trade', *AP/RN*, 10 October 1991. 'IRA orders shooting victims to quit country', *The Independent*, 7 October 1991.
24. 'Loyalist group threatens Catholic massacre', *The Independent*, 7 November 1992. 'IRA claims demise of death group', *The Times*, 7 November 1992.
25. 'Action against drugs puts gunmen in "policing" role', *The Independent*, 3 November 1992. 'RUC chief fears IRA plans to intensify mainland campaign', *The Times*, 3 November 1992. 'IRA looks set for victory over terrorist faction', *The Independent*, 4 November 1992.
26. K. J. Kelley, *The Longest War*, 292. 'IRA interview: Defending the community', *AP/RN*, 19 December 1991.
27. 'Few tears over IRA rough justice', *The Independent on Sunday*, 20 December 1992.
28. 'Northern Exposure', *New Statesman and Society*, 27 May 1994.

29. K. J. Kelley, *The Longest War*, 289–92. 'Kneecap victim in IRA plea', *The Irish Times*, 9 September 1992. 'IRA expulsion order lifted', *The Irish Times*, 10 September 1992. 'Packing a picket', *Fortnight*, December 1994. 'Sanctuary pair live in fear of IRA gunmen', *The Independent*, 19 August 1991. 'IRA faces blame for beating councillor', *The Independent*, 26 March 1994. 'Godfathers of violence step up beatings to keep grip on power', *The Daily Telegraph*, 29 December 1995.
30. 'Loyalists target of sustained campaign', *The Independent*, 25 October 1993. 'Catholic front line waits in fear for retribution', *The Independent*, 26 October 1993. 'It's going to be a tragedy for people in the Ardoyne', *The Guardian*, 25 October 1993. 'Assassins are on the rampage', *The Independent*, 27 October 1993. '"The gunmen are savage, sinful, wicked, depraved"', *The Independent*, 1 November 1993. 'Major set to invite Hume to Ulster talks', *The Times*, 1 November 1993. 'Anatomy of an atrocity', *The Guardian*, 29 November 1993. 'New wave of Ulster violence feared', *The Independent*, 20 June 1994. 'Reprisal fear after Catholic pub killings', *The Times*, 20 June 1994. 'Ulster awaits backlash after IRA guns down loyalist', *The Independent*, 12 July 1994. 'Backlash feared as IRA kills leading loyalist', *The Guardian*, 12 July 1994. 'Loyalists pledge to avenge shootings', *The Independent*, 2 August 1994. E. Mallie & D. McKittrick, *The Fight for Peace*, 198–9, 309–10. B. Rowan, *Behind the Lines*, 37, 52–3, 106–8, 111–12.
31. E. Moxon-Browne, 'The Water and the Fish', in P. Wilkinson (ed.), *British Perspectives on Terrorism* (London: George Allen & Unwin, 1981), 50.
32. M. Holland, 'The Growing Desperation of the British Army', *Magill*, December 1979.
33. C. Hewitt, 'Terrorism and Public Opinion: A Five Country Comparison', *Terrorism and Political Violence*, 2, no. 2 (Summer 1990), 152, 153, 158, 163. S. Aust, *The Baader-Meinhof Group*, 154.
34. 'Tamils kill 350 Muslims in Sri Lanka', *The Independent*, 13 August 1990. 'Civil strife makes Sri Lanka a tropical hell', *The Independent*, 8 April 1991.
35. '74 villagers killed in Sri Lankan massacres', *The Independent*, 30 April 1992.
36. M. Sutton, *Bear in mind these dead*, 60, 68.
37. T. N. Madan, 'The Double-edged Sword: Fundamentalism and the Sikh Religious Tradition', in M. E. Marty & R. S. Appleby (eds), *Fundamentalisms Observed* (Chicago: University of Chicago Press, 1993), 612. M. J. Akbar, *India: The Siege Within*, 170.
38. H. Oberoi, 'Sikh Fundamentalism: Translating History into Theory', in M. E. Marty & R. S. Appleby (eds), *Fundamentalisms and the State*, 264.
39. 'India train massacre caps year of violence', *The Independent*, 29 December 1991. 'Sikh extremists massacre factory managers', *Financial Times*, 12 March 1992. 'Sikh militants shoot 20 dead in street', *Financial Times*, 20 March 1992.
40. T. N. Madan, 'The Double-edged Sword', 607.

41. E. J. Hobsbawm, *Bandits*, second edition (Harmondsworth: Penguin, 1985), 17–29. P. F. Angiolillo, *A Criminal as Hero: Angelo Duca* (Lawrence, KS: The Regents Press of Kansas, 1979), 1–16.
42. F. Burton, *The Politics of Legitimacy*, 106–8. S. Belfrage, *The Crack: A Belfast Year* (André Deutsch, 1987; London: Grafton, 1988), 88. R. P. Clark, *The Basque Insurgents*, 169–72, 174–6, 180–2. 'Valley of violence', *Far Eastern Economic Review*, 24 May 1990. 'Indian ferocity alienates Kashmir', *The Independent*, 23 July 1990. 'Kashmiris find cold comfort in Pakistan haven', *The Times*, 23 July 1990. 'Security forces raze Kashmir town centre', *The Independent*, 3 October 1990. 'Indian villagers tell of mass rape by soldiers', *The Independent*, 19 March 1991. 'Kashmiri villagers tell of gang rapes by Indian soldiers', *The Times*, 4 April 1991. 'In the shadow of the gunmen', *The Sunday Times*, 29 December 1991.
43. S. Verba & G. A. Almond, 'National Revolutions and Political Commitment', in H. Eckstein (ed.), *Internal War*, 230. A. Jamieson, *The Heart Attacked*, 32, 51, 57. V. S. Pisano, *The Dynamics of Subversion and Violence in Contemporary Italy*, 23.
44. S. Verba & G. A. Almond, 'National Revolutions and Political Commitment', 222.
45. Ibid., 226.
46. D. Moss, *The Politics of Left-Wing Violence in Italy*, 101–4. A. Jamieson, *The Heart Attacked*, 100, 123–4.
47. 'Italian Terrorists Kill a Union Aide', *Washington Post*, 25 January 1979. 'Italian labour protest over killing', *Financial Times*, 26 January 1979. 'Hero's funeral for party victim', *Financial Times*, 29 January 1979. C. Seton-Watson, 'Terrorism in Italy', 110. A. Jamieson, *The Heart Attacked*, 100, 175–6. D. Moss, *The Politics of Left-Wing Violence in Italy*, 227, 285 n42. A. Jamieson, *The Heart Attacked*, 92, 100, 123, 126, 175–6, 186.
48. G. Adams, *The Politics of Irish Freedom*, 64.
49. A. P. Schmid & J. de Graaf, *Violence as Communication*, 43. M. Dillon, *The Enemy Within*, 211.
50. 'IRA "SCUDS" steal Gulf headlines', *AP/RN*, 14 February 1991. 'Another mortar for ould Ireland', *AP/RN*, 14 February 1991. 'London chaos through the world's eyes', *AP/RN*, 14 February 1991.
51. G. Fairbairn, *Revolutionary Guerrilla Warfare: The Countryside Version* (Harmondsworth: Penguin, 1974) 287 n7.
52. E. Behr, *The Algerian Problem* (Harmondsworth: Penguin, 1961), 112.
53. A. P. Schmid & J. de Graaf, *Violence as Communication*, 25.
54. Ibid., 48–9. N. C. Livingstone, *The War Against Terrorism* (Toronto: Lexington Books, 1982), 66.
55. 'Death in the post', *The Guardian*, supplement, 15 May 1995. 'Misfit's lonely downfall', *The Guardian*, 5 April 1996. 'Have they now caught the Unabomber', *The Independent*, 5 April 1996. 'FC', *The Unabomber Manifesto: Industrial Society and its Future* (Berkeley, CA: Jolly Roger Press, 1995; 1996).
56. P. C. Hearst & A. Moscow, *Every Secret Thing*, 78, 151, 43, 68–9.
57. M. Baumann, *Wie Alles Anfing*, 100.

58. A. Jamieson, *The Heart Attacked*, 119–71, *passim*.
59. A. P. Schmid & J. de Graaf, *Violence as Communication*, 122–37.
60. A. Jamieson, *The Heart Attacked*, 77.
61. D. Miller, *Don't Mention the War: Northern Ireland, Propaganda and the Media* (London: Pluto Press, 1994), 247–50. A. P. Schmid, 'Terrorism and the Media: The Ethics of Publicity', 558.
62. T. Bjorgo, 'Role of the Media in Racist Violence', in T. Bjorgo & R. Witte (eds), *Racist Violence in Europe*, 98–100.
63. L. Curtis, *Ireland: The Propaganda War. The British Media and the 'Battle for Hearts and Minds'* (London: Pluto Press, 1984), 190–3. 'A gag that chokes freedom', *The Independent*, 12 September 1994.
64. Article 19, *No Comment: Censorship, Secrecy and the Irish Troubles* (London: Article 19, 1989), 23–5.
65. 'Jail for Greek editors who defied terror ban', *The Independent*, 10 September 1991. 'Editors backed', *The Times*, 11 September 1991. 'Greece in the dock over gagging order on media', *The Independent*, 16 September 1991.
66. A. P. Schmid & J. de Graaf, *Violence as Communication*, 44.
67. M. Baumann, *Wie Alles Anfing*, 54–5.
68. A. Jamieson, *The Heart Attacked*, 100.
69. M. Dillon, *The Shankill Butchers*, xi. R. Bell, R. Johnstone, R. Wilson (eds), 'Troubles Chronology: 17.5.84', *Troubled Times*, 199. D. Miller, *Don't Mention the War*, 274.
70. A. Corsun, 'Group Profile: The Revolutionary Organization 17 November', 105, 118. Revolutionary Organisation 17th November, 'Communiqué on the assassination in Athens on 21 February 1985 of Nikos Momiferatos, publisher of *Apogevmatini*', in Y. Alexander & D. Pluchinsky (eds), *Europe's Red Terrorists*, 94–8.
71. 'Islamists kill 29th journalist', *The Independent*, 18 February 1995. 'Algeria murder', *The Daily Telegraph*, 18 February 1995. 'Editors fired at from both sides in a vicious war', *The Independent*, 13 March 1995. 'Algerian woman journalist killed', *The Guardian*, 9 August 1995. 'Cutting throats to create a Muslim state', *The Independent*, 6 December 1996.
72. 'France fears upsurge of Islamic terror', *The Independent on Sunday*, 10 April 1994.
73. Amnesty International, *Political Violence in Colombia*, 19.
74. J. Pearce, *Colombia: Inside the Labyrinth*, 254–5. Amnesty International, *Political Violence in Colombia*, 75–6.
75. Amnesty International, *Guatemala: Maquila workers among trade unionists targeted* (London: Amnesty International, 1995).
76. Ibid., 8.
77. Ibid., 9.
78. 'Journalist helped end building site racket', *The Independent*, 10 December 1988. S. Bruce, *The Red Hand*, 245, 248. J. Cusack & M. Taylor, 'The Resurgence of a Terrorist Organization', 6–8.
79. R. Hill & A. Bell, *The Other Face of Terror*, 99–106, 216–19.
80. 'Bombing "devastating" to IRA', *The Independent*, 11 November 1987.
81. D. Miller, *Don't Mention the War*, 279–80.

82. 'The angry south, the weary north', *The Independent on Sunday*, 28 March 1993.
83. D. McKittrick, *Endgame*, 269.
84. 'Caging the godfathers of terror', *The Independent*, 26 March 1993. E. Gorman, 'Back in the frame', *Fortnight*, June 1993.
85. A. P. Schmid & J. de Graaf, *Violence as Communication: Insurgent Terrorism and the Western News Media* (London: Sage, 1982), 184.
86. 'Are we feeding IRA bloodlust', *The Sunday Telegraph*, 28 August 1988.
87. 'Bus suicide bomber kills five Israelis', *The Daily Telegraph*, 25 July 1995.
88. 'Suicide bombs rock Middle East peace', *The Guardian*, 23 January 1995. 'Bus stop bombers kill 19 in Israel', *The Independent*, 23 January 1995. 'Bus suicide bomber kills five Israelis', *The Daily Telegraph*, 25 July 1995. 'Onward march of terrorist violence', *The Independent*, 4 March 1996. 'Calls grow for "total war" as press loses patience', *The Guardian*, 6 March 1996. 'Israel puts ring of steel around the Palestinians', *The Independent*, 7 March 1996. 'Israeli blockade keeps mother and baby apart', *The Guardian*, 19 March 1996. 'Bomber's kin await Israel's revenge', *The Independent*, 19 March 1996. 'Portrait of a suicide bomber', *The Independent*, 10 March 1996.
89. 'Suicide bus bomber kills 22', *The Daily Telegraph*, 20 October 1994. 'Israel steps up war on Hamas', *The Daily Telegraph*, 21 October 1994. 'Arab village stunned by martyrdom', *The Daily Telegraph*, 22 October 1994. 'The menacing face of Hamas', *The Daily Telegraph*, 21 October 1994. 'Arabs search for honour in the peace', *The Independent on Sunday*, 23 October 1994.
90. A. Corsun, 'Group Profile: The Revolutionary Organization 17 November', 98, 105–8, 115–16, 117.
91. 'Greek bombers target the tourists', *The Independent*, 13 June 1994.
92. A. Corsun, 'Group Profile: The Revolutionary Organization 17 November', 106, 11.
93. Revolutionary Organisation 17 November, 'Communiqué on the assassination of Ronald Stewart, a US Air Force Sergeant, in Athens on 12 March 1991', in Y. Alexander & D. Pluchinsky (eds), *Europe's Red Terrorists*, 111.
94. US Department of State, Press Statement, 4 March 1991. First of October Anti-Fascist Resistance Groups, 'Communiqué on the Bombing of Oil Pipelines in Spain on 22 February 1991'; Revolutionary Left, 'Undated Dev Sol communiqué on "Operation Desert Storm"', and editors' comments, in Y. Alexander & D. Pluchinsky (eds), *Europe's Red Terrorists*, 23, 58, 93, 117, 130–1, 233, 249–50.
95. M. L. R. Smith, *The Role of the Military Instrument in Irish Republican Strategic Thinking: An Evolutionary Analysis*, Ph.D., King's College, University of London, 1991, 345.
96. 'The Armalite and the Ballot Box', *Magill*, July 1983.
97. M. L. R. Smith, *The Role of the Military Instrument in Irish Republican Strategic Thinking*, 311–14.
98. P. Bishop & E. Mallie, *The Provisional IRA*, 251. J. Bowyer Bell, *The Secret Army*, 398.

99. '"We are doing all in our power to shorten this war" – IRA', *AP/RN*, 12 March 1992.
100. Ibid.
101. 'London counts the cost of IRA bombs', *The Independent*, 13 April 1992. 'Insured loss may hit £150m', *Lloyd's List*, 12 February 1996.
102. '"The ceasefire is over": IRA bombers blast London', *The Independent*, 10 February 1996. 'Bomb shatters IRA ceasefire', *The Times*, 10 February 1996. 'IRA statement', *The Guardian*, 10 February 1996. 'Statements from republican sources and the prime minister', *Financial Times*, 10–11 February 1996. 'Damage adds up to £85m', *The Independent on Sunday*, 11 February 1996. 'Insured loss may hit £150m', *Lloyd's List*, 12 February 1996. 'Premiums threat as cost estimate tops £150m', *Financial Times*, 12 February 1996. 'IRA cessation ends after 527 days', 'IRA blames Major for end of cessation', both in *AP/RN*, 15 February 1996.
103. C. Dobson & R. Payne, *The Carlos Complex*, 126–7. D. Yallop, *To the Ends of the Earth*, 375–6, 378–9. 'Security alert sent to police before bombing in Brighton', *The Times*, 15 October 1984. P. Bishop & E. Mallie, *The Provisional IRA*, 423–6.

10 DECISION-MAKING

1. A. Schlesinger, 'The Historians and History', *Foreign Affairs*, 41 (April 1963), 493, quoted in B. Brodie, *War and Politics* (London: Cassell, 1973), 279. George Kennan made a similar point after his transition from the National War College to the State Department. G. Kennan, 'Planning of Foreign Policy', in G. D. Harlow & G. C. Maerz (eds), *Measures Short of War: The George F. Kennan Lectures at the National War College, 1946–47* (Washington DC: National Defense University Press, 1991), 207–10.
2. D. Beresford, *Ten Men Dead*, 152.
3. See M. Ranstorp, 'Hizbollah's Command Leadership'.
4. A. Geifman, 'Aspects of Early Twentieth-Century Russian Terrorism: The Socialist Revolutionary Combat Organization', *Terrorism and Political Violence*, 4, no. 2 (Summer 1992), 29, 34–5, 38–9. N. Schliefman, *Undercover Agents in the Russian Revolutionary Movement: The SR Party, 1902–14* (London: Macmillan, 1988), 82–118.
5. G. Grivas-Dighenis, *Guerrilla Warfare*, 25, 69.
6. A. Jamieson, 'Entry, Discipline and Exit in the Italian Red Brigades', 5. A. Jamieson, *The Heart Attacked*, 84–5. G. C. Caselli & D. della Porta, 'The history of the Red Brigades', 74. D. Moss, *The Politics of Left-Wing Violence in Italy*, 57. J. Bowyer Bell, *IRA Tactics and Targets*, 27, 48, 116.
7. S. Aust, *The Baader-Meinhof Group*, 92–3. P. C. Hearst & A. Moscow, *Every Secret Thing*, 131–2, 109.
8. 'The making of a martyr', *The Daily Telegraph*, 3 February 1995. B. A. Scharlau, *Left-Wing Terrorism in the Federal Republic of Germany*, 43. H. J. Horchem, *Terrorism in West Germany*, 6.

9. 'Far-Right entering anti-hunt groups', *The Daily Telegraph*, 7 April 1993.
10. D. Henshaw, *Animal Warfare*, 51.
11. 'The making of a martyr', *The Daily Telegraph*, 3 February 1995.
12. D. Henshaw, *Animal Warfare*, 50.
13. J. K. Zawodny, 'Guerrilla Warfare and Subversion as a Means of Political Change'. Paper presented at the 1961 Annual Meeting of the American Political Science Association, Sheraton-Jefferson Hotel, St Louis, Missouri, 6–9 September 1961, 7. J. K. Zawodny, 'Internal Organizational Problems and the Sources of Tensions of Terrorist Movements as Catalysts of Violence', *Terrorism: An International Journal*, 1, nos. 3/4, 278.
14. M. Crenshaw, 'An Organizational Approach to the Analysis of Political Terrorism', 467.
15. M. Dillon & D. Lehane, *Political Murder in Northern Ireland*, 257–8. M. L. R. Smith, *Fighting for Ireland*, 120.
16. 'A tribal past lingers in modern hate', *The Independent*, 4 June 1991. 'Rising tide of death threats sharpens fear in East Tyrone', *The Irish Times*, 8 September 1992. 'Attempt by IRA to murder church caretaker condemned as sectarian', *The Irish Times*, 10 September 1992. 'The deadly results of pub talk suspicions', *The Irish Times*, 14 September 1992. S. MacStiofain, *Revolutionary in Ireland*, 253. T. P. Coogan, *The IRA*, 472. M. Dillon & D. Lehane, *Political Murder in Northern Ireland*, 260. J. Bowyer Bell, *IRA Tactics and Targets*, 27, 48, 110–14, 116.
17. 'Bombing "devastating" to IRA', *The Independent*, 11 November 1987.
18. '11 die in Poppy Day massacre', *The Times*, 9 November 1987. P. Bishop & E. Mallie, *The Provisional IRA*, 459–61.
19. L. Crocq, M. Crocq, C. Barrois, G. Belensky, & F. D. Jones, 'Low-intensity combat psychiatric casualties', in P. Pichot, P. Berner, & K. Thau (eds), *Psychiatry: The state of the art*, 548.
20. A. Jamieson, 'Identity and Morality in the Italian Red Brigades', 514.
21. P. C. Hearst & A. Moscow, *Every Secret Thing*, 197.
22. P. C. Hearst & A. Moscow, *Every Secret Thing*, 201.
23. K. Wasmund, 'The political socialization of terrorist groups in West Germany', *Journal of Political and Military Sociology*, 11 (Fall 1983), 228, 233.
24. K. Wasmund, 'The political socialization of terrorist groups in West Germany', 236. K. Wasmund, 'The Political Socialization of West German Terrorists', in P. H. Merkl (ed.), *Political Violence and Terror*, 219.
25. R. P. Clark, *The Basques*, 121–4. R. P. Clark, 'Patterns in the Lives of ETA members', 283–4, 293–4, 303–6. F. O'Connor, *In Search of a State: Catholics in Northern Ireland* (Belfast: Blackstaff, 1993), 125. E. MacDonald, *Shoot the Women First*, 141. 'Local Hero', *Esquire*, December 1993/January 1994. P. Bishop & E. Mallie, *The Provisional IRA*, 12.
26. H. Brown, *People, Groups, and Society*, 2–7, 9, 11–15.
27. K. Heskin, *Northern Ireland: A Psychological Analysis*, 87–8. H. Brown, *People, Groups, and Society*, 16–19.
28. I. Janis, *Groupthink: Psychological Studies of Policy Decisions and Fi-

ascoes, revised and enlarged (Boston: Houghton Mifflin, 1982).
29. I. Janis, *Groupthink*, 9.
30. I. Janis, *Groupthink*, 174–5. J. E. Dougherty & R. L. Pfaltzgraf, *Contending Theories of International Relations*, third edition (New York: Harper & Row, 1990), 499.
31. A. Jamieson, *The Heart Attacked*, 281.
32. B. A. Scharlau, *Left-Wing Terrorism in the Federal Republic of Germany*, 187–8.
33. J. Bowyer Bell, *IRA Tactics and Targets*, 14, 15.
34. J. Bowyer Bell, *IRA Tactics and Targets*, 111–12.
35. For the rise of the northerners and the split in 1986 see: P. Bishop & E. Mallie, *The Provisional IRA*, 275–87, 310, 315. L. Clarke, *Broadening the Battlefield*, 29, 84–5, 228–41.
36. E. Mallie & D. McKittrick, *The Fight for Peace*, 201–2, 314–18, 381–3. B. Rowan, *Behind the Lines*, 55, 84–5.
37. A. I. Teger & D. G. Pruitt, 'Components of Group Risk Taking', *Journal of Experimental Social Psychology*, 3 (1967). S. Moscovici & M. Zavalloni, 'The Group as a Polarizer of Attitudes', *Journal of Personality and Social Psychology*, 12, no 2. R. Brown, *Group Processes: Dynamics within and between Groups* (Oxford: Blackwell, 1988), 143, 142–58 *passim*.
38. A. K. Semmel & D. Minix, 'Small-Group Dynamics and Foreign Policy Decision-Making: An Experimental Approach', in L. S. Falkowski (ed.), *Psychological Models in International Politics* (Boulder, CO: Westview Press, 1979).
39. G. McKee & R. Franey, *Time Bomb*, 330–47.
40. T. Bjorgo, 'Terrorist Violence against Immigrants and Refugees in Scandanavia', 40–2.
41. J. K. Zawodny, 'Infrastructures of Terrorist Organizations', in L. Z. Freedman & Y. Alexander (eds), *Perspectives on Nuclear Terrorism*, 67. J. K. Zawodny, 'Internal Organizational Problems and the Sources of Tensions of Terrorist Movements as Catalysts of Violence', 281–2.
42. H. Holland, *The Struggle*, 228.
43. H. Holland, *The Struggle*, 206, 219.
44. K. Wasmund, 'The political socialization of terrorist groups in West Germany', 235.
45. S. Aust, *The Baader-Meinhof Group*, 92–3. B. A. Scharlau, *Left-Wing Terrorism in the Federal Republic of Germany*, 176, 184. J. M. Post, 'Hostilite, Conformite, Fraternite', 216. J. M. Post, 'Prospects for Nuclear Terrorism: Psychological Motivations and Constraints', in P. Leventhal & Y. Alexander (eds), *Preventing Nuclear Terrorism: The Report and Papers of the International Task Force on Prevention of Nuclear Terrorism* (Lexington, MA: Lexington Books, 1987), 94. J. M. Post, 'Terrorist psycho-logic', 33–4. K. Wasmund, 'The political socialization of terrorist groups in West Germany', 235. P. Taylor, *States of Terror*, 80.
46. *Der Spiegel*, 7 August 1978, cited in G. Bass et al., *Motivations and Possible Actions of Potential Criminal Adversaries of US Nuclear Programs* (Santa Monica, CA: RAND Corporation, February 1980), 7.
47. B. M. Jenkins, *International Terrorism: A New Kind of Warfare*, 4. B. M. Jenkins, *The Likelihood of Nuclear Terrorism*, 7. B. M. Jenkins,

High Technology Terrorism and Surrogate War, 11.
48. B. M. Jenkins, *The Likelihood of Nuclear Terrorism*, 8.
49. D. Canter, *Criminal Shadows*, 125–58.
50. R. W. White & T. F. White, 'Revolution in the City', 107.
51. F. Burton, *The Politics of Legitimacy*, 23.
52. L. Clarke, *Broadening the Battlefield*, 41, 252. T. P. Coogan, *The IRA*, 580.
53. M. McKeown, *Two Seven Six Three*, 49–54. R. McKeever, 'Repartition: An Irish Solution to the Northern Irish Problem'. Paper for presentation at ECPR Joint Workshop on Theories of Political Violence in Bochum, West Germany, 2–7 April 1990, 26–32.
54. On this form of loyalist attack see M. Dillon & D. Lehane, *Political Murder in Northern Ireland*, 177–8, 182, 211–12. M. Dillon, *The Shankill Butchers*, 159.
55. R. P. Clark, *The Basque Insurgents*, 185–203.

Bibliography

OFFICIAL DOCUMENTS

Central Intelligence Agency. *Patterns of International Terrorism: 1980* (Washington DC: Government Printing Office, 1981).
GHQ Ireland. *Record of the rebellion in Ireland in 1920–21 and the part played by the Army in dealing with it. Volume II. Intelligence* (A-2448-2).
M. Maguire & C. Norris. *The Royal Commission on Criminal Justice: The Conduct and Supervision of Criminal Investigations* (London: HMSO, 1992).
Director of Housing, Oldham Metropolitan Borough. *Racial Harassment Policy*, local government report (Oldham: Oldham Metropolitan Borough, December 7, 1988).
Royal Ulster Constabulary. *Chief Constable's Annual Report 1993* (London: HMSO, 1994).
Royal Ulster Constabulary. *Chief Constable's Annual Report 1994* (London: HMSO, 1995).
Security Service. *The Security Service* (London: HMSO, 1993).
UK House of Commons, Defence Committee. *The Physical Security of Military Installations in the United Kingdom* (HC-171) (London: HMSO, 1990).
UK House of Commons, Home Affairs Committee. *Organised Crime* (HC 18– I) (London: HMSO, 1995).
US Department of State. Press Statement, March 4, 1991.
US Department of State, Bureau of Public Affairs. *Libya under Qadhafi: A Pattern of Aggression*, Special Report No. 138 (Washington DC: US Dept of State, January 1986).
US Department of State. *Patterns of Global Terrorism: 1983* (Washington DC: Government Printing Office, September 1984).
US Department of State. *Patterns of Global Terrorism: 1984* (Washington DC: Government Printing Office, November 1985).
US Department of State. *Patterns of Global Terrorism: 1985* (Washington DC: Government Printing Office, October 1986).
US Department of State. *Patterns of Global Terrorism: 1989* (Washington DC: Government Printing Office, April 1990).
US Department of State. *Patterns of Global Terrorism: 1990* (Washington DC: Government Printing Office, April 1991).
US Department of State, Overseas Security Advisory Council. *Security Guidelines for American Families Living Abroad* (Washington DC: US Dept of State, n.d).

DOCUMENTS FROM OTHER BODIES

Amnesty International. *Argentina: The Military Juntas and Human Rights, Report of the Trial of the Former Junta Members* (London: Amnesty International, 1987).

Amnesty International. *Getting Away with Murder: Political killings and 'disappearances' in the 1990s* (London: Amnesty International, 1993).
Amnesty International. *Guatemala: Maquila workers among trade unionists targeted* (London: Amnesty International, 1995).
Amnesty International. *Peru: Human Rights in a Climate of Terror* (London: Amnesty International, 1991).
Amnesty International. *Political Violence in Colombia: Myth and reality* (London: Amnesty International, 1994).
Angry Brigade. *The Angry Brigade, 1967–1984: Documents and Chronology* (Bratach Dubh Anarchist Pamphlets, 1978; London: Elephant Editions, 1985).
Argentina, Comision Nacional sobre la Desparicion de Personas. *Nunca Mas: A Report by Argentina's National Commission on Disappeared People* (English translation) (Buenos Aires: Editorial Universitaria de Buenos Aires, 1984; London: Faber & Faber/Index on Censorship, 1986).
Herri Batasuna. *The 'Herri Batasuna' the Basque Country Needs* (Herri Batasuna).
Herri Batasuna. *The Recognition of Democratic Rigths [sic] in Basque Country: Basis for Peace* (Herri Batasuna, October 1994).
Searchlight. *From Ballots to Bombs: The Inside Story of the National Front's Political Soldiers* (London: Searchlight, after 1989).

TECHNICAL SALES LITERATURE

Advanced Design Electronics & the Home Office. *The simple guide to choosing an alarm system* (Advanced Design Electronics Ltd, n.d.).
Bel-Tech Security Products. *Bel-Pac 1000 1–2 door access control: BT1000* (Ilford: Bell Security Ltd).
Modern Security Systems. *Could YOU use an extra pair of eyes?* (Hemel Hempstead: Modern Security Systems Ltd, November 1992).
Modern Security Systems. *Detection Devices: Passive Infra-Red Movement Detectors* (Hemel Hempstead: Modern Security Systems Ltd, November 1992).
PAC International. *Access Control Equipment: Data Sheet* (Stockport: PAC International Ltd, July 1993).
Sensormatic CamEra. *Sensormatic CamEra: The World Leader in Loss Prevention* (Warrington: Sesormatic CamEra Ltd, n. d).
Visonic. *Company profile & Product Catalogue* (Biggleswade: Visonic Ltd, n.d.).

ACADEMIC THESES AND PAPERS

J. T. Choi. *Acts of Violence against Civil Aviation: historical survey, perspectives and responses*, Ph.D., University of St Andrews, 1992.
D. L. G. Hall. *The Ulster Defence Association: A case of change and continuity*, M. Social Sc., Queen's University, Belfast, 1988.
Y. Katayama. *Terrorism in Japan since 1969: A study of the activities of the Japanese Red Army*, Ph.D., University of Aberdeen, 1989.

R. McKeever. 'Repartition: An Irish Solution to the Northern Irish Problem'. Paper for presentation at ECPR Joint Workshop on Theories of Political Violence, Bochum, West Germany, April 2nd to 7th 1990.
S. V. D. Samaranayake. *Political Violence in the Third World: A Case Study of Sri Lanka, 1971–1987*, Ph.D., University of St Andrews, 1990.
B. A. Scharlau. 'Chronology of Major Events' (Unpublished manuscript, 1992).
B. A. Scharlau. *Left-Wing Terrorism in the Federal Republic of Germany*, Ph.D., University of St Andrews, 1991.
M. L. R. Smith. *The Role of the Military Instrument in Irish Republican Strategic Thinking: An evolutionary analysis*, Ph.D., King's College, University of London, 1991.
J. K. Zawodny. 'Guerrilla Warfare and Subversion as a Means of Political Change'. Paper presented at the 1961 Annual Meeting of the American Political Science Association, Sheraton-Jefferson Hotel, St Louis, Missouri, September 6–9, 1961.

ARTICLES IN JOURNALS

A. J. Alexander. 'Getting the Most from Scarce Resources', *TVI Journal*, 5, no. 2 (Fall 1984).
J. D. Baldeschwieler. 'Explosive Detection for Commercial Aircraft Security', *Terrorism and Political Violence*, 5, no. 2 (Summer 1993).
M. Barkun. 'Millenarian Aspects of 'White Supremacist' Movements', *Terrorism and Political Violence*, 1, no. 4 (October 1989).
M. Barkun. 'Millenarian Groups and Law Enforcement Agencies: The Lessons of Waco', *Terrorism and Political Violence*, 6, no. 1 (Spring 1994).
J. Bowyer Bell. 'Career Moves: Reflections on the Irish Gunman', *Studies in Conflict and Terrorism*, 15, no. 1 (January–March 1992).
J. Bowyer Bell. 'Revolutionary Dynamics: The Inherent Inefficiency of the Underground', *Terrorism and Political Violence*, 2, no. 2 (Summer 1990).
E. Best. 'An Interview with Ed Best, Director of Security at the Los Angeles Olympics', *TVI Journal*, 5, no. 2 (Fall 1984).
S. Bruce. 'Criminality and Vigilante Politics; The Scottish Protestant Case', *Conflict Quarterly*, Spring 1986.
M. Bull. 'Villains of the Peace: Terrorism and the Secret Services in Italy', *Intelligence and National Security*, 7, no. 4 (October 1992).
R. Clutterbuck. 'Trends in Terrorist Weaponry', *Terrorism and Political Violence*, 5, no. 2 (Summer 1993).
M. Crenshaw. 'An Organizational Approach to the Analysis of Political Terrorism', *Orbis: A Journal of World Affairs* 29, no. 3 (Fall 1985).
M. Crenshaw. 'How terrorism declines', *Terrorism and Political Violence*, 3, no. 1 (Summer 1991).
M. Crenshaw. 'The Concept of Revolutionary Terrorism', *Journal of Conflict Resolution*, 16, no. 3 (September 1972).
M. Crenshaw. 'Political Violence in Algeria', *Terrorism and Political Violence*, 6, no. 3 (Autumn 1994).
H. M. Cubert. 'The Militant Palestinian Organizations and the Arab-Israeli

Peace Process', *Terrorism and Political Violence*, 4, no. 1 (Spring 1992).

J. Cusack & M. Taylor. 'The Resurgence of a Terrorist Organization – Part 1: The UDA, A Case Study', *Terrorism and Political Violence*, 5, no. 3 (Autumn 1993).

Y. Debay. 'The Legion tests new weapons', *RAIDS*, August 1993.

W. Enders & T. Sandler. 'The Effectiveness of Antiterrorism policies: A Vector-Autoregression-Intervention Analysis', *American Political Science Review*, 87, no. 4 (December 1993).

W. Enders, T. Sandler and J. Cauley. 'UN Conventions, Technology and Retaliation in the Fight Against Terrorism: An Econometric Evaluation', *Terrorism and Political Violence* 2, no. 1 (Spring 1990).

F. Ferracuti. 'A Sociopsychiatric Interpretation of Terrorism', *Annals of the American Academy*, 463 (September 1982).

D. Fitzpatrick. 'The Geography of Irish Nationalism: 1910–1921', *Past and Present*, 78 (February 1978).

A. Geifman. 'Aspects of Early Twentieth-Century Russian Terrorism: The Socialist Revolutionary Combat Organization', *Terrorism and Political Violence*, 4, no. 2 (Summer 1992).

W. A. Hazleton & S. Woy-Hazleton. 'Sendero Luminoso: A Communist Party Crosses a River of Blood', *Terrorism and Political Violence*, 4, no. 2 (Summer 1992).

C. Hewitt. 'Terrorism and Public Opinion: A Five Country Comparison', *Terrorism and Political Violence*, 2, no. 2 (Summer 1990).

B. Hoffman. 'Terrorist Targeting: Tactics, Trends, and Potentialities', *Terrorism and Political Violence*, 5, no. 2 (Summer 1993).

B. Hoffman & D. K. Hoffman. 'The RAND-St Andrews Chronology of International Terrorism, 1994', *Terrorism and Political Violence*, 7, no. 4 (Winter 1995).

H. Horchem. 'The Decline of the Red Army Faction', *Terrorism and Political Violence*, 3, no. 2 (Summer 1991).

R. A. Hudson. 'Colombia's Palace of Justice Tragedy Revisited: A Critique of the Conspiracy Theory', *Terrorism and Political Violence*, 7, no. 2 (Summer 1995).

E. I. Im and J. Cauley. 'Cycles and Substitutions in Terrorist Activities: A Spectral Approach', *Kyklos* 40, no. 2 (1987).

Z. Ivianski. 'Fathers and Sons: A Study of Jewish Involvement in the Revolutionary Movement and Terrorism in Tsarist Russia', *Terrorism and Political Violence*, 1, no. 2 (April 1989).

A. Jamieson. 'Entry, Discipline and Exit in the Italian Red Brigades', *Terrorism and Political Violence*, 2, no. 1 (Spring 1990).

F. Jiminez. 'Spain: The Terrorist Challenge and the Government's Response', *Terrorism and Political Violence*, 4, no. 4 (Winter 1992).

J. Kaplan. 'The Context of American Millenarian Revolutionary Theology: The Case of the 'Identity Christian' Church of Israel', *Terrorism and Political Violence*, 5, no. 1 (Spring 1993).

G. Kassimeris. 'Greece: Twenty Years of Political Terrorism', *Terrorism and Political Violence*, 7, no. 2 (Summer 1995).

M. Kotsonouris. 'Revolutionary Justice – the Dail Eireann Courts', *History Ireland*, 2, no. 3 (Autumn 1994).

M. Kramer. 'Sacrifice and Fratricide in Shiite Lebanon', *Terrorism and Political Violence*, 3, no. 3 (Autumn 1991).

P. W. Little. 'Abduction and Assassination Reconsidered', *TVI Report*, 8, no. 3.

F. Llera, J. M. Mata & C. L. Irwin. 'ETA: From Secret Army to Social Movement – The Post-Franco Schism of the Basque Nationalist Movement', *Terrorism and Political Violence*, 5, no. 3 (Autumn 1993).

F. Lopez-Alves. 'Political Crises, Strategic Choices and Terrorism: The Rise and Fall of the Uruguayan Tupamaros', *Terrorism and Political Violence*, 1, no. 2 (April 1989).

P. A. Lupsha. 'Explanation of Political Violence: Some Psychological Theories Versus Indignation', *Politics and Society*, 2, no. 1 (Fall 1971).

H. A. Lyons & H. J. Harbinson. 'A Comparison of Political and Non-Political Murderers in Northern Ireland, 1974–84', *Medicine, Science and the Law*, 26, no. 3 (1986).

T. D. Mason & C. Campany. 'Guerrillas, Drugs and Peasants: The Rational Peasant and the War on Drugs in Peru', *Terrorism and Political Violence*, 7, no. 4 (Winter 1995).

T. D. Mason & J. Swartzfager. 'Land Reform and the Rise of Sendero Luminoso in Peru', *Terrorism and Political Violence*, 1, no. 4 (October 1989).

A. Merari. 'Terrorism as a Strategy of Insurgency', *Terrorism and Political Violence*, 5, no. 4 (Winter 1993).

A. Merari, T. Prat & D. Tal. 'The Palestinian *Intifada*: An Analysis of a Popular Uprising after Seven Months', *Terrorism and Political Violence*, 1, no. 2 (April 1989).

S. Moscovici & M. Zavalloni. 'The Group as a Polarizer of Attitudes', *Journal of Personality and Social Psychology*, 12, no. 2.

K. L. Oots. 'Organizational Perspectives on the Formation and Disintegration of Terrorist Groups', *Terrorism*, 12, no. 3 (1989).

P. Paganacci. 'Weapons of the Russian Special Forces', *RAIDS*, UK edition (January 1995).

J. M. Post. 'Hostilite, Conformite, Fraternite: The Group Dynamics of Terrorist Behaviour', *International Journal of Group Psychotherapy*, 36, no. 2 (April 1986).

J. M. Post. 'Notes on a Psychodynamic Theory of Terrorist Behaviour', *Terrorism: An International Journal*, 7, no. 3 (1984).

M. Ranstorp. 'Hizbollah's Command Leadership: Its Structure, Decision Making and Relationship with Iranian Clergy and Institutions', *Terrorism and Political Violence*, 6, no. 3 (Autumn 1994).

H. J. Rosenbaum & P. C. Sederberg. 'Vigilantism', *Comparative Politics*, 6, no. 4 (1974).

I. Salan, chair. 'Psychology of leaders of terrorist groups', *International Journal of Group Tensions*, 12 (1982).

D. Salvioni & A. Stephanson. 'Reflections on the Red Brigades', *Orbis: A Journal of World Affairs*, 29, no. 3 (Fall 1985).

G. Samaranayake. 'Ethnic Conflict in Sri Lanka and Prospects of Management: An Empirical Inquiry', *Terrorism and Political Violence*, 3, no. 2 (Summer 1991).

T. Sandler, J. T. Tschirhart and J. Cauley. 'A Theoretical Analysis of Transnational Terrorism', *American Political Science Review* 77 no. 1 (March 1983).
T. Sandler, W. Enders and H. E. Lapan. 'Economic Analysis Can Help Fight International Terrorism', *Challenge*, (January/February 1991).
J. Schmeidel. 'My Enemy's Enemy: Twenty Years of Co-operation between West Germany's Red Army Faction and the GDR Ministry for State Security', *Intelligence and National Security*, 8, no. 4 (October 1993).
T. Sheehan. 'Myth and Violence: The Fascism of Julius Evola and Alain de Benoist', *Social Research*, 48 (Spring 1981).
R. H. Shultz. 'Iranian Covert Aggression: Support for Radical Political Islamists Conducting Internal Subversion Against States in the Middle East/Southwest Asia Region', *Terrorism and Political Violence*, 6, no. 3 (Autumn 1994).
J. Teenbrook. 'ERT Negotiators', *RAIDS*, UK edition, March 1993.
A. I. Teger & D. G. Pruitt. 'Components of Group Risk Taking', *Journal of Experimental Social Psychology*, 3 (1967).
B. Vaughn. 'The Use and Abuse of Intelligence Services in India', *Intelligence and National Security*, 8, no. 1 (January 1993).
J. E. Vorbach. 'Monte Melkonian: Armenian Revolutionary Leader', *Terrorism and Political Violence*, 6, no. 2 (Summer 1994).
K. Wasmund. 'The political socialization of terrorist groups in West Germany', *Journal of Political and Military Sociology*, 11 (Fall 1983).
C. Watson. 'Guerrilla Groups in Colombia: Reconstituting the Political Process', *Terrorism and Political Violence*, 4, no. 2 (Summer 1992).
L. Weinberg & W. Eubank. 'Leaders and Followers in Italian Terrorist Groups', *Terrorism and Political Violence*, 1, no. 2 (April 1989).
R. W. White & T. F. White. 'Revolution in the City: On the Resources of Urban Guerrillas', *Terrorism and Political Violence*, 3, no. 4 (Winter 1991).
P. Wilkinson. 'Designing an Effective International Aviation Security System', *Terrorism and Political Violence*, 5, no. 2 (Summer 1993).
P. Williams. 'Transnational Criminal Organisations and International Security', *Survival*, 36, no. 1 (Spring 1994).
J. K. Zawodny. 'Internal Organizational Problems and the Sources of Tensions of Terrorist Movements as Catalysts of Violence', *Terrorism: An International Journal*, 1, nos. 3/4 (1978).

ARTICLES IN EDITED BOOKS

A. Ashkenasi. 'Social-Ethnic Conflict and Paramilitary Organization in the Near East'. In P. H. Merkl (ed.) *Political Violence and Terror: Motifs and Motivations* (Berkeley: University of California Press, 1986).
C. E. Baumann. 'Diplomatic Kidnappings'. In B. M. Jenkins (ed.) *Terrorism and Personal Protection* (Stoneham, MA: Butterworth, 1985).
I. F. W. Beckett. 'Guerrilla Warfare: Insurgency and Counter-insurgency since 1945'. In C. McInnes & G. D. Sheffield (eds) *Warfare in the Twentieth Century: Theory and Practice* (London: Unwin Hyman, 1988).
R. H. Berg. 'Peasant Responses to Shining Path in Andahuaylas'. In D. S.

Palmer (ed.) *Shining Path of Peru* (London: Hurst & Co, 1992).
T. Bjorgo. 'Terrorist Violence against Immigrants and Refugees in Scandanavia: Patterns and Motives'. In T. Bjorgo & R. Witte (eds) *Racist Violence in Europe* (London: Macmillan, 1993).
T. Bjorgo. 'Role of the Media in Racist Violence'. In T. Bjorgo & R. Witte (eds) *Racist Violence in Europe* (London: Macmillan, 1993).
L. Bollinger. 'Terrorist conduct as a result of a psychosocial process'. In P. Pichot, P. Berner, & K. Thau (eds) *Psychiatry: The State of the Art Volume 6: Drug Dependence and Alcoholism, Forensic Psychiatry, Military Psychiatry* (New York: Plenum Press, 1985).
D. G. Boyce. '"A Gallous Story and a Dirty Deed": Political Martyrdom in Ireland since 1867'. In Y. Alexander & A. O'Day (eds) *Ireland's Terrorist Dilemma* (Dordrecht, The Netherlands: Martinus Nijhoff, 1986).
E. Bramall. 'The Place of the British Army in Public Order'. In P. J. Rowe & C. J. Whelan (eds) *Military Intervention in Democratic Societies* (London: Croom Helm, 1985).
A. M. Bravo. 'Frontier culture takes to cocaine'. In M. L. Smith (ed.) *Why people grow drugs: Narcotics and Development in the Third World* (London: Panos, 1992).
J. Caceres. 'Violence, National Security and Democratisation in Central America'. In M. Kirkwood (ed.) *States of Terror: Death Squads or Development?* (London: Catholic Institute for International Relations, 1989).
G. Capotorto. 'How Terrorists look at Kidnappings'. In B. M. Jenkins (ed.) *Terrorism and Personal Protection* (Stoneham, MA: Butterworth, 1985).
G. C. Caselli & D. della Porta. 'The history of the Red Brigades: organizational structures and strategies of action (1970–82)'. In R. Catanzaro (ed.) *The Red Brigades & Left-Wing Terrorism in Italy* (London: Pinter, 1991).
R. Catanzaro. 'Subjective experience and objective reality: an account of violence in the words of its protagonists'. In R. Catanzaro (ed.) *The Red Brigades & Left-Wing Terrorism in Italy* (London: Pinter, 1991).
R. P. Clark. 'Patterns in the Lives of ETA members'. In P. H. Merkl (ed.) *Political Violence and Terror: Motifs and Motivations* (Berkeley: University of California Press, 1986).
R. P. Clark. 'Patterns of Eta Violence: 1968–1980'. In P. H. Merkl (ed.) *Political Violence and Terror: Motifs and Motivations* (Berkeley: University of California Press, 1986).
A. Corsun. 'Group Profile: The Revolutionary Organization 17 November in Greece (1975–91)'. In Y. Alexander & D. Pluchinsky (eds) *European Terrorism Today & Tomorrow* (Washington DC: Brassey's (US), 1992).
R. Cox. 'Total Terrorism: Argentina, 1969 to 1979'. In M. Crenshaw (ed.) *Terrorism, Legitimacy, and Power: The Consequences of Political Violence* (Middletown, CT: Wesleyan University Press, 1983).
M. Crenshaw. 'The logic of terrorism: Terrorist behaviour as a product of strategic choice'. In W. Reich (ed.) *Origins of Terrorism: Psychologies, Ideologies, Theologies, States of Mind* (Cambridge: Cambridge University Press, 1990).
L. Crocq, M. Crocq, C. Barrois, G. Belensky, & F. D. Jones. 'Low-intensity

combat psychiatric casualties'. In P. Pichot, P. Berner, & K. Thau (eds) *Psychiatry: The State of the Art Volume 6: Drug Dependence and Alcoholism, Forensic Psychiatry, Military Psychiatry* (New York: Plenum Press, 1985).

J. Darby. 'The Historical Background'. In J. Darby (ed.) *Northern Ireland: The Background to the Conflict* (Belfast: Appletree Press, 1983).

M. S. Diokno. '"Guardians of Democracy": Vigilantes in the Philippines'. In M. Kirkwood (ed.) *States of Terror: Death Squads or Development?* (London: Catholic Institute for International Relations, 1989).

F. Doherty. 'SIGINT used by Anti-State Forces: A Case Study of Provisional IRA Operations'. In C. Bledowska (ed.) *War and Order: Researching State Structures* (London: Junction Books, 1983).

R. Drake. 'Julius Evola and the Ideological Origins of the Radical Right in Contemporary Italy'. In P. H. Merkl (ed.) *Political Violence and Terror: Motifs and Motivations* (Berkeley: University of California Press, 1986).

F. Ferracuti & F. Bruno. 'Psychiatric Aspects of Terrorism in Italy'. In I. L. Barak-Glantz & C. R. Huff (eds) *The Mad, the Bad, and the Different: Essays in Honor of Simon Dinitz* (Lexington, MA: Lexington Books, 1981).

First of October Anti-Fascist Resistance Groups. 'Communiqué on the Bombing of Oil Pipelines in Spain on 22 February 1991'. In Y. Alexander & D. Pluchinsky (eds) *Europe's Red Terrorists: The Fighting Communist Organizations* (London: Frank Cass, 1992).

A. M. Gallagher. 'Policing Northern Ireland: Attitudinal Evidence'. In A. O'Day (ed.) *Terrorism's Laboratory: The Case of Northern Ireland* (Aldershot: Dartmouth, 1995).

A. M. Gallagher. 'Civil Liberties and the State'. In P. Stringer & G. Robinson (eds) *Social Attitudes in Northern Ireland: The Second Report, 1991–1992* (Belfast: Blackstaff Press, 1992).

A. George. 'The Discipline of Terrorology'. In A. George (ed.) *Western State Terrorism* (Cambridge: Polity Press, 1991).

F. Ginsburg. 'Saving America's Souls: Operation Rescue's Crusade against Abortion'. In M. E. Marty & R. S. Appleby (eds) *Fundamentalisms and the State* (Chicago: University of Chicago Press, 1993).

J. E. Gonzales. 'Guerrillas and Coca in the Upper Huallaga Valley'. In D. S. Palmer (ed.) *Shining Path of Peru* (London: Hurst & Co, 1992).

G. Gorritti. 'Shining Path's Stalin and Trotsky'. In D. S. Palmer (ed.) *Shining Path of Peru* (London: Hurst & Co, 1992).

A. Guelke & F. Wright. 'On A "British Withdrawal" from Northern Ireland'. In P. Stringer & G. Robinson (eds) *Social Attitudes in Northern Ireland: The Second Report, 1991–1992* (Belfast: Blackstaff Press, 1992).

C. Guevara. 'Guerrilla Warfare – A Method'. In W. Laqueur (ed.) *The Guerrilla Reader: A Historical Anthology* (London: Wildwood House, 1978).

E. S. Herman & G. O'Sullivan. '"Terrorism" as Ideology and Cultural Industry'. In A. George (ed.) *Western State Terrorism* (Cambridge: Polity Press, 1991).

R. J. Healy. 'Protecting the Office'. In B. M. Jenkins (ed.) *Terrorism and Personal Protection* (Stoneham, MA: Butterworth, 1985).

K. Heskin. 'The Terrorists'. Terrorist: Vincent Browne's interview with Dominic McGlinchey'. In Y. Alexander & A. O'Day (eds) *Ireland's Terrorist Dilemma* (Dordrecht, The Netherlands: Martinus Nijhoff, 1986).

K. Heskin. 'The psychology of terrorism in Northern Ireland'. In Y. Alexander & A. O'Day (eds) *Terrorism in Ireland* (London: Croom Helm, 1984).

H. J. Horchem. 'Terrorism in Western Europe'. In R. Clutterbuck (ed.) *The Future of Political Violence: Destabilization, Disorder and Terrorism* (London: Macmillan, 1986).

C. L. Irvin. 'Terrorists' Perspectives: Interviews'. In D. L. Paletz & A. P. Schmid (eds) *Terrorism and the Media* (Newbury Park, CA: Sage, 1992).

B. J. Isbell. 'Shining Path and Peasant Responses in Rural Ayacucho'. In D. S. Palmer (ed.) *Shining Path of Peru* (London: Hurst & Co, 1992).

P. Janke. 'Europe'. In R. Clutterbuck (ed.) *The Future of Political Violence: Destabilization, Disorder and Terrorism* (London: Macmillan, 1986).

G. Kennan. 'Planning of Foreign Policy'. In G. D. Harlow & G. C. Maerz (eds) *Measures Short of War: The George F. Kennan Lectures at the National War College, 1946–47* (Washington DC: National Defense University Press, 1991).

E. Kolinsky. 'Terrorism in West Germany'. In J. Lodge (ed.) *The Threat of Terrorism* (Brighton: Wheatsheaf, 1988).

M. Kramer. 'Hizbullah: The Calculus of Jihad'. In M. E. Marty & R. S. Appleby (eds) *Fundamentalisms and the State* (Chicago: University of Chicago Press, 1993).

P. Kropotkin. 'The Spirit of Revolt'. In W. Laqueur (ed.) *The Terrorism Reader: A Historical Anthology* (New York: Meridian, 1978).

T. N. Madan. 'The Double-edged Sword: Fundamentalism and the Sikh Religious Tradition'. In M. E. Marty & R. S. Appleby (eds) *Fundamentalisms Observed* (Chicago: University of Chicago Press, 1993).

Mao Tse-tung *Basic Tactics* (New York: Praeger, 1966).

Mao Tse-tung. 'Be concerned with the well-being of the masses, pay attention to methods of work'. In *Selected Works of Mao Tse-tung*, 3 vols (Peking: Foreign Languages Press, 1965).

Mao Tse-tung. 'The Chinese Revolution and the Chinese Communist Party'. In *Selected Works of Mao Tse-tung*, 3 vols (Peking: Foreign Languages Press, 1965).

Mao Tse-tung. 'On correcting mistaken ideas in the Party'. In *Selected Works of Mao Tse-tung*, 3 vols (Peking: Foreign Languages Press, 1965).

Mao Tse-tung. 'On Protracted War'. In *Selected Works of Mao Tse-tung*, 3 vols (Peking: Foreign Languages Press, 1965).

Mao Tse-tung. 'Pay attention to economic work'. In *Selected Works of Mao Tse-tung*, 3 vols (Peking: Foreign Languages Press, 1965).

Mao Tse-tung. 'Problems of strategy in China's Revolutionary War'. In *Selected Works of Mao Tse-tung*, 3 vols (Peking: Foreign Languages Press, 1965).

Mao Tse-tung. 'Problems of strategy in guerrilla war against Japan'. In *Selected Works of Mao Tse-tung*, 3 vols (Peking: Foreign Languages Press, 1965).

Mao Tse-tung. 'Report of an investigation of the peasant movement in

Hunan'. In *Selected Works of Mao Tse-tung*, 3 vols (Peking: Foreign Languages Press, 1965).

C. Marighela. 'Guerrilla Tactics and Operations'. In C. Marighela *For the Liberation of Brazil* (Harmondsworth: Penguin, 1971).

C. Marighela. 'Handbook of Urban Guerrilla Warfare'. In C. Marighela *For the Liberation of Brazil* (Harmondsworth: Penguin, 1971).

C. Marighela. 'Problems and Principles of Strategy'. In C. Marighela *For the Liberation of Brazil* (Harmondsworth: Penguin, 1971).

R. Mark. 'Keeping the Peace in Great Britain: The Differing Roles of the Police and the Army'. In P. J. Rowe & C. J. Whelan (eds) *Military Intervention in Democratic Societies* (London: Croom Helm, 1985).

A. Merari. 'The readiness to kill and die: Suicidal terrorism in the Middle East'. In W. Reich (ed.) *Origins of Terrorism: Psychologies, Ideologies, Theologies, States of Mind* (Cambridge: Cambridge University Press, 1990).

E. Moxon-Browne. 'The Water and the Fish: Public Opinion and the Provisional IRA in Northern Ireland'. In P. Wilkinson (ed.) *British Perspectives on Terrorism* (London: George Allen & Unwin, 1981).

C. Novaro. 'Social networks and terrorism: the case of *Prima Linea*'. In R. Catanzaro (ed.) *The Red Brigades & Left-Wing Terrorism in Italy* (London: Pinter, 1991).

H. Oberoi. 'Sikh Fundamentalism: Translating History into Theory'. In M. E. Marty & R. S. Appleby (eds) *Fundamentalisms and the State* (Chicago: University of Chicago Press, 1993).

K. Oxford. 'Patterns in a Labyrinth – The Problem in Crime Detection'. In A. R. Brownlie (ed.) *Crime Investigation: Art or Science* (Edinburgh: Scottish Academic Press, 1984).

D. Pluchinsky. 'RAF Assassination of Alfred Herrhausen'. In US Department of State, Bureau of Diplomatic Security (ed.) *Terrorist Tactics and Security Practices* (Washington DC: US Department of State, 1994).

D. Pluchinsky. 'An Organizational and Operational Analysis of Germany's Red Army Faction Terrorist Group (1972–1991)'. In Y. Alexander & D. Pluchinsky (eds) *European Terrorism Today & Tomorrow* (Washington DC: Brassey's (US), 1992).

B. Pollack & G. Hunter. 'Dictatorship, Democracy and Terrorism in Spain'. In J. Lodge (ed.) *The Threat of Terrorism* (Brighton: Wheatsheaf, 1988).

J. M. Post. 'Terrorist psycho-logic: Terrorist behaviour as a product of psychological forces'. In W. Reich (ed.) *Origins of Terrorism: Psychologies, Ideologies, Theologies, States of Mind* (Cambridge: Cambridge University Press, 1990).

J. M. Post. 'Prospects for Nuclear Terrorism: Psychological Motivations and Constraints'. In P. Leventhal & Y. Alexander (eds) *Preventing Nuclear Terrorism: The Report and Papers of the International Task Force on Prevention of Nuclear Terrorism* (Lexington, MA: Lexington Books, 1987).

Red Army Faction. 'Communiqué on the Assassination of Alfred Herrhausen, Chairman of Deutsche Bank, in Frankfurt on 30 November 1989'. In Y. Alexander & D. Pluchinsky (eds) *Europe's Red Terrorists: The Fighting Communist Organizations* (London: Frank Cass, 1992).

Red Army Faction. 'Communiqué on the Assassination of Detlev Rohwedder, President of Treuhandanstalt, in Dusseldorf on 1 April 1991'. In Y. Alexander & D. Pluchinsky (eds) *Europe's Red Terrorists: The Fighting Communist Organizations* (London: Frank Cass, 1992).

Red Brigades – Fighting Communist Party. 'Communiqué on the Assassination of Ezio Tarantelli, a Rome University Economics Professor, in Rome on 27 March 1985'. In Y. Alexander & D. Pluchinsky (eds) *Europe's Red Terrorists: The Fighting Communist Organizations* (London: Frank Cass, 1992).

Red Brigades & Red Army Faction. 'Excerpts from Notes of a Meeting between the Red Brigades and Red Army Faction in January 1988'. In Y. Alexander & D. Pluchinsky (eds) *Europe's Red Terrorists: The Fighting Communist Organizations* (London: Frank Cass, 1992).

Revolutionary Left. 'Undated Dev Sol communiqué on "Operation Desert Storm"'. In Y. Alexander & D. Pluchinsky (eds) *Europe's Red Terrorists: The Fighting Communist Organizations* (London: Frank Cass, 1992).

Revolutionary Organisation 17 November. 'Communiqué on the assassination of Ronald Stewart, a US Air Force Sergeant, in Athens on 12 March 1991'. In Y. Alexander & D. Pluchinsky (eds) *Europe's Red Terrorists: The Fighting Communist Organizations* (London: Frank Cass, 1992).

Revolutionary Organisation 17th November. Communiqué on the assassination in Athens on 21 February 1985 of Nikos Momiferatos, publisher of *Apogevmatini*'. In Y. Alexander & D. Pluchinsky (eds) *Europe's Red Terrorists: The Fighting Communist Organizations* (London: Frank Cass, 1992).

R. Rumrrill. 'The highs and lows of a cocaine economy'. In M. L. Smith (ed.) *Why people grow drugs: Narcotics and Development in the Third World* (London: Panos, 1992).

C. A. Russell & B. H. Miller. 'Profile of a Terrorist'. In L. Z. Freedman & Y. Alexander (eds) *Perspectives on Nuclear Terrorism* (Wilmington, DE: Scholarly Resources Inc, 1983).

C. A. Russell & B. H. Miller. 'Terrorist Targets and the Executive Target'. In Y. Alexander & R. A. Kilmarx (eds) *Political Terrorism and Business: The Threat and Response* (New York: Praeger, 1979).

A. A. Sachedina. 'Activist Shi'ism in Iran, Iraq, and Lebanon'. In M. E. Marty & R. S. Appleby (eds) *Fundamentalisms Observed* (Chicago: University of Chicago Press, 1993).

B. A. Salamanca. 'Vehicle Bombs: Death on Wheels'. In N. C. Livingstone & T. E. Arnold (eds) *Fighting Back: Winning the War Against Terrorism* (Lexington, MA: Lexington Books, 1986).

J. Salata. 'MANPADs: The Potential for Use as a Terrorist Tactic'. In US Department of State, Bureau of Diplomatic Security (ed.) *Terrorist Tactics and Security Practices* (Washington DC: US Department of State, 1994).

T. Sandler et al. 'Economic Methods and the Study of Terrorism'. In P. Wilkinson & A. M. Stewart (eds) *Contemporary Research on Terrorism* (Aberdeen: Aberdeen University Press, 1987; 1989).

D. T. Schiller. 'The European Experience'. In B. M. Jenkins (ed.) *Terrorism and Personal Protection* (Stoneham, MA: Butterworth, 1985).

A. J. Scotti. 'Transportation Security'. In B. M. Jenkins (ed.) *Terrorism*

and Personal Protection (Stoneham, MA: Butterworth, 1985).
A. K. Semmel & D. Minix. 'Small-Group Dynamics and Foreign Policy Decision-Making: An Experimental Approach'. In L. S. Falkowski (ed.) *Psychological Models in International Politics* (Boulder, CO: Westview Press, 1979).
C. Seton-Watson. 'Terrorism in Italy'. In J. Lodge (ed.) *The Threat of Terrorism* (Brighton: Wheatsheaf, 1988).
M. L. Smith. 'Shining Path's Urban Strategy: Ate Vitarte'. In D. S. Palmer (ed.) *Shining Path of Peru* (London: Hurst & Co, 1992).
M. L. Smith. 'Taking the High Ground: Shining Path and the Andes'. In D. S. Palmer (ed.) *Shining Path of Peru* (London: Hurst & Co, 1992).
E. Sprinzak. 'From Messianic Pioneering to Vigilante Terrorism: The Case of the Gush Emunim Underground'. In D. C. Rapoport (ed.) *Inside Terrorist Organizations* (London: Frank Cass, 1988).
Z. Sternhell. 'Fascist Ideology'. In W. Laqueur (ed.) *Fascism: A Reader's Guide; Analyses, Interpretations, Bibliography* (Wildwood House, 1976, Harmondsworth: Penguin, 1979).
G. Tarnovski. 'Terrorism and Routine'. In W. Laqueur (ed.) *The Terrorism Reader: A Historical Anthology* (New York: Meridian, 1978).
J. R. Thackrah. 'Reactions to Terrorism and Riots'. In *Contemporary Policing: An examination of society in the 1980s* (London: Sphere, 1985).
T. P. Thornton. 'Terror as a Weapon of Political Agitation'. In H. Eckstein (ed.) *Internal War: Problems and Approaches* (New York: The Free Press of Glencoe, 1964).
K. Tololyan. 'Martyrdom as Legitimacy: Terrorism, Religion and Symbolic Appropriation in the Armenian Diaspora'. In P. Wilkinson & A. M. Stewart (eds) *Contemporary Research on Terrorism* (Aberdeen: Aberdeen University Press, 1987; 1989).
K. Tololyan. 'Cultural Narrative and the Motivation of the Terrorist'. In D. C. Rapoport (ed.) *Inside Terrorist Organizations* (London: Frank Cass, 1988).
R. D. Tomasek. 'Complex Interdependency Theory: Drug Barons as Transnational Groups'. In W. C. Olson & J. R. Lee (eds) *The Theory and Practice of International Relations* (Englewood Cliffs, NJ: Prentice-Hall, 1994).
H. E. Vanden. 'State Policy and the Cult of Terror in Central America'. In P. Wilkinson & A. M. Stewart (eds) *Contemporary Research on Terrorism* (Aberdeen: Aberdeen University Press, 1987; 1989).
S. Verba & G. A. Almond. 'National Revolutions and Political Commitment'. In H. Eckstein (ed.) *Internal War: Problems and Approaches* (New York: The Free Press of Glencoe, 1964).
K. Wasmund. 'The Political Socialization of West German Terrorists'. In P. H. Merkl (ed.) *Political Violence and Terror: Motifs and Motivations* (Berkeley: University of California Press, 1986).
H. Willmott. 'Kenya in Revolt'. In R. Thompson & J. Keegan (eds) *War in Peace: An Analysis of Warfare since 1945* (London: Orbis, 1981).
G. Woodcock. 'Anarchism: A Historical Introduction'. In G. Woodcock (ed.) *The Anarchist Reader* (Glasgow: Fontana/Collins, 1977).
S. Woy-Hazleton & W. A. Hazleton. 'Shining Path and the Marxist Left'.

In D. S Palmer (ed.) *Shining Path of Peru* (London: Hurst & Co, 1992).
D. E. Wurth. 'The Proper Function and use of the Private Sector Bodyguard'. In B. M. Jenkins (ed.) *Terrorism and Personal Protection* (Stoneham, MA: Butterworth, 1985).
J. K. Zawodny. 'Infrastructures of Terrorist Organizations'. In L. Z. Freedman & Y. Alexander (eds) *Perspectives on Nuclear Terrorism* (Wilmington, DE: Scholarly Resources Inc, 1983).

BOOKS AND BOOKLETS

No author named. *Punishing the Innocent: House Demolition and Sealing in the West Bank* (London: Council for the Advancement of Arab–British Understanding, 1987).
No author named. *Volunteer Seamus Twomey, 1919–89: A Tribute* (Dublin: AP/RN, 1989).
R. Adam. *Modern Handguns* (London: Quintet, 1989).
R. Adam. *The World's Most Powerful Rifles & Handguns* (London: Quintet, 1991).
G. Adams. *The Politics of Irish Freedom* (Dingle, Ireland: Brandon, 1986).
J. Adams. *The Financing of Terror* (London: New English Library, 1986; 1988).
J. Adams. *Trading in Death: The Modern Arms Race* (London: Hutchinson, 1990; Pan, 1991).
J. Adams, R. Morgan, & A. Bambridge. *Ambush: The War Between the SAS and the IRA* (London: Pan, 1988).
J. Agirre *Operation Ogro: The Execution of Admiral Luis Carrero Blanco* (New York: Quadrangle, 1975).
M. J. Akbar. *India: The Siege Within* (Harmondsworth: Penguin, 1985).
S. E. Ambrose. *Rise to Globalism: American Foreign Policy Since 1938*, seventh edition (Harmondsworth: Penguin, 1993).
P. F. Angiolillo. *A Criminal as Hero: Angelo Duca* (Lawrence: The Regents Press of Kansas, 1979).
Article 19. *No Comment: Censorship, Secrecy and the Irish Troubles* (London: Article 19, 1989).
S. Aust. *The Baader-Meinhof Group: The Inside Story of a Phenomenon* (Hamburg: Hoffman & Campe Verlag, 1985; London: Bodley Head, 1987).
R. Baldwin & R. Kinsey. *Police Powers and Politics* (London: Quartet, 1982).
T. F. Baldy. *Battle for Ulster: A Study of Internal Security* (Washington DC: National Defense University Press, 1987).
S. Banerjee. *India's Simmering Revolution: The Naxalite Uprising* (London: Zed Books, 1984).
N. Barber. *The War of the Running Dogs: The Malayan Emergency, 1948–1960* (London: 1971; New York: Bantam, 1987).
D. Barker. *Grivas: Portrait of a Terrorist* (London: Cresset, 1959).
T. Barry. *Guerrilla Days in Ireland* (Dublin: The Irish Press, 1949; Tralee: Anvil, 1962).
D. Barzilay. *The British Army in Ulster*, volume 2 (Belfast: Century Services Ltd, 1975).

G. Bass et al. *Motivations and Possible Actions of Potential Criminal Adversaries of US Nuclear Programs* (Santa Monica, CA: RAND Corporation, February 1980).
B. Baumann. *Wie Alles Anfing. How it all Began: The Personal Account of a West German Urban Guerrilla* (Munich: Trikont Verlag, 1975; Vancouver: Pulp Press, 1977).
J. Becker. *Hitler's Children: The Story of the Baader-Meinhof Gang* (London: Granada, 1978).
C. A. Beckwith & D. Knox. *Delta Force* (London: Arms and Armour Press, 1984; Fontana, 1985).
M. Begin. *The Revolt*, revised edition (1952; London: W. H. Allen, 1979).
E. Behr. *The Algerian Problem* (Harmondsworth: Penguin, 1961).
S. Belfrage. *The Crack: A Belfast Year* (Andre Deutsch, 1987; London: Grafton, 1988).
J. Bowyer Bell. *IRA Tactics and Targets: An Analysis of Tactical Aspects of the Armed Struggle, 1969–1989* (Swords, Ireland: Poolbeg, 1990).
R. Bell, R. Johnstone, R. Wilson (eds). *Troubled Times: Fortnight Magazine and the Troubles in Northern Ireland 1970–1991* (Belfast: Blackstaff Press, 1991).
D. Beresford. *Ten Men Dead: The story of the 1981 Irish hunger strike* (London: Grafton, 1987).
G. Best. *Humanity in Warfare: The Modern History of the International Law of Armed Conflicts* (London: Weidenfeld & Nicolson, 1980; Methuen, 1983).
P. Bishop & E. Mallie. *The Provisional IRA* (London: Heinemann, 1987; Corgi, 1988).
A & C. Black Ltd. *Who's Who 1988: An annual biographical dictionary* (London: A & C Black, 1988).
M. Bles & R. Low. *The Kidnap Business* (1987; London: Star, 1988).
Y. Bodansky. *Target America: Terrorism in the US Today* (New York: SPI Books, 1993).
K. Boyle, T. Hadden, & P. Hillyard. *Ten Years on in Northern Ireland: The Legal Control of Political Violence* (London: Cobden Trust, 1980).
D. Breen. *My Fight for Irish Freedom*, revised and enlarged edition (Dublin: Anvil, 1964).
British Society for Social Responsibility in Science. *TechnoCop: New Police Technologies* (London: Free Association Books, 1985).
B. Brodie. *War and Politics* (London: Cassell, 1973).
H. Brown. *People, Groups, and Society* (Milton Keynes: Open University Press, 1985).
R. Brown. *Group Processes: Dynamics within and between Groups* (Oxford: Basil Blackwell, 1988).
C. R. Browning. *Ordinary Men: Reserve Police Battalion 101 and the Final Solution in Poland* (New York: Harper Collins, 1992; 1993).
S. Bruce. *The Edge of the Union: The Ulster Loyalist Political Vision* (Oxford: Oxford University Press, 1994).
S. Bruce. *The Red Hand: Protestant Paramilitaries in Northern Ireland* (Oxford: Oxford University Press, 1992).
A. Bullock. *Hitler: A Study in Tyranny*, revised edition (London: Book Club Associates, 1973).

J. Burns. *The Land That Lost It's Heroes: Argentina, The Falklands and Alfonsin* (London: Bloomsbury, 1987).
F. Burton. *The politics of legitimacy: Struggles in a Belfast community* (London: Routledge & Kegan Paul, 1978).
E. Butler. *Barry's Flying Column: The story of the IRA's Cork No. 3 Brigade 1919–21* (London: Leo Cooper, 1971; Tandem, 1972).
A. Calder. *The People's War: Britain 1939–1945* (London: Jonathan Cape, 1969; Granada, 1982).
D. Canter. *Criminal Shadows: Inside the Mind of the Serial Killer* (London: Harper Collins, 1994; 1995).
G. Carr. *The Angry Brigade: The Cause and the Case* (London: Victor Gollancz, 1975).
R. Catanzaro. *Men of Respect: A Social History of the Sicilian Mafia* (Padua: Liviana Editrice spa, 1988; New York: Free Press, 1992).
G. Chaliand. *The Palestinian Resistance* (Harmondsworth: Penguin, 1972).
S. Christie. *Stefano Delle Chiaie: Portrait of a Black Terrorist* (London: Anarchy Magazine/Refract Publications, 1984).
A. Clark. *Diaries* (London: Weidenfeld & Nicolson, 1993; Phoenix, 1994).
R. P. Clark. *The Basques: The Franco Years and Beyond* (Reno: University of Nevada Press, 1979).
R. P. Clark. *The Basque Insurgents: ETA, 1952–1980* (Madison: University of Wisconsin Press, 1984).
L. Clarke. *Broadening the Battlefield: The H-Blocks and the Rise of Sinn Fein* (Dublin: Gill & Macmillan, 1987).
R. Clutterbuck, *Kidnap, Hijack and Extortion* (London: Macmillan, 1987).
L. Collins & D. Lapierre. *O Jerusalem!* (London: Weidenfeld and Nicholson, 1972; Pan, 1973).
T. Colman. *Incident into Evidence: Operational Police Skills* (Maidenhead: McGraw-Hill, 1989).
T. P. Coogan. *Michael Collins: A Biography* (London: Hutchinson, 1990).
T. P. Coogan. *On the Blanket: The H-Block Story* (Dublin: Ward River Press, 1980).
T. P. Coogan. *The IRA* (Glasgow: Fontana/Collins, 1987).
C. Coughlin. *Hostage: the complete story of the Lebanon captives* (London: Little, Brown & Co, 1992).
E. Crankshaw. *The Shadow of the Winter Palace: The Drift to Revolution, 1825–1917* (London: Macmillan, 1976; Harmondsworth: Penguin, 1981).
M. Crenshaw Hutchinson. *Revolutionary Terrorism: The FLN in Algeria, 1954–1962.* (Stanford, CA: Hoover Institution Press, 1978).
S. Cronin. *Irish Nationalism: A History of its Roots and Ideology* (Dublin: The Academy Press, 1980).
L. Curtis. *Ireland: The Propaganda War. The British Media and the 'Battle for Hearts and Minds'* (London: Pluto Press, 1984).
J. Darby. *Intimidation and the Control of Conflict in Northern Ireland* (Dublin: Gill and Macmillan, 1986).
N. Darbyshire & B. Hilliard. *The Flying Squad* (London: Headline, 1993).
B. Dasgupta. *The Naxalite Movement* (New Delhi: Allied Publishers, 1974).
R. Debray. *Revolution in the Revolution? Armed Struggle and Political Struggle in Latin America* (France: 1967; Harmondsworth: Penguin, 1968).

H. W. Degenhardt (ed). *Revolutionary and Dissident Movements: An International Guide* (Harlow: Longmans, 1988).
P. de Polnay. *Napoleon's Police* (London: W. H. Allen, 1970).
P. Devlin. *Straight Left: An Autobiography* (Belfast: Blackstaff, 1993).
M. Dewar. *The British Army in Northern Ireland* (London: Arms & Armour Press, 1985).
M. Dewar. *Weapons & Equipment of Counter-Terrorism* (Poole: Arms & Armour Press, 1987).
C. di Giovanni. *Light from Behind the Bars: Letters from the Red Brigades and Other Former Italian Terrorists; True Stories of Terror, Agony and Hope* (Slough: St Paul Publications, 1990).
C. Dickey. *With the Contras: A Reporter in the Wilds of Nicaragua* (New York: Simon & Schuster, 1985; London: Faber & Faber, 1986).
M. Dillon. *Killer in Clowntown: Joe Doherty, the IRA and the Special Relationship* (London: Hutchinson; Arrow, 1992).
M. Dillon. *The Dirty War* (London: Hutchinson, 1990; Arrow, 1991).
M. Dillon. *The Enemy Within* (London: Doubleday, 1994).
M. Dillon. *The Shankill Butchers: A Case Study of Mass Murder* (London: Hutchinson, 1989; Arrow, 1990).
M. Dillon & D. Lehane. *Political Murder in Northern Ireland* (Harmondsworth: Penguin, 1973).
C. Dobson & R. Payne. *The Carlos Complex: A Study in Terror*, revised edition (London: Coronet, 1978).
J. E. Dougherty & R. L. Pfaltzgraf. *Contending Theories of International Relations*, third edition (New York: Harper & Row, 1990).
T. Downes-Le Guin & B. Hoffman. *The Impact of Terrorism on Public Opinion, 1988 to 1989* (Santa Monica, CA: RAND Corporation, 1993).
R. Drake. *The Revolutionary Mystique and Terrorism in Contemporary Italy* (Bloomington, IN: Indiana University Press, 1989).
E. Duyker. *Tribal Guerrillas: The Santals of West Bengal and the Naxalite Movement* (Delhi: Oxford University Press, 1987).
J. Ellis. *The Sharp End of War: The Fighting Man in World War II* (Newton Abbot: David & Charles, 1980; London: Corgi, 1982).
S. Emerson & B. Duffy. *The Fall of Pan Am 103* (London: Futura, 1990).
E. C. Ezell. *Small Arms of the World: a basic manual of small arms*, twelfth edition (New York: Barnes & Noble, 1993).
R. Fagilot. *Britain's Military Strategy in Ireland: The Kitson Experiment* (London: Zed Books, 1983).
G. Fairbairn. *Revolutionary Guerrilla Warfare: The Countryside Version* (Harmondsworth: Penguin, 1974).
G. Falcone & M. Padovani. *Men of Honour: The Truth About the Mafia* (Paris: Edition 1, 1991; London: Fourth Estate, 1992).
W. R. Farrell. *Blood and Rage: The Story of the Japanese Red Army* (Lexington, MA: Lexington Books, 1990).
'FC'. *The Unabomber Manifesto: Industrial Society and its Future* (Berkeley, CA: Jolly Roger Press, 1995; 1996).
A. Feldman. *Formations of Violence: The Narrative of the Body and Political Terror in Northern Ireland* (Chicago: University of Chicago Press, 1991).

R. Fisk. *Pity the Nation: Lebanon at War* (London: Andre Deutsch, 1990; Oxford: Oxford University Press, 1991).
W. D. Flackes & S. Elliott. *Northern Ireland: A Political Directory 1968–93* (Belfast: Blackstaff, 1994).
R. Fleming & H. Miller. *Scotland Yard* (London: Michael Joseph, 1994).
C. Foley. *Legion of the Rearguard: The IRA and the Modern Irish State* (London: Pluto, 1992).
M. R. D. Foot. *Resistance* (Eyre Methuen, 1976; London: Granada, 1978).
F. L. Ford. *Political Murder: From Tyrannicide to Terrorism* (Cambridge, MA: Harvard University Press, 1985).
A. Frangi. *The PLO and Palestine* (Frankfurt: R. G. Fischer Verlag, 1982; London: Zed Books, 1983).
R. A. Friedlander (ed). *Terrorism: Documents of International and Local Control. Volume IV: A World on Fire* (London: Oceana Publications Inc, 1984.
T. Gander. *Combat Pistols: A manual of modern handguns* (Wellingborough: Patrick Stephens Ltd, 1989).
R. Garner. *Animal politics and morality* (Manchester: Manchester University Press, 1993).
C. Gearty. *Terror* (London: Faber & Faber, 1991; 1992).
J. Gellner. *Bayonets in the Streets: Urban guerrilla at home and abroad* (Don Mills, Ontario: Collier-Macmillan Canada, 1974).
T. Geraghty. *The Bullet-Catchers: Bodyguards and the World of Close Protection* (London: Grafton, 1988; 1989).
V. N. Giap. *People's War People's Army: The Viet Công Insurrection Manual for Underdeveloped Countries* (New York: Praeger, 1962; Bantam, 1968).
R. Gillespie. *Soldiers of Peron: Argentina's Montoneros* (Oxford: Clarendon Press, 1982).
G. Grivas – Dighenis. *Guerrilla Warfare and EOKA's Struggle* (London: Longmans, 1964).
G. Grivas – Dighenis & C. Foley (ed). *The Memoirs of General Grivas* (London: Longmans, 1964).
C. Guevara. *Guerrilla Warfare* (New York: Praeger, 1961; Harmondsworth: Penguin, 1969).
P. Gurney. *Braver Men Walk Away* (London: Harper Collins, 1993).
C. W. Gwynn. *Imperial Policing* (London: Macmillan, 1934; 1936).
D. Hamill. *Pig in the Middle: The Army in Northern Ireland, 1969–1984* (London: Methuen, 1985).
G. Harris. *The Dark Side of Europe: The Extreme Right Today*, new edition (Edinburgh: Edinburgh University Press, 1994).
I. Hasselbach & T. Reiss. *Fuhrer-Ex: Memoirs of a Former Neo-Nazi* (London: Chatto & Windus, 1996).
M. Hastings. *Bomber Command* (London: Michael Joseph, 1979; Pan, 1981).
P. C. Hearst & A. Moscow. *Every Secret Thing* (London: Methuen, 1982; Arrow, 1983).
P. Henissart. *Wolves in the City: The Death of French Algeria* (London: Rupert Hart-Davis, 1971).
D. Henshaw. *Animal Warfare: The Story of the Animal Liberation Front* (London: Fontana, 1989).

E. S. Herman. *The Real Terror Network: Terrorism in Fact and Propaganda* (Montreal: Black Rose Books, 1985).
E. S. Herman & G. O'Sullivan. *The Terrorism Industry: The Experts and Institutions That Shape Our View of Terror* (New York: Pantheon, 1989).
K. Heskin. *Northern Ireland: A Psychological Analysis* (Dublin: Gill & Macmillan, 1980).
R. Hill & A. Bell. *The Other Face of Terror: Inside Europe's Neo-Nazi Network* (London: Grafton, 1988).
R. Hingley. *The Russian Secret Police: Muscovite, Imperial Russian and Soviet Political Security Operations, 1565–1970* (London: Hutchinson, 1970).
A. Hitler. *Mein Kampf* (London: Pimlico, 1992).
D. Hobbs. *Doing the Business: Entrepreneurship, The Working Class, and Detectives in the East End of London* (Oxford: Oxford University Press, 1989).
E. J. Hobsbawm. *Bandits*, second edition (Harmondsworth: Penguin, 1985).
E. J. Hobsbawm. *Nations and Nationalism since 1780: Programme, Myth, Reality*, second edition (Cambridge: Cambridge University Press, 1992).
B. Hoffman. *Recent trends and future prospects of terrorism in the United States* (Santa Monica, CA: RAND Corporation, 1988).
B. Hoffman. *Right-Wing Terrorism in West Germany* (Santa Monica, CA: RAND Corporation, 1986).
G. Hogan & C. Walker. *Political Violence and the Law in Ireland* (Manchester: Manchester University Press, 1989).
H. Holland. *The Struggle: A History of the African National Congress* (London: Grafton, 1989).
J. Holland. *The American Connection* (New York: Viking Penguin, 1987; Dublin: Poolbeg, 1989).
J. Holland & H. McDonald. *INLA: Deadly Divisions* (Dublin: Torc, 1994).
R. Holmes. *Firing Line* (London: Jonathan Cape, 1985; Harmondsworth: Penguin, 1987).
F. Holroyd & N. Burbridge. *War Without Honour* (Hull: Medium, 1989).
H. J. Horchem. *Terrorism in West Germany* (London: Institute for the Study of Conflict, 1986).
A. Horne *A Savage War of Peace: Algeria 1954–1962* (London: Macmillan, 1977; Harmondsworth: Penguin, 1979).
M. Howard. *The Causes of War* (London: Maurice Temple Smith, 1983; Unwin, 1984).
J. Hutchinson & A. D. Smith (eds). *Nationalism* (Oxford: Oxford University Press, 1994).
Irish Information Partnership. *Agenda: Information Service on Northern Ireland and Anglo-Irish Relations*, sixth edition (London: Irish Information Partnership, 1990).
A. Iyad & E. Rouleau. *My Home My Land: A Narrative of the Palestinian Struggle* (Paris: Fayolle, 1978; New York: Times Books, 1981).
G. Jackson. *People's Prison* (Faber & Faber, 1973; Newton Abbot: Reader's Union, 1974).
A. Jamieson. *The Heart Attacked: Terrorism and Conflict in the Italian State* (London: Marion Boyars, 1989).
I. Janis. *Groupthink: Psychological Studies of Policy Decisions and Fias-*

coes, revised and enlarged (Boston: Houghton Mifflin, 1982).
K. Jeffrey & P. Hennessy. *States of Emergency: British Governments and Strikebreaking since 1919* (London: Routledge & Kegan Paul, 1983).
B. M. Jenkins. *International Terrorism: A New Kind of Warfare* (Santa Monica, CA: RAND Corporation, June 1974).
B. M. Jenkins. *International Terrorism: The Other World War* (Santa Monica, CA: RAND Corporation, November 1985).
B. M. Jenkins. *Soldiers versus Gunmen: The Challenge of Urban Guerrilla Warfare* (Santa Monica, CA: RAND Corporation, March 1974).
B. M. Jenkins. *Terrorism Works – Sometimes* (Santa Monica, CA: RAND Corporation, April 1974).
B. M. Jenkins. *The Lessons of Beirut: Testimony before the Long Commission* (Santa Monica, CA: RAND Corporation, February 1984).
J. Joll. *The Anarchists* (London: Eyre & Spottiswoode/Methuen, 1964).
N. H. Jones. *Hitler's Heralds: The Story of the Freikorps, 1918–1923* (London: John Murray, 1987).
S. M. Katz. *Guards Without Frontiers: Israel's War Against Terrorism* (London: Arms and Armour Press, 1990).
R. Kee. *The Green Flag: A History of Irish Nationalism* (London: Weidenfeld & Nicolson. 1972).
K. J. Kelley. *The Longest War: Northern Ireland and the IRA* (London: Zed Books, 1988).
R. Kirk (ed). *The Portable Conservative Reader* (Harmondsworth: Penguin, 1982).
F. Kitson. *Low Intensity Operations: Subversion, Insurgency and Peacekeeping* (London: Faber & Faber, 1971).
P. Koch & K. Hermann. *Assault at Mogadishu* (Hamburg: Stern, 1977; London: Corgi, 1977).
A. Labrousse. *The Tupamaros: Urban Guerrillas in Uruguay* (Paris: Editions du Seuil, 1970; Harmondsworth: Penguin, 1973).
B. Lane. *The Encyclopedia of Forensic Science* (London: Headline, 1992; 1993).
W. Laqueur. *The Age of Terrorism* (London: Weidenfeld & Nicolson, 1987).
V. I. Lenin. *What is to be Done? Burning Questions of our Movement*, English translation (Stuttgart: Dietz, 1902; Moscow: Progress Publishers, 1947).
N. C. Livingstone. *The War Against Terrorism* (Toronto: Lexington Books, 1982).
C. MacDonald. *The Killing of SS Obergruppenführer Reinhard Heydrich: 27 May 1942* (London: Macmillan, 1989).
E. MacDonald. *Shoot the Women First* (Fourth Estate, 1991; London: Arrow, 1992).
S. MacStiofain. *Revolutionary in Ireland* (Edinburgh: Gordon Cremonesi, 1975).
J. J. McCuen. *The Art of Counter-Revolutionary War: The Strategy of Counter-insurgency* (London: Faber & Faber, 1966).
M. McGuire. *To Take Arms: A Year in the Provisional IRA* (London: Macmillan, 1973; Quartet, 1973).
G. McKee & R. Franey. *Time Bomb* (London: Bloomsbury, 1988).
M. McKeown. *Two Seven Six Three: An analysis of fatalities attributable to*

civil disturbances in Northern Ireland in the twenty years between July 13th 1969 and July 12th 1989 (Lucan, Ireland: Murlough, 1989).
D. McKittrick. *Despatches from Belfast* (Belfast: Blackstaff, 1989).
D. McKittrick. *Endgame: The Search for Peace in Northern Ireland* (Belfast: Blackstaff, 1994).
D. Mack Smith. *Mussolini* (London: Weidenfeld & Nicolson, 1981; Granada, 1983).
M. Maclear. *Vietnam: The Ten Thousand Day War* (London: Eyre Methuen, 1981; Thames Methuen, 1982).
E. Mallie & D. McKittrick. *The Fight for Peace: The Secret Story behind the Irish Peace Process* (London: Heinemann, 1996).
P. Marnham. *Crime and the Academie Francaise: Dispatches from Paris* (Harmondsworth: Viking, 1993).
D. C. Martin & J. Walcott. *Best Laid Plans: The Inside Story of America's War Against Terrorism* (New York: Harper & Row, 1988).
K. Marx & F. Engels. *The Communist Manifesto* (Harmondsworth: Penguin, 1967).
E. F. Mickolus, T. Sandler, J. M. Murdock. *International Terrorism in the 1980s: A Chronology of Events. Volume I, 1980–1983* (Ames: Iowa State University, 1989).
E. F. Mickolus, T. Sandler, J. M. Murdock. *International Terrorism in the 1980s: A Chronology of Events. Volume II, 1984–1987* (Ames: Iowa State University, 1989).
D. Miller. *Anarchism* (London: J. M. Dent & Sons, 1984).
D. Miller. *Don't Mention the War: Northern Ireland, Propaganda and the Media* (London: Pluto Press, 1994).
H. Miller. *Traces of Guilt: Forensic Science and the Fight Against Crime* (London: BBC Books, 1995).
D. Moss. *The Politics of Left-Wing Violence in Italy, 1969–1985* (London: Macmillan, 1989).
J. Most. *Revolutionare Kriegswissenschaft* (New York: Drud und Berlag des Internationalen Zeitungs Beireins, 1885) and *The Beast of Property* (New Haven: International Workingmen's Ass'n, 1884), in one volume (New York: Kraus Reprint, 1983).
C. Mullin. *Error of Judgement: The Truth about the Birmingham Bombings* (revised edition) (Swords, Ireland: Poolbeg, 1990).
D. Neligan. *The Spy in the Castle* (London: MacGibbon & Kee, 1968).
S. Nelson. *Ulster's Uncertain Defenders: Loyalists and the Northern Ireland Conflict* (Belfast: Appletree Press, 1984).
O. North & W. Novak. *Under Fire: An American Story* (New York: Harper Collins, 1991).
G. Northam. *Shooting in the Dark: Riot Police in Britain* (London: Faber & Faber, 1989).
B. O'Brien. *The Long War: The IRA and Sinn Fein, 1985 to Today* (Dublin: O'Brien Press, 1993).
W. V. O'Brien. *Law and Morality in Israel's War with the PLO* (New York: Doubleday, 1991).
F. O'Connor. *In Search of a State: Catholics in Northern Ireland* (Belfast: Blackstaff, 1993).

S. O'Doherty. *The Volunteer: A Former IRA Man's True Story* (London: Harper Collins, 1993).
P. O'Malley. *Biting at the Grave: The Irish Hunger Strikes and the Politics of Despair* (Belfast: Blackstaff Press, 1990).
P. O'Malley. *The Uncivil Wars: Ireland Today* (Belfast: Blackstaff, 1983).
N. K. O'Sullivan. *Conservatism* (New York: St Martin's Press, 1976).
J. Parker. *The Walking Dead: A Woman's Brave Stand Against the Mafia* (London: Simon & Schuster, 1995; Pocket Books, 1996).
T. Parker. *May the Lord in His mercy be kind to Belfast* (London: Jonathan Cape, 1993).
J. Pearce. *Colombia: Inside the Labyrinth* (London: Latin American Bureau, 1990).
F. S. Pearson. *The Global Spread of Arms: Political Economy of International Security* (Boulder, CO: Westview Press, 1994).
V. S. Pisano. *The Dynamics of Subversion and Violence in Contemporary Italy* (Stanford, CA: Hoover Institution Press, 1987).
W. Powell. *The Anarchist Cookbook* (Lyle Stuart Inc, 1971; Secaucus, NJ: Barricade Books, 1989).
J. Power. *Against Oblivion: Amnesty International's fight for human rights* (Glasgow: Fontana, 1981).
J. Ranelagh. *The Agency: The Rise & Decline of the CIA* (London: Weidenfeld & Nicolson, 1986; Sceptre, 1988).
D. Raviv & Y. Melman. *Every Spy a Prince: The Complete History of Israel's Intelligence Community* (New York: Houghton Mifflin, 1990).
M. Rees. *Northern Ireland: A Personal Perspective* (London: Methuen, 1985).
S. Rimmington. *The Richard Dimbleby Lecture 1994: Security and Democracy – Is There a Conflict?* (London: BBC Education, 1994).
D. Robertson. *The Penguin Dictionary of Politics* (Harmondsworth: Penguin, 1986).
D. Ronfeldt. *The Mitrione Kidnapping in Uruguay* (Santa Monica, CA: RAND Corporation, 1987).
W. A. Rosenbaum. *Political Culture* (London: Nelson, 1975).
G. Rosie. *The Directory of International Terrorism* (Edinburgh: Mainstream Publishing, 1986).
B. Rowan. *Behind the Lines: The Story of the IRA and Loyalist Ceasefires* (Belfast: Blackstaff, 1995).
M. Ryan. *War & Peace in Ireland: Britain and the IRA in the New World Order* (London: Pluto Press, 1994).
P. B. Ryan. *The Iranian Rescue Mission: Why It Failed* (Annapolis, MD: Naval Institute Press, 1985).
C. Ryder. *The RUC: A Force Under Fire* (London: Methuen, 1989).
C. Ryder. *The Ulster Defence Regiment: An Instrument of Peace?* (London, Methuen, 1991).
B. Savinkov. *Memoirs of a Terrorist* (Millwood, NY: Kraus Reprint, 1972).
C. Schaerf, G. de Lutiis, A. Silj, F. Carlucci, F. Bellucci, S. Argentini. *Venti Anni di Violenza in Italia: 1969–1988*, two volumes (Rome: ISODARCO, n. d).
P. Schlesinger. *Media, State and Nation: Political Violence and Collective Identities* (London: Sage, 1991).

N. Schliefman. *Undercover Agents in the Russian Revolutionary Movement: The SR Party, 1902-14* (London: Macmillan, 1988).
A. P. Schmid & J. de Graaf. *Violence as Communication: Insurgent Terrorism and the Western News Media* (London: Sage, 1982).
A. P. Schmid & A. J. Jongman. *Political Terrorism: A new guide to actors, authors, concepts, data bases, theories, and literature* (Amsterdam: North-Holland Publishing, 1988).
P. D. Scott & J. Marshall. *Cocaine Politics: Drugs, Armies, and the CIA in Central America* (Berkeley: University of California Press, 1991).
R. Scruton. *The Meaning of Conservatism* (Harmondsworth: Penguin, 1980).
P. Seale. *Abu Nidal: A Gun for Hire* (New York: Random House, 1992).
Searchlight. *From Ballots to Bombs: The Inside Story of the National Front's Political Soldiers* (London: Searchlight, after 1989).
S. Segaller. *Invisible Armies: Terrorism into the 1990s*, revised edition (London: Sphere Books, 1987).
A. Selth. *Against Every Human Law: The Terrorist Threat to Diplomacy* (Rushcutter's Bay: Australian National University Press, 1988).
T. Shawcross & M. Young. *Mafia Wars: The Confessions of Tommaso Buscetta* (Glasgow: Fontana, 1988).
K. R. M. Short. *The Dynamite War: Irish-American Bombers in Victorian Britain* (Dublin: Gill & Macmillan, 1979).
M. Short. *Lundy: The Destruction of Scotland Yard's Finest Detective* (London: Grafton, 1991).
P. Singer. *Animal Liberation: A New Ethics For Our Treatment of Animals* (New York: Avon, 1977).
P. Singer. *The animal liberation movement: it's philosophy, its achievements, and its future* (Nottingham: Old Hammond Press, n.d.).
A. D. Smith. *National Identity* (Harmondsworth: Penguin, 1991).
H. Smith. *The Power Game: How Washington Works* (London: Fontana, 1989).
M. L. R. Smith. *Fighting for Ireland? The Military Strategy of the Irish Republican Movement* (London: Routledge, 1995).
P. Snow & D. Phillips. *Leila's Hijack War: The True Story of 25 Days in September 1970* (London: Pan, 1970).
W. Stevenson. *90 Minutes at Entebbe* (New York: Bantam, 1976).
A. T. Q. Stewart. *The Narrow Ground: The Roots of Conflict in Ulster*, revised edition (London: Faber, 1989).
A. Stille. *Excellent Cadavers: The Mafia and the Death of the First Italian Republic* (London: Jonathan Cape, 1995).
H. Strachan. *European Armies and the Conduct of War* (London: Unwin Hyman, 1983).
S. Strong. *Shining Path: The World's Deadliest Revolutionary Force* (London: Harper Collins, 1992).
S. Strong. *Whitewash: Pablo Escobar and the Cocaine Wars* (London: Macmillan, 1995).
Sunday Times Insight Team. *Siege: Prince's Gate, London, April 30–May 5 1980* (Feltham: Hamlyn, 1980).
M. Sutton. *Bear in mind these dead ... An Index of Deaths from the Conflict in Ireland, 1969–1993* (Belfast: Beyond the Pale Publications, 1994).

R. Taber. *The War of the Flea: Guerrilla Warfare Theory and Practice* (St Albans: Paladin, 1970).
E. Tavin & Y. Alexander (eds). *Psychological Warfare and Propaganda: Irgun Documentation* (Wilmington, DE: Scholarly Resources Inc, 1982).
P. Taylor. *Beating the Terrorists: Interrogation in Omagh, Gough and Castlereagh* (Harmondsworth: Penguin, 1980).
P. Taylor. *States of Terror: Democracy and Political Violence* (London: BBC Books, 1993).
R. Thompson. *Defeating Communist Insurgency: Experiences from Malaya and Vietnam* (London: Chatto & Windus, 1967).
D. Thomson. *Europe Since Napoleon*, revised edition (Harmondsworth: Penguin, 1966).
D. Tinnin. *Hit Team* (London: Weidenfeld & Nicolson, 1976; Futura, 1977).
K. Toolis. *Rebel Hearts: Journeys within the IRA's Soul* (London: Picador, 1995).
C. Townshend. *Political Violence in Ireland: Government and Resistance since 1848* (Oxford: Oxford University Press, 1983).
C. Townshend. *The British Campaign in Ireland, 1919–1921: The Development of Political and Military Policies* (Oxford: Oxford University Press, 1975).
R. Trinquier. *Modern Warfare: A French View of Counterinsurgency* (London: Pall Mall Press, 1964).
M. Tully & S. Jacob. *Amritsar: Mrs Gandhi's Last Battle* (London: Jonathan Cape, 1985).
S. Uglow. *Policing Liberal Society* (Oxford: Oxford University Press, 1988).
M. Urban. *Big Boys' Rules: The Secret Struggle against the IRA* (London: Faber & Faber, 1992).
J. Waldron. *Maamtrasna: The Murders and the Mystery* (Dublin: Edmund Burke, 1992).
M. Walzer. *Just and Unjust Wars: A Moral Argument with Historical Illustrations* (New York: Basic Books, 1977; Harmondsworth: Penguin, 1980).
G. Wardlaw. *Political Terrorism: Theory, tactics, and counter-measures*, revised edition (Cambridge: Cambridge University Press, 1989).
P. Wilkinson. *Political Terrorism* (London: Macmillan, 1974).
P. Wilkinson. *Terrorism and the Liberal State*, second edition (London: Macmillan, 1986).
P. Wilkinson. *The New Fascists*, revised edition (Grant McIntyre, 1981; London: Pan, 1983).
P. Willan. *Puppet Masters: The Political Use of Terrorism in Italy* (London: Constable, 1991).
M. Williams (ed). *International Relations in the Twentieth Century: A Reader* (Basingstoke: Macmillan, 1989).
R. D. Wilson. *Cordon and Search: With 6th Airborne Division in Palestine* (Aldershot: Gale & Polden, 1949).
G. Woodcock. *Anarchism: A History of Libertarian Ideas and Movements* (USA: The World Publishing Company, 1962; Harmondsworth: Penguin, 1975).
B. Woodward. *Veil: The Secret Wars of the CIA, 1981–1987* (London: Simon & Schuster, 1987).

J. Wright. *Terrorist Propaganda: The Red Army Faction and the Provisional IRA, 1968–1986* (London: Macmillan, 1991).
D. Yallop. *To the Ends of the Earth: The Hunt for the Jackal* (London: Jonathan Cape, 1993).

TELEVISION PROGRAMMES AND VIDEOS

F. Martin (dir) *Behind the Mask*, video (London: Activision, 1989).
The Cook Report, ITV, television, 13 June 1995.
Dispatches: Law of the Ghetto, Channel 4, television, 26 February 1992.
Inside Story: The Informer, BBC1, television, 24 November 1992.
Scotland Yard: Terror, ITV, television, 3 February 1994.
Scotland Yard: Trooping the Colour, ITV, television, 10 February 1994.

Index

For details of some specific attacks see the group responsible or the type of operation.

Abduction
  bank robbers', 116
  Bunge y Born [Sept 1974], 13
  definition, 6
  for finance, 95
  location, 105
  location of hostages, 134
  logistics, 55
AD (Direct Action), 140
  members and personal links, 83
ALN (Action for National Liberation), 12
AMAL (Lebanese Resistance Battalions), 43
Anarchism, 18
Anarchist terrorists in France, 14–15
ANC (African National Congress)
  aims, 18
  bomb attacks, 18, 170–1
Angry Brigade, 18, 37
ALF (Animal Liberation Front), 164
ASALA (Armenian Secret Army for the Liberation of Armenia), 15
Assassination, 5–6

B2J (June 2nd Movement), 87
  East German support, 81
  formation, 73
  trained by PLO, 81
Bombs
  letter bombs, 115
  planting, 68
BR (Red Brigades)
  clandestinity, effect of, 167
  communiqués, 29
  formation, 73
  ideology: influence on targeting, 25–6, 32–4
  information-gathering, 61; slipshod nature, 29
  leadership, 77, 78
  maiming attacks, 64, 148
  members, part-time, 55
  PL, rivalry with, 43
  planning, 63
  prisoners, 139–40
  structure, 164, 169
  support, 152–3
  targeting pattern, 33–4
  targets: Casalegno shooting [Nov 1977], 156; D'Urso abduction [Dec 1980], 139–40; legal system, 141; Moro abduction [Apr 1978], 8, 55, 69–70, 71, 80, 111, 129, 154–5; police, 11, 76, 126–7, 138; Tarentelli [Mar 1985], 26; witness, 127
  unpopular attacks, 76
British Army, 41, 132–3
  see also security forces; PIRA, targets

Cavendish and Burke assassinations, Dublin [May 1882], 105
CCC (Fighting Communist Cells), 37
communism, 18–19
conservatism, 19–20
Contras (Nicaraguan counter-revolutionaries), 90, 96; US Government support, 90, 96
couriers, 65
criminal justice system, 120

267

death squads,
  Colombia: aims, 20; military involvement, 81–2; targeting pattern, 30, 156
  Guatemala, 157
discriminate attacks, 6
drug traffickers, Colombia
  abductions, 13
  bomb attacks, 40
  intimidation of legal system, 140–1
  phone-tapping by, 58
documentation
  causes problems for terrorists, 56, 96–7

EOKA (National Organisation of Cypriot Fighters)
  aim, 17
  British intelligence officers attacked, 125
  formation, 55
  structure, 164
ETA (Basque Homeland and Liberty)
  aim, 17
  extradition from France, 135–6
  ideology, 22
  information-gathering and reconnaisance, 62
  personal links, 83
  support, 168
  targeting pattern, 29–30, 174
  targets: Carrero Blanco assassination [Dec 1973], 8, 60, 80, 106; nuclear plant engineers, 21, 148; security forces, 137 (Table 8.2)
  weapons, 91

fascism, 20–1
fascist terrorism
  European, general, 9, 45
  Italian: 4; Bologna bombing [Aug 1980], 8– 48; mass casualty bombings, 42, 47–9; Mafia links, 49; strategy of tension, 47–9; trained in Lebanon, 81

training in Lebanon, 81
United Kingdom, 157
FARC (Colombian Armed Revolutionary Force)
finance, 96
FLN (National Liberation Front)
  European civilians attacked, 27
  media, 153–4
  strategy, 43
FRC (Fatah Revolutionary Command), 91
fund-raising, 96
finances, 95–6
  bank robberies, 12
FIS (Islamic Salvation Front), 49–50
  claims Algerian government infiltrated GIA, 52
forensic evidence, 127

GAL (Anti-Terrorist Liberation Group), 3, 132
GIA (Armed Islamic Group)
  scanners used by, 58
  targets: 50–3; foreigners, 50–1; journalists, 51, 156; non-conformers, 52; teachers and academics, 51–2
Goldstein, Baruch, 66
gun attacks
  close quarter, 67–8
  snipers, 68, 75–6, 114

Hamas
  aims, 22–3, 159
  family links, 83
  Iranian govt aid, 96
  Israeli intelligence agents assassinated, 125
  suicide bombings, 66, 114–15, 159
Heydrich assassination, Prague [May 1942], 105
hijacking, 7
  Dawson's Field, Jordan [Sep 1970], 7
  TWA 847 [June 1985], 13–14
Hindawi, Nizar, attempted bombing of El Al aeroplane [Apr 1986], 6

Hizbollah, 163
  AMAL, rivalry with, 43
  family links, 83
  Iranian govt aid, 96
  Sheikh Fadlallah assassination attempt, [Mar 1985], 65
  suicide bombings, 66
  targets: Argentine-Israeli Association bomb, Buenos Aires [Jul 1994], 27–8, 117–18; Israeli Embassy bombing, Buenos Aires [Mar 1994], 117; Jews as legitimate targets, 27–8; TWA 847, 13–14; US Embassy bombings, Beirut [April 1983, Sep 1984], 66; US Embassy bombing, Kuwait [Dec 1983], 66; US Marine barracks bombing [Oct 1983], 66
hostage rescue units, 133–5

ideology, 16
  dehumanises targets, 25–7
  displaces guilt for attacks, 28
  influence on strategy, 36
  role in target selection, 23–9
  targeting pattern, 29–34
information-gathering by terrorists, 57–61
INLA (Irish National Liberation Army), 67–8, 137–8
intelligence, anti-terrorist, 122–5
IPLO (Irish Peoples' Liberation Organisation), 56, 149
IRA (Irish Republican Army)
  information-gathering, 57–8
  support, 144
  targets: British intelligence system, 11, 40, 124; Lord French assassination attempt [Dec 1919], 10
  weapons, 93
  see also PIRA
Iranian Government support: to Hamas, 96; to Hizbollah, 90, 96

Israel
  assassination of Palestinian terrorists, 196 n17
  demolition of alleged Palestinian terrorists' homes, 41–2
  security forces in occupied territories, 130–1
Italy
  low public support for institutions, 152

JRA (Japanese Red Army)
  Lod Airport attack, Israel [May 1972], 27, 62

legitimate targets
  concept, 23–5; used by states, 26–7
liberalism, 18
Libyan Government aid: to FRC, 97; to PIRA, 90, 124
Loyalist terrorism, Northern Ireland
  aims, 19–20
  dehumanised Catholics, 25
  membership, 82
  planning, 63
  security force involvement, 82
  targeting pattern, 32, 172–4
  targets: Catholic civilians, 30–1, 101; Sinn Fein members, 101; lawyers, 142
  opportunist attacks, 9
  weapons, 89, 91
LTTE (Liberation Tigers of Tamil Eelam)
  aims, 17
  deny attacks, 72
  Indian goverment support, 3, 81
  suicide attacks, 66
  targets: Muslim civilians, 151; Rajiv Gandhi assassination [Apr 1991], 6, 55, 66, 70; President Premadasa [May 1993], 66

Mafia, Sicilian
  aims, 22
  phone-tapping, 58

Mafia, Sicilian (*continued*)
  targets: investigators, 40; witnesses, 127
Marighela, Carlos, 12, 19
mass casualty attacks, 6
mass destruction attacks, 7
media censorship, 155
military dictatorships
  Argentina, 121, 136
  Uruguay, 42, 136
MLN (Tupamaros)
  abductions, 13
  strategy of provocation, 42
Montoneros, 13

Naxalites
  landowners assassinated, 64, 148
  Indian security force measures against, 129
  use of crude weapons, 64, 80–1

OAS (Secret Army Organisation), 19
organised crime, 21–2
OPEC Conference siege [Vienna, Dec 1975], 71, 161

Palestinian terrorists
  PLO (Palestinian Liberation Organisation) formation, 73
  targets: Black September attack, Munich Olympics [Sep 1972], 14, 28; Israeli intelligence officers, 125; Jewish and Israeli targets, 117–18; PFLP Dawsons Field hijacking [Sep 1970], 7, 42
Paris bombings [1985–6], 107–8
PIRA (Provisional Irish Republican Army)
  aims, 17
  blames British Government for all deaths in Northern Ireland conflict, 28
  ceasefire (Aug 1994), 35
  effect of leaders' imprisonment, 74, 165
  finance, 95
  ideology, effect on strategy, 36–7
  informers, effect of, 123–4, 129
  information-gathering, 58–9, 62
  intimidation, 148–9
  leadership, 75–6, 78–9
  legitimate targets, 24, 26, 30
  local support, 146–7, 148, 168
  media, 153, 158
  members, 82, 86; family links, 83
  prisoners, 139
  planning, 63, 76
  sensitivity to political events, 160–1
  strategy, 38, 41, 43–4
  structure, 55, 63, 165–6, 169–70
  targeting pattern, 31–2, 172–4
  targets: Balcombe Street siege, London [Dec 1975], 7, 170; Brighton bomb [Oct 1984], 68–9, 103, 127, 161; British Army, 11, 28, 112–14, 116, 118, 130–1; businessmen, 23, 148; City of London bombs [Apr 1992], 7, 66, [Apr 1993], 7, 66, 112; Derry city centre, N. Ireland, 112; Docklands bomb [Feb 1996], 161; English operations, 7, 41, 55, 66, 68, 170; Enniskillen bomb [Nov 1987], 113–14, 157–8, 165–6; continental European operations, 115–16; Gow assassination [July 1990], 25; La Mon Hotel bomb [Feb 1978], 7; legal system, 141–2; loyalists, 150; Mountbatten assassination [Apr 1979], 10; Northern Ireland Forensic Laboratory [Sep 1992], 12, 128; RUC, 11–12, 104, 118, 131; RUC officer abduction [Sep 1990], 6; UDR/RIR, 113, 118; witnesses, 127